T0329654

Electronic Health Record

Electronic Health Record

Standards, Coding Systems, Frameworks, and Infrastructures

PRADEEP SINHA
GAUR SUNDER
PRASHANT BENDALE
MANISHA MANTRI
ATREYA DANDE

IEEE PRESS

A John Wiley & Sons, Inc., Publication

Library of Congress Cataloging-in-Publication Data

Electronic health records : standards, coding systems, frameworks, and
infrastructures / Pradeep Sinha . . . [et al.].
   p. ; cm.
  ISBN 978-1-118-28134-5 (cloth)
  I. Sinha, Pradeep K. (Pradeep Kumar)
  [DNLM: 1. Electronic Health Records–standards. 2. Forms and Records
Control. 3. Medical Records Systems, Computerized. WX 175]
  610.285–dc23
                                        2012024681

10 9 8 7 6 5 4 3 2 1

Contents

PART ONE

Introduction

PART TWO

EHR Standards

6 MESSAGING STANDARD FOR HEALTHCARE DATA   57

7 MODEL-BASED MESSAGING STANDARD FOR HEALTHCARE DATA   69

8 CLINICAL DOCUMENT STANDARDS   81

PART THREE

Coding Systems

PART FOUR

Standard Frameworks

PART FIVE

Case Studies: National EHR Efforts

PART **SIX**

Findings and Conclusion

Preface

Motivation

Information Technology (IT) is playing an increasingly important role in all sectors of economy, healthcare sector being no exception. In fact, the increased role of IT in the healthcare sector has led to coining of a new terminology, "Health Informatics," which deals with the use of IT for better healthcare services. Health informatics applications often deal with the health record of individuals, in digital form, which is referred to as the *Electronic Health Record (EHR)*.

For interoperability of health informatics applications, many health informatics standards have been proposed and made available. These include structural standards, data content standards, data exchange standards, security standards, and so on.

EHR being central to most health informatics applications, several countries have initiated programs for implementing national EHR infrastructures. Building and implementing a national EHR infrastructure requires understanding of healthcare standards, coding systems, and standard frameworks. Hence, for using, developing, and promoting any health informatics application (including EHR infrastructure), it is imperative for the concerned team/group to study and evaluate existing material on past and ongoing work in these areas. Due to the lack of a book or research monograph that would consolidate this information, the concerned team/group finds it frustrating and time-consuming to collect, study, analyze, and evaluate this information from multiple sources.

The authors of this book faced similar difficulty while working toward building a national EHR service framework. This motivated the authors to compile the study and analysis research work carried out by them in the form of a book, so that this body of knowledge will be readily available at one place to other researchers, technologists, and professionals working in similar areas. This will help accelerate research and development of future standards, coding systems, frameworks, EHR infrastructures, and healthcare applications for evolving better healthcare services for the benefit of mankind at large.

Objective

The book provides an overview of different Health Informatics Standards, Healthcare Coding Systems, and Standard Healthcare Frameworks that underlie design and development of interoperable healthcare systems and applications.

The objective of the book is to provide broad-level understanding of various healthcare standards rather than to provide implementation-level details of any one particular standard for someone to become an expert of that standard. Hence, the book aims at providing an understanding of what role a particular healthcare standard plays in EHR design and overall IT-enabled healthcare services along with the issues involved. However, if one wants to actually work with that standard at the implementation level, the book provides a set of references at the end of each chapter to enable such readers to obtain implementation-level details of any standard covered in the book.

The material in the book has been drawn largely from the research literature in the field. Of the vast amount of research literature available in this field, effort was made to select and give more emphasis to those concepts that are of practical value in real systems, rather than those that are only of theoretical interest.

For each Standard/Coding system/Framework covered in the book, there is a discussion section that provides an assessment of the Standard/Coding system/Framework with respect to the following important aspects of an EHR infrastructure:

- Clinical process model
- Information model
- Exchange specifications
- Security and privacy considerations
- Legal aspects

These assessments are helpful in tackling issues involved in building national EHR infrastructures and health informatics applications. They are also useful in understanding the applicability of different standards, coding systems, and frameworks in various health informatics applications.

Organization and Contents

The book is organized into six parts covering introduction, EHR standards, coding systems, standard frameworks, case studies of national EHR efforts, and findings and conclusion. Except Part I and Part IV, each part contains separate chapters covering individual topics of that part. The six parts of the book and their chapterwise contents are briefly introduced below.

PART ONE: INTRODUCTION

This part provides an introduction to Health Informatics, the EHR concept, and the role of EHR in healthcare applications. It contains the following chapter:

Chapter 1. Introduction to EHR. This chapter introduces EHR and describes other related concepts. It covers the various functions and significance of EHR with the probable reasons that affect its adaption. Finally, it explains the role of standards, coding systems, frameworks, and national case studies in implementation of an EHR infrastructure.

PART TWO: EHR STANDARDS

This part deals with various standards related to EHR. These include standards for EHR specifications, EHR communication/exchange, EHR concepts and processes, and EHR functional specifications. It contains the following chapters:

Chapter 2. Standard for EHR Architecture Requirements. This chapter covers technical specifications defined by the International Organization for Standardization (ISO/TS 215) for EHR architecture. ISO/TS 18308 is an international standard for EHR requirements.

Chapter 3. Standard for Continuity of Care Concepts. This chapter describes European standard CEN/TC 251 EN 13940, known as CONTsys. CONTsys is a two-part standard that standardizes the concepts and processes in healthcare. The chapter includes a description of both parts of the standard, that is, EN 13940-1 and prEN 13940-2.

Chapter 4. Standard for EHR Functional Specifications. This chapter describes the EHR-S Functional Model from the perspective of supporting functional requirements of EHR.

Chapter 5. Standard for EHR Communication. This chapter describes European standard CEN/TC 251 EN 13606, which was further evolved as ISO standard, commonly known as EHRcom. It is a five-part standard that provides specifications for structure of data for representation and communication, content of data, security, and communication protocol for two healthcare applications that share part or the whole EHR.

Chapter 6. Messaging Standard for Healthcare Data. This chapter describes the American National Standards Institute (ANSI)-accredited Health Level 7 (HL7) v2.x developed by HL7 organization. The standard primarily defines specifications for exchange of health informatics data between healthcare IT applications.

Chapter 7. Model-Based Messaging Standard for Healthcare Data. This chapter describes the HL7 v3 standard developed by the HL7 organization, which is significantly modified from its previous versions described in Chapter 6. It defines information model and exchange specifications for healthcare IT applications.

Chapter 8. Clinical Document Standards. This chapter describes clinical document standards, Clinical Document Architecture (CDA) and Continuity of Care Document (CCD). These standards are specifically used in exchange of clinical documents across healthcare applications.

Chapter 9. Standard for Medical Imaging and Communication. This chapter describes Digital Imaging and Communications in Medicine

(DICOM) PS 3.0-2004 standard evolved by American College of Radiology (ACR) and National Electrical Manufacturers Association (NEMA).

Chapter 10. Standard for Patient Health Summary. This chapter describes the American Society for Testing and Materials (ASTM) standard, Continuity of Care Record (CCR). It provides analysis of the standard from the perspective of identifying minimum artifacts required for referrals that can be incorporated in an EHR system.

PART THREE: CODING SYSTEMS

This part deals with various standard code sets used for representation of health information recorded in EHRs. It contains the following chapters:

Chapter 11. Coding System for Classification of Diseases and Related Health Problems. This chapter deals with the applicability of ICD to promote standardization, as well as to improve a system's capability to search for information following common semantics.

Chapter 12. Coding System for Laboratory Tests and Observations. This chapter discusses usage of LOINC in development of EHR model. LOINC is a freely available code set developed by Regenstrief Institute Inc. for identifying laboratory results and clinical observations generated during patient care.

Chapter 13. Coding System for Patient Care Procedures. This chapter presents CPT, its code structure, application scope, and coverage of medical procedures used in health services such as medical, surgical, and diagnostic services.

Chapter 14. Extended Coding System for Patient Care Procedures. This chapter provides an overview of HCPCS, which is based on CPT. The chapter also discusses its scope and significance in improving healthcare delivery and its applicability in building EHR systems.

Chapter 15. Comprehensive Coding System for Clinical Terms. This chapter describes different areas of healthcare information covered by SNOMED CT. It also discusses its significance in representing error-free and meaningful health information in electronic health records.

Chapter 16. Unified Medical Language System. This chapter describes the Unified Medical Language System (UMLS) framework evolved by National Library of Medicine (NLM). UMLS primarily aims at providing mapping among coding systems.

Chapter 17. Other Coding Systems. This chapter covers some other widely used coding systems that provide classifications of clinical codes for a particular specialty in healthcare domain. It covers coding systems for nursing, pharmacy, functional disability, and so on.

PART FOUR: STANDARD FRAMEWORKS

This part deals with various standard frameworks for building national EHR infrastructures. It contains the following chapters:

> **Chapter 18. openEHR.** This chapter describes the openEHR framework developed by openEHR Foundation. openEHR is an open source specification for management of EHR.
>
> **Chapter 19. Integrating the Healthcare Enterprise (IHE).** This chapter describes the Integrating the Healthcare Enterprise (IHE) technical framework and integration profiles developed by IHE organization. IHE aims at facilitating integration among different healthcare systems supporting different standards (mainly HL7 and DICOM).

PART FIVE: CASE STUDIES: NATIONAL EHR EFFORTS

This part provides case studies of select national efforts to build national EHR infrastructures. It contains the following chapters:

> **Chapter 20. Australia's HealthConnect.** This chapter describes the healthcare IT initiatives in Australia, primarily carried out under the *Health Connect* program of the Government of Australia.
>
> **Chapter 21. Austria's ELGA.** This chapter describes the architecture of the national EHR project of Austria, called *Elektronische Gesundheitsakte (ELGA)*.
>
> **Chapter 22. Canada's EHRS Blueprint.** This chapter describes the national framework for EHR in Canada. This framework is called the EHRS Blueprint. It provides the architecture of *Electronic Health Record Infrastructure* (EHRi) used by EHR systems in the country.
>
> **Chapter 23. Denmark's MedCom.** This chapter describes the national IT initiatives in health in Denmark. It describes the national health data network called *MedCom*, as well as the national Basic Electronic Health Record structure called *GEPJ*.
>
> **Chapter 24. Hong Kong's eHR Infrastructure.** This chapter describes different architectural components developed under the *E-health Engagement Initiative (EEI)* in Hong Kong.
>
> **Chapter 25. India's Health IT Initiatives.** This chapter describes the health IT initiatives in India, including regulatory guidelines and recommendations for healthcare practices, concept project, and initiatives toward national EHR.
>
> **Chapter 26. Netherlands' AORTA.** This chapter describes the architecture of national health IT infrastructure of Netherlands called *AORTA*.
>
> **Chapter 27. Singapore's NEHR.** This chapter describes the various healthcare services developed under the national EHR program of Singapore.

It also covers the national interoperability framework called EMR *Exchange (EMRX)* and the *National Electronic Health Record (NEHR)* of Singapore.

Chapter 28. Sweden's NPO. This chapter describes the National IT Strategy for eHealth in Sweden. It discusses national services, national EHR, and the national EHR implementation architecture called *Nationell Patientöversikt (NPÖ)*.

Chapter 29. Taiwan's Health Information Network. This chapter describes the health IT initiatives in Taiwan. It describes the structure of *Taiwan Medical Record Template (TMT)* and the architecture of *Health Information Network (HIN)* in Taiwan.

Chapter 30. United Kingdom's Spine. This chapter describes the national EHR initiative, Spine, by the National Health Service (NHS) through the *National Program for IT (NPfIT)* in the United Kingdom.

Chapter 31. USA's EHR Meaningful Use. This chapter describes the national initiatives in the United States of America for enabling integrated healthcare practices across the nation. It covers the architecture of *Nationwide Health Information Network (NHIN)*, regulatory guidelines for *Meaningful Use of EHR*, and relevant federal regulations in the country.

PART SIX: FINDINGS AND CONCLUSION

This part concludes the book with a summary of key findings of the study and analysis research carried out by the authors. It contains the following chapter:

Chapter 32. Findings and Conclusion. This chapter concludes the book by summarizing the findings of the study and analysis of different standards, frameworks, coding systems and case studies of EHR initiatives taken by various countries.

Intended Audience

This book is designed for use by beginners as well as experts dealing with Health Informatics. For a beginner, this text will be valuable to get a broad idea about all the standards and resources that are out there and about EHRs. For an expert, this book will be useful as a ready reference. The book is particularly valuable for anyone involved in making decisions about building a large-scale (e.g., national) EHR infrastructure. More specifically, readers can benefit from this book in the following manner:

- The coverage of study of all aspects of EHR with inclusion of current situations for development of national EHR infrastructures makes it a vital resource for researchers, professionals, students, and administrators working in the health informatics area.

- Using Information Technology for storage, retrieval, and exchange of health data has become the need of the hour. This book can, therefore, help healthcare specialists, hospital administrators, and hospital consultants in acquiring knowledge of Healthcare Information Technology (HIT) standards, current international affairs and issues, while selecting and investigating health information systems and healthcare applications for their organizations.

- It can be also useful for professionals needing knowledge to advance the use and value of health informatics. The book can be used as a professional resource for analyzing methods to improve health information for building better healthcare applications.

- Information Technology (IT) professionals who want to move into health informatics domain can use the book to gain knowledge of requirement specifications for building standardized healthcare applications.

- A wide range of stakeholders from the healthcare industry and the HIT industry (such as Insurance Industry, Public Health Sector, Software Companies, Medical and Public Libraries, etc.) will also find the book a useful learning aid to improve the quality of use of HIT.

Disclaimer

The material contained herein including case studies of various national programs are compiled from the information, opinions, and analysis/reports in publically available documents. However, due to continuous advancements happening at a rapid pace in these domains and national programs, their current status might have changed from what is given in this book. The authors make no representation, expressed or implied, as to its accuracy, completeness, or correctness.

The authors hope that the material presented in this book serves the purpose stated earlier and that readers will benefit from our work in the domain by using the book as a starting point in their pursuit to explore further.

Acknowledgments

Many people have contributed to this book, either directly or indirectly. To start with, we would like to thank all the researchers who have contributed to the field of health informatics. This book is based on their research work.

The book covers various standards that are useful in the design and development of interoperable healthcare systems and applications. We thank all international standards bodies who have put efforts toward evolving such standards. National EHR efforts carried out in various countries are covered as case studies in the book. We thank the people, government bodies, health organizations, and other agencies who contributed to the healthcare/EHR initiatives in these countries.

The Department of Electronics & Information Technology (DeitY), the Ministry of Communications and Information Technology (MCIT), the Government of India and VINNOVA, and the Government of Sweden jointly approved and supported the project titled "Technology Development for Building Distributed, Scalable, and Reliable Healthcare Information Store." The project provided an opportunity to the authors to carry out research in the area of Electronic Health Record (EHR) infrastructure and associated technologies. The book is based on the knowledge gained by the authors during the project. We would like to thank both DeitY and VINNOVA for providing us this opportunity.

The Centre for Development of Advanced Computing (C-DAC), Pune, India and the Swedish Institute of Computer Science (SICS), Kista, Sweden provided the fertile ground where our ideas in this domain could grow and take this shape through the joint project. We are thankful to both C-DAC and SICS for this support. Members of the Medical Informatics Group and our staff Arpita Kulkarni and Sushma Pawar helped us in drafting the manuscript.

Lively discussions with several technical members including Mr. B. S. Bedi, Dr. S. K. Srivastava, Mr. R. C. Meharde, Dr. T. K. Sarkar, Dr. Suman Bhattacharya, Prof. A. K. Majumdar, Prof. S. K. Mishra, Dr. Jim Dowling, and Prof. Seif Haridi helped us in broadening our knowledge in this area. We are thankful to all of them.

Several anonymous reviewers of our draft manuscript provided invaluable feedback regarding the book's title, organization, topic coverage, typographical errors, and obscure parts and helped in overall improvement of the material. We thank all the reviewers for their valuable inputs.

Our production editor at IEEE PRESS Danielle Lacourciere, did an excellent job in numerous ways to present the book in its current form. IEEE PRESS Director Kenneth Moore and Senior Acquisitions Editor Taisuke Soda were of great help in improving the overall quality of the book and in bringing it out in a timely manner. We thank them all for their support and help.

We specially thank European Committee for Standardization (CEN), Health Level Seven International (HL7), National Electrical Manufacturers Association (NEMA), The Institute of Engineers and Technology (IET), IHE International Inc., International Health Terminology Standards Development Organization (IHTSDO), Canada Health Infoway Inc., National E-Health Transition Authority (nehta), The openEHR Foundation, Department for Innovation and Technology Italy, National Board of Health and Welfare Sweden, Elsevier Science Ireland Ltd, Ringholm bv, and Jan Petersen and Lone Asp for permitting us to use the material from their publication(s).

Special thanks from Pradeep K. Sinha to his wife Priti, his son Deeptanshu, and his parents for their patience, sacrifice, loving support, and understanding. Thanks to coauthors of the book for their lively discussions, dedication, and untiring efforts.

Special thanks from Gaur Sunder to his wife Sudha, his son Kartik, his parents, and his family members for being the pillar of strength and constant source of inspiration. Also thanks to coauthors, especially Dr. Pradeep Sinha, for sharing the vision and push against all odds.

Special thanks from Prashant Bendale to his wife Chetana, his son Yash, his mother Ashalata, and his family for their support and personal sacrifices. This effort is dedicated to his father the late Mr. Prabhakar Bendale. Also, thanks to Gaur Sunder and Dr. Pradeep Sinha for mentoring.

Special thanks from Manisha Mantri to her husband Dinesh, her son Aalok, her sister Sonika, and her parents and family members for being a constant source of inspiration and support during this work. Thanks to Gaur Sunder and Dr. Pradeep Sinha for their guidance and support. Also, thanks to coauthors and team members for their support and help.

Special thanks from Atreya Dande to his whole family for their continued understanding, love, and affection. Thanks go to Dr. Pradeep Sinha and Gaur Sunder for encouraging with insightful direction during this endeavor. Thanks go to co-authors for their continued support. Also, he would like to express his gratefulness to his friends and team members for their help in innumerable ways.

The authors hope that this book is useful in your work, research, and development and in exploring the exciting possibilities that may exist.

PRADEEP K. SINHA
GAUR SUNDER
PRASHANT BENDALE
MANISHA MANTRI
ATREYA DANDE

Acronyms

A

AAFP	American Academy of Family Physicians
AASM	American Academy of Sleep Medicine
ABAC	Attribute Based Access Control
ACF	Access Control Framework
ACR	American College of Radiology
ADA	American Dental Association
ADL	Archetype Definition Language
ADT	Admissions/Registration, Discharge or Transfer
AHFS	American Hospital Formulary Service
AHSL	Apollo Health Street Ltd.
AIHW	Australian Institute of Health and Welfare
AM	Archetype Model
AMA	American Medical Association
ANA	American Nurses Association
ANSI	American National Standards Institute
APA	American Psychiatric Association
ARRA	American Recovery and Reinvestment Act
ASTM	American Society for Testing and Materials
ATC	Anatomical Therapeutic Chemical
ATNA	Audit Trail and Note Authentication
AUI	Atom Unique Identifiers

B

BIF	Bastjänster för Informations Försörjning (Basic Services for Information)

BSN	Burgerservicenummer (Citizen Identification Number)

C

CA	Certification Authority
CAP	College of American Pathologies
CCD	Continuity of Care Document
CCHIT	Certification Commission for Health Informatics Technology
CCR	Continuity of Care Record
CDA	Clinical Document Architecture
C-DAC	Centre for Development of Advanced Computing
CDS	Common Data Sets
CDT	Current Dental Terminology
CFR	Code of Federal Regulations
CIR	Clinical Investigator Record
CME	Continuing Medical Education
CMS	Centers for Medicare and Medicaid Services; Clinical Management System
COBIT	Control Objectives for Information and Related Technology
CONTSys	European Standard EN 13940 for Continuity of Care
CPR	Computerized Patient Record
CPT	Current Procedural Terminology

CRS	Care Records Service
CSA	Clinical Spine Application
CT	Computed Tomography; Consistent Time
CTV	Clinical Terms Version
CUI	Concept Unique Identifiers

D

DCR	Detailed Care Record
DICOM	Digital Imaging and Communications in Medicine
DIM	Domain Information Model
DMDI	Document Meta Data Index
DMEPOS	Durable Medical Equipment Prosthetics, Orthotics and Supplies
DMERCS	Durable Medical Equipment Regional Carriers
D-MIM	Domain Message Information Model
DSM	Diagnostic and Statistical Manual of Mental Disorders
DSTU	Draft Standard for Trial Use

E

ECID	EHRi Client ID
EEI	E-Health Engagement Initiative
EHCR	Electronic Health Care Record
EHR	Electronic Health Record
EHRcom	European standard EN13606 Communication of EHR
EHRRA	Electronic Health Record Reference Architecture
EHRS	Electronic Health Record Solutions
EHR-S	Electronic Health Record-Systems
EMR	Electronic Medical Record
EMRX	EMR Exchange
EPD	Electronic Patient Dossier (Dutch Electronic Patient Record System)
EPR	Electronic Patient Record

EU	European Union
EUA	Enterprise User Authentication

F

FDA	Food and Drug Administration
FIPS	Federal Information Processing Standards

G

GEHR	Good Electronic Health Record; Good European Health Record
GEPJ	Grundstruktur for Elektronisk Patient Journal (Basic Electronic Health Record)
GP	General Practitioner

H

HA	Hospital Authority
HCA	Health Certificate Authority
HCO	Health Care Organization
HCPCS	Healthcare Common Procedure Coding System
HHS	Department of Health and Human Services
HIAL	Health Information Access Layer
HIMSS	Health Information Management and Systems
HIN	Health Information Network
HIPAA	Health Insurance Portability and Accountability Act
HIS	Health Information System; Hospital Information System
HIT	Health Information Technology
HITSP	Healthcare Information Technology Standards Panel
HKCVT	Hong Kong Clinical Vocabulary Table
HKPMI	Hong Kong Patient Master Index
HL7	Health Level 7
HSA	Hälso-och sjukvårdens Adresskatalog (Electronic Catalog for Health and Social Care)

I

ICD	International Classification of Diseases
ICF	International Classification of Functioning
ICSD	International Classification of Sleep Disorders
ICT	Implementation of Computer Technology; Information and Communication Technology
ID	Identifier
IEHR	Integrated Care Electronic Health Record
IHE	Integrated Healthcare Enterprise
iHIND	Indian Health Information Network Development
IHTSDO	International Health Terminology Standards Development Organization
IOD	Information Object Definition
IPP	Information Privacy Principles
IRDA	Insurance Regulatory and Development Authority (of India)
ISO	International Organization For Standardization
ITIH	Information Technology Infrastructure for Health
ITIL	Information Technology Infrastructure Library

L

LDAP	Lightweight Directory Access Protocol
LIS	Laboratory Information System
LOINC	Logical Observation Identifiers Names and Codes
LRS	Longitudinal Record Services
LUI	Lexical Unique Identifiers
LVG	Lexical Variant Generator

M

MCIT	Ministry of Communication and Information Technology

MDS	Minimum Data Sets
MeSH	Medical Subject Headings
MIEC	Medical Information Exchange Centre
MMA	Medicare Modernization Act
MMS	Massachusetts Medical Society
MOH	Ministry of Health
MPI	Master Patient Index

N

NANDA	North American Nursing Diagnosis Association
NASH	National Authentication Service for Health
NCPDP	National Council for Prescription Drug Programs
NCVHS	National Committee on Vital Health Statistics
NDC	National Drug Code
NEHTA	National E-Health Transition Authority
NEMA	National Electrical Manufacturers Association
NHG	National Healthcare Group
NHIA	National Health Information Authority
NHIH	National Health Information Hub
NHP	National Health Portal
NHS	National Health Services
NIC	Nursing Interventions Classification
NICTIZ	Nationaal ICT Instituut in de Zorg (Dutch National ICT Institute for Healthcare)
NIST	National Institute of Standards and Technology
NKC	National Knowledge Commission
NLM	National Library of Medicine
NOC	Nursing Outcomes Classification
NPfIT	Nation Program for IT
NPO	National Patient Summary
NPP	National Privacy Principles
NRAS	National Registration and Accreditation Scheme

O

OASIS	Open Architecture for Secure Interworking Services
ONC	Office of National Coordinator
ORF	Original Release Format

P

PACS	Picture Archival and Communications Services
PCEHR	Personally Controlled EHR
PCS	Procedure Coding System
PDQ	Patient Demographics Query
PDU	Protocol Data Unit
PID	Public ID
PIPEDA	Personal Information Protection and Electronic Documents Act
PIX	Patient Identifier Cross-referencing
PKI	Public Key Infrastructure
PLI	Patient Lookup Index
PoS	Point of Service
PQRI	Physician Quality Reporting Initiative
PSA	Patient Synchronized Applications
PSIS	Personal Spine Information Service
PWP	Personal White Pages

Q

QHIS	Qualified Healthcare Information Systems

R

RBAC	Role-Based Access Control
RHIO	Regional Health Information Organizations
RID	Retrieve Information and Display
RIM	Reference Information Model
RLE	Run Length Encoding
RM	Reference Model
R-MIM	Refined Message Information Model
RRF	Rich Release Format

S

SADMERC	Statistical Analysis Durable Medical Equipment Regional Carriers
SAMBA	Structured Architecture for Medical Business Activities
SAML	Security Assertion Markup Language
SCR	Summary Care Record
SDOs	Standard Development Organizations
SDS	Spine Directory Service
SDT	Structured Document Template
SICS	Swedish Institute of Computer Science
SIGs	Special Interest Groups
SingHealth	Singapore Health Services
SITHS	Säker IT i Hälso-och Sjukvård (Secure IT in Health Services)
SM	Services Model
SNOMED CT	Systematized Nomenclature of Medicine–Clinical Terms
SNOMED RT	Systematized Nomenclature of Medicine–Reference Terminology
SOA	Service-Oriented Architecture
SOP	Service-Object Pair
SR	Structured Reports
SSL	Secured Socket Layer
STS	Security Token Service
SUI	String Unique Identifiers
SUP	Acronym of Standardized Extracts of Patients Data
SUS	Secondary Uses Service

T

TC	Technical Committee
TMT	Taiwan Medical Record Template

TPA	Third-Party Administrators
TSL	Transport Layer Security
TSPID	Telemedicine Service Provider ID

U

UCL	University College of London
UHI	Unique Healthcare Identifier
UMLS	Unified Medical Language System

V

| VPN | Virtual Private Network |

W

| WADO | Web Access to DICOM Objects |
| WHO | World Health Organization |

X

| XDS | Cross-Enterprise Document Sharing |

PART ONE

Introduction

CHAPTER ONE

Introduction to EHR

1.1 Introduction

Use of Information Technology (IT) is common in all areas, including health-care. Many healthcare organizations use IT-enabled healthcare applications for simplifying healthcare processes such as administration, managing health records across departments, and billing. On the other hand, some organizations are still struggling with conventional healthcare processes and paper-based health records.

Increase in population, complemented with new and complex treatments for diseases, have increased demand for better and more efficient healthcare services globally. Due to complexity of health problems, multiple healthcare providers are involved in treatment of a patient, making healthcare process more complex. Need for complete health information of a patient—such as patient's history, allergies, laboratory tests, medication, and so on—at one place for his/her better care is increasing. Researchers have now realized that increased application of IT to healthcare with Electronic Health Record (EHR) is a way to deal with these issues. Hence, many countries are promoting increased use of IT in healthcare services and use of EHR for enhancing continuity of care to patients.

In the fifth century B.C., Hippocrates developed the first known medical record with two specific goals [EHR Overview 2006]:

1. Preserving course of a disease
2. Indicating probable cause of a disease

Electronic Health Record: Standards, Coding Systems, Frameworks, and Infrastructures, Pradeep Sinha, Gaur Sunder, Prashant Bendale, Manisha Mantri, and Atreya Dande.
© 2013 by The Institute of Electrical and Electronics Engineers, Inc. Published 2013 by John Wiley & Sons, Inc.

These goals are still precise. However, with advancement in IT and introduction of EHR, expectations have increased, such as depicting healthcare workflow, secured and authorized access to health information, faster access to health records irrespective of place and time, and so on.

1.2 Definition of EHR

A simple generic definition of an EHR is health records of a patient in electronic form. However, this definition is not comprehensive. Some definitions of EHR and associated terminologies as found in the literature are:

An ***Integrated Care EHR*** defined by ISO/DTR 20514: *"A repository of information regarding the health of a subject of care in computer processable form, stored and transmitted securely, and accessible by multiple authorized users. It has a standardized information model, which is independent of EHR systems. Its primary purpose is the support of continuing efficient and quality-integrated healthcare and it contains information, which is retrospective, concurrent, and prospective"* [ISO/TR 20514]

An EHR defined by Health Information and Management Systems Society (HIMSS): *"EHR is a longitudinal electronic record of patient health information generated by one or more encounters in any care delivery setting. Included in this information are patient demographics, progress notes, problems, medications, vital signs, past medical history, immunizations, laboratory data, and radiology reports. The EHR automates and streamlines the clinician's workflow. The EHR has the ability to generate a complete record of a clinical patient encounter, as well as supporting other care-related activities directly or indirectly via interface including evidence-based decision support, quality management, and outcomes reporting"* [HIMSS 2011]

From both definitions it is clear that EHR is not owned by any single healthcare provider and contains complete records of encounters of a patient throughout the visited healthcare organizations for that particular encounter. EHR aims at providing care to a patient across healthcare organizations.

While surveying the literature, we came across many terminologies that have evolved together with EHR. These terminologies are either subsets of EHR or used by different groups to mean the same thing. However, our analysis indicates that the term EHR is more widely accepted globally, which defines the broadest scope of health information systems. Below we provide definitions of some commonly used related terminologies found in the literature [Diweesh and Garg 2006]:

- ***Electronic Medical Record (EMR).*** EMR is often used in parallel with EHR. It is a fully interoperable electronic health record of a patient within a healthcare organization. However, some people consider EMR as a set of records of a patient related to a single encounter or a single care episode. According to this view, EMR is a point-in-time view of a larger EHR. This approach considers an EHR to be sum total of all EMRs of a patient.

- **Computer-Based Patient Record (CPR).** CPR was first used to conceptualize the idea of EHR [Richard et al. 1997]. It is a lifetime health record of a patient, which includes information from all specialties. It requires full interoperability (potentially international interoperability) that may be achieved in the near future.

- **Electronic Patient Record (EPR).** EPR is similar to CPR, but does not necessarily contain a lifetime record and focuses on relevant information only.

- **Personal Health Record (PHR).** PHR is managed and controlled by a patient. It is mostly considered to be web-based. Usually, PHR is another patient-side view of an EHR/EMR maintained by a particular group of healthcare providers.

1.3 Functions of EHR

Margaret and Steven [2005] described EHR as a system of hardware, software, people, policy, and processes that work together to collect data from multiple resources, thus providing information and decision support to multiple healthcare providers irrespective of time and place.

Accordingly, an EHR system should offer the following basic functions:

- **Health Information and Data.** It should store and provide access to health information of patients such as patient's history, allergies, laboratory reports, diagnosis, current medications, and so on, to healthcare providers for taking appropriate clinical decisions for better patient care. It should integrate data from various sources and make it available to the people involved in the care of a patient.

- **Replicate the Workflow.** It should be able to work in-sync with the original workflow of the healthcare organization.

- **Efficient Interaction.** It should be able to work effectively, saving time of care providers by keeping things concise.

- **Clinical Decision Support (CDS).** It should support provision of reminders, prompts, and alerts. Such features help in improving clinical and preventive practices and reduce frequency of adverse events.

- **Patient Support.** It should empower patients to access their health information, enabling them to be involved in their own healthcare.

- **Messaging and Data Processing Capability.** It should enable exchange of data in known/standard formats for interoperability of healthcare applications. Additionally, it should enable processing of incoming data in known/standard formats.

- *Administrative Tools.* It should provide administrative tools, such as scheduling systems, for improving efficiency of clinical practices and timely service to patients.

1.4 Significance of EHR

An EHR system helps to provide an integrated view of healthcare records by enabling integration of various healthcare applications such as Hospital Information Systems (HIS), Pharmaceutical Systems, Imaging Systems, and Health Insurance Systems. In turn, an EHR system plays a significant role in better healthcare services by offering the following advantages [IOM 2003]:

- *Ease of Maintaining Health Information of Patients.* An EHR system enables paperless medical treatment with less space required for storing health data of patients. Additionally, with proper backup policies, the lifespan of EHRs can be increased. This reduces the cost of generating, storing, and maintaining patient records in healthcare organizations.

- *Efficient in Complex Environments.* Large healthcare organizations have many specialty departments, laboratories, training and research centers, and so on. An EHR system helps in improving clinical processes or workflow efficiency across these units of a healthcare organization. For example, it enables an administrator to obtain data for billing, a physician to see progress of treatments, a nurse to report an adverse reaction, and a researcher to analyze efficacy of medications on patients.

- *Better Patient Care.* Often, multiple healthcare providers are involved in treatment of a patient. An EHR system allows sharing of the patient's information among them. Moreover, it enables point-in-time data insertion, retrieval, and update, thereby providing immediate access of patient data from any specialty center whenever required. This enables healthcare providers to make timely decisions for better patient care. Availability of health information, such as past medical history, family medical history, and immunization, through EHR helps in taking preventive measures and managing chronic diseases more effectively.

- *Improve Quality of Care.* EHR helps to decrease reporting and charting time during treatment, thereby improving quality of care. EHR also helps in improving risk management and accurate diagnosis, thereby improving quality of care.

- *Reduce Healthcare Delivery Costs.* Due to the availability of health information data from all healthcare organizations, a healthcare provider can refer to the required test reports, thus avoiding repetition of expensive tests.

- *Accelerates Research and Helps Build Effective Medical Practices.* EHR provides a large database at one place, enabling its use for disease surveillance for providing preventive measures. It also helps in analyzing treatment patterns of medicine, providing new ideas and ways of drug discovery. Decision support with EHR enables effective medical practices.

- **Better Safety.** Through access, audit, and authorization control mechanisms, an EHR system provides better safety to a patient's health records as compared to a paper-based system.

1.5 Factors Affecting Implementation of EHR

An EHR system needs to deal with multiple healthcare applications and various types of healthcare providers. Hence, its implementation is a complex task that usually requires more time and effort than implementation of several other IT applications. The following factors usually affect the implementation of an EHR system and need to be dealt with properly:

- **Significant Changes in Clinical Workflow.** Implementation of an EHR system in a healthcare organization often requires significant changes in the organization's clinical workflow. Hence, it is always good to make EHR a part of the strategic vision of the organization. Design of the system needs involvement of clinical staff with inclusion of organization's policies and workflow processes [Hamilton 2011].

  Although an EHR can be customized for a specific medical practice, clinical workflow varies from one specialty to another. Thus, an EHR having a specific workflow for practicing medicine is usually not adaptable easily.

- **Privacy and Security.** An EHR implementation must deal with privacy and security issues with great care because health care providers are concerned about alteration of EHR without their knowledge, and patients are concerned about unauthorized access to their private data.

  An EHR system must also meet the privacy and security regulations for health data imposed by regulatory bodies in the country. This provides assurance to patients and providers that the health data is securely stored and privacy is maintained, while healthcare applications deliver appropriate services. The system should audit log the accesses made to an EHR with strict access policies.

- **Unique Identification.** Duplication of EHR records of a patient in the same EHR system is an important issue in EHR usage. This issue arises because healthcare data of a patient is often collected from various healthcare organizations, with each organization having its own registration process. In the process, different organizations assign different identifiers to the same patient. While integrating such data, an EHR system must properly link all data of a patient to create his/her single EHR.

- **Interoperability.** An EHR system consolidates patients' healthcare data generated from various healthcare systems. Hence, it should be capable of integrating data from all such systems. Moreover, it should enable interoperability among various healthcare applications and systems that are developed independently.

- *Consistent Use of Standards.* To support interoperability and information sharing across various healthcare applications and systems, an EHR system requires consistent use of standards such as clinical vocabulary and standardized data formats. Different healthcare applications usually offer different sets of features supporting different structures and data formats. Additionally, these applications usually do not make consistent use of security and data integrity standards. An EHR system must, therefore, make consistent use of standards and upgrade consistently to newly developed standards for addressing these issues.

- *Ethical and Legal Issues.* An EHR system must also carefully handle ethical and legal issues that are linked to accuracy, confidentiality and access rights of healthcare data.

- *Unknown Return on Investment (ROI).* An EHR system mostly provides intangible benefits. These include improved quality and patient care, patient safety, more efficient tracking of patient data, improved documentation, and better audit of accessed information. Certainly, an EHR system also provides some financial ROI, such as increase in income with expanded patient load due to time efficiency, and reduced material costs such as paper, charts, and printing supplies. Convincing an organization's decision makers to invest in implementing an EHR system on the basis of intangible benefits or related saving only is rather difficult.

- *Difficult to Operate.* Some healthcare providers find it more difficult and time-consuming to use computers for data entry than handwriting. Therefore, they need special training, which adds to the cost of implementing an EHR system.

- Additionally, paper-based records have some advantage over EHR. For example, they are less structured and hence offer more flexibility in terms of writing text and putting diagrams. Also, reading text on paper is 40% faster than reading text on a computer screen [Walsh 2004; Lewis 2009].

In spite of the issues listed above for EHR implementation, the question of moving from paper-based system to an EHR system does not arise today. The whole world is moving toward it, and several implementation issues are being addressed gradually.

1.6 Role of Standards

Implementation of an EHR system requires healthcare applications to be interoperable, enabling sharing of data across all such applications. Health Information Technology (HIT) standards provide a foundation for interoperability of healthcare applications. Additionally, implementation of a regionwide or nationwide healthcare information store requires uniformity in:

1. Clinical and business processes of healthcare service providers
2. Information structure for healthcare data
3. Quality of healthcare services
4. Privacy and security regulations and techniques in healthcare services, and so on

Internationally accepted standards are the way to achieve this.

Many Standard Development Organizations (SDOs) and Special Interest Groups (SIGs) are working toward addressing these issues and have evolved and proposed several Healthcare IT standards for the same. The second part of the book includes study of various such standards that have become popular. Standards for EHR specifications, EHR communication/exchange, EHR concepts and processes, and EHR functional specifications are discussed in separate chapters in the first part of this book.

1.7 Role of Clinical Coding Systems

For natural interoperability and common semantics, the healthcare community at large identified the need for developing standard codes for commonly used concepts and terms in healthcare delivery. Hence, code-based vocabularies, terminologies, and classifications were developed. Standardization work in this area involves development of standard code-sets for generally used concepts, terms, disease names, procedures, entity names, laboratory tests, observations, devices, clinical findings, body structure names, pharmaceutical products, organisms, and so on. These code sets primarily assist in meaningful interpretation of healthcare information exchanged across healthcare systems.

Many international organizations have built standard code sets for various categories of health information recorded in electronic health records. To develop an interoperable EHR framework, knowledge of these coding systems is essential to understand their scope, structure, and importance in representing healthcare information. The third part of the book deals with various coding systems supporting different clinical specialties.

1.8 Role of Standard Frameworks

A framework is a complete specification of a system with all structures and operations to be performed for a given objective. Frameworks usually adhere to standard guidelines/specifications for a system and provide mechanisms through APIs or components to build such a system. In healthcare IT, well-developed frameworks for EHRs, coding systems, and clinical data interoperability help in achieving integrated healthcare environment. Thus, it is important to study frameworks in healthcare IT to analyze them for their applicability to enable integrated healthcare environment. The fourth part of this book describes standard healthcare IT frameworks.

1.9 Case Studies of National EHR Implementations

A single EHR for every individual in a nation has been the dream of many countries. This requires a nation to build a nationwide healthcare IT infrastructure. Hence, the prime design focus for a nationwide EHR is to identify requirements for building a national healthcare IT infrastructure. Because the health of an individual is an important issue with social and private implications, such an infrastructure requires proper consideration for security, legal, and ethical aspects.

Countries with ongoing initiatives for building such an infrastructure are good candidates for case studies of applicability of standards discussed in this book for creating a national EHR framework. Although parameters differ from one country to another due to diversity in expectations, as well as rules and regulations, study of national EHR efforts of various countries will be helpful in visualizing a rich set of situations and their solutions. Such a comprehensive study also helps in listing out issues resulting from geographically, legally, and ethically diverse conditions. Finally, it helps in evolving a matured architecture for a national EHR framework that takes care of existing issues and incorporates the best-known solutions to circumvent those issues.

The fifth part of this book covers case studies of various countries that are building an operational model for a national IT infrastructure, enabling exchange of healthcare information across various healthcare facilities and systems.

BIBLIOGRAPHY

[Diween and Garg 2006] Diween A., and Garg M., Electronic health record—Improving quality of care, reducing costs and empowering patients, *Calance* (February 2006); http://www.calance.com/in/pdfs/CAL_WP_EHR.pdf.

[EHR Overview 2006] National Institutes of Health (NIH), National Center for Research Resources (NCRR) and MITRE Corporation, *Electronic Health Records Overview* (April 2006).

[Hamilton 2011] Hamilton, B. R., *An Introduction to Electronic Health Records*, second edition, McGraw-Hill, Chapter 1 (2011).

[Hillestad et al. 2005] Hillestad, R., Bigelow, J., Bower, A., Girosi, F., Meili, R., Scoville, R., and Taylor, R., Can electronic medical record systems transform health care? Potential health benefits, savings, and Costs, *Health Affairs*, Vol. 24, 1103–1117 (2005).

[HIMSS 2011] Healthcare Information and Management Systems Society (HIMSS), *Definition of EHR*; http://www.himss.org/ASP/topics_ehr.asp.

[IOM 2003] Institute of Medicine Committee (IOM) on Data Standards for Patient Safety, Key Capabilities of an Electronic Health Record System, Letter Report (2003); http://www.providersedge.com/ehdocs/ehr_articles/Key_Capabilities_of_an_EHR_System.pdf.

[ISO/TR 20514] International Organization for Standardization, *Health Informatics: Electronic Health Record—Definition, Scope and Context*, ISO/TR 20514 (2005).

[Lewis 2009] Lewis B., *The Electronic Health Record* (June 2009).

[Margaret and Steven 2005] Margaret, K. A. and Steven, S. L., *Electronic Health Records: Transforming Your Medical Practice*, first edition, Medical Group of Management Association (MGMA), Chapter 1, p. 7 (2005).

[Richard et al. 1997] Richard, S. D., Elaine, B. S., and Don, E. D., *The Computer-Based Patient Record: An Essential Technology for Health Care*, Institute of Medicine (IOM) (1997).

[Sinha and Gaur Sunder 2011] Sinha, P., and Gaur Sunder, Addressing India's skewed-doctor-to-patient ratio issue through ICT. In: *Proceedings of National Conference on Future Trends in Information & Communication Technology & Applications (NCICT-2011)*, pp. 29–33 (September 2011).

[Walsh 2004] Walsh, S. H., The clinician's perspective on electronic health records and how they affect patient care, *British Medical Journal*, Vol. 328, 1184–1187 (2004).

PART TWO

EHR Standards

CHAPTER TWO

Standard for EHR Architecture Requirements

2.1 Introduction

Over the past several years, several countries have made efforts to develop electronic health record models and systems to maintain it. These efforts have resulted in several publications dealing with architecture, model, and implementation mechanisms of EHR. The diversified approaches found in these publications created a need for defining a common specification for the principal requirements of EHR content and its architecture. *International Organization for Standardization (ISO)* initiated efforts to address this requirement and published ISO/TS 18308.

ISO/TC 215 is a Technical Committee (TC) of ISO working in the area of Health Informatics. Its primary goal is to standardize health information and achieve interoperability across EHR systems. It has published various standards for healthcare information. These include standards for data structures, messaging and communications, privacy and security, devices, and so on. It also published ISO/TS 18308, which defines a common specification for EHR architecture.

Electronic Health Record: Standards, Coding Systems, Frameworks, and Infrastructures, Pradeep Sinha, Gaur Sunder, Prashant Bendale, Manisha Mantri, and Atreya Dande.
© 2013 by The Institute of Electrical and Electronics Engineers, Inc. Published 2013 by John Wiley & Sons, Inc.

2.2 ISO/TS 18308 Requirement Specification

ISO/TS 18308 Health Informatics—Requirements for an electronic health record architecture [ISO/TS 18308 2002] is a specification for defining user and technical requirements of an EHR and its architecture. It projects EHR as a longitudinal health record and enlists requirements about the structure, content, form, and type of content. It also defines requirements for reference architecture of an EHR for exchanging or sharing health information.

The standard discusses different names of EHR such as Electronic Patient Record (EPR), Electronic Health Care Record (EHCR), Computerized Patient Record (CPR), Electronic Medical Record (EMR), and so on. Various bodies associate different meanings with each one of them. Although EHR has different names, the requirements specified in ISO/TS 18308 are the same for all its variants. These terminologies, including EHR, were described in Chapter 1.

ISO/TS 18308 defines a "reference architecture" for EHR that enlists requirements for various EHR contents to be accessible and exchangeable across healthcare systems. This architecture forms the basis of EHR system architecture. Other systems can adopt this architecture for developing EHR applications. Hence, the reference architecture forms the abstract specification, while the system architecture forms the technological specification for implementing a product.

The structural, functional, securities, and legal requirements of an EHR system, as given by ISO/TS 18308, are discussed below.

2.2.1 CONTENT STRUCTURE MODEL

ISO/TS 18308 specifies the requirements for the content structure model that an EHR system should conform to. Accordingly, an EHR should have structural elements that encapsulate contained data. The encapsulation enables interoperability and automatic processing of EHR. An EHR should also support exchange of its structural elements across healthcare systems and should be independent of hardware, software, and so on. It should be possible to extract information from EHR for other nonprimary uses such as for research, study, and so on.

Information stored in an EHR may be clinical or administrative. Clinical information contains tabular records, images, scans, raw text, and so on. Administrative information contains information related to patient identification, demographic, insurance, encounters, financials, legal status, and so on. An EHR should be able to contain both structured and nonstructured data with suitable data types to represent all possible types of clinical information. It should be able to contain the information representation structure specified by various standards, coding systems, and terminologies. It should be possible to translate information in an EHR into any human readable language, keeping faithfulness and reliability of original information.

2.2.2 INCLUSION OF CLINICAL AND RECORD PROCESSES

An EHR can be acted upon by either a clinical process or a record process. Clinical processes include orders, care plans, clinical guidelines, decision support, and so on. It should be possible to create and instantiate a clinical process and maintain various states of the process within the EHR acted upon. For example, a clinical process can include an order. Various events in this clinical process can be:

1. Order for test to be conducted on a patient, which represents the state INITIATED.
2. Execution of the order that represents the state IN-PROCESS.
3. Generation of results that represents COMPLETED.
4. Verification of the results by ordered entity for "VERIFIED."

Record processes include processes for capturing, editing, updating, querying, and presentation of data. It should be possible to implement the rules for inserting, updating, and deleting of data (if need to be supported). It should also be possible to retrieve partial structure of EHR and represent it into different views for different types of users such as physicians, patients, and so on.

2.2.3 CONTENT EXCHANGE

Interoperability enables exchange of records between healthcare systems having different EHR record structures. HIS, EHR systems, and clinical systems developed by different vendors or organizations often need to interoperate. ISO/TS 18308 defines standards for data representation and exchange services. According to ISO/TS 18308, it should be possible to exchange partial or complete record while maintaining integrity and context of EHR data. Additionally, it should provide support for authentication and audit trail of exchange process.

2.2.4 PRIVACY AND SECURITY

ISO/TS 18308 stipulates that for personal healthcare information, EHR should incorporate ethical and legal requirements. For security, EHR should support authentication, data integrity, confidentiality, nonrepudiation, and audit of accessed information. It should restrict access to a group of users on a part or whole of EHR, defining the level of what actions (read, write, update, verify, transmit) could be allowed. Data integrity is to be ensured at the time of storage and transfer of a part or whole of EHR. Audit control mechanisms should keep track of who, when, and what type of accesses were made to EHR data.

2.2.5 LEGAL CONSIDERATIONS

ISO/TS 18308 makes it mandatory to record the chronology of events happening on an EHR and the actors involved in the events. Every action (read, write, insert, update, verify, transmit) performed by an actor to the EHR along with the details of the action such as its date, time, location, and so on, must be recorded. It must also maintain versions of part or whole of EHR for every amendment made to it. This requirement enables re-creation of an older state of the EHR at any specific point of time in the past.

2.2.6 ETHICAL, CONSUMER/CULTURAL ASPECTS

Ethical and moral responsibility on part of the actors accessing EHR records is an important factor in maintaining patient autonomy and in delivering highest standard of clinical care. ISO/TS 18308 requires recording of approval for any nonprimary usage of EHR.

ISO/TS 18308 suggests that patients should access EHR through user interfaces that have health improvement advices for the patient and that enables patients to self-monitor their health condition. Additionally, EHR should promote communication between clinicians and patients. ISO/TS 18308 stresses the need to include patient's comments, rating on delivery of healthcare, expectations, and so on, in EHR.

Certain cultural issues impose restrictions on sharing parts of clinical information. ISO/TS 18308 requires that EHR architecture should address such issues and maintain processes for any local customs. It must also make information accessible across jurisdictions.

2.2.7 FUTURE-PROOF FRAMEWORK

ISO/TS 18308 recognizes that due to rapid changes in technologies, an EHR architecture should be "future-proof" in the sense that it should be able to represent new types of data, incorporate new record types, and generally be extensible in nature.

2.3 Discussion

ISO/TS 18308 is a set of user and technical requirements for building a platform-independent reference EHR architecture. It is a set of guidelines based on which one can derive detailed specifications for EHR structure and system architecture.

ISO/TS 18308 refers to EHCR-SupA specification as a source material to formulate the requirements. EHCR-SupA [EHCR-SupA 2000] is a requirement specification document generated under the EHCR project, which describes requirements for EHR and its architecture.

ISO/TS 18308 is a set of abstract specifications for a conceptual medical and administrative record structure. It is not a complete technical specification for a particular EHR architecture. The reference architecture requirements specified by ISO/TS 18308 are followed by CEN/ISO EN 13606 [EN 13606 Association] standard. Further details of this standard are covered in Chapter 5.

Clinical Process Model. ISO/TS 18308 is a technical requirements specification for EHR reference architecture. It does not define a clinical process model or a concept model for care. The defined requirements focus on content structure, content type and forms, exchange, privacy, and security aspects.

Structural Model. According to ISO/TS 18308, an EHR structure should constitute various sections containing different components representing health information content. It should be possible to create different views of each section of EHR.

Although ISO/TS 18308 defines sections in an EHR, it does not discuss about structural design of the "section" as to what kind of form will it take such as, will it support nested sections, or are there separate types of sections identified based on the content it represents.

ISO/TS 18308 requires reference architecture to support archiving of EHR. However, it does not disintegrate this requirement to the level of defining what content has to be archived, how to archive it, and for how much time one can keep the archived data.

ISO/TS 18308 specifies a list of clinical data such as patient history, physical examination, and so on, that shall be recorded at minimum, but does not mandate presence of a minimum confirmed list of contents.

Security/Privacy Considerations. ISO/TS 18308 specifies requirements for privacy, confidentiality, consent, access and audit control, and non-repudiation. However, it does not detail any technical requirements for achieving them. It does not specify what frameworks should be in place to implement security and privacy, since frameworks depend on the jurisdiction where they are applied.

In case of access control, ISO/TS 18308 specifies that grant, revocation, and update of access rights on an EHR should be applicable per section or per attribute. This is a minor guideline for an access control service, rather than an exhaustive list of requirements needed for defining a complete access control service.

Enabling anonymization of EHR data when accessed by certain class of users as part of security requirements is not included. However, there is a reference for "secondary use" of EHR specified under structural requirements of EHR.

Legal Aspects. ISO/TS 18308 specifies actor identification for actions done on a record and provides a thoughtful list of various factors involved in health care events. This is an important requirement from legal point of view. It also requires recording of intended clinical meanings in EHR that should not change when representation is converted to some other format. This requirement fulfills the need for non-repudiation. Requirements such as re-creation of a previous state of EHR and disallowing deletion of any amendment made to EHR are of utmost legal importance.

Exchange Specifications. For exchange specifications, ISO/TS 18308 suggests use of medical informatics standards such as HL7, DICOM, and so on, but does not mandate any of the standards. Hence, a conforming EHR system is free to choose any suitable exchange standard.

ISO/TS 18308 specifies requirements for record management to maintain record entries in EHR. For example, it should be possible to exchange part or all of EHR across healthcare settings, and so on. This is an important requirement for any EHR structure, since exchange of part or whole of EHR should be possible.

Technical Guidelines. ISO/TS 18308 lists a set of technologies to be used in EHR architecture. However, it does not mandate use of these technologies. They are used specifically in exchanging EHR record entries. The technologies mentioned are XML, CORBA, and .NET.

2.4 Conclusion

ISO/TS 18308 is a broad requirement specification for an EHR model. It defines a nonexhaustive set of requirements for EHR architecture. The listed requirements are based on reference EHR architecture, rather than study and statistical analysis of overall requirements. ISO/TS 18308 can be used to validate an EHR model against a set of specified requirements.

This chapter covered the technical requirements of an EHR system. However, other than the technical requirements, an EHR system should also address the clinical requirements. It should depict the clinical workflows that are followed in an integrated healthcare environment. It should incorporate the clinical and legal concepts in EHR. The next chapter focuses on such requirements that should be incorporated in an EHR.

BIBLIOGRAPHY

[**Begoyan 2007**] Begoyan., A. (University of Westminster), An overview of interoperability standards for electronic health records. In: *Integrated Design and Process Technology (IDPT)* (2007); http://citeseerx.ist.psu.edu/viewdoc/download?doi= 10.1.1.131.4421&rep=rep1&type=pdf.

[**EHCR-SupA 2000**] Electronic Healthcare Record Support Action (EHCR-SupA) Deliverable 1.4, *Consolidated List of Requirements* (2000); http://eprints.ucl.ac.uk/ 1603/1/R5.pdf.

[**EN 13606 Association**] EN 13606 Association; www.en13606.org.

[**ISO/TS 18308 2002**] International Organization for Standardization (ISO), Health Informatics—Requirements for an electronic health record architecture, ISO/TS 18308 (2002).

[**Lloyd and Kalra**] Lloyd, D., and Kalra, D., EHR Requirements, Centre for Health Informatics and Multiprofessional Education (CHIME), University College London; http://eprints.ucl.ac.uk/1583/1/A5.pdf.

[**NEHTA 2006**] National E-Health Transition Authority (NEHTA, *Review of Shared Electronic Health Record Standards*, Version 1.0 (February 2006); http://publicaa.ansi. org/sites/apdl/Documents/Standards%20Activities/Healthcare%20Informatics% 20Technology%20Standards%20Panel/Standardization%20Committees/International %20Landscape/NEHTA%20EHR%20Standards%20Report%20v1%200.pdf.

[**openEHR 2007**] openEHR Foundation, ISO 18308 Conformance; http://www. openehr.org/releases/1.0.2/requirements/iso18308_conformance.pdf.

CHAPTER THREE

Standard for Healthcare Concepts

3.1 Introduction

Processes with defined concepts help healthcare professionals take better decisions during referral, transfer, and supportive care. Standardization of such concepts and processes contributes significantly to interoperability of systems across organizations. EN 13940 is such a standard developed by European Standardization Committee (CEN). The standard is called CONTsys and its full form is "Health informatics—System of concepts to support continuity of care" [CONTsys site]. CEN technical committee, CEN/TC 251, evolved it to deal with standardization in health information and communication technology for interoperability between systems. Hence, the standard is named CEN/TC 251 EN 13940.

CONTsys has two parts. The first part describes basic concepts within healthcare, while the second part describes various core processes involved in healthcare along with workflows for different scenarios. CONTsys describes management of health information to support continuous care of an individual within an organization as well as across organizations. Information usually shared between different healthcare providers includes patient's information, healthcare provider's information, information about patient's health problem(s), information about ongoing treatment, and so on. CONTsys aims to identify, analyze, and model all these information as different concepts to provide continuity of care.

Electronic Health Record: Standards, Coding Systems, Frameworks, and Infrastructures, Pradeep Sinha, Gaur Sunder, Prashant Bendale, Manisha Mantri, and Atreya Dande.
© 2013 by The Institute of Electrical and Electronics Engineers, Inc. Published 2013 by John Wiley & Sons, Inc.

As mentioned earlier, the two parts of CONTsys are:

1. *Health informatics—System of concepts to support continuity of care, Part 1: Basic concepts* (published in 2007 as CEN standard), EN 13940-1 [EN 13940-1 2007]

2. *Health informatics—System of concepts to support continuity of care, Part 2: Core process and work flow in health care*, prEN 13940-2 [prEN 13940-2 2009]

The first part (EN 13940-1) describes about 58 concepts with their definitions, multiplicity, attributes, and relationships with other concepts. Description of concepts includes their diagrammatical representation using Unified Modeling Language (UML). The standard describes concepts such as *who are all the actors involved in healthcare* (actors include patient, healthcare provider, and third parties), *for what* (health issues), and *when* (time-related concepts such as episode), *what is done* (decisions, clinical activities), and *how* (management of data).

The second part (prEN 13940-2) is supportive extension of the first part and describes all concepts in terms of processes. It explains applicability of the concepts in hospital workflow and core processes in healthcare, focusing on curing health state of the patient. It uses the process-modeling technique for describing objects as inputs and outputs, processes for management of patient care activities, communication of information, and clinical activities assuring quality control and responsibilities of doctors.

The two parts are described below.

3.2 CEN/TC EN 13940-1

EN 13940-1 describes the following healthcare concepts:

1. Actors in continuity of care
2. Health issues and their management
3. Concepts related to responsibility in continuity of care
4. Time-related concepts in continuity of care
5. Concepts related to knowledge, activities, and decision support
6. Health data management

3.2.1 ACTORS IN CONTINUITY OF CARE

Actors are entities involved in healthcare activities and are classified as either *healthcare device* or *healthcare party*. Healthcare party is further classified as *subject of care, healthcare provider*, and *healthcare third party*. Healthcare provider can be a *healthcare organization* or *healthcare professional*. A healthcare organization has

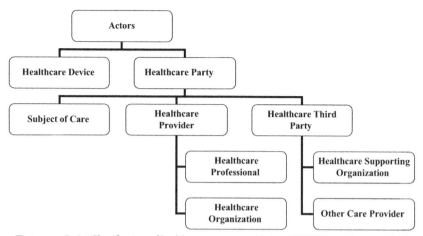

FIGURE 3.1 Classification of healthcare actors provided in CEN/TC 13940-1 standard.

one or more appointed healthcare professionals, who actually deliver care to the subject of care. A healthcare third party can be a *healthcare supporting organization* or an independent organization (called *other carer*) related to the subject of care and affecting the care of subject. Figure 3.1 summarizes the classification of healthcare actors provided in the standard.

3.2.2 HEALTH ISSUES AND THEIR MANAGEMENT

Health issue is the health problem of a subject of care (patient) identified by a healthcare party (doctor or hospital). Its interpretation can change over time depending on efforts taken to solve the health issue. Thus, a single health issue can spawn into none or many *Health threads* having different interpretations of the health issue; for example, a health issue such as "an accident" can be further interpreted as "fracture" in diagnosis process.

3.2.3 CONCEPTS RELATED TO RESPONSIBILITY

The authorization given to a healthcare provider for treating a health issue of a subject of care is called *Health mandate*. Health mandates are categorized into:

1. Demand mandate
2. Care mandate
3. Mandate to export personal data
4. Continuity facilitator mandate

Demand mandate signifies that a patient has demanded the care, either explicitly or implicitly. *Care mandate* is the authorization given to a healthcare provider for being responsible for care of the patient. The healthcare provider can either accept or reject the same. After receiving a care mandate for a patient, the healthcare provider can refer the patient to another healthcare provider by transferring the care mandate. A care mandate sender cannot send or share the patient data with a care mandate receiver before getting the *Mandate to export personal data*. It allows sharing of the patient data with the other healthcare provider during the care process. Healthcare providers can provide continuous sharing of information for supporting continuity of care to a patient through the *continuity facilitator mandate*.

Transfer of responsibilities and permissions during the care process of a patient should be traceable from the demand mandate given by the patient. Health mandate notifications are used to notify transfer and assignment of mandates for health issue of the patient. The information will be sent to the patient and other users having access rights as per other mandates.

3.2.4 TIME-RELATED CONCEPTS

Time-related concepts describe the timeframes in which interactions among the involved healthcare actors takes place for treating the subject of care. These concepts include:

1. Period of care
2. Contact
3. Episode of care

Period of care is the duration during which clinical activities are performed for multiple health issues of a patient within a single mandate by one or more healthcare providers. A new period of care can be started within a period of care for a new health thread with a new health mandate.

Contact is a meeting between a patient and a healthcare professional for addressing one or more health issues. Every contact is generally responsible for some change in the EHR of the patient. A contact can be either an *encounter* or a *record contact*. In the case of an encounter, the patient is directly or indirectly involved, whereas in the case of a record contact, the patient's information is generated during clinical activities. During a contact, the patient information generated for each health issue is called a *contact element*.

Collection of contact elements (clinical activities performed by a healthcare provider) for one particular health issue is called an *Episode of care*. An episode of care is usually divided into multiple *sub-episodes of care*, where each sub-episode of care is aimed at achieving a specific goal for the care of the patient. For example, diagnosis can be a sub-episode of care during the care of a patient for one health issue. Collection of all clinical activities by multiple healthcare providers for a single health issue (all episodes of care for a single health issue from multiple healthcare providers) is called *Cumulative episode of care*.

Figure 3.2 describes the relationship among the time-related concepts. It represents a *Period of care* for three *Health issues* having multiple *Contact elements* created during three different *Contacts* for a single patient by a single healthcare provider.

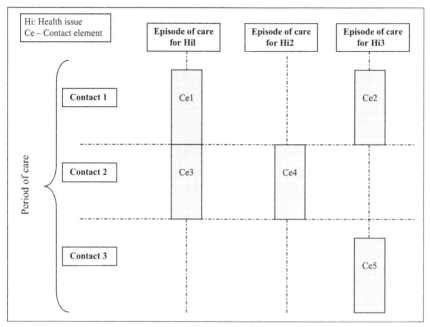

FIGURE 3.2 Time-related concepts in continuity of care.

Each *contact element* contains one or more records of clinical activities performed during a *contact* for a specific *episode of care*.

3.2.5 CONCEPTS RELATED TO KNOWLEDGE, ACTIVITIES, AND DECISION SUPPORT

This section of the standard deals with the concepts related to the activities preformed in healthcare during the treatment of a patient. It includes healthcare activities, clinical guidelines and protocols, programs of care, and care plans. A healthcare activity is a health-related activity performed by any *healthcare party* such as a doctor (e.g., surgery), a patient for her self-care (e.g., physical exercise), a third party who supports patient care (e.g., health insurance company), or an automated device (e.g., X-ray or CT machine) that generates test reports of a patient. Various types of healthcare activities are:

1. Healthcare provider activity
2. Health self-care activity
3. Healthcare contributing activity
4. Healthcare automated activity

The collection of all these activities for one health issue is called *healthcare activities bundle*.

Healthcare activities are performed based on generic clinical guidelines that refer to the protocols for various treatments followed by healthcare provider organizations. *Program of care* refers to the protocol followed for the care of a patient within a Health care organization by its multiple Health care professionals. A Program of care can have a number of Care plans within it. Thus, we treat a Program of care as a healthcare objective and its care plans as specific healthcare goals.

3.2.6 HEALTH DATA MANAGEMENT

Management of health data is detailed at two levels: managing it within a hospital and managing it while sending it to another hospital. To address the issue of health data management at both levels, the standard specifies that a health informatics application should be used to manage health data for the mentioned healthcare activities, transfer of mandates, and complete EHR of a patient. It also specifies that such data when transferred to a common shared repository should be in electronic form.

The standard also deals with assuring correctness of such data generated by means of clinical devices. For this, it specifies that data should be accepted only after verification and approval of a clinician, and clinical record data in electronic form should be stored in a shared repository after verification only. Additionally, all data access operations must be through access rights verification, and all access information should be logged in the EHR of a patient.

3.3 CEN/TC prEN 13940-2

CEN/TC prEN 13940 is the second part of CONTsys standard. It describes the usability aspects of the concepts defined in Part 1 of the standard in terms of processes, entities involved in the processes, and workflow for various scenarios in hospitals. It uses the concepts drawn from the Swedish process modeling project titled *Structured Architecture for Medical Business Activities (SAMBA)* [SAMBA]. The project aims to identify core processes and workflows in healthcare.

The standard defines a *process* as the *set of interrelated or interacting activities, which transform inputs into outputs*—ISO 9000:2005. This describes characteristics of a process.

A process has one *refinement object* that converts input into output with a defined objective. Sometimes, a process may be used to add value to the refinement object. An actor involved in a process may be responsible for it. A process might use resources for achieving its defined objective. It has a definite time course with clearly defined start and end points.

A core process in healthcare is a *clinical process* that deals with a patient's condition as a refinement object with a fixed objective of curing it. Two other types of processes influencing a clinical process include *management process* and *support process*. A process model comprises of activities and conditions. It can be applied to an organization where multiple professionals are involved in the care of a *subject of care*. A workflow model describes activities in a process with identified actors and their roles. It also describes the flow of communication among the participants involved in the care, enabling continuity of care activities.

The standard describes the following types of processes with their relationships and interactions in a healthcare provider organization having healthcare professionals contributing to the care of a patient:

1. **Healthcare Process.** It is the core process in the organization. It consists of clinical, resource management, and clinical management processes.

2. **Healthcare Provider Research Process.** This process aims to improve clinical knowledge of healthcare professionals in the organization.

3. **Healthcare Provider Educational Process.** This process aims to improve the skills of healthcare professionals by enabling them to learn the practical implementation of the clinical knowledge for the care of patients.

4. **Healthcare Administrative Process.** This process is used to control and support the healthcare process.

Healthcare process further comprises of the following processes:

1. **Clinical Process.** This is the core process of health care process and includes all the clinical activities in healthcare.

2. **Clinical Management Process.** This process deals with the management of clinical process activities, such as planning and monitoring of the clinical activities.

3. **Documentation and Communication Process.** This process deals with the recording of clinical data and activities during clinical process. It interacts with all the clinical processes.

4. **Healthcare Quality Management Process.** This process monitors healthcare activities and evaluates them to assure quality of health care delivery.

5. **Healthcare Resources Management Process.** This process manages the availability, transfer, and usability of resources required in the healthcare process.

3.3.1 HEALTHCARE PROCESS

A healthcare process is a set of healthcare activities having a specific healthcare goal. For achieving this goal, a healthcare activity includes one or more healthcare tasks having an explicit purpose. A healthcare process may include one or more healthcare processes, depending on the complexity and requirement of the goal.

A healthcare process may have two types of inputs: major/primary process input and secondary process input. The former is a refinement object that results in a major process output, while the latter acts as a supportive input that will be utilized during the process. Major input to a clinical process might be health state of a subject of care with the aim to improve and stabilize health state through healthcare activities.

Health state of a patient is classified depending on healthcare activities preformed on it. The input to the healthcare process is called *actual health state* of the patient. The first encounter with a healthcare professional is called *initial contact*, and the reason for making initial contact is called *health issue*.

During clinical process, the subjective observation obtained during the healthcare process is called *Initial health condition*. Afterwards, a healthcare professional performs activities on the health condition of the patient. This assessed condition of the patient is called *Assessed health condition*. At the same time, a targeted health condition is set, which will be the desired health condition of the patient during the clinical process. Various clinical activities will be performed to achieve the targeted goals, ultimately resulting in a *Resulted health condition*.

A patient starts a clinical process through a demand of care. A healthcare process for the patient's continuity of care is represented as:

1. Initial contact of the patient—that is, the first encounter for health issue showing the process for demand of care.
2. Clinical process showing the activities that contribute to any change in health condition of the patient.
3. Healthcare workflow with healthcare resources during program of care for multiple health issues and health issue threads.
4. Healthcare activities (decision, diagnostic activities, plans, etc.) and their relationship with other objects such as, mandate, health condition, and so on.

3.4 Discussion

The first part of CONTsys standard is comprehensive and includes normative and informative sections. The second part provides diagrammatical representation of the processes in healthcare, using concepts specified in the first part.

It does not impose use of information technology in healthcare, but focuses more on the processes, workflows, and concepts in healthcare. This enables standardization of healthcare processes that can lead to interoperability between health informatics systems used in organizations following this standard.

Since the standard is newly evolved, its worldwide popularity and adaptability is considerably less. In a national program, Sweden adapted this standard for implementing its national EHR model.

Clinical Process Model. The second part of the standard covers the clinical process model, which deals with the processes used in healthcare and workflow for those processes to support concepts explained in part one. It describes general flow and relationships between healthcare processes such as clinical process, management process, communication process, educational process, and research process.

Clinical process is influenced by the Swedish national process model of EHR, which is based on changing the health state of a patient. Various health conditions are described as output of clinical activities during a clinical process. Activities include subjective observation, diagnosis/assessment, and care plan. The standard considers diagnosis and assessment at the same level.

Structural Model. The standard does not provide specifications for the various types of clinical information with contents that must be generated during continuous care of a patient. However, it describes the concepts that should be involved during continuous care such as mandate, care plan, contact, and contact elements.

The standard suggests use of CEN/ISO EN 13606 [EN13606] part 1 standard for representing clinical data and information in the form of *Record Components*. Further details of structural specifications of EN 13606 are covered in Chapter 5.

Security Considerations. The standard focuses completely on healthcare processes and thus does not define security management. It suggests that security is a part of EHR communication, and security aspects can be followed as explained in EN 13606 part 4.

Privacy/Consent Considerations. The standard suggests preserving access logs of all accesses to shared data of patients, all transfers of mandates from one healthcare professional to another, and all encounters using health informatics system. However, it does not specify how and what should be preserved for tracing access of a patient's data.

The standard describes use of healthcare mandates for permitting healthcare professionals to treat a patient, share data with other professionals, and provide continuous data to a shared repository such as a national store.

Legal Aspects. The standard imposes validation and approval of electronically generated clinical data before sending, storing, or exporting it to a shared repository. The regulation ensures that data will be legally assured and clinically correct. This can be useful for evaluating processes and quality control in hospitals and can be referred while developing information systems.

Exchange Specifications. The standard suggests use of EN 13606 for exchange specifications. It does not provide any further requirements for EHR communication. The details of exchange specifications provided by EN 13606 are covered in Chapter 5.

Technical Guidelines. The standard only describes concepts and processes in healthcare, considering legal aspects for continuity of care. It does not provide any technical guidelines.

3.5 Conclusion

CONTsys describes clinical concepts and processes and aims to adapt semantic processes at organizations to support continuous care to patients.

Standardization of concepts in healthcare can be helpful in providing a smooth process for treating common diseases in hospitals. Application of this standard can help in building a regulation for treatment at organizations across countries.

The standard can be referred for development of health informatics systems to support most healthcare processes. In addition, it can help in evaluating processes and workflow for storing shared clinical data in a national distributed EHR store for ratification of data.

After studying the workflow specifications in the form of processes and concepts for an EHR system, the next chapter covers the remaining requirement specifications of an EHR system—that is, functional requirement through HL7 EHR-S Functional Model.

BIBLIOGRAPHY

[**Areblad et al. 2005**] Areblad, M., Fogelberg, M., Karlsson, D., Åhlfeldt, H., SAMBA—Structured architecture for medical business activities. In: *Proceedings of Medical Informatics Europe, Geneva, Switzerland*, pp. 1225–1230 (August 2005).

[**CONTSys site**] European ehealth continuity site; http://www.contsys.eu/.

[**EN13606**] European Committee for Standardization (CEN), Health Informatics—Electronic Health Record Communication, EN13606-1, EN13606-2, EN13606-3, EN13606-4, EN13606-5.

[**EN 13940-1 2007**] European Committee for Standardization (CEN), *Health Informatics—System of Concepts to Support Continuity of Care—Part 1: Basic Concepts, EN 13940-1*; http://www.tc215wg3.nhs.uk/docs/isotc215wg3_n386.pdf.

[**prEN 13940-2 2009**] European Committee for Standardization (CEN), Health Informatics—System of Concepts to Support Continuity of Care–Part 2: Core Process and Work Flow in Health Care, prEN 13940-2; http://www.contsys.eu/documents/prEN13940-2_(E)_WD_2009-11-26khl.doc.

[**SAMBA**] Structured Architecture for Medical Business Activities (SAMBA), *Process and Concept Analysis of the Workflow in Swedish Health Care for Care of One Individual Subject of Care* (November 2003); http://www.contsys.eu/documents/samba/samba_en_short_1_3.pdf.

CHAPTER FOUR

Standard for EHR Functional Specifications

4.1 Introduction

In 2003, the *HL7 EHR Special Interest Group (HL7 EHR SIG)* initiated the development of a functional guidelines document to cover expectations from an EHR system. This set of requirements is called the *HL7 EHR-System Functional Model (HL7 EHR-S FM)*. This standard defines the guidelines that are neither messaging specifications nor EHR specifications, but are descriptive understanding of functions expected in a system claiming to be an EHR system. The guidelines refer to a functional profile template that represents various categories of functionalities in terms of codes. An entity providing/requiring some capability has to refer to these profiles while specifying its capabilities/requirements. Since these codes provide a thoughtful description of each of the activities, specifying an entity need not describe its functional details. In addition, as vendors can thoroughly examine what each code refers to, they can claim clear assurance to each of the expected functionality [Overview of EHR-S FM 2007].

HL7 EHR-SIG defined a template for specifying functional profiles in medical specialties. It keeps on adding new functional profiles to the template. Users can submit new functional profiles for addition to the template by following the HL7 EHR-S FM template. The HL7 EHR-S FM approved by ANSI covers more than 160 functional profiles related to EHR systems.

Electronic Health Record: Standards, Coding Systems, Frameworks, and Infrastructures, Pradeep Sinha, Gaur Sunder, Prashant Bendale, Manisha Mantri, and Atreya Dande.
© 2013 by The Institute of Electrical and Electronics Engineers, Inc. Published 2013 by John Wiley & Sons, Inc.

HL7 EHR-SIG has also developed *EHR Interoperability Model (EHR/IM)*, which specifies how EHRs could be interoperable during transmission and reception.

HL7 EHR-SIG's ongoing work on EHR standards development includes profile descriptions for a wide category of EHR systems. These categories include EHR Behavioral Health Functional Profile, EHR Child Health Functional Profile, and EHR Interoperability Model. These components show HL7's view of EHR system [HL7 HER/PHR 2007].

HL7 EHR-S FM refers functional descriptions from various guidelines developed by EHR standards like ISO/TS 18308, ISO 20514, and CEN 13606. These standards provide guidelines for requirements of an EHR system. HL7 EHR-S SIG reviews these guidelines and incorporates their recommendations while defining specifications in functional profiles [Donald 2010].

4.2 HL7 EHR-S Functional Model

4.2.1 FUNCTIONAL PROFILES

The functional profiles template defined in ANSI-approved HL7 EHR-S FM contains overview, set of functions, and guidelines on creating custom functional profiles as per needs of users. Table 4.1 shows the EHR functional profiles template. As shown, the set of functions are divided into three categories including Direct Care, Supportive, and Information Infrastructure. Each category has various functional areas with specific codes assigned to them.

HL7 EHR-SIG defined a set of functional profiles based on the EHR-S template. These profiles are:

TABLE 4.1   **Template of HL7 EHR-S Functional Model**

Category	Code	Functional Areas
Direct Care	DC.1	Care management
	DC.2	Clinical decision support
	DC.3	Operations management and communication
Supportive	S.1	Clinical support
	S.2	Measurement, analysis, research, and reports
	S.3	Administrative and financial
Information Infrastructure	IN.1	Security
	IN.2	Health record information and management
	IN.3	Registry and directory
	IN.4	Standard terminology and terminology services
	IN.5	Standards-based interoperability
	IN.6	Business rules management
	IN.7	Workflow management

Source: Adapted from [Donald 2010].

1. *EHR Child Health Functional Profile.* Pediatrics Data Standards Special Interest Group of HL7 organization has developed ANSI-approved EHR Child Health Functional Profile. This profile conforms to EHR-S FM and aims to provide guidelines for development of EHR systems used in healthcare delivery to children. Major functional topics covered in this profile include immunization management, growth tracking, medication dosing, pediatric data norms, and privacy of health records [ANSI/HL7 EHR CHFP 2008].

2. *EHR Clinical Research Profile.* Functional profile for EHR Clinical Research aims to develop EHR systems that assist in clinical research. Using these guidelines, vendors can develop EHR systems that make provisions for functions where EHR data can be used as resource for clinical research. The group has developed this functional profile keeping in mind the present growth of EHR systems and the countrywide healthcare IT networks. This functional profile provides guidelines on how to utilize current health information in these systems/networks without creating redundant collection of data. This profile describes access mechanisms for clinical data stored in EHR systems while meeting regulatory requirements [HL7 EHR/CR FP 2008].

3. *EHR Interoperability Model.* EHR Interoperability Model (IM) specifies guidelines and requirements for standards developed to exchange health information from one source to another. Examples of such standards are HL7 v2/3, Clinical Document Architecture (CDA), Continuity of Care Record (CCR), Continuity of Care Document (CCD). HL7 EHR IM Committee provides guidance on how to achieve technical, semantic, and process level interoperability. According to the model,

   - **Technical interoperability** is all about knowing and preserving structure of information among systems while transmitting and receiving data.

   - **Semantic interoperability** goes beyond that and attaches semantics and validations to the structural information, which is very useful in health-care. The absence of one set of information in a larger structure would not fail technical interoperability, but will fail semantic interoperability if that information is semantically vital for the receiver.

   - **Process interoperability** goes yet further, and it incorporates the received data into its own process and triggers action based on the contents of data to achieve process/workflow level interoperability [Gibbons et al. 2007].

▣ EXAMPLE 4.1 **Direct Care Function for Managing Patient Demographics**

> Table 4.2 is an example of specification of a function in the category of Direct Care from EHR-S FM. It exemplifies the depth of description that EHR-S FM guidelines provide for a function of EHR system.
>
> Table 4.2 explains functional requirements for capturing Patient Demographics Information. Function statement specifies action to be taken, and Conformance Criteria specifies finer expectations from the system for managing demographics information [Direct Care Functions 2007].

TABLE 4.2   **Direct Care Function Specification from EHR-S FM**

ID#	Name	Statement/Description	Conformance Criteria
DC.1.1.2	Manage patient demographics	**Statement:** Capture and maintain demographic information. Where appropriate, the data should be clinically relevant and reportable. **Description:** Contact information including addresses and phone numbers, as well as key demographic information such as date of birth, time of birth, gestation, gender, and other information is stored and maintained for unique patient identification, reporting purposes and for the provision of care. Patient demographics are captured and maintained as discrete fields (e.g., patient names and addresses) and may be enumerated, numeric or codified. Key patient identifiers are shown on all patient information output (such as name and ID# on each screen of a patient's record). The system will track who updates demographic information, and when is the demographic information updated.	1. The system *shall* capture demographic information as part of the patient record. 2. The system *shall* store and retrieve demographic information as discrete data. 3. The system *shall* provide the ability to retrieve demographic data as part of the patient record. 4. The system *shall* provide the ability to update demographic data. 5. The system *should* provide the ability to report demographic data. 6. The system *should* store historical values of demographic data over time. 7. The system *shall* present a set of patient-identifying information at each interaction with the patient record. 8. The system *should* conform to the function IN.1.4 (Patient Access Management). 9. The system *shall* conform to the function IN.2.2 (Auditable Records).

Source: Adapted from [Direct Care Functions 2007].

4.2.2 EXCHANGE

Functional requirements specified for information exchange describe usage of existing medical informatics standards for messaging. Functional Model also encourages use of coding terminologies for better search and information representation in healthcare domain. Interoperability Model specified by the

EHR committee describes use of HL7 v3 and HL7 CDA standards for exchange and medical record representation respectively [EHR Data Exchange 2007]. Further details of these standards are covered in Chapters 7 and 8.

4.2.3 SECURITY/PRIVACY

Legal EHR-S Functional Profile describes security and privacy related functional requirements along with legal rationale behind them. Various functions included in this profile are as follows [Legal EHR-S FM 2007]:

- Entity authentication
- Entity Authorization
- Entity Access Control
- Patient Access Management
- Nonrepudiation
- Secure Data Exchange
- Secure Data Routing
- Provider Information
- Provider Access Levels
- Provider Registry or Directory
- Report Generation
- Ad Hoc Query and Report Generation

- Patient Privacy and Confidentiality
- Health Record Information and Management
- Data Retention, Availability, and Destruction
- Legal Hold
- Legal Hold Notice
- Auditable Records
- System and Record Metadata
- Manage Record States
- Health Record Completeness
- Chronology of Events
- Registry and Directory Services
- Standard Terminologies and Terminology Services

- Support Remote Healthcare Services
- Manage Practitioner/Patient Relationships
- Provider Information
- Standards-based Interoperability
- Interchange Agreements
- Manage Record States
- Clinical Decision Support
- Information Attestation
- Extraction of Health Information
- Workflow Management
- Genealogical Access

Legal EHR-S Functional Profile covers a wide range of functional requirements that are helpful in managing healthcare information in secure manner, conforming to legal requirements. Table 4.3 shows a functional guideline for "legal hold." This function describes the activities that an EHR system should support in a scenario where a particular patient's legal case mandates the EHR system to keep his/her EHR on hold and to suspend normal EHR operations.

TABLE 4.3   **Example Function: Legal Hold**

ID#	Name	Statement/Description	Conformance Criteria
NEW 72 A IN.2.1.1	Legal hold	**Statement:** EHR systems must support a duty to preserve material evidence (suspend normal destruction practices) when the organization reasonably should know that the evidence (health information) may be relevant to anticipated litigation. **Description/Legal rationale:** Organizations have a duty to preserve information that is or could be relevant to a legal proceeding whether litigation is threatened (the potential for) or impending. The organization must take steps to place a legal hold (suspend their normal destruction practices for all potentially relevant information) and prevent from loss, destruction, unauthorized use or alteration. Audit trail functionality helps identify access and alterations to the record.	1. The system *shall* provide the ability to secure data/records for the purpose of suspending the normal destruction process for information considered relevant to potential or pending litigation. 2. The system *shall* identify the locations of data/records and identify the associated custodian of the record. 3. The system *should* provide the ability to identify the information involved in the legal hold by type, class, or encounter (for example: medical record entry or report, email, metadata, etc.). 4. The system *shall* provide the ability to designate the status of information subject to legal hold as active, historical/archived or future data. 5. The system *shall* provide the ability to monitor and age the ongoing status of a legal hold and provide reports for management. 6. The system *should* provide a report that indicates file size, format, and retention of data on legal hold to be used for determining costs.

Source: Adapted from [Legal EHR FM 2007].

4.3 Comparison of HL7 EHR-S FM and ISO/TS 18308

ISO/TS 18308-Requirements for an Electronic Health Record Architecture is a specification for user and technical requirements of an EHR and its architecture [ISO/TS 18308 2011]. Since requirements translate into functions of the resulting system, HL7 EHR-S FM is comparable with ISO/TS 18308 standard. Some notable points in this comparison are:

- ISO/TS 18308 describes requirements for the structure, contents, and type of contents in an EHR, whereas HL7 EHR-S FM describes the functions requiring structure of an EHR in the system. For example, data capture functions in HL7 EHR-S FM specify several mechanisms and formats of data to be accepted by an EHR system. However, it does not constrain specific structure requirements on EHR itself.

- EHR system designers need to refer to both the standards to build an EHR system because ISO/TS 18308 defines the EHR architecture and HL7 EHR-S FM defines the functional requirements. Considering constraints posed by both standards, the resulting system will satisfy a wide range of requirements from users' perspective.

- Both the standards require that the content structure of an EHR should be representable in messaging standards for ensuring interoperability.

- ISO/TS 18308 describes the inclusion of clinical process or record process that associates workflow with an EHR structure, while HL7 EHR-S FM describes functions required at each stage of such a workflow instead of describing any workflow.

- Both these standards specify privacy/security requirements. The requirements given by ISO/TS 18308 are similar to the functional expectations given in HL7 EHR-S FM.

- HL7 EHR-S FM defines a profile related to legal requirements of an EHR system that gives many details about several legal situations related to EHR as discussed in the security/privacy section of this chapter. ISO/TS 18308 defines legal requirements purely from a security perspective, including authentication, audit log, nonrepudiation, and so on.

Details of ISO/TS 18308 standard have already been presented in Chapter 2.

4.4 Discussion

Development work in the area of EHR standards at HL7 primarily focused on functional profiles. HL7 has now started developing a wide variety of such profiles targeting specific areas in healthcare domain. Various functional profiles defined by HL7 EHR-SIG are helpful in defining the functional requirements of EHR systems. The descriptions and conformance criteria provide clear guidelines for these functions.

Clinical Process Model. Since HL7 EHR-S Functional Model describes only the functional characteristics of an EHR system, a clinical process model is not its objective. This functional model still provides a much better insight into what kinds of functionalities users expect from an EHR system.

Structural Model. Since the EHR-S Functional Model aims at specifying function-oriented guidelines, it does not describe any structural characteristics of the EHR model. However, functional guidelines are definitely helpful in designing the EHR structural model of any EHR framework.

Security/Privacy Considerations. Security- and privacy-related functionality specified by the Functional Model is of great help in identifying the responsibilities of the security module in an EHR framework. Detailed functional description given in Table 4.3 can help in defining the security policies. These functional descriptions can also work as validation criteria for an EHR framework [Legal EHR-S FM 2007].

Legal Aspects. Legal EHR functional profile is a good resource to refer while designing and developing an EHR system. This profile describes various functions that are applicable to an EHR system for security, privacy, and legal purposes. Though the standard does not specify exact technologies or mechanisms to implement these features, functional guidelines are helpful in ensuring that the EHR framework caters to all these requirements. These functional guidelines also include legal rationale with every requirement that help designers understand the importance of functionality and thus helps in designing systems that are better legally compliant [Legal EHR-S FM 2007].

Exchange Specifications. While specifying syntactic, semantic and process-based interoperability, the HL7 EHR committee specified use of HL7 v3 and HL7 CDA standards for interoperability. However, using some set of standards over the other has its own disadvantages. Other entities adhering to different standards need modification. This may also cause data loss during conversion from one standard to another.

Adhering to one standard for interoperability is a good suggestion if all systems adhere to the same standard. However, in an ecosystem of EHRs adhering to diverse standards, ensuring this is a difficult task.

Technical Guidelines. HL7 EHR-S FM being a functional specification, it does not provide technical guidelines for implementation.

4.5 Conclusion

HL7 EHR-S Functional Model is a set of functional requirements that any EHR system should fulfill. Thus, it does not specify the clinical process model and structural model of an EHR system.

Functional profiles are useful for setting validation criteria while evaluating an EHR system. While designing an EHR system, functional profiles are good candidates for performing requirement analysis. Another major useful component of this standard is its interoperability model. Semantic and process interoperability emphasizes use of HL7 v2/3, CDA, CCR, and CCD standards as means of interoperability. Security/privacy and legal functional specifications of the standard are very clear and helpful while developing an EHR system.

Until now, we have covered technical, workflow, and functional requirement specifications of an EHR system. The next chapter presents structural specifications of an EHR system for enabling sharing of information across different healthcare systems.

BIBLIOGRAPHY

[**Alam et al. 2011**] Alam, M., Hussain, M., Afzal, M., Maqbool, M., Ahmad, H.F., and Razzaq, S., Design and implementation of HL7 V3 standard-based service aware system. In: *Proceedings of 10th International Symposium on Autonomous Decentralized Systems (ISADS)* (2011).

[**ANSI/HL7 EHR CHFP 2008**] Pediatric data standards special interest group—HL7, *The Health Level Seven EHR Child Health Functional Profile Release 1* (2008).

[**Direct Care Functions 2007**] HL7 EHR TC, *Electronic Health Record—System Functional Model, Release 1 Chapter Three: Direct Care Functions* (2007).

[**Donald 2010**] Donald T. Mon, EHR & PHR system functional model (EHR-S FM & PHR-S FM) and standard. In: *Proceedings of European HL7 Interoperability Meeting*, (2010).

[**Donald 2011**] Donald, T. Mon, HL7 EHR system functional model and standard. In: *Proceedings of HIMSS Annual Conference*, (2011); http://www.hl7.org/documentcenter/public_temp_AE292405-1C23-BA17-0C6CAD376EC04F1B/calendarofevents/himss/2011/HL7_EHR-S_Functional_Model_2011_HIMSS_presentation.pdf.

[**EHR Data Exchange 2007**] HL7 EHR TC, *EHR Interoperability Model with EHR Data Exchange Criteria*, 2007.

[**EHR Functional Profiles 2011**] HL7 EHR-S Functional Profiles; http://xreg2.nist.gov:8080/ehrsRegistry/view/listFunctionalProfiles.jsp?filter=all.

[**Gibbons et al. 2007**] Gibbons, P., Arzt, N., Burke-Beebe, S., Chute, C., Dickinson, G., Flewelling, T., Jepsen, T., Kamens, D., Larson, J., Ritter, J., Rozen, M., Selover, S., and Stanford, J., *Coming to Terms: Scoping Interoperability for Health Care* (2007).

[**HL7 EHR 2011**] HL7 Electronic Health Record; http://www.hl7.org/EHR/.

[**HL7 EHR FM 2007**] EHR-S Functional and Interoperability Model; http://www.hl7.org/ehr/downloads/index_2007.asp.

[**HL7 EHR/CR FP 2008**] EHR/CR Functional Profile Working Group, *Electronic Health Records/Clinical Research Functional Profile* (2008).

[**HL7 EHR/PHR 2007**] Electronic Health Record/Personal Health record; http://www.hl7.org/implement/standards/ehrphr.cfm.

[**Information Infrastructure Functions 2007**] HL7 EHR TC, *Electronic Health Record—System Functional Model, Release 1 Chapter Three: Information Infrastructure Functions*, 2007.

[**ISO/TS 18308 2011**] International Organization for Standardization (ISO), *ISO/TS 18308—Requirements for an Electronic Health Record Architecture*, (2011); http://www.iso.org/iso/iso_catalogue/catalogue_tc/catalogue_detail.htm?csnumber=52823

[Janjua et al. 2011] Janjua, N.K., Hussain, M., Afzal, M., and Ahmad, H.F., Digital health care ecosystem: SOA compliant HL7 based health care information interchange. In: *Proceedings of 10th International Symposium on Autonomous Decentralized Systems (ISADS)*, 2011.

[Kibbe 2007] Kibbe, D., *The ASTM Continuity of Care Record, CCR, Standard: A Brief Description for a Non-Technical Audience* (2007).

[Legal EHR-S FM 2007] HL7 EHR TC—Legal EHR-S Functional Profile Workgroup, *Legal Electronic Health Record-System Functional Profile* (2007).

[Overview of EHR-S FM 2007] HL7 EHR TC, *Electronic Health Record—System Functional Model, Release 1 Chapter One: Overview* (2007).

[Supportive Functions 2007] HL7 EHR TC, *Electronic Health Record—System Functional Model, Release 1 Chapter Four: Supportive Functions* (2007).

CHAPTER FIVE

Standard for EHR Communication

5.1 Introduction

During the last decade, sharing of clinical information has acquired great emphasis due to various reasons such as increase in chronic diseases, increase in complex treatment methodologies, and need for secured access to healthcare data. However, EHR structures and their exchange protocols differ from application to application and from country to country. Various standards have been evolved to address this issue. CEN/ISO EN 13606 is one such initiative for standardizing the structure, content, communication, and security policies for communication of EHR in European countries. It is also called *EHRcom*.

European Standardization Committee (CEN) [CEN] develops standards in various domains for European Union (EU) and some associated countries outside EU. CEN has a number of committees, each focusing on development of standards in a particular domain. The TC 251 committee of CEN is responsible for development of standards in the medical domain. It evolved the EN 13606 [EN 13606 Association] [Kalra 2009] standard from European pre-standard ENV 13606. The standard was further drafted jointly by CEN and ISO for

Electronic Health Record: Standards, Coding Systems, Frameworks, and Infrastructures, Pradeep Sinha, Gaur Sunder, Prashant Bendale, Manisha Mantri, and Atreya Dande.

publication. *ISO 13606* and *CEN/ISO EN 13606* are referred to as ISO and CEN standards, respectively.

The CEN/ISO EN 13606 standard provides specifications for achieving semantic interoperability during exchange of EHR information. It primarily focuses on interoperability between EHR frameworks/standards that are popular in European countries (i.e., HL7 and openEHR) with base requirements from ISO/TS 18308 standard [ISO/TS 18308 2002]. It is a five-part standard. The EHR framework of this standard is based on the two-level modeling approach of openEHR. This is reflected in Part 1 and Part 2 of the published standard. Additionally, it provides mapping to HL7 CDA and openEHR for facilitating interoperability.

The five parts of the standard are:

1. ***Health informatics–Electronic health record communication, Part 1.*** *Reference model* (published in 2007 as CEN standard and in 2008 as ISO standard). This part describes a generic reference information model of a part or complete EHR of a patient for communication [EN13606-1 2007].

2. ***Health informatics–Electronic health record communication, Part 2.*** *Archetypes interchange specification* (published in 2007 as CEN standard and in 2008 as ISO standard). This part provides a definition of clinical records that are built from the generic reference model by applying rules required for representation of those clinical records [EN13606-2 2007].

3. ***Health informatics–Electronic health record communication, Part 3.*** *Reference archetypes and term lists* (published in 2008 as CEN standard and in 2009 as ISO standard). This part describes the basic set of archetypes in order to illustrate mapping (representation) of archetypes to other relevant standards. In addition, the standard describes use of terminologies within the reference model [EN13606-3 2008].

4. ***Health informatics–Electronic health record communication, Part 4.*** *Security* (published in 2007 as CEN standard and in 2009 as ISO standard). This part provides specifications for supporting access control, mandate and audit trails during EHR exchange [EN13606-4 2007].

5. ***Health informatics–Electronic health record communication, Part 5.*** *Exchange models* (published jointly by ISO and CEN in 2010). This part describes interfaces for message/service-based communication functioning on top of the components described in other parts [EN13606-5 2010].

The standard considers EHR as a consolidated record of care of a single patient from different organizations across nations. EHR Extract from Part 1 of the standard is compliant to Information Viewpoint of *ISO/IEC 10746 Open Distributed Processing (ODP)*. ISO/IEC 10746 defines specifications for developing large-scale distributed systems from five viewpoints, namely Enterprise, Information, Computational, Engineering, and Technology [Kalra 2010].

5.2 CEN/ISO EN 13606 Requirement Specification

5.2.1 PART 1: REFERENCE MODEL

This part of EHRcom standard describes requirements for a generic model named *EHR Extract*. EHR Extract is required for transferring health information of a patient during continuous care in a healthcare environment consisting of heterogeneous EHR systems. Figure 5.1 shows the structure of EHR Extract. It has a number of components arranged in a manner similar to that of generally used clinical documents. It is influenced by the EHR model of openEHR with certain changes in it to make it generic (e.g., it has removed certain specifications from openEHR such as ENTRY Types) [openEHR IM]. Further details of openEHR are given in Chapter 18.

EHR Extract is the top-level container that contains a part of or the complete EHR of a patient. Folders are a high-level collection of information of the EHR relating to diseases, episode of care, organization, doctor, and so on. A composition in a folder represents a single clinical record of the patient produced at a single encounter by a single clinician for a single goal. A section represents a clinical heading such as allergy, family history, reason for encounter, subjective observations, and so on. A composition can have multiple and nested sections arranged logically in human readable form. A section has multiple Entry nodes that represent the clinical actions for the clinical records known as clinical statements. Cluster and Element are data structures to hold the data within an Entry. A Cluster holds complex data types and an Element holds simple data types. Data can be text and coded terms, quantities including ratios, intervals and durations, dates and time, graphical data, and MIME types.

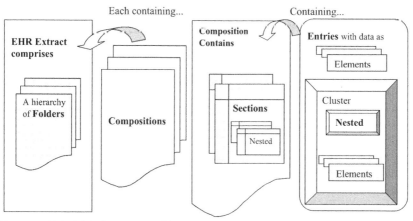

FIGURE 5.1 EHR Extract record hierarchy. Adapted from [EN13606-1 2007]. © CEN, reproduced with permission.

The standard provides specification for this generic EHR model for communication in terms of the following four packages:

1. **EXTRACT Package.** It consists of classes corresponding to the above-mentioned components of EHR Extract. These classes support Identity, Access, Security, Role, and References as the context information for supporting ethical and legal requirements. Those supportive classes include ATTESTATION_INFO, AUDIT_INFO, FUNCTIONAL_ROLE, LINK, and so on.

2. **DEMOGRAPHIC Package.** It consists of classes corresponding to all the entities involved in the care process with their identification, address, and contact details.

3. **SUPPORT Package.** It consists of structures for certain repetitive fields used in EHR Extract and taken from data types defined in CEN TS 14796 [prCEN TS 14796 2003]. It includes data type for representing code from the coding system for a particular version, data type for representing raw byte data with specified algorithm used for compression, data type for representing the path (URI), and so on.

4. **PRIMITIVES Package.** It includes all the primitive data types available at any of the technology platforms such as Boolean, Byte, Character, Double, Integer, Real, String, Array, Set, and List.

Part 1 of the standard provides detailed description of each attribute of each class of each package with the cardinality and optionality. The representation of the packages is in UML notation.

CEN/ISO EN 13606 standard provides mapping between other health informatics standards. Those include *CEN/TC 215 EN13940-part 1* (CONTsys) [CONTsys 2007] (it maps health informatics clinical concepts of EN 13940 standard to the components of EHR Extract), *CEN EN 12967 (HISA), CEN EN 14822 (GPIC)*, and *IHE XDS specification* [Rinner et al. 2007; NHS SC Pilot Study 2007].

5.2.2 PART 2: ARCHETYPES INTERCHANGE SPECIFICATION

EHRcom standard follows a two-level modeling approach by separating the structure (generic EHR model – EHR Extract) and the meaning as *Archetypes* of health information. EHR Extract (defined in Part 1) represents generic structures as building blocks, while archetypes (defined in Part 2) define the structure of a specific clinical record with data types and validation rules on it. This enables defining of different medical domain concepts at different times without any change in EHR Extract. The approach, therefore, provides a future-proof EHR model.

The standard describes an archetype model and a language for creating them. The language is called Archetype Definition Language (ADL). Both archetype model and ADL are adapted from openEHR. The archetypes are instances of an archetype model defined in ADL.

While defining archetypes, it is required to give proper identification (such as identifier of archetype, identifier for repository where archetype will be stored, language used for describing archetype, domain in which archetype is applicable, etc.) and description (such as archetype version, reason for creating a newer version, targeted age group of patients, etc.) of an archetype.

Archetype is a schema of hierarchical nodes defining clinical record, where a node can be one of the root structure represented in the generic EHR model (COMPOSITION, SECTION, ENTRY, CLUSTER, etc.). We can form an archetype by including other archetypes in order to provide modularity. We can also derive an archetype to make a specialized archetype. It is necessary to describe each archetype node in terms of clinical code for supporting identification of archetypes. Formats, cardinality, and multiplicity for different used data types are also needed.

Archetype Model. Figure 5.2 depicts the archetype model, which consists of the following packages:

1. Archetype package consisting of archetype description, constraint model, and ontology
2. Support package for identification and text
3. Domain extensions

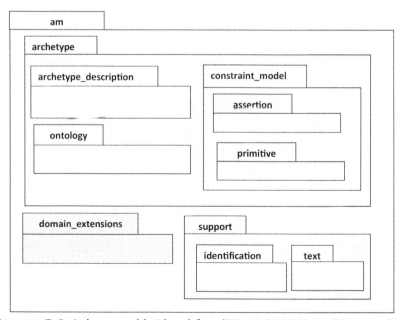

FIGURE 5.2 Archetype model. Adapted from [EN13606-2 2007]. © CEN, reproduced with permission.

ARCHETYPE class, from *archetype* package, holds identification information of the archetype, the language used for its description, type of the archetype, and so on.

Archetype_description package deals with details of repository URL where archetype gets created and stored, the reason for using a particular language, audit information, and conversion details if converted from one language to another (e.g., original archetype id, URL to the repository of original archetype, reason for conversion, etc.).

Constrain_model package describes constraints applied on complex data types (container objects such as COMPOSITION, ENTRY, SECTION, etc.). Constrained representation of these complex data types is an instance of an archetype including their cardinality, optionality, and other choices. The generic class corresponding to these complex types is called C_COMPLEX_OBJECT. This package consists of derived classes for all complex structures from this class. A complex data type can include primitive data types as well as another complex data type.

Primitive package defines all constrained primitive types by deriving them from base C_PRIMITIVE_OBJECT.

Assertion package defines rules for using expressions such as defining archetype constraint, defining constants in complex data types (container objects), and defining manifest constants. The syntax used for defining assertion statement is compliant with Object Constraint Language (OCL) specified by Object Management Group (OMG) [OCL].

Ontology package includes the classes for term definitions and constraint definitions that describe the meaning of terminology or constraint. It also contains the classes for defining term binding and constraint binding, which are used for mapping local terms to external terminologies.

Domain_extensions package provides constraints to data types other than generic constraints (C_PRIMITIVE_OBJECT, C_COMPLEX_OBJECT). It is achieved by deriving the data type from C_DOMAIN_TYPE.

Support package defines additionally required types to the archetype model of this part. These types include ARCHETYPE_ID, HIER_OBJECT_ID, TERMINOLOGY_ID, CODE_PHRASE, and CODED_TEXT. Basic, assumed, and generic types are referred from the basic data-type package of EHR Extract model, whose specification depends on the technology used for implementation.

Archetype Definition Language (ADL). EHRcom standard uses ADL as a formal language for expressing archetypes (that are constraint-based representation of domain content). ADL is a way to represent the archetype for exchange. It consists of two types of syntax:

1. *dADL.* Provides syntax for representing the data that is an instance of domain-specific information model.
2. *cADL.* Provides syntax for expressing constraints on the data.

ADL provides syntaxes for defining various parts of archetypes. They include:

1. **Header.** Contains the archetype identification information, such as its identifier, name, and specialization information.
2. **Description.** Contains the author information, lifecycle status (publication status such as Test/demo, Tentative, Draft, Private, Public, Preferred, Deprecated), and the purpose of the archetype.
3. **Definition.** Includes the clinical concept represented by the archetype, described in terms of its reference model entities.
4. **Ontology.** Contains links to the terminologies and mapping.

The standard also describes various other elements and language syntaxes.

5.2.3 PART 3: REFERENCE ARCHETYPES AND TERM LISTS

This part of EHRcom standard includes specifications for values used as coded terms (one of the data types provided by generic EHR Extract) for constant data in the reference model. Codes for known or applicable values in attributes of the reference model are provided to contribute to uniformity in definition while exchanging EHR. It does not provide any medical terminology. Codes are provided for the following:

1. Subject of information in the EHR including patient, relative, infant, mother, donor, and others.
2. Different types of information represented by ELEMENT and CLUSTERS in the reference model.
3. Version status of COMPONENT (e.g., finished, draft, deleted, etc.).
4. Mode of documentation of clinical information (e.g., verbal, electronic, dictated, telephone, videoconference, e-mail, etc.).
5. Status of action performed (provided codes are compatible with HL7 v3 Mood codes).
6. While providing a link as reference in a record of EHR, codes can be used to define the nature of the link such as "related to" (similar problem or some other disease) and "confirmed by" (certain evidence, test) and to link an attribute to a role.
7. Types of clusters like Table and List.

The standard also provides reference archetypes that are mapped to HL7 v3 Acts and are part of Clinical Statement Domain Message Information Model and openEHR ENTRY types.

5.2.4 PART 4: SECURITY

Security is an important aspect while sharing of patient health data. EHRcom standard describes the access model and security model for EHR Extract and

TABLE 5.1 **Access Policies via Functional roles to RECORD_COMPONENT Sensitivity**

	RECORD_COMPONENT Sensitivity				
Functional Role	Care Management	Clinical Management	Clinical Care	Privileged Care	Personal Care
Subject of care	√	√	√	√	√
Subject of care agent	√	√	√	√	√
Personal healthcare professional	√	√	√	√	√
Privileged healthcare professional	√	√	√	√*	√**
Healthcare professional	√	√	√		
Health-related professional	√	√			
Administrator	√				

Indicators:

√ Allowed to RECORD_COMPONENTs of respective sensitivity unless there is no specialized policy that constrains access.

* Allowed if the user belongs to the same specialty as that of requested or in emergency of care (if authorized).

** Allowed by agreement in some care settings for special conditions.

Source: Adapted from [EN13606-4 2007].

© CEN, reproduced with permission.

provides specifications for it. It describes sensitivity of clinical data in terms of accessibility and functional roles. The data can be accessible for performing different functions to only eligible healthcare providers. Thus, functional roles are mapped to permissions for performing certain operations (Read, Write, Update, Delete, etc.) on particular parts of EHR (Demographics, Observations, etc.).

Although the standard does not provide any rule for "who is allowed," it provides a way to specify the rules for access and security.

Table 5.1 provides various access types defined depending on the legal aspects and the type of data. Data can be accessible depending on the functional role.

The standard also specifies mechanisms for auditing the data while accessing the EHR. It refers to the security requirements of ISO/TS 18308 standard. It also mentions ways to provide security through authentication, authorization, data integrity, and so on.

5.2.5 PART 5: EXCHANGE MODELS

This part of EHRcom standard describes a set of protocols used for message-based or service-based communication of clinical information. The standard defines interfaces/protocols for requesting EHR Extract from an EHR system,

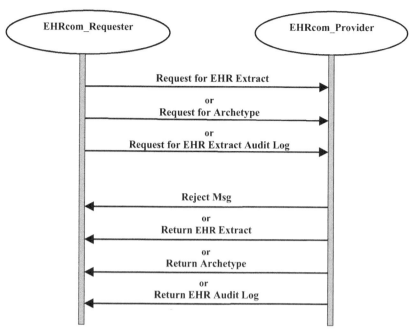

FIGURE 5.3 Interaction diagram for exchange of information. Adapted from [EN13606-5 2010]. © CEN, reproduced with permission.

Archetypes stored at the repository, and Audit log information of an EHR from an EHR system for a given subject of care.

Figure 5.3 describes the communication and flow of information. The communication is between (a) an EHRcom Requester that needs the data and (b) an EHRcom Provider that contains and can return the requested data. For each request, it provides a list of attributes with their optionality. The requests for fetching the data such as EHR Extract, can be Archetype, or EHR Extract Audit Log.

5.3 Discussion

EHRcom standard is one of the best and complete specifications that covers structure, representation, and communication of EHR. The standard enables interoperability among heterogeneous EHR systems to exchange a part of or the complete EHR of a patient. The standard specifications are like a bridge between already existing standards such as, HL7 v3, HL7 CDA, CEN/TC, CEN/TC EN12967, IHE XDS, and standard frameworks like openEHR.

Due to advancements in medical domain, many different requirements come up with new research in areas of medical procedures, diagnosis, biomedical information, and so on. This leads to the enhancement of EHR systems as well as the standards used by those systems to meet the new requirements. EN 13606 uses a two-level modeling approach that helps in developing a stable information model by separating clinical knowledge from its representation.

CEN/ISO EN 13606 is being adapted as a standard in the European Union (EU). The healthcare systems in the EU need to be interoperable with EHRcom for getting national compliance. The national EHR model of Sweden is based on EHRcom. The archetype exchange part of the standard is used in national EHR implementation in the United Kingdom.

Clinical Process Model. The primary focus of EHRcom standard is on communication of EHR. Hence, it does not contain any clinical process model for EHR. However, it does provide mapping to the concepts defined in CEN/TC EN13940 CONTsys, which describes concepts and processes in healthcare to provide continuity of care to patients. Thus, EHRcom can be easily adapted to CONTsys standard and can be used to build a complete standard based process-oriented EHR system. Details of CONTsys specifications have already been presented in Chapter 3.

Structural Model. EHRcom standard provides structure of a generic EHR model called EHR EXTRACT. The detailed structure of packages with classes and their attributes, constraints, data types, and description is provided through a normative way (UML modeling). EHR EXTRACT structure is more of open-EHR Information Model type. It has generalized openEHR ENTRY to GENERIC ENTRY because openEHR ENTRY types are classified in specific artifacts as Observation, Opinion, Instruction, and Action. These ENTRY types produce ambiguity during mapping of certain clinical records (as other EHR standards/systems may not use similar classification for record types).

Part 2 of the standard also describes the detailed structure of the archetype model. However, the concept of archetype is itself difficult to understand, and thus understanding of the archetype model by mapping structures with use of archetype becomes difficult.

The standard provides basic level mapping with HL7 CDA Release 2 and mapping of its demographic classes with HL7 v3 classes. The standard uses data-type specifications compliant to ISO 21090 health informatics data types specification and HL7 data types. Thus, it provides flexibility of conversion from one standard to another while exchanging data across heterogeneous healthcare applications.

Security/Privacy Considerations. EHRcom standard specifies the use of functional, role-based access control. It also provides recommendations for security aspects covered in ISO/TS 18308 standard. The information model of the standard is structured to cover various security aspects. EHR Extract consists of an Audit Log package with versioning, identification, and provision for describing functional role for role-based access.

Legal Aspects. EHRcom standard provides support for medico-legal requirements specified by the ISO/TS 18308 standard. It allows EHR access along with access log by including specific structures and providing specifications for exchanging them in Part 5 of the standard. The standard provides structures for validation and verification of EHR information that is being stored in repository or transferred to any other system. However, it does not provide any policy for anonymization of data during transfer/exchange.

Exchange Specifications. Archetypes built from ADL are used for data representation and communication formats. openEHR provides mapping between various standards/frameworks such as HL7 v3 in terms of archetypes. However, for a nonstandard complex system, adoption of Archetypes will be quite difficult since it needs to change the data storage and retrieval mechanism of the system in terms of archetypes. In addition, conversion of nonstandard data to the archetype format could be a cumbersome task. In many countries, most EHR systems used in healthcare organizations are proprietary in nature. Hence, archetypes make it difficult to enable quick data conversion and collection from hospitals for creating a national repository of EHRs. However, the standard provides mapping to appropriate sections of CEN EN 12967 (HISA) and registry metadata of IHE XDS, enabling use of standardized exchange mechanisms for EHR.

Technical Guidelines. The two-level modelling approach of the EHRcom standard is adopted from openEHR, which can be considered as a demonstration of implementation of the standard. In addition, the standard suggests use of archetypes already developed by openEHR at openEHR Clinical Knowledge Manager [openEHR].

An open source tool is available for developing archetypes called LinkEHR Archetype Editor [LinkEHR]. It refers to multiple reference models including CEN/ISO EN13606, openEHR, HL7 CDA, CCR, and OpenMRS. The openEHR Archetype Editor can create archetypes. In addition, an open source EHR system is available that supports the CEN/ISO EN13606 reference model called EHRflex [EHRflex].

5.4 Conclusion

CEN/ISO EN13606 focuses on interoperability among diverse healthcare systems, which should be able to exchange a part of or the complete information about patient's health data. Interoperability among various EHR standards such as HL7 v3, HL7 CDA, the standard itself, openEHR, and so on, is provided by working in harmonization with each other. The standard accommodates most of the published requirements of EHR considering multi-enterprise exchange of health data.

Being an accepted specification for EHR communication across standards, EHR systems will benefit from supporting archetype exchange of the standard to enable interoperability with international standards.

Although CEN/ISO EN 13606 provides specifications for communication of an EHR, many other standards are widely used for exchange of healthcare data between healthcare applications. The next chapter covers study of one such standard series i.e. HL7 v2.x.

BIBLIOGRAPHY

[CEN] European Standardization Committee; http://www.cen.eu.

[CONTsys 2007] European Committee for Standardization (CEN), *Health Informatics–System of Concepts to Support Continuity of Care*, EN 13940-1, prEN 13940-2 (2007).

[EHRflex] CEN EN13606 based EHR System; http://ehrflex.sourceforge.net.

[EN 13606 Association] EN 13606 Association; www.en13606.org.

[EN13606-1 2007] European Committee for Standardization (CEN), *Health Informatics–Electronic Health Record Communication, Part 1: Reference Model*, EN13606-1 (2007).

[EN13606-2 2007] European Committee for Standardization (CEN), *Health Informatics–Electronic Health Record Communication, Part 2: Archetypes*, EN13606-2 (2007).

[EN13606-3 2008] European Committee for Standardization (CEN), *Health Informatics–Electronic Health Record Communication, Part 3: Reference Archetypes and Term Lists*, EN13606-3 (2008).

[EN13606-4 2007] European Committee for Standardization (CEN), *Health Informatics–Electronic Health Record Communication, Part 4: Security*, EN13606-4 (2007).

[EN13606-5 2010] European Committee for Standardization (CEN), *Health Informatics–Electronic Health Record Communication, Part 5: Exchange Models*, EN13606-5 (2010).

[Fernández-Breis et al. 2006] Fernández-Breis, J. T., Vivancos-Vicente, P. J., Menarguez-Tortosa, M., Moner, D., Maldonado, J. A., Valencia-García, R., and Miranda-Mena, T, Using semantic technologies to promote interoperability between electronic healthcare record's information models. In: *Proceedings of 28th Annual International Conference IEEE Engineering in Medicine and Biology*, New York, EEUU, pp. 2614–2617 (March 2006).

[GPIC 2005] European Committee for Standardization (CEN), *Health Informatics–General Purpose, Information Components–Message Headers*, CEN EN 14822 (2005).

[HISA 2011] European Committee for Standardization (CEN), *Health Informatics–Service Architecture*, CEN EN 12967-1, CEN EN 12967-2, and CEN EN 12967-3 (2011).

[ISO] International Organization for Standardization; www.iso.org/.

[ISO/TS 18308 2002] International Organization for Standardization (ISO), *Health Informatics–Requirements for an Electronic Health Record Architecture*, ISO/TS 18308 (2002).

[ISO/IEC 10746-3 1998] International Organization for Standardization (ISO), *Information Technology–Open Distributed Processing–Reference Model: Architecture*, ISO/IEC 10746-3 (1998).

[ISO/IEC 10746-4 1998] International Organization for Standardization (ISO), *Information Technology–Open Distributed Processing–Reference Model: Architecture Semantics*, ISO/IEC 10746-4 (1998).

[Kalra 2009] Kalra, D. (CHIME, UCL) ISO EN 13606 electronic health communication (EHRCom): The contribution of archetypes towards eHealth semantic interoperability. In: *Norwegian Seminar on Archetypes and Architecture Oslo* (November 2009); www.kith.no/upload/5414/EHRCOM-Archetypes-DipakKalra-20091126.pdf.

[Kalra 2010] Kalra, D., EHR standards landscape. In: *CEN/ISO EN13606 Invitational Workshop*, Madrid, Spain (June 2010).

[LinkEHR] LinkEHR Archetype Editor; www.linkehr.com.

[Maldonado et al. 2008] Maldonado, J. A., Moner, D., Bosca, D., Fernández-Breis, T. F., Angulo, C., and Robles, M., Semantic upgrade and normalization of existing EHR extracts. In: *Proceedings of 30th Annual International Conference of the IEEE Engineering in Medicine and Biology Society*, Technical University of Valencia, Spain, pp. 1466–1469 (August 2008).

[Moner et al. 2006] Moner, D., Maldonado, J. A., Bosca, D., Fernández-Breis, J. T., Angulo, C., Crespo, P., Vivancos-Vicente, P. J., and Robles, M. Archetype-based semantic integration and standardization of clinical data. In: *Proceedings of 28th Annual International Conference IEEE Engineering in Medicine and Biology*, New York, EEUU, pp. 5141–5144 (2006).

[NHS SC Pilot Study 2007] National Health Service for Scotland (NHS Scotland), CEN/ISO 13606 Pilot Study Final Report (2007); www.ehr.chime.ucl.ac.uk/download/attachments/3833859/NHSCFH_13606-Pilot-Final-Rpt_v1-0.pdf.

[OCL] Object Management Group (OMG), *Object Constraint Language (OCL)*, Version 2.2 (February 2010); http://www.omg.org/spec/OCL/2.2.

[*open*EHR] *open*EHR Community, open*EHR Archetype Repository*; http://www.openehr.org/knowledge.

[openEHR IM] openEHR Community, *openEHR Information Model*; www.openehr.org/releases/1.0.2/architecture/rm/ehr_im.pdf.

[prCEN TS 14796 2003] European Committee for Standardization (CEN), *Health Informatics–Data Types* (2003).

[Rinner et al. 2007] Rinner, C., Wrba, T., and Duftschmid, G., CEN prEN 13606 compliant export of medical data from an entity-attribute-value based patient record system. In: *Proceedings of Die diesjährige TELEMED* (2007).

CHAPTER SIX

Messaging Standard for Healthcare Data

6.1 Introduction

Health Level Seven (HL7) family of standards is one of the most widely discussed and used application data exchange standards in the health information technology industry. The family consists of several standards, namely, HL7 v2.x, HL7 v3, Clinical Document Architecture (CDA), and Continuity of Care Document (CCD), and so on. These standards are widely used worldwide by healthcare application providers.

Health Level Seven International [HL7] is a not-for-profit, ANSI-accredited standards developing organization. It is dedicated to providing a comprehensive framework and related standards for exchange, integration, sharing, and retrieval of electronic health information. It also works for supporting clinical practices, delivery, and evaluation of health services. This chapter provides an overview of HL7 v2.x standards family, describes its features, and discusses its usage in achieving interoperability.

The main objective of developing HL7 v2.x standards was to support electronic exchange of healthcare data across various healthcare applications supporting different communication environments, ranging from full OSI-compliant to point-to-point interconnections, and even transferring data on removable media such as compact disks (CDs) or tape. The standard simplifies

Electronic Health Record: Standards, Coding Systems, Frameworks, and Infrastructures, Pradeep Sinha, Gaur Sunder, Prashant Bendale, Manisha Mantri, and Atreya Dande.
© 2013 by The Institute of Electrical and Electronics Engineers, Inc. Published 2013 by John Wiley & Sons, Inc.

implementation of interfaces between computer applications from different, and often competing, vendors. It supports exchange of healthcare data among different departments of a hospital, chain of hospitals, regional/national healthcare framework. HL7 v2.x serves as a way of communication between inherently disparate applications having disparate data architectures and operating in a heterogeneous system environment.

6.2 HL7 v2.x

HL7 v2.x represents message structures for different functions in healthcare environment, namely, Patient Administration (ADT), Clinical Laboratory and Observation Reporting, Medical Record Management, (MDM), and so on. For the purpose of further discussion, version 2.5 of the HL7 standard is assumed.

There are in all 12 different functions of healthcare environment supported by ANSI HL7 v2.5 standard. These are covered in separate chapters in the standard for convenience. The 12 chapters are as follows:

1. *Patient Administration (ADT).* It consists of messages containing information related to patients during various healthcare events such as Patient Admit, Visit, Discharge, Change Patient Status, Update Patient Demographics, Merge Patient, Query Patient, and so on. These messages are used to either notify change or query the status of a patient. This message set contains messages for Patient Administration (ADT) and Acknowledgment (ACK).

2. *Order Entry.* It consists of messages for request, update, or query orders that are given by physicians to avail a health service. Orders are meant for patients and may include orders related to medications, clinical observations, laboratory tests, diagnostic images, and so on. This message set contains messages for General Order and Response (ORM and ORR), Order Query Response Status (OSQ and OSR), General Clinical Order and Acknowledgment (OMG and ORG), Laboratory Order and Response (OML and ORL), and Imaging Order and Response (OMI and ORI).

3. *Financial Management.* It consists of messages for billing, insurance payments, and accounts management. This message set contains messages for Detail Financial Transaction (DTF), Add/Change Billing account (BAR), and general Acknowledgment (ACK).

4. *Observation Reporting.* It consists of messages for searching, querying, and reporting of laboratory test results or clinical observations. This message set contains messages for Unsolicited Observation and Laboratory (ORU and OUL) and Query for Observation Results (QRY and ORF).

5. *Master Files.* Master files are maintained for preserving information of different entities involved in healthcare information transactions, namely,

medical staff, practitioners, location of health organization, medical equipment location, patient status master, and so on. Any addition or update in such master files needs to be communicated to all the available healthcare applications involved in the healthcare environment to synchronize information about the specified entities. This message set contains messages for Master File Notification and Acknowledgment (MFN and MFK) and Master File Query and Response (MFQ and MFR).

6. *Medical Records Management.* It consists of messages related to document management that can be used to maintain documents related to patient consent, chart location and tracking, and so on. The messages support functions to append, archive, cancel, authenticate, and thereby maintain status of documents such as new, updated, obsolete, restricted, revised, and so on. This message set contains messages for Medical Record Management (MDM) and General Acknowledgment (ACK).

7. *Scheduling.* It consists of messages for scheduling of various resources existing in the healthcare environment. The schedule can be for a service, staff, or practitioner. This message set contains messages for Scheduling Request and Response (SRM and SRR) and Scheduling Query and Response (SQM and SQR).

8. *Patient Referral.* It consists of messages for referring a patient across healthcare organizations and transferring the patient information during such a referral. This message set contains messages for Patient Information Query and Response (RQI and RPI), Clinical Information Query and Response (RQC and RCI), Unsolicited Insurance Information and General Acknowledgment (PIN and ACK), Patient Authorization Request and Response (RQA and RPA), and Patient Referral Request and Response (REF and RRI).

9. *Patient Care.* It consists of messages related to the health problem of a patient. It supports exchange of health problems, goals set during treatment, pathway to carry out treatments, and so on. This message set contains messages for Patient Goal Request and Response (PGL and PPV), Patient Problem Request and Response (PPR and PRR), Patient Pathway (PPP, PPG), Query Patient Care Problem (QRY), and General Acknowledgment (ACK).

10. *Clinical Laboratory Automation.* It consists of messages for interfacing medical equipment with a Laboratory Information System (LIS). The information transferred in these messages includes device status, specimen status, patient orders and related results, and so on. This message set contains messages for Automated Equipment Status Update, Request (ESU, ESR), Specimen Update, Request (SSU, SSR), Automated Equipment Inventory Update, Request (INU, INR), and General Acknowledgment (ACK).

11. *Application Management.* It consists of messages related to application-level information exchange. The information regarding software versions, system clock, migration of file system, and so on can be transferred using

these messages. This message set contains messages for Application Management Query and Data (NMQ and NMD).

12. *Personal Management.* It consists of messages related to administrative activities in healthcare environment such as recruitment and relieving of medical staff, permission change to access master files for a specific user, and so on. This message set contains messages for Personal Record addition, update, deletion, deactivation, and termination (PMU) and General Acknowledgment (ACK).

6.2.1 MESSAGE STRUCTURE

Messages in HL7 v2.x standards are of two basic types:

1. *Event.* These messages represent real-world events happening in healthcare environment that involve transfer of health-related data. They are basically used by interacting healthcare applications for notifications and are responded to by acknowledgment messages. A message can be identified as an event by looking at the message-type field of MSH segment (discussed later in the chapter). For example, Patient Admit event is represented by ADT_A01 where ADT is the message type and A01 is the event code.

2. *Query.* These messages are used to query health care information of one or more patients. They are responded to by using respective response messages containing the required information. For example, Patient Information Query is represented by QRY_A19 and respective response message is ADR_A19.

Apart from the message type field, every message has a structure defined in the standard. Every HL7 v2.x communication has the following components:

1. *Message.* It is the main component of data transfer in HL7 v2.x standard. It describes a real-world healthcare event or query and the healthcare data to be transferred. It comprises a collection of Segments described in a fixed sequence that defines the structure of the message. Each message contains an MSH (Message Header) as a mandatory segment that describes the message transaction identifier, message type, event code, HL7 standard version, healthcare application identifier, and related information. For example, ORU_R01 is a Unsolicited Observation Result message used to communicate laboratory test results and related observations. HL7 messages are developed devoid of any dependency on any software, hardware, or application/platform.

2. *Segment and Groups.* A segment represents a set of packaged data units for a specific kind of information such as Patient Identification (PID), Patient Visit (PV1), Observation Result (OBX), Specimen (SPM), and so on. Each segment contains a number of fields. These small packaged data units are independent of messages and are reused in many messages. However, their

internal composition may vary from one message to another. Segments in a message can be mandatory, optional, or repeatable.

Groups are logical collection of segments that represent related health information. For example, insurance-related information is held by an insurance group that contains IN1 and IN2 segments. This collection of segments is used across messages to represent the same kind of data. However, the group composition may vary from one message to another. Such groups are predefined in the standard.

3. *Fields and Data Value Tables.* A field is the smallest unit of health-related information used in HL7 v2.x messages. HL7 v2.x provides a comprehensive list of fields along with their identifier, data type, data value table, and so on. Fields from this list are reused in multiple segments. For example, patient identifier list is a field containing all public identifiers related to a patient.

Data Value Tables contain enumerated values represented by specific fields such as, Marital Status of a patient. HL7 defines probable values used in such a field.

4. *Data Types.* Each field has a data type. Data types are categorized as Primitive and Composite. Primitive data types are the basic data types that can represent a single unit of information. These are ST, IS, ID, FT, and NM. Composite data types contain multiple primitive data types or other composite data types. For example, AD (Address) contains Street Address (ST), Other Designation (ST), City (ST), State or Province (ST), Country (ID), Address Type (ID), and Other geographical destination (ST).

6.2.2 AUXILIARY MESSAGING PROTOCOLS

Apart from being a specification for messages, HL7 v2.x standard also defines various protocols for exchange of messages in an orderly fashion. Following are the protocols supported by HL7 v2.x standard:

1. *Message or Segment Continuation.* Messages containing large data are sometimes required to be fragmented during transmission. This auxiliary protocol defines the use of ADD and DSC special segments to break a longer message into smaller fragments and then transmit them. The receiver application needs to remove these two segments and re-create the original message to interpret it correctly.

2. *Batch Transfer.* Sometimes it is required to transmit number of messages against a query message pertaining to multiple patients. In such a case, the batch transfer protocol is used to transfer a set of messages. The protocol works in two ways:

   • An HL7 Batch File message containing special segments, File Header Segment (FHS) at the start and File Trailer Segment (FTS) at the end of the batch file. This type of batch transfer is used to send multiple batches of messages at a time.

- An HL7 Batch message containing special segments, Batch Header Segment (BHS) at the start and Batch Trailer Segment (BTS) at the end. This type of batch transfer is used to send a single batch of messages.

  DSC segment is used at the end of each message, except the last one in the batch, to specify batch continuation.

3. *Interactive Continuation.* It is used in case of large response to a query. To keep the interaction going on during such a long transaction, the requestor application should specify the amount of data acceptable at a time by using the second field of the RCP segment. This segment is commonly used in query messages. The responding application then sends the response limiting its size to that specified in RCP segment's second field.

4. *Query Cancelation.* This protocol is used in a scenario where the requestor application wants to cancel a recent query initiated by it. Such a cancelation request can be posted before the responding system generates the response. The cancelation request is done using a special message QCN_Q01 specifying the message transaction identifier of the query to be canceled.

5. *Sequence Number.* This protocol is used to number the responses sent against a query message. When multiple responses are sent against a query message, all the responses are sent using a sequence number. This is to track whether all the responses are received in the correct sequence.

6. *Publish and Subscribe.* This protocol implements the publish-subscribe model of message transmission in a healthcare application. Different applications subscribe with a publisher application based on the type of message. The publisher publishes messages that are then broadcasted to subscribing applications. The subscription message is sent using QSB_Q16 special message.

7. *Local Extension.* This protocol is used to extend existing messages and create new messages according to the requirements of healthcare applications. This protocol can be implemented to extend a message, a segment, or a data type.

6.2.3 USAGE SCENARIO

The example in Table 6.1 clarifies usage of HL7 v2.x messages in a real-world scenario. It demonstrates various events happening during a patient's care episode and respective HL7 v2.x messages being generated between various application interfaces such as, Patient Administration System, Clinical Laboratory System, and Billing System.

6.2.4 EXAMPLE OF HL7 v2.x MESSAGE

Figure 6.1 shows an example of an HL7 v2.x message for sending the result generated from a glucose test. The segments in the message are made bold, and

TABLE 6.1   Use of HL7 in a Real-World Scenario

Real-World Event	HL7 Message
A patient visits a hospital for the first time.	Patient registration is completed at the Patient Administration System and Patient Register event is sent to other systems in the hospital. E.g. Financial Management System for creation of billing account.
The primary physician at the hospital consults the patient for high fever, severe cough, cold, and sore throat and H1N1 test order is placed.	An order message is sent from order entry system to the Clinical Laboratory System.
Reports for the H1N1 test are acquired.	A report message is sent from the dictation system to the Clinical Laboratory System. Message is also recorded for billing in account.
The patient is admitted to the hospital for H1N1 Treatment (patient diagnosed of H1N1 flu).	A Patient Admit message is sent to other systems in the hospital. Message is also recorded by the Billing System to issue bills.
The patient is prescribed medications during the treatment.	A medication Order message is sent to the Pharmacy system for medications and to the Billing system for bill generation.
The patient is discharged from the hospital after recovery.	A discharge message is sent from the Patient Administration System to other systems in the hospital. The Billing System generates bills.

MSH|^~\&|Sending Application^Universal Id^x400|Path Lab^Universal Id^x400|Receiving Application^ Universal Id^x400|NID ^UniversalId ^x400|20000320^D|Security|ORU^R01 ^ ORU_R01 |MSG0001 |T^T|2.5^^|||AL|AL|IN|ASCII|LDLP^TEXT2^99^AI3^AT3^99|ISO 2022-1994| Entity Identifier ^NAMESPACE^UniversalId^x500

PID|1|||WJYYU11556^^^REGAD1&IncomeTax Department&GUID^^^^^^|105^^^REGAD1 &Hospital A&GUID^^^^^^|Jim&^Toe^^^^^^^^^^^ ||19950815^D|M||| ^^^ 411089 ^^ ^^^^^^|||||||105^^^REGAD1&Hospital A&GUID^^^^^^||MH122000435623^ RTO^|||||||||||||||

PV1|1|O||||||Reg No:6643^John&^Doe^^^^^^^^^^^^^^^^^^^^|||||||||||||||||||||||||||||||||||||||

OBR|1|||52041-1^BloodGlucose^LN^^^|||20110506^D|||||||||||||||F||||||DR102&Tom&Ray& &&&MD&&&||||||||||||||

OBX|1|CE|166921001^Blood Glucose Normal^SNOMED CT^^^||281301001^Within Reference Range^SNOMED CT^00^00^00|UNIT^%^^^^|Reference range|N|||F|||||||SPM|1||| BBL^ Blood Bag ^HL7^^^^^^||||||

FIGURE 6.1   An example of an HL7 v2.x ORU_R01 message.

only the fields that are necessary for understanding are filled. Following is the list of segments and their description.

Message Header Segment (MSH). It is the header segment of any HL7 v2.x message. It specifies the fields describing the message syntax. It contains information about the delimiters, sending and receiving application name and identifiers, message type, message identifier, version of HL7 standard, message response type, country code, encoding of characters, and so on.

Patient Identification Segment (PID). It is the primary segment used for exchanging patient identification and demographic information. It contains fields such as, patient identifier list, patient name, race, temporary and permanent address, country code, date of birth, birth place, patient account number, and so on.

Patient Visit Segment (PV1). It records the information related to a patient's hospital visit. It contains fields such as patient class, attending doctor, referral doctor, patient type, visit number, and so on.

Observation Request Segment (OBR). It is the header segment of a report generated for recording the result of a test. It contains lab test order-related information, specimen, priority, and so on.

Observation/Result Segment (OBX). It is the segment used to exchange information related to a single observation. It is a generic segment that contains the record value in any HL7 v2.x specified data type. It contains fields such as observation value type, identifier, observation value, unit of value, result status, and so on.

6.3 Discussion

HL7 v2.x messages are widely used for exchanging clinical and administrative information most of the EMR/EHR systems. It is also the primary standard of data exchange of EHR frameworks of many countries such as Australia, Hong Kong, Singapore, United States, and so on. For example,

- Australia used HL7 v2.x for implementing its Event Model. It also used it as the initial exchange standard for achieving quick adoption of HealthConnect project in the country.

- Hong Kong uses HL7 v2.5 data types and fields to describe the content part of its information model.

- Singapore initially used HL7 v2.3 messages in exchanging clinical documents between the two major health clusters.

- The United States of America mandates usage of HL7 v2.5.1 for order and laboratory tests and results. It specifies HL7 v2.3.1 and v2.5.1 for public health and surveillance reports and immunization.

Clinical Process Model. HL7 v2.x does not support a clinical process model for EHR. However, it provides standardized message constructs to enable exchange of healthcare information among healthcare applications.

Structural Model. The message structure provided in HL7 v2.x versions consists of tightly coupled elements separated by delimiters. There are standard characters used for distinguishing various elements of the message, but it does not make it mandatory to use them.

The data types listed does not support any collection or set of other data. This makes the application use platform-dependent data types when it comes to creating a collection of data values.

Structural relationships among the data fields in messages are not clear. In many messages, Segments are re-used. Many trigger events also reuse message definitions. To accommodate this extensive reuse, most data fields are optional. Optional fields in a message make the standard unreliable, since different implementers would interpret these fields differently.

HL7 v2.x is silent about logical and physical construction of electronic health record of an individual as development of these messages is not the focus area of HL7 standard organization. Hence, this standard can be used only as an exchange medium rather than for constructing a longitudinal health record of an individual.

HL7 v2.x has an implicit information model based on a dictionary of fields, segments, groups, and messages. It does not have an explicit formally described information model for EHR. Many of the fields in the messages support text that can contain any arbitrary text which would be accepted by validation rules specified in the standard. The standard does not mandate use of values from its data value tables, rather declares them as only suggestive values. A user application can extend or replace them with local values. This often leads to inconsistencies during exchange of information.

Introduction of Z-Segments and Z-Fields may seem to be a good feature, but it introduces localized messages and fields that are not universal and may hamper interoperability.

The standard does not provide a mechanism to find a link between health problems, identified during a treatment, and visits made to treat these health problems. This is one of the basic requirements to develop a problem-based EHR model.

Security/Privacy Considerations. HL7 v2.x is silent about the security, confidentiality, and data integrity of clinical information exchanged using its messages. It does not specify any security mechanism (such as encryption algorithms) and leaves it to applications to support their own mechanisms for the desired type of security/privacy.

HL7 v2.x messages do not support anonimization of data. Anonymized clinical information does not disclose a patient or provider's identification. Although we can create such a message by using existing message formats, it would be out of validation rules of HL7 and might have a patient identification field with no data. In a strict HL7 validated environment, this may be treated as an invalid message.

The standard does not support any mechanism for a handshake between interacting healthcare applications before they begin message transmission between them. From security perspective, such a handshake is important to identify the applications and then decide whether to allow message transmission or not.

The standard does not support any protocol or specifies any profile for recording message transmission logs for audit trail. This is an important requirement for implementing a secure EHR system. The standard leaves it to the application to implement such mechanisms.

Exchange Specifications. HL7 v2.x, being an exchange standard, specifies a comprehensive set of messaging constructs for various healthcare functions. Apart from these messages, it provides a set of auxiliary protocols for supporting various scenarios of message transmission between healthcare applications. However, HL7 v2.x does not describe any formal functional roles that describe the responsibility of interacting applications during a message transmission. The standard does not specify any healthcare workflow that defines the actors and the messages flowing between them.

ORU_R01 message described in the standard is used for reporting laboratory results and observations. It consists of a single OBR segment defining header of a report and multiple OBX segments for each of the fields to be recorded in the report. There are two problems identified with this construct:

1. The single message is used to communicate a single report for a single patient, multiple reports for multiple patients, time-based results where an OBR is followed by multiple OBX that contains values recorded at specific intervals, waveform reports, and narrative reports. Many optional fields exist for using this single message for incorporating all such scenarios. Hence, it becomes difficult to interpret such a message correctly.

2. Since a single message is used to report all types of results generated in a laboratory, it becomes difficult to identify the exact report type.

These problems are supposed to be alleviated by using the code sets such as LOINC. However, it means that systems should be able to process LOINC codes to differentiate between report types and then may subclassify the report message into different record types.

Technical Guidelines. HL7 v2.x does not list any specific technical guidelines for use or integration of technologies with it. The standard is independent of any software, hardware, or technology. The messages are exchanged as string stream. Applications can do so over network connections or in files. Few vendors have created an XML schema document for message structure and support an XML file or stream as well.

Few middle-ware implementations of this standard are available in open as well as proprietary forums. C-DAC, an R&D organization in India, publishes

APIs for HL7 v2.5 as a Software Development Kit (SDK) available in both .NET and Java platforms.

6.4 Conclusion

HL7 v2.x has widespread support in existing vendor-specific HIS/EHR applications due to its simplicity of message structure and flexibility in validation rules. Hence, HL7 v2.x can be used as a data integration standard that makes integration between existing HIS/EHR/EMR applications possible. Several national EHR and data exchange programs make use of this standard as well. Its support is necessary in health informatics applications.

The issues related to HL7 v2.x standards (some of which are covered in the discussion part of this chapter) were identified by the HL7 committee, which evolved a new version of the standard. This standard is based on object-oriented principles and is known as HL7 v3. The next chapter describes HL7 v3.

BIBLIOGRAPHY

[**HL7**] Health Level 7; http://www.hl7.org.

[**HL7 v2.5 SDK**] C-DAC's Medical Informatics Standards Software Development Kit for HL7; http://medinfo.cdac.in/products/sdk/hl7/medinfo_hl7_home.aspx.

[**Huang et al. 2002**] Huang, E. W., Shiao, S. H., Liuo, D. M., Design and Implementation of a Web-Based HL7 Message Generation and Validation System, (2002); http://www.ijmijournal.com/article/S1386-5056%2803%2900006-6/abstract.

[**Oemig and Blobel 2009**] Oemig, F., and Blobel, B., Semantic interoperability between health communication standards through formal ontologies. In: *IOS Press*, (2009); http://person.hst.aau.dk/ska/MIE2009/papers/MIE2009p0200.pdf.

[**Shafarman 2007**] Shafarman, M., Trends in Practical Deployment of HL7 Standards: Supporting Regional Electronic Healthcare Records (2007); http://www.google.com/url?sa=t&rct=j&q=&esrc=s&source=web&cd=12&ved=0CDAQFjABO Ao&url=http%3A%2F%2Fwww.hl7.org%2Fdocumentcenter%2Fpublic%2Fwg %2Fimpl%2FBogota_future.trends.in.practical.deployment.of.HL7.fin.ppt&ei= pZrKTs6hNI7PrQfPtNSzDg&usg=AFQjCNHfoj2nSfbT7PxDacGQBY_RlZ yvsA&sig2=M0fwjqoMDz5EM7_0RmmArg.

[**Xiaoqi et al. 2011**] Xiaoqi, X., Yu, G., Jianfeng, Z., Ning, Y., and Weitao, J., Research and implementation of medical information format conversion based on HL7 Version 2.x. In: *IEEE Computer Science and Service System (CSSS) Conference*, pp. 2440–2443.

[**Xiaoqi et al. 2010**] Xiaoqi, L., Yu, G., Lidong, Y., Weitao, J., and Wang, L., Research and implementation of transmitting and interchanging medical information based on HL7. In: *The 2nd International Conference on Information Science and Engineering (ICISE)*, pp. 457–460.

[**Ping et al. 2007**] Ping, X., Ko, L., Shang, R., Lai, F., Chen, C., and Huang, K, S, D., Dynamic Messages Creation Method for HL7 based Healthcare Information System. In: *9th International Conference on e-Health Networking, Application and Services*, pp. 150–155.

CHAPTER SEVEN

Model-Based Messaging Standard for Healthcare Data

7.1 Introduction

From the learning of HL7 v2.x standards (studied in earlier chapter), the Health Level Seven International organization has developed a model-based standard based on HL7 Development Framework (HDF) methodology and object-oriented principles. Under this methodology, message specifications for healthcare workflows are developed and continuously harmonized, depending on EHR architectural requirements.

Over the years, HL7 has introduced standards for exchange, integration, sharing, and retrieval of electronic health information. HL7 family of standards covering HL7 v2.x, HL7 v3, and HL7 CDA are the most used application data exchange standards for health informatics applications.

This chapter describes HL7 v3 standard, its features, and its usage in achieving interoperability.

7.2 HL7 v3

Although HL7 v3 defines a set of messages exchanged between computer systems, HL7 has changed the way messages are evolved by introducing a process called

Electronic Health Record: Standards, Coding Systems, Frameworks, and Infrastructures, Pradeep Sinha, Gaur Sunder, Prashant Bendale, Manisha Mantri, and Atreya Dande.
© 2013 by The Institute of Electrical and Electronics Engineers, Inc. Published 2013 by John Wiley & Sons, Inc.

"harmonization." HL7 v3 messages are based on the basic models built from object-oriented techniques, vocabulary of attributes, and a set of data types to support medical data content. Apart from messages that transfer data across systems, it introduces the concept of message wrappers for exchange of a message across healthcare systems. The message wrappers provide more information about a message being exchanged and describe the role of the sender/receiver as to what action has to be taken in response to the message. HL7 also introduces healthcare-specific interactions that are typically executed during patient care delivery, thereby supporting healthcare workflows.

HL7 v3 has domains similar to HL7 v2.x functions. The domain categories are as follows:

1. **Administrative Domains.** Administrative domains do not involve direct patient care, but are required to carry out supportive functions such as, administrative functions, in healthcare environment. Following are the eight domains defined under this category:

Accounting and Billing	Master File/Registry Infrastructure
Claims and Reimbursement	Medical Records
Data Access Consent	Personnel Management
Drug Stability Reporting	Scheduling

2. **Clinical Domains.** Clinical domains directly involve patient care and related services. Following are the 11 domains defined under this category:

Care Provision	Care Record Topic
Care Structures Topic	Care Transfer Topic
Clinical Genomics	Implantable Device Cardiac—Follow-up
Individual Case Safety Report	Device Summary
Queries Care Record Topic	Notifiable Condition Report
Regulated Studies Annotate	Regulated Product Submission

7.2.1 MESSAGE STRUCTURE

The messages defined in HL7 v3 are based on XML. The different concepts assisting in constituting the HL7 v3 messages are described below:

Reference Information Model (RIM). The *Reference Information Model (RIM)* forms a shared view of information domain used across all HL7 messages and is independent of message structures. It is based on object-oriented fundamentals and consists of the following components:

1. Classes, their attributes, and relationships among the classes
2. State-transition models for some classes
3. Data types and constraints

RIM is only one model of healthcare information. Abstract style of RIM and the ability to extend RIM through vocabulary specifications make RIM applicable to any conceivable Healthcare System information interchange scenario. In fact, it is conceptually applicable to any information domain involving entities playing roles and participating in acts.

RIM describes six major classes, namely, Act, Entity, Role, Participation, Role_Link, and Act_Relationship. A message is based on associative and generalized relationships between these classes [HL7v3].

1. **Act:** It is an intentional action done by the actors. Examples can be orders, plans, and so on. An Act is played by the Entities under a specific Role.

2. **Entity:** It represents people, organization, and so on.

3. **Role:** It defines the professional position of an individual. An Entity involves an Act under a specific Role.

4. **Participation:** It defines association between a Role and an Act. It represents the function of the Role under the context of the Act.

5. **Role_Link:** It describes a relationship between two roles. An example can be linking the Patient Role and Physician Role with the Organization, thereby describing patient–physician relationship.

6. **Act_Relationship:** It defines the relation between two Acts. One Act can be the successor of another Act.

RIM is the base of all message specifications listed in HL7 v3. HL7 v3 methodology of evolving messages is through a process called Message Development Framework. As per the methodology, a separate committee is formed for each expertise domain say, patient administration, observation reporting, and so on. Each such committee evolves a *Domain Message Information Model (D-MIM)* that constitutes classes, relationships extending the five core classes, and defining acts, roles, and entities for that particular domain. D-MIM is then refined to *Refined Message Information Model (R-MIM)* that uses part of the D-MIM and develops a particular message based on class relationships.

Artifacts and Wrappers. The various artifacts generated during the message development process are discussed below:

- *Domain Information Model (D-MIM).* D-MIM is a subset of RIM and a D-MIM is developed for each domain of HL7 v3. A D-MIM describes all the classes, attributes, and associations required to create messages in its corresponding domain.

- *Refined Message Information Model (R-MIM).* R-MIM describes messages for a particular scenario in a domain. It includes the set of classes, attributes, and associations from the corresponding D-MIM, required for creating one or more messages for that domain. R-MIM is a diagrammatic representation of the message, which can be represented in XML format.

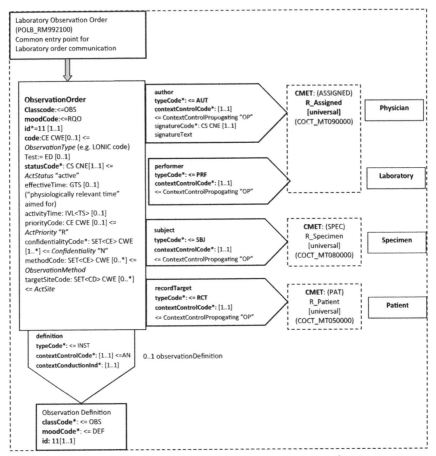

FIGURE 7.1 An R-MIM of laboratory observation order.

Figure 7.1 depicts an R-MIM of laboratory observation order. It shows Act as Observation Order, Entities as author, performer, subject, and recordTarget, CMET for Person in the role of Physician, Laboratory, Specimen, and Patient, and Act_Relationship as Ordered Test Definition [Beeler 2007].

- **Hierarchical Message Descriptor (HMD).** It is a tabular representation of an R-MIM. This is the basic message template and has no corresponding event defined in real-world context. All other messages based on R-MIM are derived from this template.

- **Message Type (MT).** Each HMD is extended and constrained to represent a real-world event in healthcare domain to define an actual message.

- **Story Board (ST).** A story board describes a series of events occurring while healthcare applications exchange messages for interactions taking place among them. The diagrammatic representation of a story board depicts the series of events, messages being exchanged, and formal roles of healthcare applications involved.

- **Storyboard Narrative (SN).** It is associated with a storyboard and narrates the real-world event for which this storyboard is being described in context of HL7 v3.

- **Transmission Wrapper.** These define the envelope messages that act as wrappers over the healthcare data messages during transmission. The wrapper messages are mostly the same for all messages. Each such wrapper includes the attributes related to the sender and receiver application identities, their roles, and the message type that carry actual healthcare data.

- **Control Act Wrapper.** It provides information regarding interaction needs to be communicated in the message to be sent. They are used when interactions are not explicitly defined in the interaction model. Normally, transmission of query-based interactions is required to use these wrappers— for example, queries related to master patient index (MPI).

Vocabulary Domain. *Vocabulary domains* describe common attributes and their constraints on data contents held in messages. This is like a data dictionary used by messages to define the content types and important attributes that must be included. Vocabulary domain contains a list of enumerated values for some attributes of the messages. This list constrains data value to be from the list only and provides all possible values to be inserted (for example, marital status).

Data type specification evolved by HL7 v3 methodology now supports the data types related to collection or set of contents. Hence, data types like BAG, LIST, and TABLE now support representation of sequence of contents that was not there in earlier 2.x versions. The XML ITS Data Types R1 specification defines HL7 v3 data types in XML.

Base Infrastructure. The basic infrastructure for HL7 v3 comprises important specifications used commonly for messages in administrative and clinical domains are as below:

- **Common Message Element Types (CMET).** This specification describes CMETs that are fragments of a Message Type consisting of classes, attributes, and associations. CMETs are created to represent such concepts that are commonly used in numerous message types. For example, a person under the role of Physician can be represented as a CMET and used in many message types involving a person playing the role of a Physician.

- **Infrastructure Management.** This specification includes information regarding domains such as Transmission and Control Act Wrappers, Master Files, and Query domains. Message Type represents only the actual health-related data and has no information regarding transmission or registry/master file-based query. To support these functions, separate messages acting as "wrappers" over Message Type are defined in this specification.

- *v3 Message Refinement.* This specification includes information regarding various constraints, refinements, and local environment-related modifications to support conformance profiles specified by implemented applications. It also defines the rules for conformance and nonconformance for interacting healthcare applications.

- *Shared Messages.* This specification includes common messages, such as Acknowledgments, used by all the domains in HL7 v3 standard.

- *Minimum Lower Layer Protocol (MLLP).* This specification defines the Minimum Lower Layer Protocol (MLLP) that specifies the rules for achieving reliable messaging.

- *UML and XML ITS Data Types and Structures.* These are three different Implementable Technology Specifications (ITS) used to provide mapping of HL7 v3 data types with UML and XML types and to create representations for Hierarchical Message Definition (HMD) in XML.

7.2.2 INTERACTION MODEL

Interaction Model describes the HL7 messages and information that flow between healthcare systems. It provides the concepts that define messaging behavior required for various functional roles found in healthcare systems. It also provides a tool for specification of information flow in the standard form defined by HL7 Version 3 messages.

An interaction defines a specific instance for information exchange. It specifies the trigger event and precondition on a message and defines the responsibilities of its receiver.

Every interaction defines the following two applications under "Application Roles":

1. Type of message payloads being exchanged

2. Trigger event, on which this interaction is performed

7.2.3 ROLE-BASED ACCESS CONTROL

Apart from defining a common message specification, HL7 is evolving a *Role-Based Access Control (RBAC)* specification for role and permissions-based access control over health information of patients stored in EHR.

RBAC describes the method to manage access to resources used in an information system. It facilitates in controlling user permissions on such resources. Use of such an access control system in any information system would give the following benefits:

- Simplify processes involved in access control.

- Facilitate in achieving interoperability securely.

- Implement application level as well as network-level RBAC service.

- Reduce costs required in such an implementation.
- Provide security to patient health information.

7.2.4 HL7 v3 AND SNOMED CT

HL7 has also released an implementation guide for interoperability between SNOMED CT and HL7 v3. This guide describes how to represent SNOMED CT codes in HL7 Version 3 standard for transferring clinical information and achieving semantic interoperability. Details of SNOMED CT coding system are given in Chapter 15.

7.2.5 HL7 v3 AND SERVICE-ORIENTED ARCHITECTURE (SOA)

HL7 v3 has also released its implementation guide for implementing HL7 v3 on a Service-Oriented Architecture (SOA), thereby supporting healthcare data exchange in a distributed environment.

7.3 HL7 v2.x and v3 Comparison

Table 7.1 provides a comparison between HL7 v2.x and HL7 v3.

7.4 Discussion

HL7 v3 is a widely used standard for exchange of clinical and administrative information in EHR implementation of many countries such as, Austria, Canada, Denmark, England, Hong Kong, Netherland, Sweden, Singapore, and so on. Its usage in some of the countries is as follows:

- Austria's ELGA program adopted HL7 v3 Reference Information Model (RIM) as the basis for developing its EHR Data Model.
- Canada's EHR Infostructure (EHRi) adopted a message-centric approach for their countrywide EHR implementation which is based completely on HL7 v3. Point-of-Service (PoS) systems can still use HL7 v2.x, HL7 v3 standard is used for interacting with EHRi.
- Denmark earlier used MedCom EDIFACT as exchange standard which is now being mapped to HL7 v3 standard.
- England uses HL7 CDA in its information model which is based on HL7 v3 RIM that can be transmitted using HL7 v3 messages.
- Hong Kong's eHR implements its information model based on HL7 v3 and HL7 CDA. HL7 v3 is specifically used for exchange of patient administration information and clinical information using HL7 CDA documents.

TABLE 7.1   **HL7 v2.x and HL7 v3 Comparison**

Criteria	HL7 v2.x	HL7 v3
Information model	Implicit information model used	Reference Information Model (RIM)
Message development model	Need-based message generation	Formal process of message development called as Message Development Framework (MDF)
Message-level constraints	Optional fields make achieving interoperability difficult	Message-level constraints
Data types	Collection data types not supported	Collection data types such as LIST, BAG, etc. are supported
Transport specification	No explicit transport specification provided. Messages are directly exchanged over wire	Transport specification provided in terms of Transmission and Control-Act Wrappers
Interaction model	Implicit. Cursory description of interactions in documentation No formal functional roles defined for interacting applications	Explicit. Interactions depicting flow of messages and formal application roles are defined for interacting applications
Secure transmission	No security related specifications used or defined for secure message transmission	Attributes and classes provided for carrying information regarding secure transmission of messages
Authorization model	No explicit mention of authorization model	Role-Based Access Control (RBAC) specification evolved

- Netherland has mandated use of HL7 v3 as the standard for communicating administrative and clinical information between healthcare applications and its National Healthcare Information Hub.
- Sweden supports exchange of its EHR using HL7 v3 standard.
- Singapore's EMRX project used HL7 v2.3 in enabling exchange between its two major health clusters but faced issues using the standard. Hence, HL7 v3 was used as one of the standards for exchange of medical data in NEHR project.

Clinical Process Model. HL7 v3 supports clinical workflow, but does not provide a clinical process model for EHR. However, it provides a specification for standardizing exchange of healthcare and related data between healthcare systems.

Structural Model. Reference Information Model (RIM) of HL7 v3 provides a complete set of classes, attributes and data types that form the content of any available clinical information. This constitutes an object-oriented information model for messages.

The limitation, if not elimination, of "optionality" is one of the primary goals of HL7 v3 as compared to v2 specifications. Many of the constructs within this Message Development Framework were designed to develop strict constraints on use of fields in messages and to provide exhaustive list of coded values for enumerated fields.

To create messages for a domain, Reference Information Model (RIM) is refined using D-MIM and R-MIM. Such a process would elongate and complicate enabling support for a new domain of healthcare such as Pharmacy [Barry and Werner 2006].

Ambiguity in defining Acts as associated object containing attribute values rather than being represented as processes or actions is another point of discussion [Barry and Werner 2006].

Security/Privacy Considerations. HL7 v3 does not suggest any data security mechanism, but specifies data formats and data fields in messages that can carry such information within a message for its security. However, processing of such messages is at the discretion of the implementation system.

Role-Based Access Control (RBAC) specification covers authorization and access control aspects of security. In a distributed healthcare system implementation, such a policy framework comes as a necessary add-on over a message exchange.

Exchange Specifications. HL7 v3 standard envisages supporting all healthcare workflows existing in different domains of a healthcare enterprise. It describes each "interaction" happening between healthcare systems that are triggered by an event. According to HL7 v3 methodology, an interaction is triggered by an event and it involves two healthcare systems working under defined application roles. It also specifies exchange messages, which contain the actual clinical information, during the interaction.

Implementation guide for interoperability with coding system like SNOMED CT [IHTSDO] extends HL7 v3's reach to incorporate all types of clinical information including coded type. HL7 v3 Data type Specification describes data types for coded data and can be used for any coding system. The interpretation of such data fields based on the specified coding system is left to the implementer.

Technical Guidelines. Implementation guides for SOA-based implementation of HL7 v3 cater to the demands of a service-based framework for a national EHR implementation. This enhances the scope of HL7 v3 from single-interface systems to service-based systems that can contribute to multiple, diverse healthcare systems.

7.5 Conclusion

The support of HL7 v3 for storing and querying messages for maintaining separate Patient and Provider registries makes it a favorable standard for patient and provider identification workflows (IHE PID/PDQ Profile). These messages find their use in the EHR frameworks of many countries. In fact, use of HL7 v3 with IHE PID/PDQ profile was drafted during the implementation of Canada's EHR.

Additionally, application of HL7 v3 over a Service-Oriented Architecture has generated industry's interest toward use of HL7 v3 in service-based frameworks of EHR. Thus, we can use HL7 v3 as a communication and exchange standard between the Local Integration Platform, residing at Hospital end for data integration, and the Central Distributed EHR Store, which hosts a SOA platform.

As seen in this chapter, HL7 v3 provides a data model and exchange for structured data and only exchange for non-structured data. However, non-structured data such as clinical documents are an important part of an EHR. For supporting such data, new standard named HL7 CDA was evolved by HL7. We will study about this standard in the next chapter. In the next chapter, we will also study about CCD, which uses HL7 v3 and HL7 CDA.

BIBLIOGRAPHY

[Barry and Werner 2006] Barry, S., and Werner, C., HL7 RIM: An incoherent standard In: *Medical Informatics Europe*, pp. 133–138, (2006); http://www.google.co.in/url?sa=t&rct=j&q=HL7+rim+an+incoherent+standard&source=web&cd=1&ved=0CCYQFjAA&url=http%3A%2F%2Fciteseerx.ist.psu.edu%2Fviewdoc%2Fdownload%3Fdoi%3D10.1.1.145.4676%26rep%3Drep1%26type%3Dpdf& ei=BQ7STpuMB8borAfT7aiqDA&usg=AFQjCNEvBqSe5xAdSUugNfrGvAOxqOKz_w.

[Beeler 2007] Beeler, G. W., HL7 v3 Basics: RIM to Message Design, HL7 Tools: The Comprehensive Guide, (2007).

[Beeler 1998] Beeler, G. W., HL7 Version 3-An object-oriented methodology for collaborative standards development, *International Journal of Medical Informatics*, pp. 151–161, (1998).

[Benson 2009] Benson, T., *Principles of Health Interoperability HL7 and SNOMED*, first edition, Springer (2009).

[Blobel and Marshall 2008] Blobel, B., and Marshall, G., Role Based Access Control (RBAC): Role Engineering Overview, ANSI/HL7 V3 RBAC, R1-2008 (2008).

[Corepoint Health 2010] Corepoint Health, The HL7 Evolution—Comparing HL7 Version 2 to Version 3, Including a History of Version 2, While paper (2010); http://www.corepointhealth.com/sites/default/files/whitepapers/hl7-v2-v3-evolution.pdf.

[HL7] Health Level 7; http://www.hl7.org.

[HL7 v3] Introduction to HL7v3; http://www.cihi.ca/cihiweb/en/downloads/v3Intro_e.pdf.

[HL7 Book] HL7 Standards Material and Related Artifacts; http://hl7book.net/index.php.

[IHTSDO] International Health Terminology Standards Development; www.ihtsdo.org.

[Orvis and Hufnagel 2009] Orvis, N., Hufnagel, S., SOA in Healthcare: Value in a Time of Change, Chicago (June 2009); http://www.omg.org/news/meetings/workshops/SOA-HC/presentations-09/03-18_Hufnagel-Orvis.pdf.

[Roos 2007] Roos, G., A critical evaluation of HL7 version 3 as an interoperable EHR standard; http://albertderoos.nl/pdf/A%20critical%20evaluation%20of%20HL7%20version%203%20as%20an%20interoperable%20EHR%20standard%20v1_art.pdf.

[Schloeffel et al. 2006] Schloeffel, P., Thomas B., Hayworth, G., Heard, S., Leslie, H., The relationship between CEN 13606, HL7, and openEHR. In: *Health Informatics Conference (HIC)*, (2006); http://www.openehr.org/wiki/download/attachments/2949261/005_schloeffel.pdf?version=1.

[Schadow et al.] Schadow, G., Mead, C. N., Walker, D., and Mead, D. W., The HL7 Reference Information Model under Scrutiny; http://aurora.regenstrief.org/~schadow/Schadow-MIE06-r3.pdf.

[Spronk 2010] Spronk, R., The HL7 MIF—Model Interchange Format; http://www.ringholm.de/docs/03060_en_HL7_MIF.htm.http://albertderoos.nl/pdf/A%20critical%20evaluation%20of%20HL7%20version%203%20as%20an%20interoperable%20EHR%20standard%20v1_art.pdf.

CHAPTER EIGHT

Clinical Document Standards

8.1 Introduction

Many efforts were ongoing for development of standards for exchanging clinical information. However, clinical documents and health reports are an integral part of EHR and hence need standardization. Several Standard Development Organizations (SDOs) identified this need and took initiatives in this regard. *Health Level Seven International (HL7)* and *American Society for Testing Materials (ASTM)* have developed such document standards.

The HL7 organization has developed the HL7 *Clinical Document Architecture (CDA)* standard with the aim to bring a real-world view to medical records that medical practitioners can understand and machines can process. For this purpose, CDA represents a medical record as a document having a structure that XML technology can represent and that the information model called *Reference Information Model (RIM)* can represent. Medical records represented as CDA document format are easy to understand by doctors [HL7 CDA 2011]. CDA is a very small set compared to complete v2.x or v3 messages. It is currently in its second revision.

ASTM had earlier developed the *Continuity of Care Record (CCR)* standard catering to the need of sharing sufficient information among healthcare practitioners during patient transfer/discharge activities in hospitals of Massachusetts County. The ASTM refined the CCR standard to include most of the record types involved during the episode of care. Spurred by the popularity of document-based structure like CDA, ASTM and HL7 organization together

Electronic Health Record: Standards, Coding Systems, Frameworks, and Infrastructures, Pradeep Sinha,
Gaur Sunder, Prashant Bendale, Manisha Mantri, and Atreya Dande.
© 2013 by The Institute of Electrical and Electronics Engineers, Inc. Published 2013 by John Wiley & Sons, Inc.

worked on representing CCR standard using the CDA vocabulary and RIM model. *Continuity of Care Document (CCD)* standard is the result of these efforts [ASTM International Inc. 2011] [HL7 CCD and CCR 2010]. Today, CCD standard has become properly structured, rich in vocabulary, and can be transmitted in HL7 v3 messages.

8.2 Clinical Document Architecture (CDA)

CDA Release 2.0 provides a model for exchange of clinical documents like discharge summaries, prescriptions, and aims to cater to the needs of an actual electronic medical record. CDA uses XML document format and is based on HL7 v3 RIM and its vocabularies to represent content data. Thus, CDA makes the documents both machine-readable and human-readable. CDA documents can be displayed using XML-aware Web browsers or wireless applications such as cell phones. CDA is a schema standard that specifies the structure and semantics of "clinical documents" for the purpose of exchange [CDA QSG].

8.2.1 DOCUMENT STRUCTURES

Figure 8.1 shows the structure of a document in CDA standard. CDA document has a root tag *ClinicalDocument* element and contains a header and a body. ClinicalDocument and *structuredBody* elements enclose header information that identifies and classifies the document providing information on authentication, encounter, patient, and involved providers.

The body of the document contains a clinical report that may be an unstructured data or a structured markup. The example in Figure 8.1 shows a structured body, which is wrapped by the *structuredBody* element and is divided into recursively nestable document sections.

A CDA document section has wrapper of *section* element. Each section can contain a single narrative block and any number of CDA entries and external references. The *text* element wraps a CDA narrative block containing human readable content for rendering purpose. CDA entries represent structured content provided for further computer processing (e.g., decision support applications). CDA entries typically encode the content present in the narrative block of the same section. The example in Figure 8.1 shows two *observation* CDA entries, along with a *substanceAdministration* entry containing a nested *supply* entry.

CDA entries can nest and reference external objects. CDA external references always occur within the context of a CDA entry. External references refer to the content that exists outside this CDA document—such as some other image, some other procedure, or some other observation. *externalObservation* element wraps these external references. Authentication of the document does not cover externally referenced material (e.g., links). Hence, a user who has been authenticated for accessing this document may not be having access to external references in the document.

```
<ClinicalDocument>

    ... CDA Header ...

    <structuredBody>

        <section>

            <text>...</text>

            <observation>...</observation>

            <substanceAdministration>

                <supply>...</supply>

            </substanceAdministration>

            <observation>

            <externalObservation>...</externalObservation>

            </observation>

        </section>

        <section>

            <section>...</section>

        </section>

    </structuredBody>

</ClinicalDocument>
```

FIGURE 8.1   Example of HL7 CDA document format. Adapted from [CDA 2006].

8.2.2 EXAMPLE OF CDA COMPONENT

Figure 8.2 shows a portion of CDA document representing Medical allergy using the CDA vocabulary and templates. The example shows the use of coding systems for representation of record type and disorder. For example, LOINC code 11382-9 represents medication allergy record. SNOMED CT code 91936005 represents allergy to penicillin as a disorder. In this example, a practitioner can describe a list of medication allergies in the medical history of that patient. For example, medication allergy of this patient describes three allergies:

1. Allergy to penicillin
2. Aspirin allergy
3. Ibuprofen allergy

It also shows a mechanism of referencing a health problem through a coding system. For example, the first item in the health problem list uses content ID as

```
<component>
    <section>
     <code code="11382-9" codeSystem="2.16.840.1.113883.6.1"
         codeSystemName="LOINC"/>
     <title>Medication allergy</title>
     <text>
      <list>
       <item>
        <content ID="a1">Allergy to penicillin</content>
       </item>
       <item>Aspirin allergy</item>
       <item>Ibuprofen allergy</item>
      </list>
     </text>
     <entry>
      <observation classCode="COND" moodCode="EVN">
       <code code="91936005" codeSystem="2.16.840.1.113883.6.96"
codeSystemName="SNOMED CT" displayName=" Allergy to penicillin ">
        <originalText>
         <reference value="#a1"/>
        </originalText>
       </code>
       <statusCode code="completed"/>
       <effectiveTime value="1950"/>
      </observation>
     </entry>
    </section>
</component>
```

FIGURE 8.2 Example of Past Medical History in CDA.

a1, which is referred by an *observation* node as *#a1* with SNOMED CT code [CDA QSG].

HL7 CDA uses a *vocabulary domain* from the HL7 v3 messaging standard. The vocabulary domain includes coded value sets from international coding terminologies. CDA documents refer these coded terms while referring to a health problem, procedure, and so on.

CDA Templates. In CDA, templates define the mechanism of customization of particular parts of a CDA document. For example, HL7 CDA allows two types of templates:

> **Section-level templates:** These templates constrain the contents of a document based on its type.

Following is the list of section-level templates in HL7 CDA standard [HL7 CDA Section Templates 2007]:

Active Problems	Hospital Discharge Physical Exam
Acuity Assessment	Discharge Diagnosis
Admission Medication History	Discharge Diet
Allergies and Other Adverse Reactions	Encounter Histories
Family Medical History	Medications
Care Plan	Pregnancy History
History of Present Illness	Progress Note
History of Tobacco Use	Vital Signs
Hospital Admission Diagnosis	Procedure

Entry-level templates: These templates constrain the contents of the entry part of a CDA document.

Following is the list of entry-level templates in HL7 CDA standard [HL7 CDA Entry Templates 2007]:

Severity	Allergy and Intolerance Concern
Problem Status Observation	Problem Entry
Health Status	Immunizations
Comments	Supply Entry
Patient Medication Instructions	Product Entry
Medication Fulfillment Instructions	Simple Observations
External References	Vital Signs Observation
Internal References	Procedure Entry
Concern Entry	Payer Entry
Problem Concern Entry	Pregnancy Observation

Since HL7 CDA uses an HL7 v3 RIM model, HL7 v3 templates can also be referred from HL7 CDA documents [Dolin et al. 2004].

8.3 Continuity of Care Document (CCD)

CCD uses the vocabulary defined by the HL7 CDA standard. Document structure of a CCD document includes some templates from the CDA domain that are applicable to represent referral information. Using HL7 v3 RIM model, vocabulary, and CDA's structural concepts, a CCD document defines the structure for the following record types [CCD QSG]:

Purpose	Medications
Problems	Immunizations
Procedures	Medical Equipment
Family History	Vital Signs
Social History	Functional Status
Payers	Results
Advance Directives	Encounters
Alerts (Allergies, Adverse Reactions)	Plan of Care

8.3.1 EXAMPLE OF CCD COMPONENT

Figure 8.3 shows the Result Observation record in a CCD document. The root node describes record type in the CCD standard using the *Result Observation*

```
<observation classCode="OBS" moodCode="EVN">

  <templateId root="2.16.840.1.113883.10.20.1.31"/>

    <!-- Result observation template -->

  <id root="someIdString"/>

  <code        code="30313-1"        codeSystem="2.16.840.1.113883.6.1"
displayName="HGB"/>

  <statusCode code="completed"/>

  <effectiveTime value="200003231430"/>

  <value xsi:type="PQ" value="13.2" unit="g/dl"/>

  <interpretationCode code="N" codeSystem="2.16.840.1.113883.5.83"/>

  <methodCode code="14104" codeSystem=" 2.16.840.1.113883.5.84">

    <referenceRange>

      <observationRange>

        <text>M 13-18 g/dl; F 12-16 g/dl</text>

      </observationRange>

    </referenceRange>

  </methodCode>

</observation>
```

FIGURE 8.3 Fragment of CCD document. Adapted from [CCD QSG].

Template from the HL7 CDA standard. The terms classCode and moodCode represent HL7 message types and segments as they were in HL7 v2.5 standard. In this example, the message or classCode is OBS, which represents observation message, and segment or moodCode is EVN, which represents event-related information.

This example describes a hemoglobin result including measured value at the specified time. In this observation, it defines code 30313-1 for hemoglobin and uses PQ data type for representing measured value. It also represents normal range in *referenceRange* node [CCD QSG].

8.4 Clinical Document Exchange

HL7 CDA and CCD standards use HL7 v3 messaging specifications for transmitting documents over network. Being document standards, they represent the structure of a document. While defining this structure, these standards use the vocabulary and RIM model concepts from HL7 v3. This way, HL7 v3 messages can carry these documents during transmission. These standards don't define transmission-specific structures and make use of the available constructs in the HL7 v3 standard.

Since these standards define XML representation of the structure, these documents can also be communicated in XML format without HL7 v3 messages. However, it requires sending and receiving entities to first establish the communication mechanism, then receive these documents, and finally use these standards to understand these documents. HL7 v3 messaging standard also defines transmission level constructs and adds these documents inside those constructs, making it possible to interoperate regardless of which document standard is being used.

8.5 Discussion

HL7 CDA is widely used as a clinical document exchange standard in many countries' EHR Frameworks such as Australia, Austria, Canada, England, Hong Kong, Singapore, Taiwan, United States, and so on. HL7 CCD is used in United States for creating and exchanging Patient Summary Care Record.

Clinical Process Model. HL7 CDA and CCD standards, being document standards, concentrate on structural specifications and contents in terms of record types. Hence, there is no EHR clinical process model in these structural specifications.

Structural Model. The structural model of HL7 CDA Release 2.0 and CCD uses the vocabulary and RIM model of HL7 v3. CCD uses templates defined by HL7 CDA for identified record types and structural concepts from HL7 v3. The advantage of using these document standards is that XML, a language neutral technology, can represent these documents. However, sending and receiving entities need to convert existing healthcare information in these document formats before interacting with each other.

These standards help in identifying various record types in an EHR of a patient. They also assist the designers in identifying the coding systems that are applicable to each of these record types. The advantage of CDA is that it creates a structural schema for representing information as a structured document. Hence, it is easy to map newer standards in a manner representable by CDA terminology. The CCD standard is ASTM's CCR representation using CDA's structural concepts. This way, the represented information becomes structural and readable by both humans and machines.

Both these standards highly promote the use of coding terminologies. Several constructs in these standards have codes as an integral part. This makes the information represented in these standards to have necessary codes from available terminologies.

The structure of CCD document limits itself to healthcare information required during a patient's discharge/referral from hospital, whereas HL7 CDA describes base constructs for representing any record in a structured manner. Hence, HL7 CDA is not bound to a particular set of record types.

A structural model of the HL7 CDA standard is extensible as users can add templates to it for specific record types; for example, the CCD standard defines templates for identified record types using constructs in HL7 CDA. Similarly, to use HL7 CDA standard to represent custom record types in an EHR, designers can define templates specifying required constraints on each of the nodes in that template. Hence, the HL7 CDA structure appears as a language for representing healthcare information as a document and CCD standard as an example of using this language to define patient-discharge/transfer/referral-related records and contents.

Security/Privacy Considerations. Being in XML format, security mechanisms applicable in XML technology such as signing XML documents are applicable to these standards also. As such, no specific information is available in public documentation about security constructs provided by these standards. Underlying transmission standards such as HL7 v3 may provide security wrappers for ensuring security of the information being transmitted.

Legal Aspects. HL7 CDA and CCD standards, being document standards, do not specify legal requirements about healthcare information.

Exchange Specifications. HL7 CDA and CCD standards use HL7 v3 or plain XML as communication mechanism. Hence, they do not depend on the underlying communication mechanism. They are useful from the perspective of how EHR systems can represent healthcare information. They provide a way of representing healthcare information as document format.

8.6 Conclusion

HL7 CDA and CCD standards represent medical records. They closely relate to a medical practitioner's view toward medical records. However, since they use the vocabulary and RIM model of HL7 v3, it requires quite an investment in understanding those terms and relationships. Solutions handling these documents need to properly understand HL7 v3 concepts. Such solutions can effectively render these documents in a user-friendly manner.

Since these standards aim at representing healthcare information in document format, users should not look at these standards as a complete EHR standard. For exchange purpose, they use the available standards such as HL7 v3 or plain XML technology. For security purpose, they use the underlying platform's security capabilities.

EHR framework designers can consider the HL7 CDA standard for representing the constructs of identified record types in the EHR model. CCD standard is applicable to a patient's discharge/referral information and may not capture the entire depth of healthcare information available in a patient's EHR.

HL7 CDA and CCD are the clinical document standards that cover application level communication and medical record representation. However, exchange of data between medical devices and healthcare applications also needs to be standardized. In the next chapter, we will study DICOM, which is a widely used standard in radiological domain that enables communication between medical devices and healthcare applications.

BIBLIOGRAPHY

[ASTM International Inc. 2011] American Society for Testing Materials Organization (2011); http://www.astm.org/.

[Bendale and Gaur Sunder 2009] Bendale, P., and Gaur Sunder, Combining DICOM and HL7 into a single effective protocol in health informatics—Opportunities and challenges. In: *Proceedings of 5th National Congress of Telemedicine Society of India (Telemedicon'09)*, (November 2009).

[Bilykh 2006] Bilykh, I., Jahnke, J. H., McCallum, G., and Price, M., Using the clinical document architecture as open data exchange format for interfacing EMRs with clinical decision support systems. In: *Proceedings of 19th IEEE International Symposium on Computer-Based Medical Systems (CBMS)*, pp. 855–860 (2006).

[CCD QSG] CCD Quick Start Guide; http://www.lantanagroup.com/resources/quick-start-guides/.

[CDA 2006] Health Level 7 (HL7), HL7 Clinical Document Architecture (CDA) Release 2, Non-normative publication, (2006); http://hl7book.net/index.php?title=CDA

[CDA QSG] HL7 CDA Quick Start Guide; http://www.lantanagroup.com/resources/quick-start-guides/.

[Chang et al. 2007] Chang, Y. J., Lai, J. S., Cheng, P. H., and Lai, F., Portable CDA for the exchange of clinical documents. In: *Proceedings of 9th International Conference on e-Health Networking, Application and Services*, pp. 1–5 (2007).

[Chronaki et al. 2001] Chronaki, C. E., Lelis, P., Demou, C., Tsiknakis, M., and Orphanoudakis, S. C., An HL7/CDA Framework for the design and deployment of telemedicine services. In: *Proceedings of IEEE EMBC*, pp. 25–28 (2001).

[Dolin et al. 2004] Dolin, R., Alschuler, L., Boyer, S., Beebe, C., Behlen, F., and Biron, P., HL7 Clinical Document Architecture, Release 2.0 (2004); http://xml.coverpages. org/CDA-Release2-Unofficial.html#Major_Components_of_a_CDA_Document.

[HL7 2011] Health Level 7 Organization (2011); http://www.hl7.org.

[HL7 CCD and CCR 2010] Discussion on CCD and CCR comparison (2010); http:// www.hl7standards.com/blog/2010/03/10/ccd-and-ccr-the-discussion-continues/.

[HL7 CDA 2011] HL7 Clinical Document Architecture (CDA) Standard (2011); http:// www.hl7.org/implement/standards/cda.cfm.

[HL7 CDA Entry Templates 2007] CDA Entry Content Modules (2007); http://wiki. ihe.net/index.php?title=CDA_Entry_Content_Modules.

[HL7 CDA Section Templates 2007] HL7 CDA Section Templates (2007); http://wiki. ihe.net/index.php?title=Category:CDA_Section_Templates&until=Sample.

[Huang et al. 2010] Huang, E., Tseng, T., Chang, M., Pan, M., and Liou, D., Generating standardized clinical documents for medical information exchanges. In: *Proceedings of IT Professional*, pp. 26–32 (2010).

[Kabak et al. 2008] Kabak, Y., Dogac, A., Kose, I., Akpinar, N., Gurel, M., Arslan, Y., Özer, H., Yurt N., Özcam, A., Kirici, S., Yüksel, M., and Sabur, E., The use of HL7 CDA in the National Health Information System (NHIS) of Turkey. In: *Proceedings of 9th Int. HL7 Interoperability Conference* (2008).

[Kazemzadeh and Sartipi 2005] Kazemzadeh, R. S., and Sartipi, K., Interoperability of Data and Knowledge in Distributed Health Care Systems. In: *Proceedings of 13th IEEE International Workshop on Software Technology and Engineering Practice*, pp. 230–240 (2005).

[Kilic and Dogac 2009] Kilic, O., and Dogac, A., Achieving clinical statement interoperability using R-MIM and archetype-based semantic transformations. In: *Proceedings of IEEE Transactions on Information Technology in Biomedicine*, pp. 467–477 (2009).

[Kim et al. 2006] Kim, H., Tung, T., and Cho, H., A clinical document architecture (CDA) to generate clinical documents within a hospital information system for E-healthcare services. In: *Proceedings of Sixth IEEE International Conference on Computer and Information Technology (CIT)*, p. 254 (2006).

[Lupse et al. 2011] Lupse, O., Vida, M., Stoicu-Tivadar, L., and Stoicu-Tivadar, V., Using HL7 CDA and CCD standards to improve communication between health-care information systems. In: *Proceedings of IEEE 9th International Symposium on Intelligent Systems and Informatics (SISY)*, pp. 453–457 (2011).

[Marcheschi 2005] Marcheschi, P., Mazzarisi, A., Dalmiani, S., and Benassi, A., New standards for cardiology report and data communication: An experience with HL7 CDA release 2 and EbXML. In: *Proceedings of Computers in Cardiology*, pp. 383–386 (2005).

[Mazzarisi et al. 2004] Mazzarisi, A., Marcheschi, P., Dalmiani, S., Marraccini, P., Startari, U., and Piacenti, M., System for electrophysiology integration with other departments using clinical document architecture technologies and HL7 V3. In: *Proceedings of Computers in Cardiology*, pp. 625–628 (2004).

[Treins 2006] Treins, M., Cure, O., and Salzano, G., On the interest of using HL7 CDA Release 2 for the exchange of annotated medical documents. In: *Proceedings on 19th IEEE International Symposium on Computer-Based Medical Systems,* pp. 524–532 (2006).

[Vida et al. 2011] Vida, M., Lupse, O., Stoicu-Tivadar, L., and Stoicu-Tivadar, V., ICT solution supporting continuity of care in children healthcare services. In: *Proceedings of 6th IEEE International Symposium on Applied Computational Intelligence and Informatics (SACI),* pp. 635–639 (2011).

[Xie et al. 2010] Xie, L., Yu, C., Liu, L., and Yao, Z., XML-based Personal Health Record system. In: *Proceedings of 3rd International Conference on Biomedical Engineering and Informatics (BMEI),* pp. 2536–2540 (2010).

[Yun and Kim 2007] Yun, J., and Kim, I., Processing HL7-CDA Entry for Semantic Interoperability. In: *Proceedings of International Conference on Convergence Information Technology,* pp. 1939–1944 (2007).

[Zhengxing et al. 2007] Zhengxing, H., Xudong, L., Huilong, D., and Haomin, L., Enhanced CDA with Electronic Signature. In: *Proceedings of 1st International Conference on Bioinformatics and Biomedical Engineering (ICBBE),* pp. 1161–1164 (2007).

CHAPTER NINE

Standard for Medical Imaging and Communication

9.1 Introduction

With increasing use of computers in radiology, *American College of Radiology (ACR)* and *National Electrical Manufacturers Association (NEMA)* started work in 1983 for defining a standard for structure and transmission of images between medical devices and computer systems. Their effort resulted in a standard called DICOM (Digital Imaging and Communications in Medicine). The standard deals with the structure and transmission of medical images in digital form. It encompasses Information Entities for Patient Information, Study, and Series-related Information and Image data that are useful from the perspective of a patient's EHR.

The recent editions of the standard have improved upon its predecessors. Some notable improvements are its applicability to a network environment, usage specifications for offline media environment, standard command-based interface among communicating systems, multilevel conformance criteria specification, use of explicit information objects for imagery and nonimagery medical data, structured as multipart document, unique identification mechanism for each information object, and conversion of DICOM data sets into HL7 CDA document structure [NEMA's DICOM].

Electronic Health Record: Standards, Coding Systems, Frameworks, and Infrastructures, Pradeep Sinha, Gaur Sunder, Prashant Bendale, Manisha Mantri, and Atreya Dande.
© 2013 by The Institute of Electrical and Electronics Engineers, Inc. Published 2013 by John Wiley & Sons, Inc.

Various workflows defined in the DICOM standard, such as Modality Work Lists, General-Purpose Performed Procedure Step, Scheduled Procedure Step, and Modality Performed Procedure Step, help in automating clinical workflows in computer systems and medical devices, for details, refer to 11_04P4 of [DICOM PS 3.0 2011]. Through these workflows, a clinician can schedule a procedure, and the target medical device automatically performs the procedure and stores the result in a repository, minimizing need for any manual intervention. Security profiles of the standard tackle the issue of security management in communication and storage. It also defines access to DICOM objects over the web.

9.2 DICOM

The DICOM standard supports a wide range of features to facilitate interoperability between communicating entities. These include:

1. Specification for network communication
2. Syntactic and semantic level description of network level commands
3. Interchange media support through standard description of file format and media directory structure
4. Concrete conformance statement framework.

These features enable those entities that adhere to DICOM standard to communicate in a seamless and effective manner.

The DICOM standard provides separate mechanisms for representing information and exchange of information while communicating [Mustra et al. 2008]. It consists of types such as Data Sets, Data Elements, Information Object Definitions, and Protocol Data Units. Data Sets and Information Object Definitions together define the Information Model of the standard, while Protocol Data Units define its Message Exchange Model.

DICOM architecture describes its Information Model and Message Exchange Model and the relationships between them. The architecture is described below [DICOM PS 3.0 2011].

9.2.1 INFORMATION MODEL

Figure 9.1 shows the DICOM Information Model depicting relationships among its structural entities. These relationships define how Information Model relates to the Message Exchange Model in DICOM standard. This representation helps the communicating entities negotiate their capabilities with minimal information by exchanging some set of identifiers for these relationships. DICOM Data Dictionary defines these identifiers and their meanings for details, refer to 11_06pu of [DICOM PS 3.0 2011].

The major structural components of the standard are Data Set, Information Object Definitions, and Message Structures. The underlying data structure of the

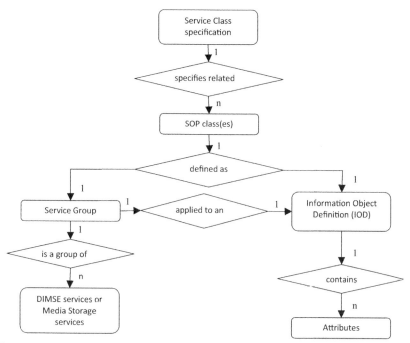

FIGURE 9.1 Major Structures of DICOM Information Molel. Adapted from [DICOM PS 3.0 2011].

DICOM standard is composed of Data elements. Data elements together constitute Data Set to form a composite entity. Communicating entities talk in terms of data sets. Logically, Information Object Definition (IOD) wraps Data Set that represents the characteristics of patient, study, series and imagery data in an object-oriented manner. This representation makes it easy to understand what DICOM information represents for details, refer to 11_03pu of [DICOM PS 3.0 2011]. Besides these structural components, the standard clearly describes network level wrappers over DICOM data. These wrappers are message structures and Protocol Data Units (PDUs). Hence, adherence to DICOM standard means building software/firmware components that understand and construct these structures and communicate in DICOM-specified language for details, refer to 11_08pu of [DICOM PS 3.0 2011].

The DICOM standard builds logical models on top of these constructs to support specific procedures and workflows in healthcare practices. It defines Composite IODs as constructs holding the entire information of a patient, study, series and image and defines Normalized IODs as constructs holding information specific to either a patient or study or series or imagery data. Service-Object Pair (SOP), an important concept in DICOM, specifies conformance and pre-communication negotiation among communicating entities. For example, the C-STORE service with Computed Tomography (CT) object informs the receiver that the sender is willing to store CT image object at the receiver end in a particular syntactic structure. This clear negotiation prior to actual transfer enables the receiver to respond in a positive or negative manner. It makes network communication efficient because the sender sends actual data only when it has assurance that the receiver will store it for details, refer to 11_07pu of [DICOM PS 3.0 2011].

9.2.2 MESSAGE EXCHANGE MODEL

DICOM, being a health information exchange standard, clearly defines the handshaking protocol between communicating entities. It describes PDUs as communication data units in structured format. A healthcare provider entity can communicate with another entity through transmission of these PDUs. The PDUs provide elements for handshake-level configuration, network-level and data-level security negotiations. Various parameters supported by exchange units of DICOM standard include security settings like, Transport Level Security (TLS) security, Public Key Cryptography Standards (PKCS), and so on, with support for infrastructure for properly validating these structures.

The validation mechanism is useful in identifying whether healthcare data is completely or partially valid for transmission from one healthcare provider to another or from one entity to another. DICOM standard also defines a set of workflows using which exchange of health data occurs amongst radiological equipment and/or health information or EMR/EHR systems. These sets of exchanges define a standard workflow process. DICOM standard ensures that the communicating entities adhere to it through association negotiation mechanisms, for details, refer to 11_08pu of [DICOM PS 3.0 2011].

9.3 Improvements in DICOM Standard

A committee appointed by NEMA refines DICOM standard every year. The committee follows a process in which the members submit change proposals and the committee reviews and integrates modifications in the standard. These improvements mostly include addition/removal of IODs, modification of validation rules for attributes in IODs, and addition of advanced technological concepts in imaging like 3D imaging support. Note that the network communication layer of DICOM standard has remained the same with minimal changes over a long period. Validations affect implementations, and thus it is important that communicating parties should know the version of DICOM standard that they are using. NEMA committee also revises the conformance statement part of the standard, which helps implementers in specifying the capabilities of the applications/medical devices. Recent versions of the standard have added example conformance statements that have also helped bring clarity in use of the standard [Clunie 2011].

9.4 Discussion

DICOM is widely adapted for exchanging radiological information in healthcare applications in national health IT programs of many countries such as Australia,

Denmark, Hong Kong, Taiwan, United Kingdom, and United States. For example, Canada's national EHR implementation supports DICOM and DICOM Structured Report (SR) for exchange of diagnostics images and reports while Austria's national EHR project uses DICOM with support of Web Access to DICOM Persistent Objects (WADO).

Clinical Process Model. The EHR model should ideally be process-based to represent various workflow processes in regular medical practices. To achieve this, decoupling of the information model from the clinical process model may be necessary. The standard represents data in Data Set and IODs such as Patient Information Model, Study Information Model, and so on and defines various workflows on top such as Modality Work Lists, Scheduled Procedure Steps, Performed Procedure Steps, and so on. These models and procedures cater to the need of a particular workflow in clinical practices. For example, when a doctor advises a patient to take an X-ray, the doctor actually schedules an X-ray work list item that the X-ray machine receives. The patient receives information about the timings of the test, the lab operator can review the scheduled procedures on the X-ray machine to conduct the X-ray procedure, and then the machine sends the X-ray test results to the central image archive. Doctors can then retrieve it from the archive, analyze it, and suggest treatment.

When we analyze the participating constructs in this entire process, it is clear that the workflow process utilizes the Information Model by taking specific Data Elements at each conceptual level like Patient, Study, and Series into account, and a set of services/actions helps in completion of the workflow. However, it is noteworthy that the Information Model coupled with workflow is not functionally the same as the process-based health record model. Nonetheless, this concept adds value while thinking of an EHR framework as an Information Model capable of representing a process and a set of workflows on top, for details, refer to 11_04pu of [DICOM PS 3.0 2011].

Structural Model

Useful Data Set and Data Element Design. DICOM provides a well-designed structure for Data Set and Data Element. EHR frameworks can utilize these structures for holding value data as a set of attributes. The design of Data Element allows representation of medical information in uniquely identifiable attributes along with detailed description of their data types, length, and so on. This mechanism can help in defining search criteria for patient records, because a Data Element is easy to search using its unique identification.

Co-existence of Syntactic and Semantic Model. Data Set represents syntactic model, whereas Information Object Definitions represent semantic model of the Information Model. The semantic model acts like a logical wrapper over the syntactic model, and it represents a view that is easy to understand for medical practitioners and lab technicians as well as suites Object Oriented Design. This concept is useful for any EHR framework. At the semantic level, the EHR model can be process-based and content-based, whereas at syntactic level, structures like Data Set represent actual contents.

Limited Radiology Specific Hierarchical Model. Hierarchical design of DICOM Information Objects appears quite specific to Radiology. For radiological medical data, DICOM provides probably the most comprehensive set for building a model. Most EHR models can simply adopt the DICOM Information Model for radiological records. While analyzing a patient's problem, a radiologist needs a series of images taken under a study. The DICOM Model only talks up to this level. Hence, from a model point of view, DICOM standard is not generic. Hierarchical and dual model design providing Data and Workflow Models in the DICOM standard is useful and applicable in various other domains such as pathology. The DICOM standard committee is refining the DICOM standard in this direction and adding pathological procedures to make it useful for supporting workflows during interoperability [DICOM Standard Supplement 2010].

Categorization of Medical Information. A composite IOD structure in DICOM reveals hierarchical structure of medical records. It properly attaches patient information to imagery data. It also arranges various studies and various series hierarchically so that any DICOM image depicts information about the concerned patient, study, and associate set of images. This model describes radiological process of conducting studies of a series of images for a particular problem of a patient. Since the model is radiology-specific, it is not a complete model for designing an EHR framework that can cater to all kinds of clinical records. However, one can take the hierarchical model design as an idea for health problem analysis and treatment.

Security/Privacy Considerations. The DICOM standard provides for Application Entity level security policies; that is, the sender and receiver entities can implement security policies. It describes an approach of specifying additional data/command elements to specify security parameters that the communicating entities can validate before starting communication. This measure ensures primary level of security. As far as the security framework supported by DICOM is concerned, EHR frameworks can utilize it while importing and exporting medical data in DICOM communication. DICOM provides a plethora of security mechanisms at various levels such as secure transport connection, digital signature, and media storage security. *Technical Guidelines* section given later in this chapter describes security profiles in technical details and their applicability from the perspective of EHR frameworks.

However, in any EHR framework, security restrictions can be a complex mix of authentication and authorization. Architects can evaluate other complex security policies frameworks also. *eXtensible Access Control Markup Language* (XACML)-based security policy frameworks may be useful [XACML Overview].

Legal Aspects. The DICOM standard, being a messaging standard, does not provide legal or ethical aspects of the represented and transmitted information.

Exchange Specifications. NEMA defined the DICOM standard to facilitate communication among medical applications/devices. Hence, the protocol architecture of the standard is such that it naturally fits as an exchange standard.

Messaging Standard (. . . and not an EHR Standard). The DICOM standard is a messaging standard to facilitate interoperability among medical devices/applications. It provides syntactical requirements and communication details. Although it does specify a structure for radiological medical data through its Data Set and IODs, from the perspective of EHR model, the standard can be thought of as a delivery vehicle for medical data. It helps in achieving interoperability among communicating entities through clear structural and communicational specifications. Hence, the standard can be utilized for importing/exporting medical data from local systems in hospitals to an EHR framework.

Support for Coding Systems. DICOM standard supports use of coding systems. It allows the users to specify the codes along with the details of the coding scheme used. Coding systems avoid ambiguity in representing the intention while specifying disease, procedure, findings, and so on. The Information Model of an EHR framework must provide support for coding systems so that it will have a place for attaching coding scheme designators with medical records.

Technical Guidelines. The DICOM standard is a complete technical specification for imagery medical data and its communication. Some of the technical guidelines derived from this industry-accepted standard that may be useful while designing EHR frameworks are as follows:

1. The data structures and the information model concept in DICOM can help in designing EHR frameworks.
2. While designing the interactions for various components of an EHR framework, its architect can refer to the network model of the DICOM standard. Various parameters considered in the DICOM standard for network communication can help in designing a comprehensive network communication protocol for EHR frameworks.
3. An excellent feature of adding security profiles to the underlying communication layer is a nice design concept for pluggable components of EHR frameworks. Since these profiles are pluggable, users can select the type of security needed while communicating.
4. Various security profiles such as secure transport connection, digital signature, and media storage security are good resources to refer to while designing security aspects of EHR frameworks. All these techniques are helpful in protecting healthcare information.

9.5 Conclusion

DICOM is a messaging standard for communication structures. However, architects can utilize many of its excellent design concepts while designing an EHR framework, particularly Data Model and Workflow Models. Though the model of the standard does not appear as an EHR Model due to its specificity for radiology domain, the idea of decoupling Data from Information Object representation is useful.

Though DICOM provides well-designed security policies and structure for carrying security information, it only talks about Application Entity level authentication. EHR framework security requirements can be quite complex and hence, users need to analyze other security policy frameworks also. However, security profiles used in DICOM standard describe end-to-end information communication security that EHR framework architects can refer.

Various Information Entities like Patient, Study, Series, and Image level are useful for identifying attributes at each level. This information is useful while defining one's own set of attributes for each type of medical record and patient information. In addition, for identification purposes at various levels in an EHR framework, one can utilize the concept of unique ID in DICOM SOPs and IODs.

After reviewing improvements in DICOM standard over a decade, it is clear that extending and enhancing DICOM is easy as the base architecture is well-thought and robust allowing flexibility. Hence, the applications/devices adhering to DICOM standard need minimal investment while upgrading to newer versions of the standard.

The previous chapters in this part of the book covered many standards for exchange of medical data and standards such as CEN/ISO EN 13606 that provide specifications for structure and content of EHR while exchanging medical data. In the next chapter, we will study the CCR standard that provides specifications for generating a summary care record for exchanging such information across healthcare organizations in an integrated care environment.

BIBLIOGRAPHY

[Becker et al. 2001] Becker, T., Onnasch, D., and Simon, R., Interoperability for image and non-image data in the DICOM standard investigated from different vendor implementations. In: *Proceedings of IEEE Conference on Computers in Cardiology*, pp. 675–678 (2001).

[Bendale and Gaur Sunder 2009] Bendale, P., and Gaur Sunder, Combining DICOM and HL7 into a single effective protocol in health informatics—Opportunities and challenges. In: *Proceedings of 5th National Congress of Telemedicine Society of India (Telemedicon'09)* (November 2009).

[Clunie 2011] Clunie, David A., DICOM Standard Status; http://www.dclunie.com/dicom-status/status.html.

[DICOM PS 3.0 2011] Digital Imaging and Communications in Medicine (DICOM) (2011); ftp://medical.nema.org/medical/dicom/2011.

[DICOM Standard Supplement 2010] DICOM Standards Committee, Working Group 26, Pathology, *Supplement 145: Whole Slide Microscopic Image IOD and SOP Classes* (August 2010); ftp://medical.nema.org/medical/dicom/final/sup145_ft.pdf.

[Huang and Su 2007] Huang, C. Y., and Su, J. L., A middleware of DICOM and web service for home-based elder healthcare information system. In: *Proceedings of 6th International Special Topic Conference on Information Technology Applications in Biomedicine*, pp. 182–185 (2007).

[Koutelakis and Lymberopoulos 2009] Koutelakis, G.V., and Lymberopoulos, D. K., WADA service: an extension of DICOM WADO service. In: *Proceedings of IEEE Transactions on Information Technology in Biomedicine*, pp. 121–130 (2009).

[Lin et al. 2010] Lin, H., Chen, Z., and Wang, W., XML schemas representation of DICOM data model. In: *Proceedings of 4th International Conference on Bioinformatics and Biomedical Engineering (iCBBE)*, pp. 1–3 (2010).

[Mustra et al. 2008] Mustra, M., Delac, K., Grgic, F M., Overview of the DICOM standard. In: *Proceedings of 50th International Symposium ELMAR* (2008).

[NEMA's DICOM] DICOM Standard; http://medical.nema.org/.

[Neri et al. 1998] Neri, E., Thiran, J. P., Caramella, D., Petri, C., Bartolozzi, C., Piscaglia, B., Macq, B., Duprez, T., Cosnard, G., Maldague, B., and De Pauw, J., Interactive DICOM image transmission and telediagnosis over the European ATM network. In: *Proceedings of IEEE Transactions on Information Technology in Biomedicine*, pp. 35–38 (1998).

[Ran and Guo 2011] Ran, C., and Guo, G., Security XACML access control model based on SOAP encapsulate. In: *Proceedings of International Conference on Computer Science and Service System (CSSS)*, pp. 2543–2546 (2011).

[Sahu and Verma 2011] Sahu, B. K., and Verma, R., DICOM search in medical image archive solution e-Sushrut Chhavi. In: *Proceedings of 3rd International Conference on Electronics Computer Technology (ICECT)*, pp. 256–260 (2011).

[Wahle et al. 1996a] Wahle, A., Builtjes, J. H., Oswald, H., and Fleck, E., Secure inter-institutional image communication by using DICOM-to-DICOM gateways. In: *Proceedings of Computers in Cardiology*, pp. 309–312 (1996).

[Wahle et al. 1996b] Wahle, A., Builtjes, J. H., Oswald, H., and Fleck, E., DICOM-integration in a heterogeneous environment. In: *Proceedings of the 18th Annual International Conference of the IEEE Engineering in Medicine and Biology Society—Bridging Disciplines for Biomedicine*, Vol. 3, pp. 1228–1229 (1996).

[Wang and Huang 2010] Wang, C., and Huang, Y., DICOM communication mechanism and engineering project integration based on ESB. In: *Proceedings of WASE International Conference on Information Engineering*, pp. 119–122 (2010).

[XACML Overview] A Brief Introduction to XACML; http://www.oasis-open.org/committees/download.php/2713/Brief_Introduction_to_XACML.html.

CHAPTER TEN

Standard for Patient Health Summary

10.1 Introduction

Clinical and other medical data that are available while referring, transferring, or discharging a patient must be recorded. Moreover, to ensure interoperability, it is wise to follow a specification or guideline for recording such data. Continuity of Care Record (CCR) standard specification was developed to address this need by ASTM International, Massachusetts Medical Society (MMS), Health Information and Management Systems Society (HIMSS), and American Academy of Family Physicians (AAFP).

The CCR standard enables export or import of relevant data from EHR systems as Patient Health Summary. This helps to minimize disruption during transfer of a patient. It describes relevant medical information as the minimum data set required for representing health summary of the patient [Tessier et al. 2003].

10.2 Continuity of Care Record (CCR)

The CCR standard defines specifications that facilitate exchange of clinical information by way of summary notes. However, it should not be considered

Electronic Health Record: Standards, Coding Systems, Frameworks, and Infrastructures, Pradeep Sinha, Gaur Sunder, Prashant Bendale, Manisha Mantri, and Atreya Dande.
© 2013 by The Institute of Electrical and Electronics Engineers, Inc. Published 2013 by John Wiley & Sons, Inc.

TABLE 10.1   **CCR Structural Model**

Sections	Additional Information	Category of Additional Information
1 Document Identifying Information	Optional	
"From/To" info of Provider/clinician	Extension	
Reason for Referral/Transfer		
2 Patient Identifying Information	Optional	
	Extension	
3 Insurance and Financial Info	Extension	Eligibility, Co-payment, etc.
4 Health Status of Patient	Extension	Med. Specialty-specific Info
Diagnosis/Problems/Conditions	Extension	Disease Management-specific Info
Adverse Reaction/Alerts	Extension	Personal Health Record Info
Current Medications		Documented by the Patient
Immunizations		
Vital Signs		
Lab Results		
Procedural/Assessments		
5 Care Documentation	Extension	Med. Specialty-specific Info
	Extension	Disease Management-specific Info
	Extension	Institution-specific Information
	Extension	Care Documentation for Payers (Attachments)
	Extension	Personal Health Record Info Documented by the Patient
6 Care Plan Recommendation (Text)		

only as a specification of clinician's note like, consultation note, progress note, or discharge summary. It helps in further treatment of a patient or helps the next clinician in understanding the previous treatment of the patient, follow-ups, and care plan given by the referring clinician.

10.2.1 STRUCTURAL MODEL

Table 10.1 shows the structure of a CCR Document. It consists of six sections, each of which can have extensions depending on requirements.

Mandated Core Elements of CCR are as follows:

Section. CCR, being a structure document, contains sections with each section describing specific information as shown in Table 10.1.

Extension. CCR provides extensions to enable implementers of CCR standard to support specific information as per user's needs. For example, Medical Specialty-specific Info extension allows implementers to support additional fields for a particular medical specialty.

Header or Document Identifying Information. This section describes the referring clinician, referred clinician, date, and purpose of the document.

1. *Patient Identifying Information.* This section includes the minimum information required to uniquely identify a patient across hospitals. However, CCR clearly mentions that it neither defines a distributed system nor specifies any kind of patient identification scheme. It only provides the minimum available information required to uniquely identify a patient.

2. *Patient's Insurance and Financial Information.* This section describes the information related to health insurance of a patient. It describes the minimum data elements for this information, such as Insurance Company Name, Subscriber's Name, Subscriber's Date of Birth, Subscriber's Member ID, and so on.

3. *Health Status of Patient.* The CCR standard describes the health status of patients by including several types of records. It includes diagnoses, problems, adverse reactions/alerts, current medications, immunizations, vital signs, laboratory results, procedures, and assessments with a provision for extension of record types, depending on the need of specific medical specialty. The extensions available are Medical Specialty-specific Information, Disease Management-specific Information, and Personal Health Record Information Documented by patient. These extensions serve the purpose of providing ability to add more information specific to user needs.

4. *Care Documentation.* While recording all current medications and care, the CCR standard also includes care documentation including links to previous encounters along with date and time of patient with clinicians. The extensions available are Medical Specialty-Specific Information, Disease Management-Specific Information, Institute-specific Information, Care Documentation for Payers (Attachments), and Personal Health Record Information Documented by a patient.

5. *Care Plan Recommendation.* This section includes the details of medication plans, tests, and treatment description. It allows free text so that clinicians can provide free-form description of a diagnosis.

Along with these mandatory sections, the CCR standard provides for the following five extensions:

- *Institution-Specific Information*
- *Medical Specialties* for providing the minimal data set
- *Specific Disease Management Information*, Personal Health Record Information to enable a patient to keep private information
- *Payer-Specific Information* (in case of insurance)

These extensions allow addition of any specific information to the mandatory core elements. The CCR standard also provides a mechanism for a patient to enter his/her personal health record information for Care Documentation and Health Status. Patients can add more information that enables representation of an EHR as *Personal Health Record (PHR)* [Tessier 2009].

10.2.2 EXCHANGE

As the CCR standard is very similar to Clinical Document Architecture (CDA) of HL7, HL7 v3 model also has provision to send CCR documents from source to destination. The detailed structure of HL7 CDA is given in Chapter 8.

XML constructs can represent structure of CCR documents [W3C XML 2011]. Figure 10.1 represents detailed hierarchical structure of a CCR document. It consists of a CCR Header, a CCR Body, and a CCR Footer. It represents various components described in the *Architecture* section of this chapter in XML representation format. The CCR Body section of the document describes various record types supported by the standard. However, detailed structural description of each of the record types is not available. CCR specifications describe the use of

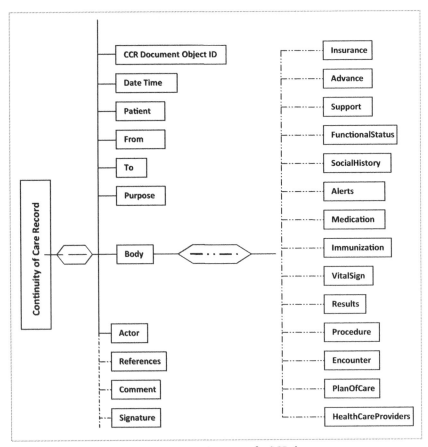

FIGURE 10.1 XML Structure of a CCR document.

a signature section in the CCR Footer for securing the entire document digitally [Tessier 2009]. It also provides for references where this document can refer to other documents. ASTM E31.20 committee defines CCR privacy and security guidelines. It recommends the use of PKI infrastructure [PKI Wiki 2011] and digital signature standard for ensuring security of CCR documents [Cooper 2010].

10.3 Discussion

Structural Model. CCR is an expansion of "Patient Care Referral Form (PCRF)" that was in wide circulation in Massachusetts County for referring/ transferring/discharging of patients. The CCR document includes the summary part of each of the identified categories mentioned in the *Architecture* section and hence the dataset is not comprehensive enough to use as an EHR Model. Since, CCR aims at avoiding medical errors due to misinterpretation of opinions/ remarks of clinicians during referral/transfer processes; Health Status of a patient requires only summarized data even in case of Lab Result, Procedures and Assessments [Larsen and Sensmeier 2003].

Although CCR standard is not a complete EHR specification, it does help in identifying categories in medical information of a patient. It divides the entire medical information into three parts – Administrative, Demographic, and Clinical. In Administrative part, it identifies Care Purpose, Financial and Insurance information of the patient. The Demographics part describes the patient's identification information that healthcare providers need to manage in secure manner. The Clinical part consists of Health Status of patient, Care Documentation, and Care Plan Recommendation. This section mentions various types of status including Diagnosis, Problem, Condition, Adverse Reaction or Alert, Current Medication, Immunization, Vital Sign, Lab Result, Procedure, and Assessment. This is useful while identifying top-level broad structures of an EHR.

CCR is supported in United Kingdom's national EHR service implementation project called *Spine* as the standard of exchange. The shared record Summary Care Record (SCR) in Spine in England can be transferred as CCR. Further details of Spine are given in Chapter 24.

Security/Privacy Considerations. CCR specification describes the use of XML constructs while transmission of CCR documents. ASTM E31.20 committee recommendations are helpful in knowing the security/privacy mechanisms applicable to an EHR framework. These recommendations are clear from a technology perspective also. Some of them are use of PKI infrastructure, digital signatures, encryption, and so on. EHR frameworks can use these techniques for securing information during transmission.

Exchange Specifications. ASTM Committee E31.25 specifies the CCR standard as a mechanism for exchanging health summary among care providers.

Hence, communication of health records is possible through CCR. Since the committee specifies the XML format of a CCR document, it makes CCR document representation simple and technology-neutral. These efforts by standard organizations emphasize the use of technology-neutral representations of exchange messages during communication [Spyropoulos et al. 2006].

10.4 Conclusion

CCR standard describes only one part of healthcare delivery i.e. referral cases. Therefore, CCR is useful for designing referral kind of artifacts of an EHR Model. However, categories identified for summary purpose are useful for identifying a set of record types for any EHR model.

Security and privacy guidelines considered in CCR specifications are also helpful in devising security and privacy policies for an EHR framework. Representation of EHR data in XML format is also a welcome recommendation considering adoption of XML in health domain during communication.

BIBLIOGRAPHY

[AAFP CCR 2005] American Academy of Family Physicians, Essential Similarities and Differences between the HL7 CDA/CRS and ASTM CCR. In: *Proceedings of AAFP* (2005); http://www.centerforhit.org/online/etc/medialib/chit/documents/proj-ctr/simdif.Par.0001.File.tmp/chit_ccrhl7.pdf.

[ASTM E2369-05e2 CCR 2011] Computerized System Standards E31.25, ASTM E2369-05e2, ASTM E2369-05e2 Standard Specification for Continuity of Care Record (CCR) (2011); http://www.astm.org/Standards/E2369.htm.

[CCR FAQ 2011] American Academy of Family Physicians, Unofficial FAQs about the ASTM CCR Standard (20011); http://www.centerforhit.org/online/chit/home/project-ctr/astm/unofficialfaq.html.

[CCR Standard 2010] Continuity of Care Record (CCR) Standard; http://wiki.medpedia.com/Continuity_of_Care_Record_(CCR)_Standard.

[Chheda 2005] Chheda, N. C., Electronic Medical Records and Continuity of Care Records—the Utility Theory. In: *Proceedings of Application of Information Technology & Economics*, (2005); http://www.nainil.com/research/whitepapers/CCR_A_Utility_Theory.pdf.

[Cooper 2010] Cooper, T., ASTM E31 Security Standards. In *Proceedings of ASTM*, (2010); http://www.ncvhs.hhs.gov/010201h9.pdf.

[CorepointHealth CCR view] Understanding the Continuity of Care Record; http://www.corepointhealth.com/whitepapers/understanding-continuity-care-record.

[Dunnagan and Terida 2008] Dunnagan, M. and Terida, Practical application of simple principles and technology to HIE. In: *Proceedings of Continuity of Care Record (CCR) A Symposium on Present and Future Uses*, (2008); http://www.massmed.org/AM/Template.cfm?Section=Calendar&CONTENTID=23067&TEMPLATE=/CM/ContentDisplay.cfm.

[Ferranti et al. 2006] Ferranti, J. M., Musser, R. C., Kawamoto, K., and Hammond, W., The clinical document architecture and the continuity of care record: A critical analysis. In: *Proceedings of American Medical Informatics Association*, (2006); http://www.ncbi.nlm.nih.gov/pmc/articles/PMC1513652/.

[Kibbe 2005] Kibbe, D. C. An overview of the ASTM continuity of care record (CCR). In: *Proceedings of AAFP, AAP, ASTM International* (2005); http://www.nchica.org/Past/06/presentations/Kibbe.pdf.

[Kibbe and Peters 2005] Kibbe, D. C. and Peters, R., The ASTM continuity of care record, CCR, a tool for health data exchange. In: *Proceedings of Center for Health Information Technology* (2005); http://www.centerforhit.org/online/etc/medialib/chit/documents/proj-ctr/astmccr.Par.0001.File.tmp/chit_ccrnyc.pdf.

[Larsen and Sensmeier 2003] Larsen, E. and Sensmeier, J., Standards insight an analysis of health information standards development initiatives. In: *Proceedings of HIMSS* (2003).

[PKI Wiki 2011] Public Key Infrastructure (2011); http://en.wikipedia.org/wiki/Public_key_infrastructure.

[Spyropoulos et al. 2006] Spyropoulos, B., Botsivaly, M., Tzavaras, A., and Koutsourakis, K., Extending the use of DRGs to estimate mean home-care cost by employing an adapted ASTM E2369-05 continuity of care record. In: *Proceedings of 28th Annual International Conference of the IEEE on Engineering in Medicine and Biology Society* (2006).

[Tessier et al. 2003] Tessier, C., Sullivan, T., Waegeman, P., Kibbe, D., Bellisle, K., Smith, D., and Brewer, P., The concept paper of the CCR. In: *Proceedings of ASTM* (2003).

[Tessier 2009] Tessier, C., Status and projects of the CCR (continuity of care record). In: *Proceedings of EHR Summit II, Los Angeles* (2009).

[Waldren 2005] Waldren, S. E., ASTM E2369-05, Standard specification for the continuity of care record (CCR). In: *Proceedings of WEDI Conference* (2005); http://www.centerforhit.org/PreBuilt/chit_wedi2005.pdf.

[W3C XML 2011] World Wide Web Consortium (W3C) Extended Markup Language (XML); http://www.w3.org/XML/.

PART THREE

Coding Systems

CHAPTER ELEVEN

Coding System for Classification of Diseases and Related Health Problems

11.1 Introduction

The World Health Organization (WHO) in association with 10 other International Centers came out with International Statistical Classification of Diseases and Related Health Problems (ICD). Their main purpose was to provide a code set that will assist in analyzing mortality rates across the world. The ICD provides a set of codes for diseases, health problems, and procedures to identify medical records and to facilitate national or international level survey about health conditions, mortality rates, and so on. These codes are useful for analysis of epidemiological situations in a country or across the globe. The primary intention of these codes is to conduct statistical health surveys across the globe. ICD-10, the tenth revision of this standard, is currently in use.

ICD identifies a set of health conditions and health practices and tries to assign alphanumeric codes to them. This mechanism improves searchability of medical records, and thus analysis becomes faster and efficient. According to the United Nations Statistics Division, the ICD standard serves the purpose of systematic recording, analysis, interpretation, and comparison of mortality and

Electronic Health Record: Standards, Coding Systems, Frameworks, and Infrastructures, Pradeep Sinha, Gaur Sunder, Prashant Bendale, Manisha Mantri, and Atreya Dande.
© 2013 by The Institute of Electrical and Electronics Engineers, Inc. Published 2013 by John Wiley & Sons, Inc.

morbidity data collected in different countries or areas and at different times. [United Nations Statistics Division].

11.2 ICD

ICD provides a set of codes that medical practitioners can attach with the medical records of their patients. Once healthcare providers start using health information systems that adhere to the ICD standard, the entire health information base becomes available for easy searching, retrieval, and analysis through ICD codes. This has proved to be very useful for researchers, government agencies, and pharmaceutical industry in many ways.

WHO publishes the online version of ICD standard describing all its codes and their structural descriptions. The ICD-10 List of Chapters describes classification of diseases into categories and assignment of codes according to these categories [ICD-10 structure].

11.2.1 CHAPTERS

ICD standard is organized into chapters. ICD-10 has 22 chapters, whose contents are listed in Table 11.1. Notice that Chapters 1 to 17 deal with a specific type of disease, whereas Chapters 18 to 22 deal with other types of health problems.

11.2.2 BLOCKS

A block describes diseases of a group of similar categories based on their characteristics. Multiple blocks constitute a chapter. For example, Chapter 11 describes diseases of the digestive system. This chapter consists of 10 blocks. One of the blocks is related to the diseases of appendix. Blocks further include specializations of diseases. For example, diseases of the appendix include types of appendicitis. The ICD standard assigns codes for these specialized classifications. Figure 11.1 shows the hierarchical structure of ICD-10 code-set. For example, the ICD code *B973* actually refers to Block number *B97* having specific disease *B97.3* as *Retrovirus* [Nath].

11.3 Improvements in ICD-10

ICD-10 differs slightly from its predecessor ICD-9. ICD-9 uses numeric codes for representing diseases whereas ICD-10 uses alphanumeric codes. For example, ICD-10 represents *Cholera* using code *A00* whereas ICD-9 represents it as *001*.

Fine tunings in ICD-10 are as follows:

1. Exclusion points giving explanatory notes about exclusion of diseases.
2. Two codes for certain conditions using the dagger (†) and asterisk (*) system representing generalized and specialized forms of diseases and associated codes.

TABLE 11.1   **Chapterwise details of ICD-10**

Chapter No.	Contents
1	Certain infectious and parasitic diseases
2	Neoplasms
3	Diseases of the blood and blood-forming organs and certain disorders involving the immune mechanism
4	Endocrine, nutritional and metabolic diseases
5	Mental and behavioral disorders
6	Diseases of the nervous system
7	Diseases of the eye and adnexa
8	Diseases of the ear and mastoid process
9	Diseases of the circulatory system
10	Diseases of the respiratory system
11	Diseases of the digestive system
12	Diseases of the skin and subcutaneous tissue
13	Diseases of the musculoskeletal system and connective tissue
14	Diseases of the genitourinary system
15	Pregnancy, childbirth and the puerperium
16	Certain conditions originating in the perinatal period
17	Congenital malformations, deformations and chromosomal abnormalities
18	Symptoms, signs and abnormal clinical and laboratory findings, not elsewhere classified
19	Injury, poisoning and certain other consequences of external causes
20	External causes of morbidity and mortality
21	Factors influencing health status and contact with health services
22	Codes for special purposes

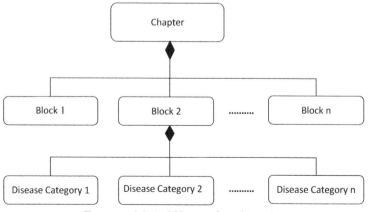

FIGURE 11.1   ICD-10 code-set hierarchy.

For example, categories G20 and G21 are for forms of Parkinsonism that are not manifestations of other diseases assigned elsewhere, while category G22* is for "Parkinsonism in diseases classified elsewhere." Corresponding dagger codes are given for conditions mentioned in asterisk categories; for example, for Syphilitic Parkinsonism in G22*, the dagger code is A52.1† [CDC 2009].

11.4 Discussion

Applicable Scope. WHO developed ICD codes to facilitate analysis and reporting during epidemic situations and to compare mortality rates at international level. ICD-10 contains over 68,000 codes, and each code contains three to seven characters. Each new version of ICD refines the already defined codes and adds more diseases and associated health information related codes to the standard. This makes it comprehensive and useful for any EHR system. Though there are many coding terminologies in existence, their combined use will only improve efficiency in storage, searching, and retrieval of medical records.

ICD standard nomenclature, being simply organized into chapters and blocks, is easy to implement in healthcare IT applications. It is useful for assigning codes to diagnoses because diagnoses normally refer to a particular health problem.

11.5 Conclusion

ICD-10 coding terminology provides a comprehensive set of codes for identified diseases and symptoms. Hence, it can be used to describe a health problem in standard manner in EHR frameworks. Based on these codes, searching and retrieval of disease related information from EHR systems becomes faster and efficient.

ICD code-set is in continuous improvement. This is a good sign as it ensures that the code set will gradually cover more codes to meet the future needs of medical practitioners internationally. The structure of the ICD-10 coding system does not make any provision for extensions. This limits its usage in scenarios where systems are using it along with local codes in a particular geographical region. But it is good in a way because extensions to incorporate local terms may prohibit the possibility of acceptance of the EHR system at the international level.

Other standards that deal with healthcare terminologies also incorporate codes for diseases. SNOMED CT is one such standard that has wide coverage of clinical terms. Its further details are covered in Chapter 15. ICD is focused on defining codes for diseases for health survey purposes internationally, and ICD codes (specifically for diseases) can be a super set for those in other terminology systems. Also, ICD codes appear to be the simplest of all in terms of structure.

ICD-10 specifies codes for identified diseases and symptoms which are recorded at the end of a problem's diagnosis phase. However, laboratory tests and observations conducted during diagnosis need specific identification codes which are covered by LOINC. The next chapter deals with LOINC.

BIBLIOGRAPHY

[CDC 2009] Dagger and Asterisk System (2009); http://wonder.cdc.gov/wonder/help/icd.html#ICD10 Dagger and Asterisk.

[Chen and Wang 2010] Chen, Y., and Wang, Z., A semantic method for coding of ICD Diagnoses. In: *Proceedings of 3rd International Conference on Biomedical Engineering and Informatics (BMEI)*, pp. 2876–2879 (2010).

[Chen et al. 2010] Chen, P., Barrera, A., and Rhodes, C., "Semantic Analysis of Free Text and its Application on Automatically Assigning ICD-9-CM Codes to Patient Records," In: *Proceedings of 9th IEEE International Conference on Cognitive Informatics (ICCI)*, pp. 68–74, (2010).

[Eder and Koncilia 2002] Eder, J. and Koncilia, C., Incorporating ICD-9 and ICD-10 data in a Warehouse. In: *Proceedings of the 15th IEEE Symposium on Computer-Based Medical Systems (CBMS)*, pp. 91–96 (2002).

[ICD 2010] International Statistical Classification of Diseases and Related Health Problems (ICD); http://www.who.int/classifications/icd/en/.

[ICD-10 Online Browser] ICD-10 Standard Details; http://apps.who.int/classifications/icd10/browse/2010/en.

[ICD-10 structure] Detailed structural description of ICD-10; http://apps.who.int/classifications/apps/icd/icd10online/.

[Nath] Nath, S. K., Introduction to ICD-10: Importance, Structure and Principles of Classification; http://cbhidghs.nic.in/S%20K%20Nath,%20Annexure%20B.ppt.

[United Nations Statistics Division] United Nations Statistics Division; http://unstats.un.org/unsd/class/family/family2.asp?Cl=219.

CHAPTER TWELVE

Coding System for Laboratory Tests and Observations

12.1 Introduction

Medical standards, terminologies, and codes play a vital role in representation of standardized clinical information in an EHR. Their purpose is to achieve semantic interoperability between healthcare systems.

Earlier, each clinical laboratory had its own set of identifier codes for representing clinical observations and laboratory test results. This created a problem in exchanging such information across different clinical laboratory systems. Although this problem was partially addressed by sharing identifier sets and providing mapping between code sets of different clinical laboratories, this solution soon became crippled with an increase in number of clinical laboratories and when such information had to be shared between clinical laboratories located in different states/countries. Another problem that the healthcare industry faced during the early days of computerization of healthcare services was that clinical observations or test results made by physicians often contained long character strings. Handling (storing, searching, sorting, etc.) this information in string form was highly inefficient and cumbersome. Even exchange of such information

Electronic Health Record: Standards, Coding Systems, Frameworks, and Infrastructures, Pradeep Sinha, Gaur Sunder, Prashant Bendale, Manisha Mantri, and Atreya Dande.
© 2013 by The Institute of Electrical and Electronics Engineers, Inc. Published 2013 by John Wiley & Sons, Inc.

between subsystems (such as Clinical Laboratory System and Patient Administration System) of an HIS was difficult. *Logical Observation Identifiers Names and Codes (LOINC)* was developed to address all these issues.

LOINC is a universal standard that provides standard identifiers, names, and codes for representing clinical observations and laboratory test results. It was developed and is maintained by Regenstrief Institute, Inc., a non-profit medical research organization associated with Indiana University, USA. LOINC facilitates clinical data exchange and management across healthcare systems. The LOINC database includes medical and laboratory code names, nursing diagnosis, nursing interventions, outcomes classification, and patient care data set [LOINC].

The Regenstrief Institute initiated work toward creating LOINC in 1994 for electronic exchange of clinical data among laboratories [LOINC Development].

12.2 LOINC

LOINC facilitates exchange and pooling of results, such as blood hemoglobin, serum potassium, or vital signs, for clinical care, outcomes management, and research. Standards such as ASTM E1238 [ASTM E1238] (now transferred to National Committee for Clinical Laboratory Standards (NCCLS) and named as NCCLS LIS5-A) [ANSI/ASTM E1238-97] or HL7 [HL7] can be used to send laboratory results electronically from production laboratories to clinical care systems in hospitals. These standards specify messages that carry laboratory test results.

LOINC has international appeal because it provides translations of its documents and terms into various languages such as Simplified Chinese, German, Spanish, Korean, Portuguese, Estonian, and so on.

12.2.1 CODE CLASSIFICATION

LOINC codes are classified as Laboratory and Clinical. Under each of these main categories, codes are distributed into specific categories. Figure 12.1 shows the specific categories under the two main categories.

12.2.2 CODE STRUCTURE

Each LOINC name code corresponds to a single test result or panel. The name code includes the following five to six fields (sixth field being optional) [LOINC Guide]:

1. *Component (Analyte).* This field identifies the component being measured during the laboratory test. It has three subfields:

   a. This subfield contains the principal name of the component that can be an analyte or measurement. It can contain any number of subclassifications of the component separated by dots. For example, Calcium.ionized is a

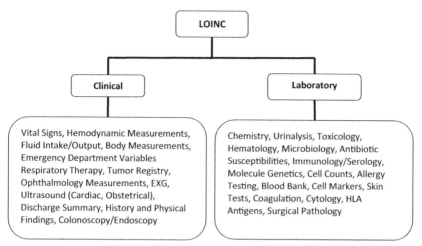

FIGURE 12.1 LOINC code categories.

subclassification of Calcium component. Other examples of this subfield are hemoglobin, potassium, and so on.

b. This subfield defines a specific situation when the component was measured. It is relevant because measurement taken at a specific time or after a laboratory test poses a challenge on the measured value. This subfield contains the name of the tolerance test, if relevant, and the time delay after which the component was measured. For example, glucose measured post 12 hours of fast is represented as Glucose ^ post 12H.

c. This subfield specifies the standardization or adjustment done during measurement. It is relevant when the measured value is adjusted according to some standard. These adjustments are coded as plain text since they are unique to the test being done. For example, Calcium.ionized adjusted to pH 7.4 is represented as

Calcium.ionized^^adjusted to pH 7.4.

2. **Property.** This field describes the property of the measured component. It is categorized into Mass, Substance, Catalytic Activity, Arbitrary, or Number. This field can be further classified into concentration, rate, contents, and ratios. For example, Glucose^10 AM:MCnc represents glucose recorded at 10 AM and measured in mass quantity (unit milligrams).

3. **Timing.** This field describes the point in time or series of time interval over which the property of the component was measured. The point in time is denoted by 'Pt' and interval by <units>/<time-interval> e.g. mg/24H.

4. **Sample Type.** This field describes the type of sample being measured. It optionally includes the name of the parent type of the sample. The parent type is included only when the subject of test is not a patient. For example, sample type can be urine, blood, fluid, serum, plasma, and parent type can be bone marrow donor, fetus, and so on.

5. *Type of Scale.* This field describes the type of measured value that is categorized as Quantitative, Ordinal, Quantitative or Ordinal, Nominal, Narrative, Multi, Document, and Set. It is like the data type of the measured value. For example, measurement is quantitative (a true measurement), ordinal (a ranked set of options), or nominal (e.g., *E. coli*; *Staphylococcus aureus*), or narrative (e.g., dictation results from X rays).

6. *Type of Method.* This optional field is sometimes required to distinguish two similar tests that differ only by the method of performing the test. It is mostly used in microbiology and coagulation tests. For example, computerized tomography (CT) and ultrasound (US).

Based on the above fields, the LOINC format for a fully specified name code of a test result or a clinical observation is given using

<Component> : <Property Measured> : <Timing> : <Type of Sample> : <Type of scale> : <method used to produce result>

The character ":" is the delimiter between various parts of the code.

12.2.3 REGENSTRIEF LOINC MAPPING ASSISTANT (RELMA)

Regenstrief LOINC Mapping Assistant (RELMA) [RELMA] is a free to download and use tool for browsing LOINC database. It is used to develop mapping between local code sets and LOINC code sets. RELMA has options for exporting and importing local map files for mapping local code sets.

12.3 Discussion

LOINC contains over 56,000 codes, with each code containing over 55 fields. Such an elaborate code structure needs a deep understanding of code descriptions to use them correctly. LOINC committee updates the code set based on the issues reported by its users. Such updates require the users to upgrade their codes at specific time intervals. However, LOINC ranks higher than other coding systems, when it comes to popularity amongst its users.

Applicable Scope. LOINC code set covers clinical observations and laboratory test results. There are other coding systems (like SNOMED CT) for a similar purpose. Let us take an example to understand the difference between LOINC and other coding systems. Each attribute in healthcare information has an identifier, a meaning, and a value. For example, an attribute "Hemoglobin level of a patient" can be identified in LOINC as 718-7: Hemoglobin: MCnc:PL:Bld: Qn. SNOMED CT provides the meaning of the attribute, and the value is represented by unit number [LOINC Introduction].

LOINC supports numerous laboratory tests such as chemistry, urinalysis, toxicology, hematology, microbiology, antibiotic susceptibilities, and so on vital signs, hemodynamic measurements, fluid intake/output, and so on (a complete list is available on LOINC's official website). Its widespread support for laboratory and clinical test results makes it a popular standard. Support for representing LOINC codes is available in DICOM, CEN TC215, ASTM E1238, and HL7 standards for exchange through use of observation messages.

LOINC, however, excludes some information that is usually communicated in laboratory test results. It is expected that exchange test result messages should contain such information. Following attributes are currently not specified by LOINC in its code set:

- Instrument used in carrying out the test
- Finer details about the sample or the site of collection such as, right antecubital fossa
- Priority of testing (e.g., whether statistical or routine)
- Verifier of the result
- Size of the sample collected
- Place of testing (e.g., home, bedside, clinical lab)

LOINC codes coverage in representing laboratory and clinical observations makes it a suitable choice for encoding of information in electronic health records.

12.4 Conclusion

LOINC defines unique identifier code sets for clinical observations and laboratory test results. It is useful in differentiating among various test results and observations that assist EHR Systems in categorization of records. LOINC can also be used as a code set for searching records from an EHR.

Since LOINC is limited to clinical observations and laboratory test results only, other coding systems (such as SNOMED CT) should be used to standardize information for other types of records in EHR. SNOMED CT is covered in Chapter 15.

LOINC specifies codes for ordering and resulting laboratory tests. After conducting these tests, bills from financial system need to be generated. The next chapter discusses about CPT that is used to specify codes for medical procedures mentioned in financial bills.

BIBLIOGRAPHY

[ANSI/ASTM E1238-97] American National Standards Institute (ANSI), Clinical and Laboratory Standards Institute (CLSI, formerly NCCLS), ANSI/ASTM E1238-97-Standard Specifications for Transferring Clinical Observations between Independent Computer Systems; http://www.clsi.org/source/orders/free/lis5-a.pdf.

[ASTM E1238] American Society of Testing and Materials (ASTM)—E1238; http://www.astm.org/Standards/E1238.htm.

[Case 2008] Case, J.T., Using RELMA, *LOINC Workshop*, (2008); http://www.slideshare.net/dvreeman/20080609-loinc-workshop.

[Eric 2011] Eric, Health Informatics—Issues and Practical Solutions, HealthBase Australia; http://blog.healthbase.info/?p=253.

[HL7] Health Level 7; http://www.hl7.org.

[LOINC] Logical Observations Identifiers, Names and Codes; http://en.wikipedia.org/wiki/LOINC.

[LOINC Development] Logical Observations Identifiers, Names and Codes Development; http://loinc.org/background/loinc-development.

[LOINC Guide] Guide for Logical Observation Identifiers, Names and Codes; http://loinc.org/downloads/files/LOINCManual.pdf.

[LOINC Introduction] Introduction and Overview of LOINC; http://loinc.org/slideshows/loinc-overview-and-introduction.

[NPRM Draft 2001] Logical Observations Identifiers, Names and Codes, NRPM Draft, LOINC Modifier Codes—for use with ASC X12N 277 Implementation Guides when Requesting Additional Information (December 2001); http://www.acbhcs.org/HIPAA/Implementation%20Guides/ModCodes.pdf.

[Pubmed 2003] McDonald, C.J., Huff, S.M., Suicom, J.G., Hill, G., Leavelle, D., Aller, R., Forrey, A., Mercer, K., DeMoor, G., Hook, J., Williams, W., Case, J., and Maloney, P., LOINC, a universal standard for identifying laboratory observations: A 5-year update, *PubMed, Source/Vol: Clinical Chemistry, Vol. 49*, pp. 624–633 (2003); http://www.ncbi.nlm.nih.gov/pubmed/12651816. http://www.clinchem.org/content/49/4/624.full.

[RELMA] Regenstrief LOINC Mapping Assistant (RELMA); http://loinc.org/relma.

[Wurtz 2005] Wurtz, R., ELR, LOINC, SNOMED, and Limitations in Public Health. (2004); http://www.stchome.com/media/white_papers/WHP0042-A.pdf.

CHAPTER THIRTEEN

Coding System for Patient Care Procedures

13.1 Introduction

Although healthcare applications are patient-centric, the clinical data that they deal with are specific to the health care profession. Healthcare coding systems enable interchange of such data between different healthcare applications by preserving the meaning and the scope of the clinical terminologies used. In addition to being helpful in patient care, representation of clinical data in coded form has various other uses such as research, analysis and statistics building, decision support, and so on. There are various standard coding systems for representation of clinical data in coded form. Current Procedural Terminology (CPT) is one of the widely used clinical terminologies for services and procedures performed on patients by health care providers, such as physicians, home healthcare providers, hospital agencies, nurses, and so on.

CPT [CPT] was developed in 1966 by the American Medical Association (AMA) [AMA] to provide consistency in describing and identifying medical procedures in terms of codes. These codes helped address health insurance claims for medical and surgical procedures. CPT evolved with time to support other fields in healthcare such as diagnostic and therapeutic procedures. The CPT Editorial Panel maintains CPT code sets. It is governed by AMA Board of Trustees and has 17 members responsible for modification, addition, and

Electronic Health Record: Standards, Coding Systems, Frameworks, and Infrastructures, Pradeep Sinha,
Gaur Sunder, Prashant Bendale, Manisha Mantri, and Atreya Dande.
© 2013 by The Institute of Electrical and Electronics Engineers, Inc. Published 2013 by John Wiley & Sons, Inc.

deletion of the codes. Its current version is CPT 2010, which provides a wide range of codes for describing medical, surgical, and diagnostic services with support for administrative services.

Centers for Medicare and Medicaid Services (CMS) adapted CPT codes and made its use mandatory in their coding system called Healthcare Common Procedure Coding System (HCPCS). It is widely used across the United States of America (USA). CMS is a national agency of the United States Department of Health and Human Services (HHS) that manages the Medicare program. It also works with state governments to manage Medicaid, State Children's Health Insurance Program, and standards related to health insurance portability.

The Health Insurance Portability and Accountability Act of 1996 (HIPAA) of USA has listed CPT and HCPCS in its final rule for transactions and code sets for medical and surgical procedures, physician services, diagnostic procedures, and transportation services. HIPAA deals with portable health insurance coverage and provides the rules for standardization of healthcare information systems for simplification of administrative work.

13.2 CPT

The first edition of CPT mainly covered surgical procedures. To incorporate diagnostic and therapeutic procedure codes in detail, the second edition evolved in 1970. The third and the fourth editions evolved successively with increase in number of codes and use of five digits instead of four for representing them.

Subsequently, the AMA initiated the development of the fifth edition due to the requirement of Electronic Data Interchange rule mentioned by the HIPAA [Rallins et al. 2006]. As HIPAA listed CPT code sets primarily for payments for medical procedures, it was necessary to make CPT codes interoperable with other clinical code sets (e.g., SNOMED CT). The CPT-4 edition was file based with no relevant concepts and relationships between codes. Hence, there were difficulties in mapping CPT codes with other coding systems. Thus, CPT-5 was developed to support interoperability by evolving a CPT Data Model, with concepts and relationships between them. The CPT-5 Data Model is currently in use with updates.

The CPT coding system comprises of the following components:

1. Data Model
2. CPT Sections
3. CPT Index
4. CPT Symbols
5. CPT Modifiers
6. Descriptive Qualifiers

These architecture components of the CPT coding system are described below.

13.2.1 DATA MODEL

The CPT Data Model consists of three categories of CPT codes as shown in Figure 13.1.

Category I Codes. Category I codes represent codes for procedures or services performed by healthcare providers on patients. Each of these codes is a five-digit code with a descriptor that tells about its classification. These codes are the core codes taken from CPT-4 and divided into six sections, namely, Evaluation and Management (E/M), Anesthesia, Surgery, Radiology, Pathology and Laboratory, and Medicine (see Figure 13.1).

Category II Codes. Category II codes are used for tracking certain services and tests for reviewing the quality of services. Each of these codes is a five-character alphanumeric code, with the first four characters as digits and the last character as alphabet. These codes are optional and located after the Medicine section.

Category III Codes. Category III codes represent codes for procedures and services that are currently under research or approval. These are the temporarily allocated codes approved by CPT Editorial Board on request to add them in the CPT code list. These codes represent a collection of such data that prove the usability of new services and procedures. The approach helps in getting the approval of procedures and services to be added to Category I codes by Food and Drug Administration (FDA). FDA is an agency of the United States Department of Health and Human Services (HHS), which is responsible for protecting and promoting public health through regulation and supervision of health-related aspects of services and products.

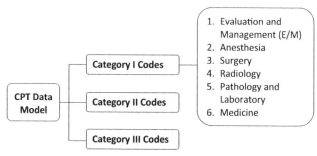

FIGURE 13.1 CPT-5 Data Model.

13.2.2 CPT SECTIONS

As mentioned earlier, CPT codes are divided into the following six sections:

1. *Anesthesia.* This section has about 1900 codes for anesthesia services provided by healthcare professionals, such as local and regional anesthesia.
2. *Surgery.* This section has about 60000 codes covering surgical procedures done by health care professionals on patients.
3. *Radiology.* This section has about 10000 codes representing radiology services provided or controlled by healthcare professionals.
4. *Pathology and Laboratory.* This section has about 9000 codes representing pathology and laboratory services provided or controlled by healthcare professionals.
5. *Medicine.* This section has about 9000 codes for procedure-oriented services, such as immunization, pregnancy, and so on, provided by healthcare professionals in various fields.
6. *Evaluation and Management (E/M).* This section has about 300 codes for services provided by physicians to determine best ways of treating a patient.

Each CPT section consists of a subsection, a heading (category), a subheading (subcategory), notes, and a descriptive qualifier describing the code and its description. They classify and describe each code in detail.

13.2.3 CPT INDEX

The CPT coding system uses a CPT Index to organize sections in terms of *service/procedure* (e.g., surgery), *anatomy* (e.g., brain), *condition* (e.g., fracture), *abbreviation* (e.g., ECG), *synonym*, and so on. The CPT Index is arranged in alphabetical order by the main term (with sub terms sorted within the main term).

13.2.4 CPT SYMBOLS

The CPT coding system uses CPT symbols to track changes in codes. It uses various symbols to indicate new added terms, revised description, and so on.

13.2.5 CPT MODIFIERS

The CPT coding system uses CPT modifiers with CPT codes to clarify the description of a code. For example, a modifier may be used with a code for a particular surgery to indicate that two surgeons performed the surgery. In this manner, modifiers are used to specify the exact meaning of the used codes. Modifiers are two-digit numbers appended to the five-digit CPT codes (e.g., 11999-25).

13.2.6 DESCRIPTIVE QUALIFIERS

Based on the description associated with CPT codes, they are classified into the following two types:

1. *Standalone Codes.* The description associated with such a code is self-contained and complete to understand its meaning.
2. *Intended Codes.* The description associated with such a code is not self-contained and complete. Hence, its description is dependent on the former standalone code's description for completeness of its meaning. Intended codes are applicable from a separator (semicolon) in the former standalone code e.g.,:

Code	Description
27780	Closed treatment of fibula fracture; without manipulation
27781	with manipulation

In this example, code 27780 is a standalone code, while 27781 is an intended code whose description is dependent on the standalone code 227780 [Green 2009].

13.3 Discussion

CPT-5 was initiated by AMA for representing CPT codes in the form of data model. Hence, it focuses only on the terminologies in healthcare. It does not have any kind of clinical process model. CPT-5 comprises of over 8000 five-digit numeric codes.

The CPT-5 edition from the CPT 2003 version had a structural model named the CPT Data Model. It evolved to support mapping and inter-terminology conversion to achieve interoperability and satisfy HIPAA rules. This data model represents a wide procedural classification with support for searching codes with a number of options by providing sections, subsections, headings, subheadings, index, and so on. It provides the structure and classification of codes.

Applicable Scope. CPT supports only medical procedures. It does not cover overall clinical terminologies such as diagnosis codes, observation codes, and so on. However, it covers codes for nearly all types of healthcare procedures with in-depth classification. The CPT coding system is more complex than ICD in terms of searching a particular code. For example, to search a code for a particular type of procedure, it requires more specific details of the procedure such as the time taken to perform, physicians involved, body parts examined or operated, and so on.

HIPAA recommends the use of CPT codes for all types of services provided by physicians to reduce the administrative burden of billing against medical insurance claims. For a system to be compliant with HIPAA, it should incorporate CPT codes for procedures.

In legal aspects, CPT codes are useful for analytical validity of performed medical procedures as mentioned in the claims by a patient/provider. In addition, Category II codes are useful for testing results of procedures performed on a patient to analyze clinical usefulness of tests and performance of the organization that provided the service.

13.4 Conclusion

Healthcare services need to abide by legal and regulatory schemes. Coded data for delivered healthcare services help in appropriate reimbursement of claims. CPT covers a wide variety of procedural codes and is recommended by many regulatory and standard bodies. Although CPT does not cover clinical terminologies in all fields of health care, its importance in medical procedural codes is well established. It is widely accepted by many health insurance companies. EHR systems and national healthcare storage should be capable of integrating CPT codes for providing healthcare services through interoperable healthcare applications.

CPT specifies codes for medical procedures used for billing purposes. However, there are auxiliary health services for which codes are needed in insurance claim processing. HCPCS is such a coding system that extends the CPT code set. The next chapter describes HCPCS.

BIBLIOGRAPHY

[AMA] American Medical Association; http://www.ama-assn.org.

[Category III codes] American Medical Association, CPT Category III codes, www.codingbooks.com; http://www.codingbooks.com/Assets/AMA_CPT_Cateogory_III_Codes_Update_August_2010(1).pdf.

[CPT] Current Procedural Terminology, American Medical Association; http://www.ama-assn.org/ama/pub/physician-resources/solutions-managing-your-practice/coding-billing-insurance/cpt.shtml.

[Green 2009] Green, M. A., *3-2-1 Code It!*, second, edition, Cengage Learning, pp. 290–321 (2009).

[Rallins et al. 2006] Rallins, M., Sperzel, D., Beebe, M., and Mays, E., Emergence of health information technology motivates the evolution of CPT. In: *Proceedings of AMIA Symposium*, pp. 1185–1186 (2006).

CHAPTER FOURTEEN

Extended Coding System for Patient Care Procedures

14.1 Introduction

Current Procedure Terminology (CPT) [CPT] is a coding system used in the delivery of healthcare services. CPT provides codes for medical, surgical, and diagnostic services. It is designed to communicate semantically uniform information about medical services and procedures among various roles of users in healthcare such as coders, physicians, patients, accreditation organizations, and insurance companies. Its code set is used mainly for administrative, financial, and analytical purposes. Healthcare Common Procedure Coding System (HCPCS) extends CPT's code set by including codes for external health services (such as ambulatory services, durable medical equipment, prosthetics, etc.). This chapter introduces HCPCS and proposes its use in standardization of terminologies and codes in a national healthcare scenario.

Centers for Medicare and Medicaid Services (CMS) [CMS] introduced HCPCS codes for use in orderly insurance claims processing. CMS, a federal agency in United States, is a branch of Department of Health and Human Services. It monitors the Medicare [Medicare] and Medicaid [Medicaid] Programs of the US administration.

HCPCS is an integral part of Medicare, Medicaid, and other health insurance programs that ensure consistent insurance claims processing. Health

Electronic Health Record: Standards, Coding Systems, Frameworks, and Infrastructures, Pradeep Sinha,
Gaur Sunder, Prashant Bendale, Manisha Mantri, and Atreya Dande.
© 2013 by The Institute of Electrical and Electronics Engineers, Inc. Published 2013 by John Wiley & Sons, Inc.

Insurance Portability and Accountability Act of 1996 (HIPAA) [HIPAA] mandatorily requires that HCPCS be used for transactions involving healthcare information. Unlike CPT, HCPCS is freely available to the masses.

14.2 HCPCS

HCPCS codes are alphanumeric having five characters. They start with a letter A through V followed by four digits. They are maintained by the CMS. HCPCS divides the entire code set into two levels:

14.2.1 LEVEL I CODES

Level I codes comprise the code set adopted from CPT.

CPT was developed by the American Medical Association (AMA) [AMA] in the 1960s, and soon it became part of the standard code set for Medicare and Medicaid. In subsequent decades, it was adopted by private insurance carriers and managed care companies, and it became the de facto standard. Its further details are covered in Chapter 13.

14.2.2 LEVEL II CODES

Level II codes were introduced in 1983. It primarily includes codes for items used in ancillary healthcare services such as prosthetic devices, ambulatory service, and durable supplies that are not covered under CPT codes. HCPCS is used to analyze claims data in an orderly fashion.

HCPCS Level II codes are categorized according to the entities responsible for establishing and maintaining them. The defined categories are: [Gail 2006]

1. **Permanent National Codes.** The HCPCS National Panel maintains HCPCS Level II Permanent National Codes. These codes are intended for use by private and public insurers. They pertain to claim submission and processing. There are roughly 4000 categories of items or services that cover millions of products from different manufacturers. These codes must appear on claims for items billed.

2. **Dental Codes.** Code series D0000–D9999 of the HCPCS Level II classify dental procedures and supplies. The American Dental Association (ADA) [ADA] maintains these codes. These codes are adopted from Current Dental Terminology (CDT) of the ADA.

3. **Miscellaneous Codes.** Miscellaneous codes are identified when a dealer of Durable Medical Equipment Prosthetics, Orthotics and Supplies (DMEPOS) submits a claim for a product or service for which no code is supplied by HCPCS Level II Permanent National Codes. This allows a supplier to start billing as soon as FDA approval is received. This code group increases the efficiency of maintaining Permanent National Codes by allowing only

selected miscellaneous codes to be finalized. This avoids creation of Permanent National Codes for case items that are billed in few cases only. Before using a code from this category, a supplier should check for the availability of a Permanent National Code with Durable Medical Equipment Regional Carriers (DMERCS) and Statistical Analysis Durable Medical Equipment Regional Carriers (SADMERC). In case no code exists, SADMERC can instruct the supplier to submit its claim using miscellaneous code, and it can also request CMS to include this code in Level II HCPCS code set.

4. **Temporary Codes.** Temporary codes are defined for usage before the annual update of Permanent National Codes. During the annual update, temporary codes either are made permanent or are maintained as temporary codes indefinitely. This gives the flexibility to use such codes even if they are not currently recorded as permanent. These codes begin with the letter C, G, H, K, Q, S, or T. Each one's use is described below:

- C codes cover billing of items under Hospital Outpatient Prospective Payment System (HOPPS). All claims submitted by a hospital's outpatient department contain codes from this code group.

- G codes are used for healthcare procedures and services that have no existing code in Level I of the HCPCS code set.

- H codes are used to identify mental health services in claim processing.

- K codes are used to implement DMERC's medical review policy when no such code is present in Permanent National Codes. These codes are used to identify various products and services listed under medical review policies.

- Q codes are used for other health services and equipment for which there are no codes in Permanent National Codes or Level I HCPCS code set.

- S codes are implemented to be used in private organizations for drugs, health services, and supplies that are not represented in Permanent National Codes. Medicaid program uses this code group.

- T codes are used for administrative services provided by Medicaid program.

Temporary codes are updated, converted to permanent, deleted, or added on a quarterly basis.

5. **Modifiers.** These codes are used to give additional information about the products and services and are attached with HCPCS Level I or Level II codes. They are two-digit numeric or alphanumeric characters. For example, in a medical procedure code, modifiers could describe the exact body part (hands, fingers, etc.) where the medical procedure was performed. There are almost 300 modifiers available in HCPCS Level II codes. HCPCS Level I and Level II modifiers both can coexist in a code with the condition that a Level II modifier is applied first. [CHPW 2011]

The major difference between CPT and HCPCS is that CPT focuses on providing codes defining medical procedures carried out by physicians, whereas HCPCS provides codes for other services such as supplies, pharmacies, dental, and so on, that are important for billing.

14.3 Discussion

Applicable Scope. HCPCS covers codes for healthcare procedure and accessory services for delivery of healthcare. Major users of these codes are suppliers and insurers that process insurance claims and use these codes to manage claim procedures. HCPCS mainly concentrates on providing information for insurance claim processing rather than clinical care. If an EHR includes insurance data, then interpretation of these code sets is necessary.

As HCPCS coding system is used mostly in insurance claim processing, it is important to identify the need of such codes in a country and to develop such codes for efficient electronic transactions.

14.4 Conclusion

The intention of CMS behind implementing HCPCS was to cover healthcare services that were not covered initially by CPT and thereby standardize the procedure for health insurance claim processing. Thus, these codes may be used for adding insurance related information in an EHR. An EHR Model should provide content types and content data structures for holding such coded information. Inclusion of such coded structures would support storing and searching of EHRs based on such codes.

After having discussed about auxiliary and external health services, we will now study about a comprehensive, multilingual clinical healthcare terminology, SNOMED CT, in the next chapter.

BIBLIOGRAPHY

[ADA] American Dental Association; http://www.ada.org.

[AMA] American Medical Association; http://www.ama-assn.org.

[CHPW 2011] Community Health Plan of Washington (CHPW), HCPCS Level II Coding Fundamentals Training; http://www.chpw.org/assets/file/Course_4-HCPCS_Level_II_Coding.pdf.

[CMS] Centre for Medicare and Medicaid; https://www.cms.gov/medhcpcsgeninfo/01_overview.asp.

[CPT] Current Procedure Terminology; http://www.ama-assn.org/ama/pub/physician-resources/solutions-managing-your-practice/coding-billing-insurance/cpt.shtml.

[Gail 2006] Gail, S.I., *Basic CPT/HCPCS Coding*, AHIMA, 2006 edition; http://library.ahima.org/xpedio/groups/public/documents/ahima/bok1_009346.pdf.

[**HIPAA**] Health Insurance Portability and Accountability Act (HIPAA); http://www. hipaa.org.

[**HIPAA & HCPCS**] HIPAA—Electronic Transactions and Code Sets; https://www. cms.gov/educationmaterials/downloads/whateelectronictransactionsandcodesets-4. pdf.

[**HIPAASpace 2010**] HIPAASpace, *HCPCS Code Online Book*; http://www.hipaaspace. com/Medical_Webcast/Digest/HCPCS_Codes_HCPCS_code_online_book.aspx.

[**Medicare**] Medicare Health Insurance Program; http://www.cms.gov/home/medicare. asp.

[**Medicaid**] Medicaid Health Services Program; http://www.cms.gov/home/medicaid. asp.

CHAPTER FIFTEEN

Comprehensive Coding System for Clinical Terms

15.1 Introduction

Coding of clinical terms and concepts helps to provide unambiguous information about clinical processes. Coded information in clinical terms is always useful in conveying clinical information in standard format that anybody can browse and refer. For example, a clinical procedure can have a code that represents a standard operating procedure steps, possible adverse effects, and outcomes. Looking at a record containing that code, a clinician can immediately understand the standard steps involved in performing that procedure. Absence of this coding information leaves the clinicians clueless about the possible parameters observed during the procedure.

Systematized Nomenclature of Medicine—Clinical Terms (SNOMED CT) is a standardized comprehensive clinical terminology code set that provides clinical content and expressivity for clinical documentation and reporting. SNOMED Reference Terminology (SNOMED RT) developed by College of American Pathologies (CAP) and Clinical Terms Version 3 (CTV3) developed by National Health Service (NHS) of United Kingdom were merged together to form SNOMED CT vocabulary. The comprehensive SNOMED CT vocabulary consists of concepts, terms, and their relationships in a clinical process. It has a concept model that represents each of the clinical terms as a concept having relationships with other clinical terms (concepts).

Electronic Health Record: Standards, Coding Systems, Frameworks, and Infrastructures, Pradeep Sinha, Gaur Sunder, Prashant Bendale, Manisha Mantri, and Atreya Dande.
© 2013 by The Institute of Electrical and Electronics Engineers, Inc. Published 2013 by John Wiley & Sons, Inc.

SNOMED CT is an internationally accepted vocabulary of clinical terms that helps in avoiding misinterpretations of diagnoses, treatments, and procedures carried out across geographically diverse regions. It acts as a common language for accurately conveying health concepts among diverse medical practitioners. The *International Health Terminology Standards Development Organization (IHTSDO)* promotes use of SNOMED CT, to standardize the process of coding health information in widely accepted standard clinical terms [SNOMED CT User Guide 2009].

15.2 SNOMED CT

SNOMED CT is a collection of concepts, terms, and their relationships. It describes each of these components in detail with examples to understand their usage while conveying the meaning of clinical information.

15.2.1 CONCEPTS

SNOMED CT Concepts are clinical terms used in documentation and reporting. These concepts can be clinical findings, procedures, or diseases. For example, *Procedure on lymph node* is a concept in SNOMED CT. SNOMED CT organizes these concepts in hierarchical manner to describe specific to general clinical terms/processes—for example, *Biopsy on lymph node IS-A procedure* on lymph node IS-A procedure. Each of these concepts has a unique identifier called *Concept-Id,* which defines hierarchies of concepts such as

1. Clinical finding
2. Physical force
3. Procedure
4. Event
5. Observable entity
6. Environment or geographical location
7. Body structure
8. Social context
9. Organism, situation with explicit context
10. Substance
11. Staging and scales
12. Pharmaceutical/biologic product
13. Linkage concept
14. Specimen
15. Qualifier value
16. Special concept

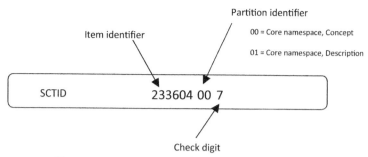

FIGURE 15.1 Structure of SNOMED CT Concept-Id.

17. Record artifact

18. Physical object

These hierarchies are identified according to their areas in clinical recordings.

Figure 15.1 depicts the structure of a concept identifier for the concept pneumonia (disorder). It consists of three parts, namely:

1. *Item identifier:* It identifies a particular concept.
2. *Partition identifier:* It represents the namespace for the identifier (e.g., Concept, Description, or Relationship).
3. *Check digit:* It represents validity of the Concept-Id and acts as a checksum digit.

Descriptions. SNOMED CT uses Descriptions to describe the terms or names of the concepts. Usually, these descriptions are phrases describing that concept. For example, description of Concept-Id *22298006* is *Myocardial Infarction* having Description-Id *751689013*. It is synonymous to *Heart Attack* having Description-Id *37443015*. The same concept can have multiple descriptions because different health practices may describe it in different manner, but essentially meaning the same. IHTSDO provides SNOMED CT Concept Identifier Lookup Service, where one can know more about concept identifiers [Description Lookup Service 2011].

Relationships. Relationships are very important from a SNOMED CT perspective because they define the meaning of concepts in relation to other concepts. Different concepts are related with IS-A relationship, called defining relationship, to describe general to specific categories of a particular health problem—for example, *Open fracture foot IS-A Fracture of foot IS-A Injury of foot IS-A Disorder of foot.* SNOMED CT defines the following types of relationships:

1. *Defining:* relationships represent IS-A relationships to define an attribute.
2. *Qualifying:* relationships represent nondefining, qualifying attributes.

3. **Historical:** relationships assist in retiring concepts in SNOMED CT. These relationships relate retired/inactive concepts to active concepts.

4. **Additional:** relationships represent other nondefining characteristics. For example, previous version of SNOMED CT, called SNOMED RT, had a relationship called PART_OF. SNOMED CT retains this as an additional relationship.

The public documentation available describes examples for Defining relationships but does not contain specific examples for other relationships.

15.2.2 STRUCTURE OF SNOMED CT CODE

SNOMED CT coding terminology uses concept identifiers and their relationships to represent health status of a patient. For example, Figure 15.2 depicts *severe pain in left thumb.*

Figure 15.2 describes the representation of a health problem using SNOMED CT codes. It includes the description of the health problem, finding site, position of organ, and characteristics of the problem. For example, *Hand Pain* is a health problem having *Thumb structure* as a finding site with a position/laterality as *Left* and description/characteristics of the problem as *severe.* For representing this diagnosis, SNOMED CT defines expressions language having the following concepts [Spackman 2009]:

1. **Attribute:** represented as *attributeName"="attributeValue,* where left side of "=" represents attribute name and right side of "=" represents attribute value.

2. **Refinements:** represented by ":" explaining parameters of preceding code. For example, *53057004:363698007* represents *53057004 (Hand pain)* having *363698007 (Finding Site).*

3. **Attribute Set:** represented by *(attribute, attribute)* defining list of attributes refining previously described concept.

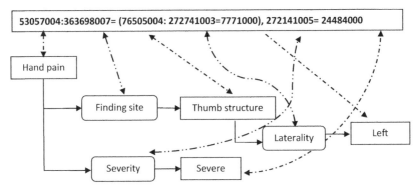

FIGURE 15.2 Example—Severe pain in left thumb. Adapted from [IHTSDO SNOMED CT Basics 2008].

SNOMED CT defines codes for all of them. Using these codes together, SNOMED CT enables coded representation of a particular health problem of a patient.

15.3 SNOMED CT Database Browsers

Many browsers provide the facility to browse SNOMED CT database [SNOMED CT® Browsers 2011]. For example, free registration at Dataline SNOMED CT Browser provides online access to SNOMED CT terminologies. This browser displays the relationships among concepts in a graphical manner along with good in-depth search for clinical concepts. For example, searching for pneumonia will display 50+ various kinds of pneumonia in a listing and graphical manner. One can navigate through each type in detail and know more about the related concepts [Dataline Browser 2011; Rogers and Bodenreider 2008].

15.4 Discussion

Since the purpose of SNOMED CT is to provide internationally accepted coded terms with their standardized description to facilitate interoperability at the clinical information level, it is very useful in associating identifiers with every possible piece of health information in a health record.

Applicable Scope. SNOMED CT coding system provides a detailed description of technical implementation of SNOMED terminologies. SNOMED CT contains more than 3,11,000 concepts with each one identified by an eight-digit numeric number. Its three main components are Concepts, Descriptions, and Relationships. SNOMED CT database represents them as table structures along with added tables for extensions. This technical description helps build application components on top of the database, and it facilitates coded linkages among various medical records.

All existing medical informatics standards such as DICOM, HL7 v2/3, CDA, and CCR support the representation of the SNOMED CT code with every medical record. This facility enables linking of medical records represented in different standards together. For example, a medical record in DICOM and a medical record in HL7 carrying the same SNOMED CT code would assist the system in identifying the problem record across the standards. Coded terminology also helps in searching across multiple standards.

Like SNOMED CT, there are other terminology standards developed for the same purpose such as *Logical Observation Identifiers Names and Codes (LOINC)* and *International Statistical Classification of Diseases and Related Health Problems (ICD)*. LOINC and ICD were already covered in Chapter 12 and Chapter 11, respectively. LOINC coding system mostly defines codes for observations and tests, and ICD coding system defines codes for problems and diseases. The National Library of Medicine under the U.S. National Institutes of Health conducted a survey for identifying the coverage of patient safety terms and concepts in LOINC, SNOMED CT, and ICD-CM coding terminologies. Their study showed that LOINC provides the maximum coverage of the concepts present in patient safety (ICD-CM 63%; LOINC 72%; SNOMED CT 65%). This experiment considers the observations/tests-related concepts in patient safety, and hence LOINC provides wider coverage in this particular scenario. However, a combinatorial vocabulary provided the most comprehensive coverage (ICD-CM/LOINC/SNOMED CT 93%). LOINC covered 59% (95 in number) and SNOMED CT covered 58% (92 in number) of single and compositional concepts completely [Chang et al. 2005]. This study shows that the use of coded terminologies available as of today in conjunction can provide maximum coverage of clinical concepts in various medical disciplines.

15.5 Conclusion

SNOMED CT vocabulary standard is applicable in linking medical records, improving their searchability, and reducing medical errors by avoiding misinterpretation of clinical information. Since every content and exchange standard in healthcare domain provides a place for associating codes specified in one or the other terminology standards, EHR systems should promote the use of these codes.

In this part of the book until now, we have discussed different coding systems and categories of clinical information covered by them. In the next chapter, we will study the UMLS, which is a compendium of many coding terminologies.

BIBLIOGRAPHY

[Chang et al. 2005] Chang, A., Castro, G., Shearer, A., and Frazier, P., Comparison of SNOMED CT, LOINC, and ICD-CM coverage of patient safety terms and concepts. In: *Proceedings of Academy Health Meeting of NLM Gateway A service of the U.S. National Institutes of Health* (2005); http://gateway.nlm.nih.gov/MeetingAbstracts/ma?f=103623884.html.

[Ciolko et al. 2010] Ciolko, E., Lu, F., and Joshi, A., Intelligent clinical decision support systems based on SNOMED CT. In: *Proceedings of Annual International Conference of the IEEE on Engineering in Medicine and Biology Society (EMBC)*, pp. 6781–6784 (2010).

[Dataline Browser 2011] Dataline SNOMED CT Browser, UK (2011); http://snomed.dataline.co.uk/.

[Description Lookup Service 2011] International Health Terminology Standards Development Organization (IHTSDO) SNOMED CT Concept Identifier Lookup Service (2011); https://mgr.servers.aceworkspace.net/apps/descriptionlookup/home.seam.

[ICD-10-CM 2011] International Statistical Classification of Diseases and Related Health Problems, Tenth Revision, Clinical Modification (ICD-10-CM); http://www.cdc.gov/nchs/icd/icd10cm.htm.

[IHTSDO SNOMED CT Basics 2008] International Health Terminology Standards Development Organization, "SNOMED Clinical Terms® Basics," (2008); http://www. ihtsdo.org/fileadmin/user_upload/Docs_01/Recourses/Introducing_SNOMED_CT/ SNOMED_CT_Basics_IHTSDO_Taping_Aug08.pdf.

[LOINC 2011] Logical Observation Identifiers Names and Codes; http://loinc.org/.

[Rogers and Bodenreider 2008] Rogers, J. and Bodenreider, O., SNOMED CT: Browsing the Browsers. In: *Proceedings of 3rd International Conference on Knowledge Representation in Medicine (KR-MED)*, (2008); http://mor.nlm.nih.gov/pubs/pdf/ 2008-krmed-jr.pdf.

[SNOMED CT® 2011] SNOMED CT homepage (2011); http://www.ihtsdo.org/ snomed-ct/.

[SNOMED CT® Browsers 2011] SNOMED CT® Browsers, (2011); http://www.nlm. nih.gov/research/umls/Snomed/snomed_browsers.html.

[SNOMED CT Release 2011] International Health Terminology Standards Development Organization, *SNOMED Clinical Terms® (SNOMED CT®) International Release*, (2011); http://www.cap.org/apps/docs/snomed/documents/january_ 2011_international_release.pdf.

[SNOMED CT Technical Reference 2009] International Health Terminology Standards Development Organization, *SNOMED Clinical Terms® Technical Reference Guide* (2009).

[SNOMED CT User Guide 2009] International Health Terminology Standards Development Organization, *SNOMED Clinical Terms® User Guide*, (2009); http://www.ihtsdo.org/fileadmin/user_upload/Docs_01/SNOMED_CT/About_ SNOMED_CT/Use_of_SNOMED_CT/SNOMED_CT_User_Guide_20090731. pdf.

[Spackman 2009] Spackman, K., Expressions and Context Patterns (2009); http://www. openehr.org/wiki/download/attachments/5997269/SNOMED+CT+expressions+ and+context+patterns.pdf?version=1&modificationDate=1256156421000.

CHAPTER SIXTEEN

Unified Medical Language System

16.1 Introduction

Many coding systems, such as ICD, CPT, LOINC, SNOMED CT, MeSH, and Read Codes, are available in the healthcare domain for standardized representation of clinical concepts. However, each coding system has its own format and contents, depending on the perspective with which it was evolved. Thus, mapping between these coding systems is a requirement when working in an integrated healthcare environment where healthcare systems need to share data among each other. Unified Medical Language System (UMLS) [UMLS a] is one such effort that attempts to integrate more than 100 coding systems for providing a seamless view of biomedical concepts across all coding systems [UMLS b].

The UMLS project was started at the National Library of Medicine (NLM) in 1986 to support retrieval of computerized health information in an effective manner. It aims to provide uniformity in clinical concepts retrieved from different sources and by different users. By virtue of uniformity, it enables sharing of meaningful information across distinct healthcare systems and databases. It helps in automation of mapping of clinical concepts defined in different coding systems.

Electronic Health Record: Standards, Coding Systems, Frameworks, and Infrastructures, Pradeep Sinha, Gaur Sunder, Prashant Bendale, Manisha Mantri, and Atreya Dande.
© 2013 by The Institute of Electrical and Electronics Engineers, Inc. Published 2013 by John Wiley & Sons, Inc.

The NLM provides UMLS databases (that integrate data for different coding systems) and tools for supporting exchange of clinical concepts between different coding systems that different healthcare applications may use.

16.2 UMLS-Supported Coding Systems

UMLS supports a large set of coding systems. It broadly classifies them as:

1. Diagnosis (e.g., LOINC)
2. Procedures and Supplies (e.g., CPT)
3. Diseases (e.g., ICD-10)
4. Comprehensive Vocabularies/Thesauri (e.g., SNOMED CT)

It covers 153 coding systems with different source content categories including drugs, procedures, diseases, insurance claim reporting, diagnosis, nursing, laboratory techniques and procedures, medical devices, adverse drug reaction reporting, anatomy, complementary therapies, consumer health information, disabilities, subject headings, dentistry, and phylogeny [UMLS b]. Although it supports multiple languages, a large amount of content is in English.

16.3 UMLS Architecture

The UMLS comprises the following three major resources, called the UMLS Knowledge Source:

1. ***Metathesaurus.*** It is a core component of UMLS, which arranges similar biomedical concepts from multiple coding systems and provides mapping between them.
2. ***Semantic Network.*** It defines and categorizes different biomedical concepts and provides relationship between these concepts.
3. ***SPECIALIST Lexicon and Lexical Tools.*** SPECIALIST Lexicon is a set of vocabularies used for the Natural Language Processing (NLP) System, whereas Lexical Tools help in resolving natural words, terms, and sentences into standard terms from coding systems.

16.3.1 METATHESAURUS

The Metathesaurus database is built by collecting the terms with identical meaning from multiple sources and giving a preferred name collectively to all those terms. This preferred name is called the *Metathesaurus Concept*. Thus, identical biomedical terms/codes from different coding systems are linked together to a unique Metathesaurus Concept. Metathesaurus has more than one million such Concepts. Each Metathesaurus Concept has a unique identifier called *Concept Unique Identifier (CUI)*.

Every Metathesaurus Concept is created with the following four levels of specifications:

1. **Concept Unique Identifiers (CUI).** This identifier uniquely identifies a Concept that links all identical terms from all sources. A Concept can have many synonyms.

2. **Lexical Unique Identifiers (LUI).** This identifier links the terms that vary in representation but have same meaning in different coding systems. For detecting lexical variants, UMLS lexical tools are available at a UMLS website.

3. **String Unique Identifiers (SUI).** This identifier links the terms (called strings) that have exact representation in different coding systems. Any variation in character set, case, or punctuation is considered a different string with a separate SUI.

4. **Atom Unique Identifiers (AUI).** This identifier is given to every term from every coding system. Every term/name is an *Atom* and thus an AUI is given to it. Metathesaurus is constructed by collecting all Atoms for different coding systems and gradually constructing a Concept. Thus, an Atom is also called a building block of Metathesaurus.

Figure 16.1 illustrates the structure of a Metathesaurus Concept with an example of a Metathesaurus Concept "Back Pain" of type "Symptom." Every

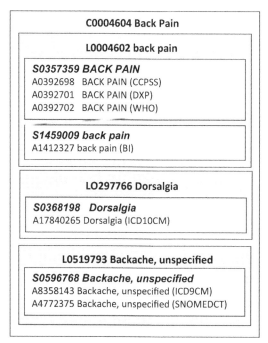

FIGURE 16.1 Structure of a metathesaurus concept.

concept has a seven-digit CUI starting with the letter C, whereas, LUI, SUI, and AUI start with the letters L, S, and A, respectively. In this example, the concept "Back Pain" has three different lexical meanings, each having a different LUI. Similarly, for every LUI there can be one or more SUIs and for every SUI there can be one or more AUIs representing a term from a particular coding system. The example of a CUI in the figure clearly shows that SUI for "back pain (BI)" is not the same as that of SUI for "BACK PAIN (WHO)" because they are in different character case. (Note that this example does not cover the complete structure of this Metathesaurus Concept and only refers to a part of it.)

Metathesaurus data are stored in a set of files. It consists of *Data, Metadata,* and *Index* files. The Data files store a collection of terms from different coding systems linking them together with CUIs. Metadata files provide information about data stored in Metathesaurus, and Index files keep indexes that can be used for faster searching of terms. The Metathesaurus database view can be customized through UMLS tools depending on requirements—that is, Metathesaurus for a specific language (e.g., English) or Metathesaurus for a specific coding system. UMLS provides two subsets of Metathesaurus:

1. ***Original Release Format (ORF).*** This format gives a Metathesaurus-centric view, where information is represented at the Metathesaurus Concept (CUI) level.

2. ***Rich Release Format (RRF).*** This format gives a source-centric view, where information is represented at a source vocabulary (AUI) level.

16.3.2 SEMANTIC NETWORK

The Semantic Network consists of a classification of biomedical concepts called *Semantic Types,* and the relationships between these biomedical concepts are called *Semantic Relationships.*

The Semantic Network has 135 Semantic Types and 54 Semantic Relationships between them. Each Metathesaurus concept has a Semantic Type assigned. These types and relations help in identifying the meaning assigned to a Metathesaurus Concept.

Semantic Type. Semantic Types are classified into two main categories: *Entity* (such as Virus, Finding, Anatomical Structure, Substance, etc.) and *Event* (such as Laboratory Procedure, Tissue Function, Mental Process, etc.). Semantic Types are classified in a hierarchical manner to form a tree structure. Each type has a unique identifier, a tree number indicating its position in the hierarchy, its definition, and its immediate parent and children.

All 135 Semantic Types are arranged into 15 Semantic Groups as follows:

1. Activities and Behavior
2. Anatomy
3. Chemicals and Drugs

4. Concepts and Ideas

5. Devices

6. Disorders

7. Genes and Molecular Sequences

8. Geographic Areas

9. Living Beings

10. Objects

11. Occupations

12. Organizations

13. Phenomena

14. Physiology

15. Procedures

Semantic Relationship. Semantic Relationship links Semantic Types together. There are different forms of Semantic Relationships. A primary relation between Semantic Types is "is-a" relationship. For example, Virus is-a Organism. Hence, there are two major relationships:

1. is-a relationship

2. associated_with relationship

The associated_with relationship is further classified into five types as follows:

1. Physically related to (further classified such as contains, part_of, consists_of, etc.)

2. Spatially related to (further classified such as surrounds, location_of, adjacent_to, etc.)

3. Functionally related to (further classified such as affects, causes, treats, prevents, etc.)

4. Temporally related to (further classified such as co-occurs_with, etc.)

5. Conceptually related to (further classified such as analyzes, measures, diagnosis, etc.)

Figure 16.2 shows an example of relationships between semantic types.

16.3.3 SPECIALIST LEXICON AND LEXICAL TOOLS

SPECIALIST Lexicon is an English dictionary that contains words as biomedical terminologies and their general English equivalent. Each word is called a lexical entry having one or more spellings with respect to syntax, origin, and orthography.

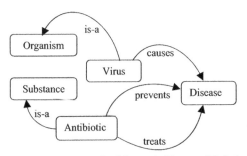

FIGURE 16.2 An example of Semantic Types and Relationships.

SPECIALIST Lexicon contains more than 200,000 entries that are collected from several medical dictionaries. UMLS Lexical Tools use SPECIALIST Lexicon for supporting term conversions and mapping.

Apart from Lexical tools, many other UMLS tools are also available. They are:

1. *UMLS Knowledge Source Server (UMLKSS).* It provides access to the UMLS Knowledge Sources.
2. *MetamorphoSys.* It is a free platform-independent tool for creating custom Metathesaurus (Subsets).
3. *RRF Subset Browser.* It can be used for searching the RRF Subset for quickly locating terms for the coding systems.
4. *Metathesaurus Browser.* It can be used for searching Metathesaurus Concepts with detailed information including CUI, LUI, SUI, and AUI.

16.4 UMLS Licensing

The sources (coding systems) covered by UMLS are grouped into different categories depending on their usage license. UMLS does not hold any ownership on sources and does not charge usage fees or royalties. However, users should have licenses for the actually used coding. All NLM-created UMLS resources can be accessed freely.

16.5 Discussion

Applicable Scope. UMLS is one of the most profound efforts to promote interoperability among various healthcare systems that use different coding systems or have their own ways of representing and defining terms. It covers over two million terms from over 100 terminologies. UMLS acts as a "middleware" that provides a set of multipurpose tools to system developers for mapping among different code sets.

By using RRF Subset of UMLS Metathesaurus, it is possible to always keep track of the original code set with mapping of all other similar concepts. However, in terms of accuracy for mapping, as per resources related to research, it doesn't provide 100% mapping between some of the standard coding systems and may be inadequate at some places [Fung and Bodenreider 2005]. Practical analysis of accuracy of mapping between specific terminologies should be done to decide its applicability.

UMLS does not charge anything for using UMLS sources. However, for using certain terminologies (e.g., SNOMED CT), the user needs to pay a separate license fee to its copyright holder. In addition, UMLS has defined various restriction levels under which different terminologies can be used in UMLS Metathesaurus (e.g., CPT falls under Level 3 category where users can use CPT codes from UMLS Metathesaurus only for internal use such as analysis, research, etc.). Additionally, to access full terminology codes, a user has to go through a separate license agreement with the copyright holder. This may lead to acquiring multiple licenses for fully utilizing UMLS sources, which is cumbersome [UMLS License].

There are two options for accessing UMLS resources. One is directly from UMLKSS through web tools and APIs that use Java as open source technology, and the other is by downloading all Metathesaurus files locally from UMLKSS through UMLS tools. The former option is not very useful because UMLKSS is not available consistently due to enormous activities going on frequently at UMLS. The latter option requires a relatively faster system in terms of storage and processing to handle huge Metathesaurus files, along with a regular update from UMLKSS for changes (addition/update of Metathesaurus).

16.6 Conclusion

In an integrated healthcare environment, data are collected from various health informatics systems that may use different code sets. UMLS provides a way to map different terminologies to a standard common vocabulary to assist in seamless exchange of medical data and achieve interoperability among health-care systems.

Additionally, statically searching for a particular set of diseases or procedures performed for a particular diagnosis requires either mapping between coding systems or conversion to a single coding system. This can be easily achieved through UMLS in national context.

BIBLIOGRAPHY

[Bo-Yeong et al. 2009] Bo-Yeong, K., Dae-Won K., and Hong-Gee K., Two-phase chief complaint mapping to the UMLS Metathesaurus in Korean electronic medical records," *Journal of IEEE Transactions on Information Technology in Biomedicine*, Vol. 13, 78–86 (June 2009).

[Cimino et al. 1994] Cimino, J.J., Johnson, S., B., Ping, P., and Aguirre, A., From ICD-9-CM to MeSH using the UMLS: A how-to guide. In: *Proceedings of American Medical Informatics Association (AMIA) Symposium*, pp. 730–734 (1994); http://www.ncbi.nlm.nih.gov/pmc/articles/PMC2850671/pdf/procascamc00002-0740.pdf.

[Fung and Bodenreider 2005] Fung, K. W., and Bodenreider, O., Utilizing the UMLS for semantic mapping between terminologies. In: *Proceedings of American Medical Informatics Association (AMIA) Symposium*, pp. 266–270 (2005); http://mor.nlm.nih.gov:8000/pubs/pdf/2005-amia-kwf.pdf.

[Lozano et al. 2003] Lozano, R., Geva, F., and Pastor, X., Relational Support for Protégé, Sixth International Protégé Workshop (2003); http://protege.stanford.edu/conference/2003/Raimundo_Lozano_Protege.pdf.

[McInnes et al. 2007] McInnes, B. T., Pedersen, T., and Carlis, J., Using UMLS Concept unique identifiers (CUIs) for word sense disambiguation in the biomedical domain. In: *Proceedings of American Medical Informatics Association (AMIA) Symposium* (2007).

[Pathak et al. 2009] Pathak, J., Peters, L., Chute, C.G., and Bodenreider, O., Comparing and evaluating terminology services APIs: RxNav, UMLSKSS, and LexBIG. In: *Proceedings of American Medical Informatics Association (AMIA) Annual Symposium*, p. 515 (2009).

[Pisanelli et al. 1998] Pisanelli, D. M., Gangemi, A., and Geri, S., An ontological analysis of the UMLS Metathesaurus. In: *Proceedings of American Medical Informatics Association (AMIA) Symposium*, pp. 810–814 (1998).

[Taboada et al. 2009] Taboada, M., Lalin, R., and Martinez, D., An automated approach to mapping external terminologies to the UMLS, *Journal of IEEE Transections on Biomedical Engineeing*, Vol. 56, 1598–1605 (June 2009).

[UMLS a] Unified Medical language System (UMLS), National Library of Medicine, US; https://uts.nlm.nih.gov/home.html.

[UMLS b] Unified Medical Language System (UMLS), UMLS Source Release Documentation 2011; http://www.nlm.nih.gov/research/umls/sourcereleasedocs/index.html.

[UMLS License] Unified Medical language System (UMLS), License Agreement for Use of the UMLS Metathesaurus; https://uts.nlm.nih.gov/help/license/LicenseAgreement.pdf.

[Zong et al. 2002] Zong C., Perl, Y., Halper, M., Geller, J., and Huanying Gu., Partitioning the UMLS semantic network," *Journal of IEEE Transactions on Information Technology in Biomedicine*, Vol. 6, 102–108 (June 2002).

CHAPTER SEVENTEEN

Other Coding Systems

17.1 Introduction

Apart from the coding systems covered in the previous chapters, there are many other coding systems, which were developed primarily to cater to the needs of a particular specialty in the healthcare domain. Healthcare data generated through applications that use such coding systems are also an integral part of an EHR system. Hence, knowledge of such coding systems is important from the point of study, analysis, and implementation of an EHR system. Many such coding systems are available today. In this chapter, we provide an overview of the more commonly known ones and provide their references for those readers who might be interested in more details. These include:

1. AHFS Drug Information (AHFS DI)
2. Current Dental Terminology (CDT)
3. International Classification of Diseases for Oncology (ICD-O)
4. International Classification of Functioning, Disability and Health (ICF)
5. Coding systems for Nursing Practices
   a. North American Nursing Diagnosis Association (NANDA)
   b. Nursing Interventions Classification (NIC)
   c. Nursing Outcomes Classification (NOC)

Electronic Health Record: Standards, Coding Systems, Frameworks, and Infrastructures, Pradeep Sinha,
Gaur Sunder, Prashant Bendale, Manisha Mantri, and Atreya Dande.
© 2013 by The Institute of Electrical and Electronics Engineers, Inc. Published 2013 by John Wiley & Sons, Inc.

6. Radiological Lexicon (RadLex)
7. RxNorm

17.2 AHFS Drug Information (AHFS DI)

The American Society of Health-System Pharmacists (ASHP) developed the American Hospital Formulary Service (AHFS) to provide uniform identification and description of drugs in 1959. Later on, it renamed it to *AHFS Drug Information* (AHFS DI). AHFS DI helps in many ways such as to understand drug therapies, especially in formulary management and promoting evidence-based medication [AHFS DI].

ASHP developed a pharmacologic–therapeutic classification of drugs for building AHFS DI. This classification is named as *AHFS Pharmacologic–Therapeutic Classification* [AHFS Classification].

AHFS Pharmacologic-Therapeutic Classification a compressive classification of drugs and is adapted in many other pharmaceutical databases and coding systems (such as First DataBank, Lexi-Comp, Medispan, Micromedex, McKesson, Health Information Designs, Affiliated Computer Systems and EDS). The classification is done in hierarchical manner based on pharmacologic, therapeutic, and chemical characteristics of a drug [ASHP Technical Guide].

The classification is also adapted by ICD for coding adverse effects and poisonings by drugs, Centers for Medicare & Medicaid Services (CMS) and Health Canada for Utilization Review of Drugs (URDs), and National Council for Prescription Drug Programs (NCPDP).

17.3 Current Dental Terminology (CDT)

Current Dental Terminology (CDT) is a reference manual developed by American Dental Association (ADA) to provide standard code sets for documenting and transferring precise information of dental procedures and services performed. The codes provided with CDT are called Code on Dental Procedures and Nomenclature (Code) (from now onwards referred to as CDT code). CDT additionally includes guidelines and instructions for using the codes, instructions for filling dental claims, and other relevant knowledge for practicing dentistry [CDT].

CDT codes are five-character alphanumeric codes that provide codes for dental procedures, services, and supplies. Each code starts with the character 'D' and the codes range from D0000 to D9999. The codes are revised after every two years and get published in the CDT manual including description of changes done from previous version. The 15th version of CDT codes was published in 2011, and the next version is due in 2013 [Richeson 2011].

CDT codes are largely used in processing insurance claims for dental services. The Health Insurance Portability and Accountability Act (HIPAA) mandated use of CDT codes in 2000. The ADA is the world's largest and oldest national dental association and works in harmonization with ANSI and ISO for defining standards in dental informatics. Additionally, many CDT codes are incorporated in HCPCS codes by Centers for Medicare and Medicaid Services (CMS) as HCPCS-D codes [ADA].

CDT codes enable uniformity in understanding dental procedures performed by different healthcare providers on a patient, where the healthcare data of the patient are stored at a common place such as a regional/national healthcare store.

17.4 International Classification of Diseases for Oncology (ICD-O)

The World Health Organization (WHO) developed the International Classification of Diseases for Oncology (ICD-O) especially for defining codes for tumor diseases. It is a domain-specific extension of International Statistical Classification of Diseases and Related Health Problems (ICD) and used for coding specifics of cancer cells including topography and histology of neoplasms. It is widely used in cancer registries where the information of cancer tumors is collected for analysis. It is originally based on the American Cancer Society's Manual of Tumor Nomenclature and Coding (MOTNAC) [ICD-O-3 2011].

The codes are classified depending on site, morphology, behavior, and grading of neoplasms, where the basic typographical classification is based on ICD-10. The current version of ICD-O is *International Classification of Diseases for Oncology*, third edition (ICD-O-3), which was published in the year 2000. The previous version ICD-O-2 was used between the years 1992 and 2000 [Percy et al. 2001].

17.5 International Classification of Functioning, Disability and Health (ICF)

International Classification of Functioning, Disability and Health (ICF) was developed by the WHO with endorsement of the World Health Assembly for developing a standard framework for classification of disabilities [WHO ICF].

ICF codes are classified considering all factors affecting functional disability. The codes define functioning of an individual at body level (activities of body parts), individual level (activities performed by him/her), and social level (activities performed in all areas of life). It also describes the environmental factors affecting functionality of an individual [ICF].

ICF codes at the national level are helpful in defining and implementing policies as per requirements of people with disabilities. A separate version of ICF is developed for defining functional disabilities in children, called International Classification of Functioning, Disability and Health—Children and Youth (ICF-CY). ICF codes are helpful in providing statistics for planning and supporting long-term healthcare services for individuals. They are also helpful in defining disability policy, anti-discrimination law, and disability evaluation.

17.6 Coding Systems for Nursing Practices

The three different coding systems for classification of diagnosis codes, procedure codes, and codes for describing the results of the procedures for nursing practices are discussed below.

17.6.1 NORTH AMERICAN NURSING DIAGNOSIS ASSOCIATION (NANDA)

The North American Nursing Diagnosis Association (NANDA) was founded in 1982 with the development of the NANDA codes for providing classification of nursing diagnosis. NANDA was later renamed *NANDA International* (NANDA-I) to support international code set for nursing diagnosis [NANDA-I]. It defines nursing diagnosis as:

> *"A clinical judgment about individual, family, or community responses to actual or potential health problems/life processes"*

NANDA-I codes provide a description of diagnosis, signs and symptoms, and cause/associated risk factors. NANDA-I contains over 250 diagnoses.

NANDA-I aims to standardize the nursing language of delivering healthcare to patients. It is important to have uniform understanding of concepts of nursing assessments in an integrated environment such as regional or national EHR. NANDA-I classifications are included in SNOMED CT and integrated in UMLS [NANDA-I Media Kit 2010].

17.6.2 NURSING INTERVENTIONS CLASSIFICATION (NIC)

Nursing Interventions Classification (NIC) is a standardized nursing terminology that provides classification of nursing care activities in clinical settings. It was evolved for managing the payment of services provided by nurses.

NIC codes are classified on the basis of domains (such as Behavioral) and classes (such as Behavioral therapy) and are linked with NANDA-I codes. It includes about 433 standard codes for nursing interventions. It is recognized by the American Nurses Association (ANA) and is included in UMLS [NIC Classification; Cordova et al. 2010].

17.6.3 NURSING OUTCOMES CLASSIFICATION (NOC)

For analyzing diagnosis and treatment in nursing, there was a need to classify results based on diagnosis and treatment to introduce suitable policies for better treatment of patients. *Nursing Outcomes Classification (NOC)* was developed with similar motive and provides classification of patient outcomes depending on nursing intervention [Moorhead 2009].

NOC provides about 330 outcomes, each describing outcome details and an indicator describing the quality of the outcome. It is also recognized by ANA.

All three coding systems (i.e., NANDA-I, NIC, and NOC) work in conjunction with each other and aim to provide a comprehensive system that covers all clinical coding related to nursing practices (collectively said to be NNN-language for nursing) [Florida 2008].

17.7 Radiology Lexicon (RADLEX)

Radiology Lexicon (RadLex) is a radiological vocabulary developed by the Radiological Society of North America (RSNA) [RadLex a; RadLex b]. It aims to provide comprehensive and uniform concepts for all radiology-related information.

RadLex is publically available for use, and it currently (2012) includes more than 30,000 terms. RadLex concepts are represented in the form of *RadLex Playbook* [RadLex Playbook]. Each concept consists of a unique identifier, a short name, a long name, and a definition. RadLex concepts are accessible through *RadLex Browser* and APIs. It is also downloadable for using it in health informatics applications [RadLex Download].

The development of RadLex was harmonized with the American College of Radiology (ACR). RadLex provides complete mapping with the ACR Index for Radiological Diagnoses. It also supports mapping with SNOMED CT and provides integration with DICOM.

17.8 RxNorm

The National Library of Medicine (NLM), while integrating clinical drug-related codes in the UMLS project, felt the need for mapping drug vocabularies from different coding systems. To address this need, *RxNorm* was developed. RxNorm provides normalized name to similar drugs and related classifications from different coding systems used in pharmacy management and drug interaction. UMLS internally uses RxNorm classification of clinical drugs and drug delivery devices that provide links to similar concepts in other coding systems [RxNorm].

RxNorm normalized names for clinical drugs and drug delivery devices contain information on ingredients, strengths, and dose form (physical form in which the drug is directed). It also includes the quantity in case of drug delivery devices.

RxNorm helps in achieving interoperability between drug and drug device codes from different coding systems and enables systems to process such data. It is recommended and used in many government projects in the United States, such as Medicare Modernization Act (MMA) pilot projects.

17.9 Discussion

Apart from the coding systems covered above, there are many other coding systems. Some of them are:

- *Anatomical Therapeutic Chemical (ATC)* Classification System—maintained by WHO Collaborating Centre for Drug Statistics Methodology (WHOCC) [WHOCC]
- *Diagnostic and Statistical Manual of Mental Disorders (DSM)*—developed by American Psychiatric Association (APA) [DSM]
- *International Classification of Sleep Disorders (ICSD)*—developed by American Academy of Sleep Medicine (AASM) [ICSD] [APA]
- *Medical Subject Headings (MeSH)*—developed by NLM [MeSH]
- *National Drug Code (NDC)*—maintained by Food and Drug Administration (FDA) [NDC; NDC, 2001]

These coding systems were evolved by various clinical research standardization organizations depending on different requirements and perspectives. Many of them are widely used in their respective domains of healthcare. However, in an integrated healthcare environment where different healthcare applications catering to the needs of different specialties require communication with each other, a mechanism through which mapping of similar concepts from such different coding systems is required. A terminology system (such as UMLS) that integrates almost all widely used and international coding systems to give a uniform view to clinical concepts can be used in this context to achieve semantic interoperability in healthcare applications [Ceusters and Smith 2010; Ceusters et al. 2005].

17.10 Conclusion

Many coding systems are available that define clinical concepts particular to a healthcare domain. For implementing an integrated healthcare environment, it becomes important to integrate all such coding systems to provide semantic interoperability among healthcare applications. This can be achieved by using a terminology system like UMLS.

BIBLIOGRAPHY

[ADA] American Dental Organization; www.ada.org.

[AHFS Classification] AHFS Pharmacologic-Therapeutic Classification; www.ahfsdruginformation.com/class/index.aspx.

[AHFS DI] AHFS Drug Information; http://www.ahfsdruginformation.com.

[AHFS DI a] AHFS DI Preface, *An Evidence-Based Foundation for Safe and Effective Drug Therapy*; http://www.ahfsdruginformation.com/docs/DI_preface.pdf.

[AHFS User Guide] AHFS DI, *AHFS DI Essentials Users Guide*; http://www.ahfsdruginformation.com/docs/essentials_user_guide.pdf.

[APA] American Academy of Sleep Medicine; http://www.aasmnet.org/.

[ASHP Technical Guide] American Society of Health-System Pharmacists (ASHP), *ASHP Technical Assistance Bulletin on Drug Formularies*; http://www.ashp.org/s_ashp/docs/files/BP07/Form_TAB_Formularies.pdf.

[CDT] Code on Dental Procedures and Nomenclature (CDT); www.ada.org/3827.aspx.

[**Ceusters et al. 2005**] Ceusters, W., Smith, B., and De Moor, G., Ontology-based integration of medical coding systems and electronic patient records. In: *9th International Conference of European Federation for Medical Informatics (MIE)* (2005); http://ontology.buffalo.edu/medo/CodingAndEHCR.pdf.

[**Ceusters and Smith 2010**] Ceusters, W., and Smith, B., Semantic Interoperability in Healthcare State of the Art in the US. *A position paper with background materials prepared for the project ARGOS* (March 2010); http://ontology.buffalo.edu/medo/Semantic_Interoperability.pdf.

[**Cordova et al. 2010**] Cordova, P.B., Lucero, R.J., Hyun, S., and Price, K., Using the nursing interventions classification as a potential measure of nurse workload, *Journal of Nursing Care Quality*, 39–45 (2010); http://www.carloshaya.net/biblioteca/boletinenfermeria7p1/cordova.pdf.

[**DSM**] American Psychiatric Association (APA), *Diagnostic and Statistical Manual of Mental Disorders* (DSM); http://www.dsm5.org.

[**Florida 2008**] Florida, M., Building Evidence Using Nursing Interventions Classification (NIC) and Nursing Outcomes Classification (NOC), NANDA International (November 2008); http://www.nanda.org/Portals/0/PDFs/Conference/NNN/NNN_5_1_1_Presentation.pdf.

[**Health Canada**] Non-Insured Health Benefits (NIHB), Health Canada, *Drug Benefit List* (2010); http://www.hlthss.gov.nt.ca/english/services/health_care_plan/pdf/drug_benefit_list.pdf.

[**ICD-O-3 2000**] World Health Organization, *International Classification of Diseases for Oncology,* third edition (2000).

[**ICD-O-2 1990**] World Health Organization, *International Classification of Diseases for Oncology,* second edition (1990).

[**ICD-O-3 2011**] *International Classification of Diseases for Oncology,* third edition (ICD-O-3), (2011); www.who.int/classifications/icd/adaptations/oncology/en/.

[**ICF**] WHO–FIC Information Sheet, International Classification of Functioning, Disability and Health (ICF) (September 2010); http://www.whofic-apn.com/pdf_files/05/ICF.pdf.

[**ICSD**] American Academy of Sleep Medicine, *The International Classification of Sleep Disorders, Revised—Diagnostic and Coding Manual* (2001); http://www.esst.org/adds/ICSD.pdf.

[**Kundu et al. 2009**] Kundu, S., Itkin, M., Gervais, D.A., Krishnamurthy, V.N., Wallace, M.J., Cardella, J.F., Rubin, D.L., and Langlotz, C.P., The IR Radlex Project: An interventional radiology lexicon—a collaborative project of the Radiological Society of North America and the Society of Interventional Radiology, *Journal of Vascular Interventional Radiology*, 433–435 (2009); http://www.sirweb.org/clinical/cpg/IR_Radlex_Project.pdf.

[**Langlotz 2006**] Langlotz, C.P., RadLex: A new method for indexing online educational materials, *RadioGraphics*, 1595–1597 (2006); http://radiographics.rsna.org/content/26/6/1595.full?sid=eaef2721-0f02-4a58-b1ff-0e9fb6c30aa2.

[**Mejino et al. 2008**] Mejino, J.L.V., Rubin, D.L., and Brinkley, J.F., FMA-RadLex: An application ontology of radiological anatomy derived from the foundational model of anatomy reference ontology. In: *Proceedings of AMIA 2008*, pp. 465–469 (2008); http://stanford.edu/~rubin/pubs/097.pdf.

[**MeSH**] National Laboratory of Medicine (NLM), Medical Subject Headings (MeSH); http://www.nlm.nih.gov/mesh/

[MeSH Tutorial] MeSH, *PubMed Online Training on MeSH*; http://www.nlm.nih.gov/bsd/disted/pubmed.html

[Moorhead 2009] Moorhead, S.A., The nursing outcomes classification, *Acta Paul Enferm*, 868–871 (2009); http://www.scielo.br/pdf/ape/v22nspe/04.pdf.

[NANDA-I] NANDA International; www.careplans.com/pages/nanda.aspx. www.nanda.org.

[NANDA-I Media Kit 2010] NANDA-I, Nanda International Media Kit (2010); http://www.nanda.org/Portals/0/PR/NANDA_I_Media_Kit_01_04_10.pdf.

[NDC] National Drug Code; www.nationaldrugcode.org.

[NDC, 2001] Workgroup for Electronic Data Interchange, NDC Codes—A White-Paper Giving a General Overview and Possible Solutions Associated with NDC's Replacing HCPCS Drug Codes for Institutional and Professional Billing (2001); www.wedi.org/snip/public/articles/ndc.pdf

[NIC Classification] Nursing Interventions Classification (NIC); http://wps.prenhall.com/wps/media/objects/219/225111/CD_NIC.pdf.

[Percy et al. 2001] Percy, C., Fritz, A., and Ries, L., Conversion of Neoplasms by Topography and Morphology from ICD-O-2 to ICD-O-3, National Cancer Institute (2001); http://seer.cancer.gov/tools/conversion/ICDO2-3manual.pdf.

[RadLex a] Radiological Society of North America (RSNA), RadLex; http://www.radlex.org/.

[RadLex b] Radiological Society of North America (RSNA), RadLex; http://www.rsna.org/radlex/.

[RadLex Download] National Centers for Biomedical Computing's Bioportal; http://bioportal.bioontology.org/ontologies/40885.

[RadLex Playbook] Radiological Society of North America (RSNA), RadLex Playbook; http://www.rsna.org/Informatics/radlex_playbook.cfm.

[Richeson 2011] Richeson, J., Optimize Your Practice: Understanding the 'CODE', Council on Dental Benefit Programs, American Dental Association (2011); http://www.gcds.org/Upload/Documents/Dr.%20Richeson.pdf.

[RxNorm] National Library of Medicine (NLM), An Overview of RxNorm; www.nlm.nih.gov/research/umls/rxnorm/overview.html.

[UMLS] Unified Medical Language System (UMLS), National Library of Medicine, US; https://uts.nlm.nih.gov/home.html.

[UMLS b] Unified Medical Language System (UMLS), UMLS Source Release Documentation 2011; http://www.nlm.nih.gov/research/umls/sourcereleasedocs/index.html.

[Weng 2007] Weng, C., John, H.G., and Douglas, B.F., User-centered semantic harmonization: A case study, *Journal of Biomedical Informatics*, 353–364 (2007); http://people.dbmi.columbia.edu/~chw7007/papers/JBI07.pdf.

[WHOCC] WHO Collaborating Centre for Drug Statistics Methodology; http://www.whocc.no.

[WHO ICF] International Classification of Functioning, Disability and Health; www.who.int/classifications/icf/en/.

PART FOUR

Standard Frameworks

CHAPTER EIGHTEEN

openEHR

18.1 Introduction

openEHR [openEHR] is an open source specification for management and exchange of EHR. It evolved from an EU project named Good European Health Record (GEHR) [GEHR] under the Advanced Informatics in Medicine Programme. Several European countries participated in this project with an aim to produce a concrete EHR architecture. Later, GEHR was renamed "Good Electronic Health Record" for use in Australia. Several projects emerged from GEHR proposing different enhancements in the EHR architecture. openEHR is built on learning from these projects and inputs from different modeling approaches taken in the EHCR Support Action (EHCR-SupA) Project funded by EU [EHCR-SupA 2000].

University College of London (UCL) and Ocean Informatics (Ocean) Pt. Ltd. from Australia established the openEHR Foundation in 2000. It is a not-for-profit organization, which provides EHR specifications, open source implementation of these specifications, and development of clinically constrained specifications called *Archetypes*. The name "openEHR" applies to both specification and foundation. openEHR Foundation provides free membership to those desiring to contribute to the development and implementation of openEHR specifications using the open source development approach. A reference implementation of openEHR is available under open source licenses.

Electronic Health Record: Standards, Coding Systems, Frameworks, and Infrastructures, Pradeep Sinha, Gaur Sunder, Prashant Bendale, Manisha Mantri, and Atreya Dande.
© 2013 by The Institute of Electrical and Electronics Engineers, Inc. Published 2013 by John Wiley & Sons, Inc.

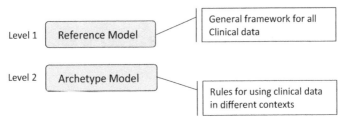

FIGURE 18.1   openEHR two-level modeling.

The EHR framework of openEHR is based on a two-level modeling approach for separating clinical concepts from the EHR information model. The first level is technical in nature and involves specification development and implementation to obtain a stable Reference Model. The second level is clinical in nature and involves domain specialists for development of ontology and archetypes based on domain constraints, called the Archetype Model. The Reference Model provides a general framework that incorporates any clinical information. Archetypes are the constraints for specifying clinical data on a specific part of the information model to achieve interoperability [Beale 2000]. Archetypes are derivable and re-usable. A collection of archetypes forms a template that can be specific to an organizational needs or GUI representation. Thus, openEHR uses the following:

1. *Reference Model,* which represents a collection of information models including generic data types and data structures.

2. *Archetype Model,* which defines the types of constraints that can be placed on generic data types and data structures to form Archetypes.

Figure 18.1 shows the two-level model of openEHR. Separation between the technical and clinical concepts helps to reduce the complexity in building and maintaining a knowledge-driven EHR system over a period.

In December 2008, "openEHR 1.0.2" was published. A reference implementation of the specification is available in various programming languages such as Java, .Net, Python, Eiffel, and Ruby.

The openEHR Foundation actively works in liaison with ISO, CEN, HL7, and IHTSDO. openEHR specifications conform to ISO/TS 18308 standard [Beale 2006]. It is also compliant with CEN/ISO EN 13606 standard [openEHR Introduction]. The detailed specifications of ISO/TS 18308 and CEN/ISO EN 13606 are given in Chapter 2 and Chapter 5, respectively.

18.2 openEHR Process Model

To incorporate all types of clinical information in an EHR, openEHR uses the problem-solving approach to represent ontology of clinical information for describing archetypes. Archetype specifies clinical information in an EHR artifact.

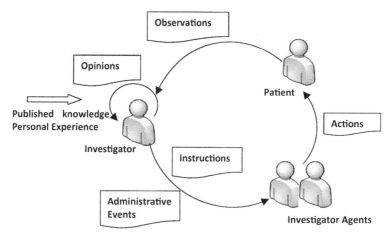

FIGURE 18.2 Clinical Investigator Model.

Clinical information is classified depending on the clinical workflow followed during patient care. Figure 18.2 depicts the generic problem solving process evolved by openEHR [Beale and Heard 2007b]. It includes the patient and the care provider (Investigator/Investigator Agents) as two participating entities. This model follows the SOAP concept (Subjective-Objective-Assessment-Plan) and is called the *Clinical Investigator Model*. Clinical information generated during the interaction between a patient and a care provider is generated in the form of different artifacts. The major types of clinical information generated in this process include:

1. *Observations* (such as measurements and tests)
2. *Opinions* (such as diagnosis)
3. *Instructions* (such as advices and medications)
4. *Actions* (such as procedures)

The entire process is controlled through *Administrative Events*. Administrative Events generate administrative data such as demographics, discharge, referrals, and so on. The above-mentioned four major types are further classified on temporal basis, observation/interventional basis, and analytical basis to obtain more specific types for recorded clinical information. The classification obtained in this manner is known as *Clinical Investigator Record(CIR) ontology* [Beale and Heard 2007b].

In openEHR Reference Model (RM) (explained later), the above-mentioned clinical information classification is represented in the form of ENTRY class, which is derived as ADMIN_ENTRY and CARE_ENTRY. The CARE_ENTRY is further classified as OBSERVATION, EVALUATION,

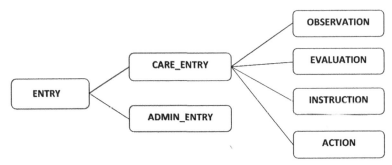

FIGURE 18.3 openEHR ENTRY.

INSTRUCTION and ACTION as shown in Figure 18.3. Since ENTRY represents single artifact containing clinical information of a particular clinical activity, most of the openEHR archetypes are based on entry types.

openEHR also classifies data depending on transactions—that is, persistence types, such as history and care plans; or event types, such as encounters or immediate treatment.

18.3 openEHR Architecture

openEHR architecture specification includes Reference Model (RM), Archetype Model (AM), and Services Model (SM). Figure 18.4 shows all high-level components of openEHR architecture [Beale and Heard 2008].

Dependency between components shown in the figure is from the bottom to top. All three models use core components from RM. All data types and data structures in openEHR adhere to the standard specifications given by CEN/ISO

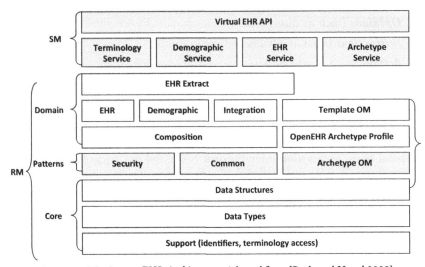

FIGURE 18.4 openEHR Architecture. Adapted from [Beale and Heard 2008].

13606 for particular structures. Additionally, they are designed to interoperate with other SDOs, including HL7 v3 and IHTDSO.

Data types defined in the *Data Types Information Model* include:

1. Text for representing plain text, coded text, and paragraphs.
2. Quantity for representing ordinal values, measured amount with units.
3. Date/times for date, time, date–time types, partial date/time, and date–time with time zone.
4. Encapsulated data type for multimedia and data for parsing.
5. Basic type for Boolean and state variable.
6. URI types for referring to objects on the Internet [Beale et al. 2008c].

The *Data Structure Information Model* includes Single, List, Table, and Tree as generic data structures. Explicit data structures are available for representing time series structure and are useful for collecting time-interval data [Beale et al. 2008b].

The *Support Information Model* includes components for definitions, identification, terminology, and measurement. All other models can use these identifiers for data processing. The terminology package in this model provides structures and interfaces for use of services that give access to coding system data. This model also provides the description of basic data types of other external systems that integrate with openEHR. openEHR supports integration with any Code Set by providing flexible data types for storing codes from standard coding systems as well as general medical terms. The data type DV_CODED_TEXT is used for representing the coded term, where the code and the defining code system are placed together.

The *Common Information Model* holds the common packages required by all models and links RM and AM. Versioning and change management are part of the common information model.

The *Security Information Model* includes the packages and classes that are related to access control and privacy setting for the data in an EHR.

The *EHR Information Model* contains *EHR* and *Composition* packages. It defines the components and their relationship with reference to EHR. It includes COMPOSITION, SECTION, and ENTRY as the major components of EHR. These concepts are similar to the concepts defined in CEN/ISO EN 13606 and closely map to the concepts defined in CDA. EHR Information Model is discussed in detail later.

The *EHR Extract Information Model* describes the various ways of building an EHR, including full and partial EHR, to support interoperability with external EHR systems.

The *Integration Information Model* supports the integration of data from legacy systems. The integration process includes the development of openEHR template (in the form of XSD) that provides mapping between message/artifact (clinical content of legacy system data) from legacy system and an openEHR archetype. The legacy message/artifact is converted into openEHR archetype through custom convertor using the openEHR template. Such openEHR templates are called *Integration Archetypes.*

The *Demographics Information Model* includes the concepts that are required to describe demographics of a person including patient, healthcare providers, and other entities participating in the care process.

The *Archetype Model* contains the models required for describing archetypes, templates, and their use. The *Archetype Definition Language* (ADL) is used for describing the rules for building archetypes [Beale and Heard 2007a].

The *Service Model* (*SM*) describes the services provided around an EHR system. They include:

1. ***Virtual EHR API.*** The API facilitates users in creating a new EHR artifact (through related archetype), requesting a part or a complete EHR, and modifying an existing EHR artifact locally.

2. ***EHR Service.*** This service provides the API for inserting, accessing, and updating EHR data at server side. Virtual EHR API calls this service for performing the above-mentioned operations on an EHR.

3. ***Archetype Service.*** This service provides the API for connecting to an online archetype repository for accessing archetypes for use and validation in an EHR application.

4. ***Terminology Service.*** This service provides the API for connecting to all available coding systems, such as ICD, CPT, SNOMED CT, and so on.

5. ***Demographic Service.*** This service provides the API for accessing, storing, and updating information of entities involved in care. In a countrywide implementation, demographic service can be viewed as a Master Patient Index (MPI), where demographic information of all patients and providers could be available.

18.3.1 EHR INFORMATION MODEL

The core part of openEHR is the EHR Information Model, which describes the various components constituting the EHR. Figure 18.5 shows the structure of this model.

Clinical data in an EHR is organized with the help of *Directories.* A directory is a logical group of *Compositions* based on some predefined criteria such as patient's cases, number of diseases, and chronological order. A Composition represents the clinical data produced during a clinical activity. Every Composition has a *Section* that acts as a heading and briefly describes the contents of composition (like headings in the document). Sections are used for searching of data in an EHR. *Cluster* and *Item* together form an ENTRY that represents a single clinical statement for representing the activity in health care process. Clusters represent complex entries such as test results, while an Item represents a single entry that contains the data value for the specific type. Item has field name, its value, and data type.

The EHR package of EHR Information model contains a root element called EHR. EHR holds an EHR ID, system ID (where EHR was created), and

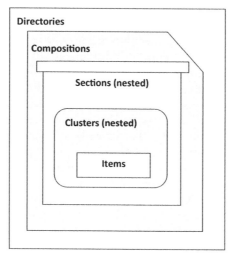

FIGURE 18.5 EHR structure of openEHR.

its time of creation as required elements. Additionally, it holds the following elements:

1. **EHR_ACCESS.** This element holds the access control settings of an EHR. It allows defining the default security policy, list of authorized users, and specialized policies for an EHR. openEHR supports the use of any security framework in EHR through its abstract ACCESS_CONTROL_SETTINGS class.

2. **EHR_STATUS.** This element keeps the status of an EHR (e.g., whether there is any activity going on in the EHR or is it inactive). This helps in identifying if an EHR is queryable for the identified purpose. It also holds the information of the patient in the form of a structure called PARTY_SELF. This structure can be made empty while anonymizing a patient's EHR data with no change in other components.

3. **Directory.** This element logically organizes Compositions (explained earlier).

4. **Compositions.** This element holds clinical/administrative information of record (explained earlier).

5. **Contributions.** This element maintains change log of an EHR.

EHR holds versioned objects of all the above elements so that it can reconstruct its previous status whenever required. The versioned objects are formed through VERSIONED_OBJECT<T>, where T is the element to be versioned (e.g., VERSIONED_OBJECT<EHR_ACCESS>). VERSIONED_OBJECT acts as a container of versions of an element in an EHR. Each Contribution keeps track of the number of versioned elements added at a time in an EHR [Beale et al. 2008a].

18.3.2 EXCHANGE

The important components of openEHR architecture are Archetypes and Templates that enable flexibility to hold any kind of clinical data. Archetypes are used for creating clinical data structures with constraint required for creating them. While describing constraints and structures, archetypes refer to RM to confirm validation against RM data structures and data types. Templates are collection of archetypes used for representing the information that is specific to requirements of the organization or application GUI. For example, the template for diagnosis of diabetes may include medical history, blood test report, urine test report, and BP measurement. However, all of them can also be independent artifacts.

openEHR provides an *Archetype Editor* for development of archetypes by using ADL that generates XML schema. It is available freely in Java, .NET, Ruby, Eiffel, and so on, with support for choosing codes from standard coding systems as field values. The openEHR approved and validated archetypes are accessible as international archetypes at archetype repository, Clinical Knowledge Manager [CKM]. Users can freely register and upload archetypes to this repository for validation and approval as standard archetype. Archetypes help in reusing clinical concepts across health domain in a standardized form.

All structures and components in RM are *archetypable* to support creation and modification of data via archetypes. Archetypes can be defined for structures such as ENTRY, COMPOSITION, CLUSTER, and so on. Archetypes can be inherited to build specialized archetypes. A specialized archetype derives properties from its parent archetype with additionally required properties. Archetypes are also composite in nature; that is, one archetype can contain/refer to an existing archetype. This ensures reusability of archetypes rather than defining the same constraints repeatedly. Such archetypes are called *Composite Archetypes*.

18.4 Discussion

Being an open source specification and software, openEHR can be used by any healthcare system to achieve interoperability. The specifications provided are in-depth and well-explained. Data types, validation rules, data structures, and so on, are described with clarity and in an easy-to-understand style. Free membership of openEHR Foundation enables involvement of any interested party. openEHR specifications are implementation-oriented.

openEHR architecture conforms to ISO/TS 18308 requirements [Beale 2006] and CEN/ISO EN 13606 standard. In turn, CEN has adapted Archetype Model of openEHR [EN13606-2 2007]. It is also compatible with HL7 v2.x messages, and work is in progress for its interoperability with HL7 CDA and HL7 v3. openEHR Foundation also works in coordination with International Health Terminology Standards Development Organization (IHTSDO) for improving semantic inter-operability with coding system [Macedo et al. 2010]. Due to compliance with standards and harmonization with SDOs, openEHR evaluation is going on in various national IT strategies for implementation of nationwide EHR (i.e., Sweden,

Singapore, Australia, Slovakia, Brazil, etc.). The Archetype Model from openEHR is more widely adapted than complete framework adaption. Thus, openEHR has made a significant impact on EHR standards.

Clinical Process Model. openEHR's problem-solving approach model for representing clinical information classification provides a realistic approach for EHR systems to run along with hospital workflow. The openEHR ontology model has been referred by various national programs for building their own national EHR models and standards for clinical information contents in EHR.

Structural Model. The two-level modeling concept of openEHR has made a significant impact on how subsequent EHR systems have been built and adapted. Stable information model reduces the cost of development, testing, and re-engineering of components for supporting upcoming medical requirements. Separation of clinical concepts in the form of archetypes enables standardization of clinical contents by involving domain specialists. Archetypes defined by openEHR are widely adapted by various national EHR initiatives. However, users should perform proof of concepts for analyzing feasibility of archetypes before adapting them.

The complete development process of openEHR involves adherence to standards in the field of EHR, coding system, data representation, EHR communication, and specification representation with clear objective of interoperability.

Security/Privacy Considerations. openEHR supports security policies such as indelibility, anonymity, and audit trailing. Indelibility requires that there be no permanent deletion of any record. In openEHR, records requested for deletion are marked as deleted and not shown to users. However, the marked records may be visible in certain scenarios like viewing previous versions of EHR. openEHR also supports encryption and digital signing of records by providing special attributes for storing such information at each node element in information model using versioned object.

Legal Aspects. Anonymity being one of the most expected features of an EHR, openEHR achieves it by separating the clinical and demographic information. EHR and demographic services of openEHR are kept separate so that the access of a clinical data does not reveal any identifiable information of the corresponding patient. All clinical artifacts are linked to the demographic details of a patient through an object called PARTY_SELF (optional in nature).

It also supports multiple languages by incorporating language attribute at Entry and Composition levels, allowing an EHR to have Composition in different languages.

It supports legal requirements for documentation of change in an EHR through versioning.

Exchange Specifications. openEHR provides flexibility in defining archetypes depending on the requirement of specialists/organizations. Additionally, use of Archetype Query Language provides flexibility to generate customized reports depending on the requirement of a particular hospital. Hence, it is useful for those scenarios where data are stored centrally and clinical reports are generated from the same data as per requirements.

However, mapping of an existing system data into Reference Model through archetype is a crucial task that may take longer time in places where most of EHR systems produce proprietary data. Additionally, it requires engaging clinicians for reviewing defined archetype. If not managed properly, use of archetypes may make it hard for immediate and short-time implementation of standard EHR systems at large organizations or in national programs.

Technical Guidelines. openEHR Reference Model is compliant with CEN-/ISO EN 13606 standard that provides specifications for communication of EHR. openEHR uses XML for communication. All architecture diagrams in specifications are represented by using UML modelling language. It provides flexibility for using code sets from various coding systems via a special kind of data type. Data structures used in openEHR adhere to standard formats and their specifications are generic enough to implement in any technology [ISO 8601]. Thus, openEHR data types could be a starting point for defining and developing structures for information model of EHR systems.

18.5 Conclusion

openEHR is compliant and interoperable with other standards. Hence, an EHR system should be able to interoperate with it. The clinical process model of openEHR can be referred to while developing an EHR model in the healthcare system due to its relevance with real-world workflow in clinical environment for treating a patient. openEHR specifications for structure of coded terms and for interfacing with coding systems are adaptable for implementing EHR systems that can support multiple coding systems.

The two-level modeling approach of openEHR by using archetypes brings stability in the EHR model. This provides flexibility in incorporating emerging clinical concepts. This design approach is generic and can be applied in any domain that uses IT. The openEHR clinical process model can be the basis for designing a workflow-oriented EHR model.

BIBLIOGRAPHY

[Barretto et al. 2004] Barretto, S. A., Warren, J., and Goodchild, A., Designing guideline-based workflow-enabled electronic health records. In: *Proceedings of the 37th Annual Hawaii International Conference in System Sciences*, pp. 10 (January 2004).

[Beale 2000] Beale, T., *Archetypes: Constraint-Based Domain Models for Future-Proof Information Systems* (2000); http://www.openehr.org/publications/archetypes/archetypes_beale_web_2000.pdf.

[Beale 2006] Beale, T., *ISO 18308 Conformance Statement*, (September 2006); http://www.openehr.org/releases/1.0.2/requirements/iso18308_conformance.pdf.

[Beale and Frankel 2007] Beale, T., and Frankel, H., openEHR Reference Model, *Extract Information Model* (2007); http://www.openehr.org/releases/1.0.2/architecture/rm/ehr_extract_im.pdf.

[Beale and Heard 2007a] Beale, T. and Heard, S., openEHR Archetype Model, *Archetype Definition Language (ADL 2)* (2007); http://www.openehr.org/releases/1.0.2/architecture/am/adl2.pdf.

[Beale and Heard 2007b] Beale, T. and Heard, S., An Ontology-based model of clinical information. In: *Proceedings of MedInfo 2007*, Kuhn et al. (eds.), IOS Publishing, pp. 760–764 (2007); http://www.openehr.org/publications/health_ict/MedInfo2007-BealeHeard.pdf.

[Beale and Heard 2008] Beale, T. and Heard, S., openEHR architecture, *Architecture Overview* (2008); http://www.openehr.org/releases/1.0.2/architecture/overview.pdf.

[Beale et al. 2008a] Beale, T., Heard, S., Kalra, D., and Lloyd, D., openEHR Reference Model, *EHR Information Model* (2008); http://www.openehr.org/releases/1.0.2/architecture/rm/ehr_im.pdf.

[Beale et al. 2008b] Beale, T., Heard, S., Kalra, D., and Lloyd, D., openEHR Reference Model, *Data Structures Information Model* (2008); http://www.openehr.org/releases/1.0.2/architecture/rm/data_structures_im.pdf.

[Beale et al. 2008c] Beale, T., Heard, S., Kalra, D., and Lloyd, D., openEHR Reference Model, *Data Type Information Model* (2008); http://www.openehr.org/releases/1.0.2/architecture/rm/data_types_im.pdf.

[Bott 2004] Bott, O. J., Electronic Health Record: Standardization and Implementation. In: *Proceedings of 2nd OpenECG Workshop, Berlin, Germany,* (2004); http://www.openecg.net/WS2_proceedings/Session08/S8.1_PA.pdf.

[Chen and Klein] Chen, R., and Klein, G., The openEHR Java Reference Implementation Project. In: *Proceedings of MedInfo 2007*, Kuhn et al. (eds.), IOS Publishing (2007); http://www.openehr.org/downloads/publications/health_ict/Medinfo2007-openehr_java-ChenKlein.pdf.

[CKM] openEHR Foundation, openEHR Clinical Knowledge Manager; http://www.openehr.org/knowledge.

[EHCR-SupA 2000] Electronic Healthcare Record Support Action (EHCR-SupA) Deliverable 1.4, *Consolidated List of Requirements* (2000); http://eprints.ucl.ac.uk/1603/1/R5.pdf.

[EN13606-1 2006] European Committee for Standardization (CEN), *Health Informatics—Electronic Health Record Communication—Part 1: Reference Model.* prEN13606-1 (2006).

[EN13606-2 2007] European Committee for Standardization (CEN), *Health Informatics—Electronic Health Record Communication—Part 2: Archetypes.* prEN13606-2 (2007).

[Fernandez-Breis et al. 2006] Fernandez-Breis, J. T., Vivancos-Vicente, P. J., Menarguez-Tortosa, M., Moner, D., Maldonado, J. A., Valencia-Garcia, R., and Miranda-Mena, T. G., Using semantic technologies to promote interoperability between electronic healthcare records' information models. In: *Proceedings of 28th Annual International Conference of the IEEE in Engineering in Medicine and Biology Society*, pp. 2614–2617 (2006).

[Fernandez-Breis et al. 2008] Fernandez-Breis, J. T., Menarguez-Tortosa, M., Martinez-Costa, C., Fernandez-Breis, E., Herrero-Sempere, J., Moner, D., Sanchez, J., Valencia-

Garcia, R., and Robles, M., A semantic web-based system for managing clinical archetypes. In: *Proceedings of 30th Annual International Conference of the IEEE in Engineering in Medicine and Biology Society (EMBS)*, pp. 1482–1485 (August 2008).

[Filgueira 2007] Filgueira, R., Odriazola, A., and Simini, F., Using openEHR in SICTI an electronic health record system for critical medicine. In: *Proceedings of 16th Argentine Bioengineering Congress and 5th Conference of Clinical Engineering, Journal of Physics*, IOP Publishing (2007).

[GEHR] Good Electronic Health Record (GEHR); http://www.gehr.org.

[GEHR GOM] Good Electronics Health Record (GEHR), *Gehr Object Model* (2001); http://www.openehr.org/downloads/usage/gehr_australia/gehr_gom.pdf.

[Hajar and Olof 2009] Hajar, K., and Olof, T., A migration to an openEHR-based clinical application, *European Federation for Medical Informatics 2009*, Adlassnig et al. (eds.), IOS Press (2009).

[ISO 8601] ISO 8601 standard describing formats for representing times, dates, and durations; http://www.mcs.vuw.ac.nz/technical/software/SGML/doc/iso8601/ISO8601.html. http://www.cl.cam.ac.uk/~mgk25/iso-time.html.

[Kalra 2002] Kalra, D., Austin, A., O'Connor, A., Patterson, D., Lloyd, D., Ingram, D., Information architecture for a federated health record server" *Electronic Health Records and Communication for Better Health care* (2002); http://eprints.ucl.ac.uk/1580/1/A2.pdf.

[Liang et al. 2004] Liang, X., Cousins, G., Hederman, L., Fahey, T., and Dimitrov, B., The design of an EHR for clinical decision support. In: *Proceedings of 3rd International Conference on Biomedical Engineering and Informatics (BMEI)*, pp. 2525–2531 (October 2010).

[Macedo et al. 2010] Macedo, N. A. M., Hilares, N.A.G., Quispe, J. P. P., and Matutti, R. A., Electronic health record: Comparative analysis of HL7 and openEHR approaches. In: *Proceedings of Health Care Exchange (PAHCE), Pan American*, pp. 105–110 (March 2010).

[openEHR] openEHR Foundation; http://www.openehr.org.

[openEHR Introduction] openEHR foundation, *Introducing openEHR*, (2006); http://www.openehr.org/releases/1.0.2/openEHR/introducing_openEHR.pdf.

[Patrick et al. 2006] Patrick, J., Ly, R., and Truran, D., Evaluation of a persistent store for openEHR. In: *Proceedings of HIC Bridging the Digital Divide: Clinician, Consumer and Computer*, Westbrook et al. (eds.), Health Informatics Society of Australia Ltd. (HISA) (2006); http://www.openehr.org/wiki/download/attachments/2949261/015_patrick.pdf.

[Paun et al. 2010] Paun, D., Sauciuc, D., Stan, O., Iosif, O., Dehelean, C., and Miclea, L., Medical information system based on electronic healthcare records. In: *Proceedings of IEEE International Conference in Automation Quality and Testing Robotics (AQTR)*, pp. 1–6 (May 2010).

[Sain et al. 2009] Sain, M., Hoonjae, Lee, and Wan-Young Chung, Personal healthcare information system. In: *INC, IMS, IDC, and NCM Fifth International Joint Conference*, pp. 1540–1545 (August 2009).

[Sauciuc et al. 2010] Sauciuc, D. G., Dehelean, S., Iosif, O., Dehelean, C., Miclea, L., and Paun, I., Romanian health informatics legislation compatibility with ISO/EN 13606 and openEHR. In: *IEEE International Conference in Automation Quality and Testing Robotics (AQTR)*, pp. 1–4 (2010).

CHAPTER NINETEEN

Integrating the Healthcare Enterprise (IHE)

19.1 Introduction

To enable interoperability among available standards, several professional bodies, including the Healthcare Information Management Systems Society (HIMSS) and the Radiological Society of North America (RSNA), started an initiative called the "Integrating the Healthcare Enterprise (IHE)" initiative. Its prime focus was to facilitate integration among diverse healthcare systems. In its approach, it does not propose any standard that EHR/HIS systems should adhere to; instead, it defines technical frameworks to achieve interoperability. These technical frameworks include existing internationally accepted standards like DICOM and HL7. They deal with the situation where systems/devices adhering to different medical informatics standards need to interact with each other. For example, a Laboratory Information System (LIS) wants to place an order for an ECG test where LIS adheres to HL7 standard and ECG device adheres to DICOM standard. In such scenarios, technical frameworks provide mapping between HL7 messages and DICOM Information Objects.

Electronic Health Record: Standards, Coding Systems, Frameworks, and Infrastructures, Pradeep Sinha, Gaur Sunder, Prashant Bendale, Manisha Mantri, and Atreya Dande.

IHE aims to facilitate integration along with adherence to industry standards. Its main goals are:

- Identify healthcare domains for facilitating seamless integration.
- Develop Technical Frameworks and Integration Profiles for identified set of processes.
- Assist healthcare providers and vendors to specify requests in common language of IHE Technical Frameworks for adherence.
- Evaluate existing products in healthcare IT domain for adherence to Technical Frameworks promoting trust in the industry.
- Ensure high level of adherence to Technical Frameworks through organizing cross-vendor testing events like Connect-a-thon.

19.2 IHE Domains

IHE's approach toward dealing with interoperability issues is process-oriented. It consists of domains, areas of healthcare, identifying processes/workflows, and providing technical frameworks to achieve interoperability among them. These domains are as follows:

1. IHE Anatomic Pathology (ANAPATH)
2. IHE Cardiology (CARD)
3. IHE Dental (DENT)
4. IHE Endoscopy (Planned to be developed till 2013)
5. IHE Eye Care (EYECARE)
6. IHE IT Infrastructure (ITI)
7. IHE Laboratory (LAB)
8. IHE Patient Care Coordination (PCC)
9. IHE Patient Care Device (PCD)
10. IHE Pharmacy (PHARM)
11. IHE Quality, Research and Public Health (QRPH)
12. IHE Radiation Oncology (RO)
13. IHE Radiology (RAD)

IHE domain consists of integration profiles, integration statements, and technical frameworks for addressing identified processes in each of its domains. It defines the following set of components for identified workflows:

19.2.1 INTEGRATION PROFILES

IHE develops integration profiles that describe workflow processes in the domain of its application, and standards applicable at each interaction point in that process. Each of the above-mentioned domains has integration profiles achieving interoperability in corresponding workflows. These integration profiles are listed in Table 19.1 [IHE Profiles].

Consider an example of Scheduled Workflow (SWF) integration profile of IHE's Radiology domain. It defines how to achieve seamless interoperability among systems involved in scheduled workflow procedure.

TABLE 19.1   IHE Integration Profiles

Anatomic Pathology

Anatomic Pathology Workflow (PWF)

Cardiology

Cardiac Cath Workflow (CATH)	Echocardiography Workflow (ECHO)
Evidence Documents (ED)	Stress Testing Workflow (STRESS)
Displayable Reports (DRPT)	

Eye Care

Eye Care Workflow (EYECARE)	Eye Care Evidence Document (ECED)
Eye Care Displayable Report (ECDR)	

IT Infrastructure

Consistent Time (CT)	Enterprise User Authentication (EUA)
Request Information for Display (RID)	Patient Synchronized Application (PSA)
Patient Identifier Cross-Referencing (PIX)	Retrieve Form for Data Capture (RFD)
Patient Demographics Query (PDQ)	Stored Query
Personnel White Pages (PWP)	Cross Enterprise Document Sharing (XDS)
Cross-Enterprise Document Reliable Interchange (XDR)	Cross-Enterprise Sharing of Scanned Documents (XDS-SD)
Patient Identifier Cross-Reference and Patient Demographics Query for HL7v3 (PIX/PDQ/v3)	Registry Stored Query Transaction for Cross-Enterprise Document Sharing Profile
Cross-Enterprise Document Media Interchange (XDM)	Audit Trail and Node Authentication (ATNA)

Laboratory

Laboratory Scheduled Workflow (LSWF)	Sharing Laboratory Reports (XD-LAB)
LOINC Test Codes Subset (LTCS)	

Patient Care Coordination

Medical Summaries (MS)	Antepartum Care Summary (APS)
Functional Status Assessments (FSA)	Query for Existing Data (QED)
Emergency Department Referral (EDR)	Basic Patient Privacy Consents (BPPC)
Pre-procedural History and Physical (PPHP)	Exchange of Personal Health Record Content (XPHR)
Emergency Department Encounter Record (EDER)	

(continued)

TABLE 19.1   **(Continued)**

Patient Care Devices	
Point-of-care Infusion Verification (PIV)	Device Enterprise Communication (DEC)
Alarm Communication Management (ACM)	Rosetta Terminology Mapping (RTM)
Implantable Device Cardiac Observation (IDCO)	
Radiation Oncology	
Normal Treatment Planning-Simple (NTPL-S)	Multimodality Registration for Radiation Oncology (MMR-RO)
Treatment Workflow (TRWF)	
Radiology	
Scheduled Workflow (SWF)	Patient Information Reconciliation (PIR)
Post-Processing Workflow (PWF)	Reporting Workflow (RWF)
Import Reconciliation Workflow (IRWF)	Portable Data for Imaging (PDI)
Nuclear Medicine Image (NM)	Mammography Image (MAMMO)
Evidence Documents (ED)	Simple Image and Numeric Report (SINR)
Key Image Note (KIN)	Consistent Presentation of Images (CPI)
Presentation of Grouped Procedures (PGP)	Image Fusion (FUS)
Cross-enterprise Document Sharing for Imaging (XDS-I)	Teaching File and Clinical Trial Export (TCE)
Access to Radiology Information (ARI)	Audit Trail and Node Authentication (ATNA)
Charge Posting (CHG)	

Figure 19.1 depicts the scheduled workflow that integrates activities related to radiology exams. These include:

1. Placing an order
2. Scheduling an order
3. Acquiring images through modalities
4. Storing acquired images
5. Viewing

Several systems perform the above-mentioned activities. Patient registration (ADT), Computerized Physician Order Entry (CPOE), and Order Scheduling (RIS) systems, adhering to HL7 messaging standard, perform activities like placing and scheduling of an order. Modalities like X-ray machines, MRI machines, etc., and Picture Archival and Communications Systems (PACS), adhering to DICOM standard, perform activities like acquiring images, storing images, and viewing them. Besides this, the integration profile also uses workflow-related services like Modality Work List service and Modality Performed Procedure Step (MPPS)

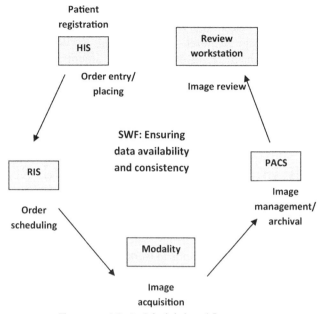

FIGURE 19.1 Scheduled workflow process.

service to ensure completeness of clinical information flow among these diverse systems [IHE SWF 2011]. As is evident, an Integration Profile combines the required systems and the relevant standards to achieve a workflow in a healthcare environment.

19.2.2 INTEGRATION STATEMENTS

Integration statements assist customers in knowing the integration profiles supported by specific HIS/RIS systems. This helps the decision makers in purchasing those systems because it assures interoperability with other systems that are already in place or planned.

19.2.3 TECHNICAL FRAMEWORKS

Technical frameworks are actual technical details that identify the entities involved in the given process and associated transactions. It addresses inter-operability concerns and provides mappings, if required, for interaction among those systems that adhere to different standards—for example, communication between an Order scheduling (RIS) system following HL7 and Modality like X-ray machine using DICOM.

IHE Technical Frameworks provide quite detailed information to the level of data type lengths of attributes. This helps in solving integration problems. It identifies a set of entities in the domain that are actively interacting with each other to complete the process flow. These entities are called *Actors*; for example, when a doctor advises an X-ray test to a patient, the CPOE system at a doctor's desk becomes Order Placer, the RIS becomes Order Filler, and the X-ray Modality becomes Image Acquirer. These three are the Actors in the profile. The next task is to define a set of interactions among these actors. These interactions are called *Transactions*. IHE defines these transactions as interactions using existing medical informatics standards. Technical framework provides integration details at the technical level to map information from one standard to another [IHE RAD-TF 2011].

19.3 IHE Initiatives on Electronic Health Record

For IHE, an Electronic Health Record is the amalgamation of records and data from several systems like Patient Management, Diagnostic Imaging, Order Communication, PACS, and Reporting Systems in a healthcare environment. Apart from the ability of these systems to work in an integrated fashion, there is another issue of EHR from one environment to another where another set of different systems exist. For a patient to carry the records from one hospital to another or for a doctor to be able to share the data across hospitals, it is important that EHR itself is portable. The IHE *Cross-Enterprise Document Sharing (XDS)* profile facilitates portability of EHRs [IHE XDS 2011].

19.4 Exchange

The entire purpose of IHE is to facilitate interoperability among diverse systems. Hence, the integration profiles provide mapping between the existing exchange standards. This is very important to complete the workflow involving systems that adhere to diverse exchange standards. Along with this, IHE also assists in exchanging healthcare information from the perspective of EHR. As EHR interoperability involves interoperability among EHR standards like *Continuity of Care Record (CCR)*, *Clinical Document Architecture (CDA)*, and so on, which are report structured exchange standards, IHE provides for sharing of records among healthcare providers.

19.4.1 CROSS-ENTERPRISE DOCUMENT SHARING (XDS)

Cross-Enterprise Document Sharing (XDS) Integration Profile uses the standards such as HL7's CDA and ASTM's CCR to achieve portability for cross-enterprise health information sharing. It describes the concepts of *Longitudinal Record (EHR-LR)* and *Care Record (EHR-CR)*. EHR-LR refers to the minimum set of patient health information from prenatal to postmortem stage across healthcare provider boundaries. EHR-CR refers to the specific clinical information within healthcare provider boundaries. This integration profile is document-centric, where every piece of medical information is represented in generic-format clinical

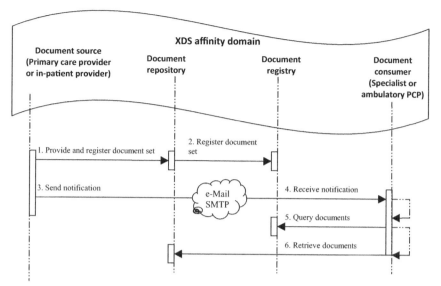

FIGURE 19.2 Cross-enterprise data sharing environment. Adapted from [IHE XDS 2011].

document. XDS profile defines the transactions using CDA and CCR standards to achieve portability of EHRs.

Figure 19.2 shows the XDS mechanism in XDS Affinity Domain. The components are:

1. *Document Source:* Provides document in the form of CCR or CDA document
2. *Document Registry:* Keeps track of available documents in the repository and facilitates searching
3. *Document Consumer:* Requests a document after searching through registry
4. *Document Repository:* Provides shared location for storage of documents

19.5 Security

IHE specifies the *Audit Trail & Node Authentication (ATNA)* profile for setting up of operational guidelines in terms of security and privacy. Some of the techniques suggested by this IHE profile are useful while designing security frameworks [IHE ATNA 2011].

19.5.1 AUDIT TRAIL & NODE AUTHENTICATION (ATNA)

ATNA profile has the following security provisions:

- *User Authentication:* ATNA profile suggests the need for user authentication, but leaves the choice open for using any of the available user authentication techniques.

- *Connection Authentication:* It suggests the use of bidirectional certificate-based node authentication among communicating nodes in a distributed network.

- *Audit Trails:* It suggests the use of audit trail and logs that will assist in system and access audit processes preventing misuse of clinical information.

- *Emergency Access:* The ATNA profile takes care of Emergency Access to the patient records by a clinician who does not have that access normally assigned. IHE suggests that a well-controlled environment under Emergency Mode can provide such access. It also makes explicit that audit logging in such a case is of prime importance.

19.6 Discussion

IHE aims to achieve interoperability and portability of health information within and across healthcare enterprises. IHE integration profiles describe integration of process workflow among systems/devices adhering to diverse standards.

Some of the IHE profiles such as XDS, ATNA, and PIX-PDQ are widely used in national health IT programs of many countries including Austria, Canada, France, Italy, Singapore, United States, and so on.

Structural Model

IHE's Electronic Health Record Concept. IHE particularly deals with workflow and data interchange in clinical processes. With this central idea, IHE assumes that the pieces of information in Radiology System, Laboratory System, Registration System, and so on, considered together represent an EHR. This concept is correct as long as we consider a particular hospital environment where these systems have some measure through which they can identify and map records to a particular patient. However, any large EHR program covering multiple healthcare service providers requires data interchange not only at the level of a particular record but across the whole EHR. IHE profiles help in addressing this requirement due to the presence of multiple standards and devices. In addition, IHE suggests conversion of clinical information between medical informatics standards that may lead to data loss. IHE's suggestions for such conversions will help exchange of clinical information provided that users are aware of the possibility of data loss.

Useful for Identifying Clinical Processes. IHE integration profiles can be useful in identifying workflow processes on top of the EHR frameworks spanning diverse standard formats.

Security/Privacy Considerations. IHE integration profiles suggest measures like encryption for secure storage and transmission. These measures are helpful in designing a security framework for any EHR framework. An ATNA profile describes useful parameters for authentication, but it does not cover authorization parameters that are of prime importance in designing any EHR framework. However, by presenting a complete profile for security and privacy, IHE makes their importance prominent in the IHE scope.

Exchange Specifications. IHE suggests portability of EHRs through Cross-Enterprise Document Sharing (XDS) using document standards like CDA or CCR. Eventually, HIS systems will need to convert the data present in any proprietary or existing medical informatics standard to these standards. This process has the drawback of not having one-to-one mapping among the standards. Furthermore, XDS does not describe the entire EHR model as such. It tackles pieces such as medical summary, allergies, and so on, that only makes it suitable for sharing these pieces of information among the systems. The main requirement of CDA and CCR standards is conformance to a specific template for each type of record. This will require healthcare providers to map their existing records to CDA templates and then provide it to the registry. Practically it is hard to implement.

IHE profiles revise mappings among different standards to keep pace with standards evolution. There may be issues where complete one-to-one mapping is not available or, worse, not possible.

19.7 Conclusion

IHE integration profiles define workflows and ensure interoperability among the various systems that take part in a workflow. The process of ensuring interoperability is very useful from the perspective of any EHR framework where records in the store are in diverse standard formats. IHE technical frameworks will be useful in such cases where a requestor entity wants the record in a particular format. For example, a system may require conversion of a record in DICOM standard to HL7 standard. IHE technical framework may assist in this process by providing data type to data type mapping among these standards.

The EHR concept suggested by IHE is the result of collaboration among the various information systems in a hospital environment. This kind of EHR lacks a process and content model that represents an EHR view. This methodology is suited for a hospital environment but cannot be used among hospitals, clinics, and individual practitioners. The information systems in diverse hospitals and clinics may be different in nature and workflows may also be different, IHE profiles may be better in a hospital environment but not for larger scales involving many hospitals. Furthermore, there are no specific details given on how an EHR should be and what all requirements it should satisfy.

IHE integration profiles are useful from the perspective of ensuring interoperability among diverse systems. It considers EHR as a federation of diverse clinical information systems in a hospital environment and not as a separate system fulfilling functions of EHR.

BIBLIOGRAPHY

[Grimes 2005] Grimes, S. L., The challenge of integrating the healthcare enterprise. In: *Proceedings of Engineering in Medicine and Biology Magazine, IEEE*, pp. 122–124 (2005).

[HIMSS 2011] Integrating Healthcare Enterprise (2011); http://www.himss.org/ASP/topics_ihe.asp.

[IHE ATNA 2011] IHE Audit Trail and Node Authentication (ATNA) Profile (2011); http://wiki.ihe.net/index.php?title=Audit_Trail_and_Node_Authentication

[IHE ATNA FAQ 2011] IHE Audit Trail and Node Authentication (ATNA) FAQ (2011); http://wiki.ihe.net/index.php?title=ATNA_Profile_FAQ.

[IHE Integration Profiles 2003] The Key to Integrated Systems, IHE Integration Profiles (2003); http://www.ihe.net/Resources/upload/iheyr3_integration_profiles.pdf.

[IHE PCC 2010] IHE International Inc. IHE Patient Care Coordination (PCC) Technical Framework Volume 1 Revision 6.0, (2010); http://www.ihe.net/Technical_Framework/upload/IHE_PCC_TF_Rev6-0_Vol_1_2010-08-30.pdf.

[IHE Profiles Wiki 2011] IHE Integration Profiles (2011); http://wiki.ihe.net/index.php?title=Profiles.

[IHE Profiles] IHE Profiles and Tools; http://ophthalmictools.com/IHE_Domains_and_profiles.aspx.

[IHE RAD-TF 2011] IHE International, Inc., IHE Radiology Technical Framework, Volume 2 (IHE RAD TF-2) (2011); http://www.ihe.net/Technical_Framework/upload/IHE_RAD_TF_Rev10-0_Vol2_2011-02-18.pdf.

[IHE SWF 2011] Scheduled Workflow Integration Profile (2011); http://wiki.ihe.net/index.php?title=Scheduled_Workflow.

[IHE XDS 2011] Cross-Enterprise Document Sharing (2011); http://wiki.ihe.net/index.php?title=Cross_Enterprise_Document_Sharing.

[Kohn 2004] Kohn, D., Integrating the healthcare enterprise (IHE): An international approach to the development of implementation guides for electronic health record systems. In: *Proceedings of IFHRO Congress & AHIMA Convention* (2004); http://library.ahima.org/xpedio/groups/public/documents/ahima/bok3_005548.hcsp?dDocName=bok3_005548.

[Noumeir 2011] Noumeir, R., Sharing medical records: The XDS architecture and communication infrastructure. In: *Proceedings of IT Professional (Journal)*, pp. 46–52 (2011).

[Vasilescu and Mun 2006] Vasilescu, E. and Mun, S. K., Service oriented architecture (SOA) implications for large scale distributed health care enterprises. In: *Proceedings of the First Distributed Diagnosis and Home Healthcare (D2H2) Conference*, pp. 91–94 (2006).

[Vasilescu et al. 2008] Vasilescu, E., Dorobantu, M., Govoni, S., Padh, S., and Mun S., WS/PIDS: Standard interoperable PIDS in web services environments. In: *Proceedings of IEEE Transactions on Information Technology in Biomedicine*, pp. 94–99 (2008).

[Vogla et al. 2006] Vogla, R., Wozak, F., Breu, M., Penz, R., Schabetsberger, T., and Wurzd, M., Architecture for a Distributed National Electronic Health Record System in Austria (2006); https://resources.oncourse.iu.edu/access/content/group/

FA06-IN-INFO-I617-28592/Additional%20Articles/Architecture%20for%20Distributed%20Electronic%20Health%20Record%20System.pdf.

[**Wang 2005**] Wang, W., Wang, M., and Zhu, S., Healthcare information system integration: A service oriented approach. In: *Proceedings of ICSSSM International Conference on Services Systems and Services Management*, Vol. 2, pp. 1475–1480 (2005).

[**Zhang et al. 2005**] Zhang, C., Tan, Y., Feng, J., Zhang, G., and Zhang, J., Building hospital EPR with IHE technical framework. In: *Proceedings of the IEEE Engineering in Medicine and Biology 27th Annual Conference*, pp. 5684–5686 (2005).

PART FIVE

Case Studies: National EHR Efforts

CHAPTER TWENTY

Australia's HealthConnect

20.1 Introduction

The government of Australia initiated the HealthConnect program to enable nationwide use of healthcare IT infrastructure. This program actively promotes coordination among healthcare information sources, like hospitals in individual states and territories. The Australian Health Ministry established the National E-Health Transition Authority (NEHTA) Limited, a not-for-profit company, for managing the HealthConnect program and for developing national e-health standards and infrastructure requirements for electronic collection and secure exchange of health information.

The NEHTA is responsible for bridging the gap between diverse healthcare sectors, implementing systems, and providing a nationwide healthcare network of systems that can generate and exchange health information in a standardized manner. For this purpose, it has proposed the model of health information representation across healthcare sectors. It works with healthcare consumers, providers, decision makers, and the entire healthcare industry to enable health-care delivery through e-health [Williams and Howard 2010].

The NEHTA works on identified priority areas in healthcare delivery. It develops reference data specifications for these priority areas. Along with the specification of clinical model, it also addresses issues like security, privacy, and legal and ethical aspects of e-health in Australia [NEHTA 2006; NEHTA 2011].

Electronic Health Record: Standards, Coding Systems, Frameworks, and Infrastructures, Pradeep Sinha, Gaur Sunder, Prashant Bendale, Manisha Mantri, and Atreya Dande.
© 2013 by The Institute of Electrical and Electronics Engineers, Inc. Published 2013 by John Wiley & Sons, Inc.

20.2 Overview

The HealthConnect program is being implemented regionwise in Australia, gradually moving toward nationwide adoption goal. It involves:

- Upgrading existing software systems to adhere to nationally accepted standards so that information sharing will be possible
- Upgrading local settings to use the network by healthcare stakeholders
- Putting national security, privacy and consent standards in place
- Allowing end-users (i.e., patients) to manage access to their records

The NEHTA works in three domains, namely, coordinated care, connecting healthcare systems, and enabling standardized electronic representation of clinical information. Coordinated care deals with EHR and its conceptual and content model. Toward connecting healthcare systems efforts, the NEHTA defines specifications for nationwide infrastructure for delivering e-health. These efforts deal with issues like security, privacy, legal and ethical practices. It deals with issues of identifying standards for exchange of information and information representation for standardizing electronic clinical information [HealthConnect 2008].

Around 2007, the second phase of HealthConnect program started with wider scope and it was renamed *Shared Electronic Health Record(SEHR)*. Its accelerated growth and rollout has continued through last few years.

20.3 Architecture

20.3.1 EHR CONCEPT

The NEHTA identifies healthcare delivery in any clinical practice as a collection of Priority events. Following are the priority health events identified by the NEHTA:

Initial Health Profile	Pharmacy Provision
Hospital Discharge—Emergency	Community-Based Health Consultation
Medical Consultation—General Practitioner	Allied Health Consultation
Medical Consultation—Specialist	Referral
Diagnostic Investigation—Imaging	Event Notification (for example, admission to hospital)
Diagnostic Investigation—Pathology	Pharmacy Provision

In each of these priority events, a set of clinical information is generated. Data Groups represent these types of clinical information. Following are the identified Data Groups:

Adverse Reaction	Observation
Alert	Reason for Encounter
Clinical Synopsis	Problem/Diagnosis and
Immunization	Clinical Intervention

For each of the identified priority events, there is a meta-model. A standard template represents the reports resulting from these events. This meta-model relates conceptual healthcare delivery process with implementation-specific constructs and their relationships [Clinical Data Specs 2005].

Figure 20.1 shows medical data resulting from a clinical event, called Hospital Discharge for an inpatient. It includes Data Groups as a collection of Data Elements. These Data Groups support clinical terminologies like SNOMED CT, ICD, CPT, and LOINC coding systems through provision for specifying value domain and classification scheme. The meta-model actually describes a set of Data Groups applicable to a particular healthcare event [NEHTA SDT Reference 2005].

20.3.2 EHR DESIGN

The structural model suggested by the NEHTA adheres to the standard specifications given by Standards Australia, which is a Government of Australia recognized standardization body. Healthcare events described by the NEHTA follow the Health Concepts Guidelines given by Standards Australia.

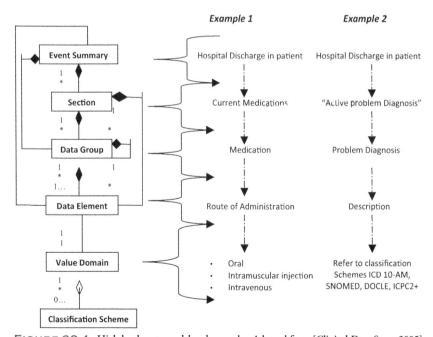

FIGURE 20.1 High level meta-model and examples. Adapted from [Clinical Data Specs 2005].

The Good Electronic Health Record (GEHR) was in use in Australia since the year 2000. The GEHR later evolved as openEHR, which is now internationally accepted. NEHTA used GEHR to evolve Structured Document Template (SDT) whose data types exactly map with the GEHR data types. SDT defines an EHR as a collection of Structured Document Templates. It describes the specifications for organizing data elements used for storing and retrieving health information.

The Structured Document Template can be specific to a clinical domain. For example, Figure 20.2 shows the applicability of a structured document template in the Pathology Result Report. The document is structured into the Header part and the Details part, where the Details part describes the result with values used from the "Blood" value domain.

The NEHTA gives several use cases having SDT as input and output from a clinical system. Once again taking the example of the Pathology Result Report, the Details part is a collection of Data Groups, and for each Data Group the Data Elements are specified in terms of data types and multiplicities. Figure 20.3 shows the contents in the Details part of the Pathology Result Report adhering to NEHTA SDT guidelines [NEHTA SDT Pathology Report 2008].

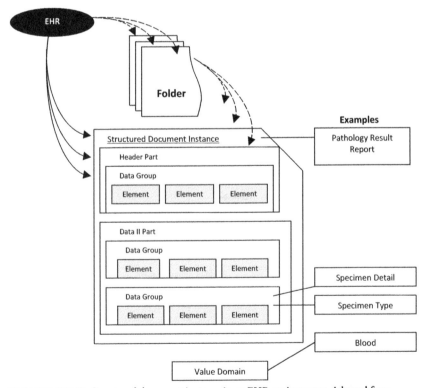

FIGURE 20.2 Structured document instance in an EHR environment. Adapted from [NEHTA SDT Pathology Report 2008].

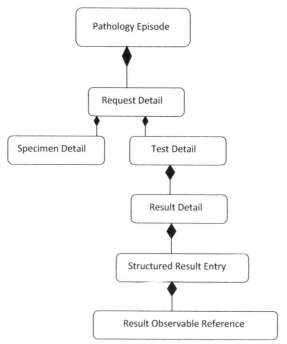

FIGURE 20.3 Structural specifications for Pathology Result Detail part.

20.3.3 e-HEALTH SERVICES

As the NEHTA suggested, the following service-oriented architecture for delivering healthcare in Australia, HealthConnect program provides e-health services for enabling health delivery through IT. It provides many services addressing various issues in healthcare delivery through IT. The services provided are:

National Authentication Service for Health (NASH). *National Authentication Service for Health (NASH)* manages security infrastructure of Health-Connect program. NASH provides strong authentication service for healthcare services in Australia. Every component over the network uses this separate authentication service. NASH service uses PKI infrastructure and multifactor authentication mechanism for issuing digital identities to the users of the network. This is essentially the same as CA infrastructure, which involves PKI and digital certificates.

Unique Healthcare Identifier (UHI) Service. The NEHTA assessed privacy issues related to healthcare information. Based on its assessment, it suggested a model that deals with privacy issues. One of the examples is the suggestion of unique healthcare identifier for healthcare users and providers. The Health-Connect program includes a Unique Healthcare Identifier (UHI) Service over healthcare network. This service provides and validates the identifiers and thus, ensures rightful access to the medical records [Privacy Study 2011].

The NEHTA considers name, date-of-birth, address, and sex as the four core fields for identifying a person. For the important issue of ensuring valid information for these core fields, while identifying a person, it follows information provided by the Medicare Database, which is legally controlled and validated by the information provider.

National Registration and Accreditation Scheme (NRAS). The Health-Connect program uses *National Registration and Accreditation Scheme (NRAS)* as a nationwide program to register healthcare consumers and providers. The e-health services can trust NRAS accredited participants.

20.3.4 NATIONAL PRIVACY PRINCIPLES (NPP)

National Privacy Principles and *Information Privacy Principles* are the two governing regulations for health in Australia. They provide guidelines for privacy issues in EMR/EHR. The NPP document is a guide for identifying the privacy issues that can occur, and it gives standard guidelines to maintain the privacy [NPP 2001]. These guidelines address various privacy issues such as:

1. Collection
2. Use
3. Data quality
4. Data security
5. Openness
6. Access and correction
7. Identifiers
8. Anonymity
9. Trans-border data flows
10. Sensitive information

It is necessary to follow these regulations to be part of the E-health infrastructure proposed by the NEHTA [Ethics and Law of eHealth 2010].

20.3.5 EXCHANGE

The NEHTA conducted a research study on evaluating existing interoperability standards [Interoperability Study 2007]. It initially suggested supporting the HL7 v2.x standard. The primary purpose was to speed up the e-transition of healthcare services. Keeping this in mind, it suggested the use of Service Oriented Architecture (SOA) in making healthcare services available to the users. The NEHTA suggested that gradually newer versions of HL7 standards are to be used for exchange of clinical information as and when they are widely accepted. The

NEHTA researched various clinical events in healthcare practices and evolved SDT which is analogous to HL7's CDA standard. These templates can be used AS-IS for recording data in healthcare events or can be extended as per the requirements. Currently, the NEHTA suggests using the CDA standard for representing this information.

20.4 Discussion

Clinical Process Model. Healthcare events and the medical information generated drive the clinical process model suggested by the NEHTA. This model helps in the identification of record types. The identified records do not provide the facility for extension through identification of "others" as one of the record types. It appears to be a rigid model.

The Healthcare Event model seems to concentrate on the types of medical information being generated. It does not represent the clinician's thought process that is responsible for these medical events. Thus, the model lacks in clarifying the "why" part of the medical information. Though a diagnosis event can give this information, the thoughtful linking of why the doctor has made this decision is missing from the model.

The Healthcare Event model is very similar to HL7 v2.x design, which is not surprising because initially the NEHTA proposed HL7 v2.x as the exchange standard. HealthConnect does not have a clinical process model explicitly designed into the system.

Structural Model. The idea of Structured Document Templates (SDTs) essentially derives from the concept of report structures because it is in CDA standard. This is helpful for clinicians because they can look at clinical information as a document report. However, the problem with any particular standard is that it may need to be extended for accommodating local requirements. This activity defeats the purpose of standardization when viewed on global scale.

The structural details of Data Groups and Data Elements are not available in public domain. But the examples available help in understanding the structure of various records types in an EHR. EHR designers can refer to the detailed structure, if available, while designing EHR systems.

Security Considerations. The concept of NASH is essential while providing federated security to national E-health infrastructure. These mechanisms are useful while developing any EHR framework for addressing large-scale problems. A nationwide healthcare IT infrastructure will definitely need such a mechanism for secure and authentic access to sensitive healthcare information. EHR framework designers must evaluate by using PKI infrastructure and federated security mechanisms while addressing security issues.

Privacy/Consent Considerations. Privacy guidelines given by NPP are useful. A detailed reference to these guidelines will help EHR designers accommodate solutions for those issues in their framework. These guidelines help designers understand the importance of consent management during activities involved in managing healthcare information.

Legal Aspects. As national level privacy principles are in place, violations of these principles are the grounds for inviting legal actions in Australia. Such guiding principles, especially for healthcare and IT domain, need to be there. These guidelines help design better solutions and solve issues arising out of malicious use of systems.

Exchange Specifications. NEHTA recommendations in Australia appear to be HL7 standards-specific. However, there are other exchange standards such as NEMA's DICOM and ASTM CCR, which need to be evaluated. Adhering to one standard requires transition of existing systems to adhere to that standard, which itself requires larger monetary and time investments.

Though standards provide the facility of extending the constructs, they lead to another problem of divergence with every system in the network. The NEHTA suggested the use of customized version of HL7 v2.x and customized version of SNOMED CT for Australia in healthcare practices. This approach may suffice the needs of a country but may create problems in standard adoption across geographical boundaries.

20.5 Conclusion

The NEHTA's approach toward e-health is very comprehensive, because it addresses not only medical records-related issues but also security, privacy, legal, and ethical issues related to e-health delivery. This program guides large-scale system developers in healthcare IT domain about tackling all these issues in an effective manner. The only approach to stick to a particular standard for information representation may prove to be a hurdle in the long run. Following are some of the components that EHR framework designers should refer in detail from the Australian HealthConnect program:

1. Unique Healthcare Identifier Service (UHI)
2. National Registration and Accreditation Service (NRAS)
3. National Authentication Service for Health (NASH)
4. Meta-model for EHR
5. Legal Frameworks such as National Privacy Principles (NPP) and Information Privacy Principles (IPP)

BIBLIOGRAPHY

[**Clinical Data Specs 2005**] National E-Health Transition Authority Ltd., *Details for Clinical Information Data Specifications—Guide for Use v0.55 [Archived]* (2005);

http://www.nehta.gov.au/component/docman/doc_details/39-clinical-information-data-specifications-guide-for-use-v055-archived.

[Ethics and Law of eHealth 2010] eHealth Australia, Ethics and Law: The Influence on eHealth Applications (2010); http://ehealthaustralia.org/ethics-and-law-the-influence-on-ehealth-applications/.

[HealthConnect 2008]   The HealthConnect Program; http://www.health.gov.au/internet/hconnect/publishing.nsf/Content/home.

[Interoperability Study 2007] National E-Health Transition Authority Ltd., Standards for E-Health Interoperability (2007); http://www.nehta.gov.au/component/docman/doc_download/252-standards-for-e-health-interoperability-v10.

[NEHTA 2006] National E-Health Transition Authority (2006); http://www.health.gov.au/internet/hconnect/publishing.nsf/Content/nehta-1lp.

[NEHTA 2011] NEHTA Official Website (2011); http://www.nehta.gov.au/.

[NEHTA SDT Pathology Report 2008] National E-Health Transition Authority Ltd., Structured Document Template Pathology Result Report (2008); http://www.google.co.in/url?sa=t&source=web&cd=1&ved=0CBUQFjAA&url=http%3A%2F%2Fwww.nehta.gov.au%2Fcomponent%2Fdocman%2Fdoc_download%2F543-structured-document-template-pathology-result-report-v04-draft-&ei=6favTMDUJoK-caXqydIN&usg=AFQjCNHVsV6wEEwCxoqeuFdEPHSBn-RlO0Q&sig2=72kGgVRz36GrGlpx17a0mA.

[NEHTA SDT Reference 2005] National E-Health Transition Authority Ltd, NEHTA Specification Template Reference Guide (2005); http://www.nehta.gov.au/component/docman/doc_download/38-clinical-information-specification-v12-template-reference-guide.

[NPP 2001] Office of the Federal Privacy Commissioner, Guidelines to The National Privacy Principles (2001); www.privacy.gov.au/materials/types/download/8774/6582.

[Privacy Study 2011] Privacy Impact Assessments, (2011); http://www.nehta.gov.au/connecting-australia/privacy/pias.

[Williams and Howard 2010]   Forum Williams, P. and Howard, A., NEHTA Presentation to AAPP Forum (2010); http://www.communiogroup.com/aapp/AAPP%20Presentation-Forum11-3-10%20vSumm.pdf.

CHAPTER TWENTY-ONE

Austria's ELGA

21.1 Introduction

Sharing of health records of a patient between different healthcare organizations can lead to efficient treatment of the patient due to availability of all required information when and where needed. To address this need, the Austrian Ministry of Health initiated a nationwide Electronic Health Record project called ELGA, an acronym for Elektronische Gesundheitsakte (Electronic Health Record). ELGA started in the year 2005 under the European eHealth Action Plan [Healthcare Reform Act 2005]. The feasibility study was completed in the year 2006 with the establishment of a national task force for EHR called Arge-ELGA [ELGA]. It is responsible for defining strategies and roadmap, planning and implementation, management of legal and ethical issues, and evaluation of results of the project. The feasibility study led to the development of an architecture framework for national EHR.

The architecture plan for ELGA was published in 2007. It described the basic components and services of ELGA. A detailed plan for each component, with selection of standards through various proofs of concepts, and the study of cost of implementation for financial planning for implementation of ELGA were completed in 2008. The implementation and development of ELGA components started in the year 2009. A foundation for national implementation was established and named *ELGA GmbH* (ELGA Limited) in 2010 [ELGA GmbH]. ELGA GmbH has the following aims:

Electronic Health Record: Standards, Coding Systems, Frameworks, and Infrastructures, Pradeep Sinha,
Gaur Sunder, Prashant Bendale, Manisha Mantri, and Atreya Dande.
© 2013 by The Institute of Electrical and Electronics Engineers, Inc. Published 2013 by John Wiley & Sons, Inc.

1. Planning and determining roadmap for EHR implementation.
2. Implementing determined projects for national EHR.
3. Integrating legal framework and national standards for EHR.
4. Ensuring smooth working of EHR at any given condition.
5. Evaluating project results.

Various implementation agencies (such as CSC) [CSC 2011] are also involved in the implementation of ELGA.

21.2 Overview

ELGA aims to consolidate the electronic health information of uniquely identified patients generated by a number of healthcare organizations. The information is stored at respective healthcare organizations, but it is accessible to an authorized caregiver at any given point of time.

The primary and secondary goals of ELGA include:

Primary Goals	Secondary Goals
Patient care	Quality management
Patient management	Automating healthcare activities
Streamlining the treatment process	Financial and Administrative processes
A lifelong EHR	Science and Research

ELGA uses a decentralized approach with distributed data storage and a central document registry that stores metadata. The central document registry links to the source data and the respective decentralize databases.

The ELGA program consists of the following components:

1. ELGA Architecture
2. Services Provided
3. Standards used for Data Content
4. Exchange and Communication Infrastructure

21.3 Architecture

The following components are part of ELGA healthcare infrastructure [Duftschmid et al. 2009]:

1. *Master Patient Index.* It stores a list of unique patient identifiers against local identifiers used by various healthcare information systems.

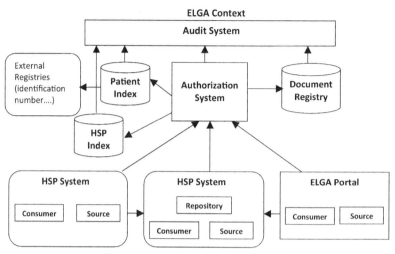

FIGURE 21.1 Architecture of ELGA.

2. **Health Service Provider (HSP) Index.** It stores a list of providers with their unique identifiers.

3. **Authorization System.** It manages data access control.

4. **HSP Systems.** These are systems at healthcare organizations that are connected together for sharing of patient data.

5. **Storage.** It is a central storage in the form of Document Registry.

6. **Network.** It is a network infrastructure used in ELGA.

7. **ELGA Portal.** It provides web-based access to ELGA network.

Figure 21.1 shows all the above-mentioned components of ELGA [Schanner 2007].

21.3.1 MASTER PATIENT INDEX

Master Patient Index (MPI) is a central component of ELGA that maintains a list of unambiguously identified persons by linking different identifiers given by different health care providers to a single patient.

21.3.2 HSP INDEX

The Healthcare Service Provider (HSP) Index maintains a list of uniquely identified health care providers throughout the nation. It provides an easily accessible list of healthcare providers, that is, doctors and healthcare organizations. The HSP list is published as a directory of nationwide healthcare providers to fulfill one of the recommendations of *Health Telematics Law* of Austria [Duftschmid et al. 2009; Brebner 2008].

21.3.3 AUTHORIZATION SYSTEM

The authorization system deals with access control of EHRs of patients. In feasibility study, role based access to users by defining profiles is recommended. A profile contains operations, which can be performed for that particular role. A patient can request for access logs and access rights on her/his EHR at any point of time. Electronic tickets can be used for giving additional authorization to a user on a patient's EHR.

21.3.4 HSP SYSTEM

The HSP systems are existing systems that provide healthcare services. Patient health records generated at various HSP systems are kept in their own repository in a decentralized manner, by converting internal data to the content format specified by ELGA using *ELGA Adapters*. ELGA Adapters are tools that convert the data of existing systems into ELGA defined format. In Figure 21.1, the *Source* produces the data (adds data in a repository), and the *Consumer* accesses it from the repository.

21.3.5 STORAGE (DOCUMENT REGISTRY)

This central registry stores indexable information of all health records of patients with location/repository information linking to the HSP Systems. Whenever required, the records can be located and retrieved independently from the respective HSP System.

No central storage for data is provided in ELGA architecture. Document Registry only contains links to the local HSP Data Repositories. After locating a record in a particular HSP repository, the record can be directly fetched from that repository. Transfer of data takes place via web services using SOAP protocol.

21.3.6 NETWORK

ELGA program uses *Integrating the Healthcare Enterprise* (IHE) based healthcare network for exchange of patients' documents called *IHE IT Infrastructure Technical Framework*. ELGA uses the following different IHE profiles:

1. Retrieve Information and Display (RID)
2. Enterprise User Authentication (EUA)
3. Patient Identifier Cross-Referencing (PIX)
4. Patient Synchronized Applications (PSA)
5. Consistent Time (CT)
6. Patient Demographics Query (PDQ)
7. Audit Trail and Note Authentication (ATNA)
8. Personal White Pages (PWP)
9. Cross-Enterprise Document Sharing (XDS)

The PIX integration profile enables cross-referencing of a patient identifier from multiple patient identifiers provider domains (multiple hospitals giving different identifiers to a patient in their hospitals) via the *Patient Identifier Cross-Reference Manager*.

The IHE XDS profile defines workflow for sharing electronic documents between healthcare providers. It includes a Document Registry, which stores a list of health records of a uniquely identified person. The healthcare providers need to register their patients' health related documents to this Document Registry that is shared with other providers. A provider/person who wants to access a document (health record of a particular patient), queries to the Document Registry. If document is available/located in the registry, then it is retrieved by referring to its HSP System.

The communication infrastructure uses Secured Socket Layer (SSL)/ Transport Layer Security (TLS) with client authentication.

21.3.7 ELGA PORTAL

ELGA Portal is a user-friendly application provided to ELGA users. It is a secured information portal for publically available information such as, health events. It also provides HSP information with personal information of users present in ELGA system in secured form.

Development of various components of ELGA and implementation of its first phase is divided into the following seven projects:

1. Master Patient Index
2. HSP Index
3. Document Registry
4. Authorization System
5. ELGA Public Portal
6. Central ELGA Architecture
7. Acceptance Management

Implementation of all ELGA core applications and services is expected to complete by the year 2012.

21.4 Functional Implementation

ELGA uses identifiers for patients from the national *Electronic Health Card* (*eCard*) *System*, which was started to make health-insurance-related activities in electronic form. An *eCard* contains identification information of a patient, such as name, gender, date of birth, social security number, and so on. Hospitals refer to a patient's eCard for identifying the patient. Every hospital has an eCard reading device that directly connects to the social insurance computing center.

Similarly, *Current Health Practice Card* is used for identifying healthcare professionals. Both these cards are used in the ELGA system for authentication and authorization during access to ELGA data [Bittschi and Kraus 2007].

Patient ID Source Service mentioned in the architecture is being implemented at national level in the form of "Central Citizen Registry," which keeps unique identification numbers given by Austrian government (called *ZMR numbers*) for the eCard System.

The HSP Index for searching healthcare providers is already implemented and named as *Central e-Health Directory Service*. The service is implemented using the Lightweight Directory Access Protocol (LDAP), for effective searching of information from the server.

A pilot project named *health@net*, for implementing the network architecture of ELGA, was carried out between 2002 and 2009. It was built using a technical infrastructure based on access to decentralized data storage through a virtual middleware in a secured manner. This infrastructure is called Medical Data GRIDs [Vogla et al. 2006]. The *health@net* project follows the IHE-XDS profile and Austrian Health Telematics Law. The network is currently used for telemedicine and other national services. The project is appraised as secure, flexible, and standardized system architecture for a regional EHR [Pfeiffer et al. 2010].

The complete architecture of health@net uses the web service technology with SOAP protocol for communication on SSL/TSL considering all web security aspects. The following core components of this network are developed as independent services [Wozak 2007]:

1. ***Document Registry Service.*** This service allows the search of documents, checks access permissions, and provides links to the originally residing data repository location of documents. It also provides *Access Nodes (AN)* for accessing services of ELGA system. It has the following internal components:

   a. ***Document Meta Data Index (DMDI).*** It keeps the index of metadata of all documents with links to the original location of the document. This is responsible for returning metadata information of a record, depending on the access permissions of that record. Multiple DMDI services are active with distributed metadata indices at a time in order to improve performance while serving multiple requests.

   b. ***Patient ID Source Service.*** It is responsible for maintaining unique identifiers of all individuals for identifying them irrespective of being treated in any of the hospitals.

   c. ***Global Index.*** On request of the identified patient's records, this component is responsible for searching a particular DMDI service where metadata of the requested records is stored and accessing those records.

2. ***Patient Lookup Index (PLI).*** The services provide the facility to search a patient, depending on his/her demographics data and other secondary identifiers such as identifiers provided by a hospital, social insurance numbers, and so on.

3. *Document Repository Service.* This service stores the health records of patients generated at healthcare organizations in the form of CDA documents. It has the following component.

    a. *Document Clearing Service.* It is responsible for mapping and converting the data from any other form (HL7, DICOM, etc.) to CDA during storage operations. It also maps a local identifier to the internal unique identifier of ELGA.

4. *HSP Index.* This service is used for searching healthcare providers and managing access control based on the digital certificates issued to them.

21.4.1 HEALTHCARE SERVICES

ELGA supports four basic records for its first phase of implementation. The templates for other type of records are planned after successful implementation of these basic record types. They include:

1. *Discharge Summary.* It stores discharge letter prepared by medical professionals.

2. *e-Report-Radiology.* It stores radiology reports with the images.

3. *e-Report-Laboratory.* It stores laboratory report details.

4. *e-Medication.* It stores prescription details for treatment of a patient. Distribution of medicines will be monitored through it.

21.5 Exchange

ELGA uses international standards for content and exchange of health data. The following standards are considered:

- IHE Technical Framework for IT Infrastructure, Patient Care Coordination, Laboratory and Radiology
- HL7 v3 RIM as basic data model
- HL7 CDA Release 2 as document standard
- LOINC codes for laboratory observations
- DICOM 3.0 and WADO for radiology data

21.6 Discussion

The ELGA implementation project has a span of nearly seven years due to the complex structure of healthcare environment surrounded by legislative policies, data standards, and interoperability issues. ELGA implementation has launched its ELGA Portal in the year 2010 [Krassnitzer 2010; ELGA Portal].

Clinical Process Model. ELGA does not use any process-based model for its EHR implementation and has directly included the commonly used health record artifacts such as discharge summary, radiology records, pathology records, medications, and so on, justifying sharing of only those documents of patients which are required by HSPs.

Structural Model. ELGA follows CDA R2 as a data content standard for structure of basic records, which is compatible with ISO and CEN standards for information content. It uses HL7 RIM as the base information model on CDA. It follows the IHE specifications for sharing of radiology reports, laboratory reports, and patient care coordination.

ELGA is compatible with HL7 v3 RIM and CDA standards with certain changes (such as putting further constraints) in original models. This was done due to the national requirements and problems in compatibility between HL7 v3 and CDA for use of certain data types in HL7v3 RIM (such as specifying preconditions for *Reference Ranges*, which, if used, causes failure while validating CDA) [Alexander et al. 2009].

It uses HL7 v3 model with German translation and constraints such as the use of text type for reference ranges to avoid validation failure.

As per an Austrian study for use of coding system, SNOMDE-CT is the best terminology among all coding systems. However, German translation of LOINC terminology is preferred in the framework for support as localization was given importance in the study [Daumke et al. 2011].

Security/Privacy Considerations. ELGA provides two levels of security for access of data by providing a decentralized approach. The first is at the central ELGA system where access to patients' registry is done through a role-based access mechanism by applying all security concerns. The second is at each HSP level that also deals with data security and access. ISO/IEC 2700X ISMS standard (called Information Security Management Systems (ISMS) standard) is followed at the ELGA system as well as at all HSP data repositories.

In role-based access control, roles are given to the job descriptions of healthcare providers to provide flexibility in access control system by allowing one person to have one or more roles.

IHE PIX integration profile used by ELGA can be used in any national context while implementing a national EHR framework. This is because a single patient having different identifiers in different hospitals is common to all countries.

IHE PDQ profile is useful for giving patient information depending on the query for that patient with certain parameters. The parameters include patient ID, name, date of birth, age, bed identifier, and so on. However, from the national EHR implementation point of view, some attributes (such as bed identifier) do not seem to be relevant. Hence, there is a need for some extra inputs on top of PDQ profile for providing search and access of patient information and visits.

A patient controls sharing of data, where he/she decides which lab reports, radiology reports, and discharge notes should be shareable/visible. The patient unique identifier is hidden from the health information systems by internally mapping data from source system to data repository. However, ELGA project has faced some access and security policies related issues. One major issue is acceptance by physicians due to the liability of physician for data misuse. Austrian government has taken initiatives in defining policies for ELGA covering such scenarios during electronic data exchange [Hofmarcher 2008] [Hackl et al. 2009; News at empirica 2010].

Legal Aspects. ELGA follows Health Telematics Law of Austria [GTelG] launched by the Federal Ministry of Health as a part of Health Reform 2005 Act. The act defines standards for a secure health data exchange and provides regulations for practicing eHealth in Austria. It also provides streamlined data security standards across the country.

It provides rules for transfer of health data in terms of confidentiality, integrity, and simplification of communication processes. It also includes regulations for issues related to information management.

Exchange Specifications. ELGA follows the exchange specifications given by IHE IT Infrastructure Technical Framework, with CDA Release 2, which uses XML as the format for representing the information. It allows HSPs to send data in either HL7 standard or DICOM standard as a source to the data repository at HSPs.

Technical Guidelines. ELGA's approach for implementation of national EHR using web services with XML (used for data representation while data transfer) and standard internet protocols can be adapted, since it gives a flexible model on top of which many healthcare services can be built.

LDAP technology, which is used for implementing an HSP Index, provides a complex control mechanism that might be helpful for a healthcare domain since information to be accessed is sensitive data. However, it is more complex in terms of configuration and modification of the queries. LDAP is also not very efficient for updates. Hence, it is useful only for storing such data, which is rarely changed and has read-only access. It can, however be considered as a methodology for keeping patient health records that are rarely updated.

Necessary grounds were already available for seamlessly implementing a nationwide EHR in Austria since the groundwork for national health infrastructures started much before planning of the National EHR. Such an approach helps in incremental enhancement and tremendous cost saving.

21.7 Conclusion

ELGA is a well-planned initiative of Austria for nationwide EHR with the use of international standards for data content, data exchange, and data structure for achieving countrywide interoperability. Its approach of using the technologies, standards, and implementation strategies should be seriously considered by a team involved in implementing regional and/or national health infrastructure in a country.

BIBLIOGRAPHY

[**Alexander et al. 2009**] Alexander, M., Stefan, S.W., and Stefan, S., An implementation guide for CDA laboratory reports in the Austrian electronic health record (ELGA). In: IHIC (2009); http://www.hl7.at/hl7_documents/Interna/mense_sabutsch_-sauermann_-_elga_laboratory_report.pdf.

[**Bittschi and Kraus 2007**] Bittschi, B., and Kraus, M., Implementation and development of the E-card, Institute for Advanced Studies (2007); http://www.hpm.org/survey/at/a10/2.

[**Brebner 2008**] Brebner, E., Confidentiality, and legal components of telemedicine, University of Aberdeen (2008); http://www.vannas.se/default.aspx?di=4552.

[**CSC 2011**] A news release at CSC, *CSC Completes Development of Master Patient Index in Austria*, (September 2011); http://www.csc.com/health_services/press_releases/74301-csc_completes_development_of_master_patient_index_in_austria. http://www.itapa.sk/data/att/3368_subor_en.pdf.

[**Daumke et al. 2011**] Daumke, P., Ingenerf, J., Daniel, C., Asholm, L., and Schulz, S., The need for SNOMED CT translations, *User Centered Networked Health Care*, A. Moen, et al., eds., In: *23 International Conference of the European Federation for Medical Informatics*, (2011). http://person.hst.aau.dk/ska/mie2011/CD/MIE_2011_Content/Posters/055_or_submission_275_2_am_ok.pdf

[**Dorda et al. 2005**] Dorda, W., Duftschmid, G., Gerhold, L., Gall, W., and Gambal, J., Introducing the electronic health record in Austria. In: *Proceedings of MIE2005— The XIXth International Congress of the European Federation for Medical Informatics/ Studies in Health Technology and Informatics*, Vol. 116, pp. 119–124 (2005); http://www.meduniwien.ac.at/msi/mias/papers/Dorda2005a.pdf.

[**Dorda et al. 2008**] Dorda W., Duftschmid G., Gerhold L., Gall W., and Gambal J., Austria's path toward nationwide electronic health records, *Methods of Information in Medicine 2008*; http://www.meduniwien.ac.at/msi/mias/papers/Dorda2007b.pdf.

[**Duftschmid et al. 2009**] Duftschmid, G., Dorda, W., and Gall, W., The ELGA initiative: A plan for implementing a nationwide electronic health records system in Austria, *Vienna, Core Unit of Medical Statistics and Informatics Section on Medical Information and Retrieval Systems (MIAS)*, Medical University of Vienna (2009); http://www.meduniwien.ac.at/msi/mias/papers/Duftschmid2009a.pdf.

[**ELGA**] Austrian National EHR official website; http://www.arge-elga.at (in German).

[**ELGA GmbH**] Elektronische Gesundheitsakte GmbH (ELGA GmbH); http://www.arge-elga.at/index.php?id=3.

[**ELGA Portal**] ELGA Portal; https://www.gesundheit.gv.at.

[**GTelG**] Austrian Health Telematics Law (GTelG); http://www.hpm.org/en/Surveys/IHS_-_Austria/06/Health_Telematics_Law_(GTelG).html.

[**Hackl et al. 2009**] Hackl, W., Hoerbst, A., and Ammenwerth, E., The electronic health record in austria: Physicians' influenced by negative emotions. *Medical Informatics in a United and Healthy Europe*, Adlassnig, K. P., et al., eds., IOS Press, pp. 140–144 (2009); http://person.hst.aau.dk/ska/MIE2009/papers/MIE2009p0140.pdf.

[**Healthcare Reform Act 2005**] Healthcare Reform Act 2005; http://www.parlament.gv.at/pls/portal/docs/page/PG/DE/XXII/I/I_00693/fname_030664.pdf.

[**Hofmarcher 2008**] Hofmarcher, M. M., Electronic health record: Developments and debates, *Survey No. 12, Health Policy Monitor, International Network Health Policy &*

Reform (2008); http://hpm.org/en/Surveys/IHS_-_Austria/12/Electronic_Health_ Record__developments_and_debates.html.

[IBM 2006]   IBM Management Summary, *Feasibility Study for Implementing the Electronic Health Record (ELGA) in the Austrian Health System*; http://www.arge-elga.at/fileadmin/user_ upload/uploads/download_Papers/Arge_Papers/Endbericht_ Folgeauftrag_en.pdf.

[Krassnitzer 2010] Krassnitzer, M., E-Health Advances in Austria, Issue published in *European Hospital* (February 2010); http://www.european-hospital.com/en/article/ 7178-E-health_advances_in_Austria.html.

[News at empirica 2010] News at empirica, *Comparative Analysis of eHealth in Austria* (October 2010); http://www.empirica.com/aktuelles/meldung_en.php?newsID= matoc-lpqcx-asqrf-ca213#.

[Pfeiffer et al. 2010] Pfeiffer, K.P., Giest, S., Dumortier, J., and Artmann J., eHealth strategies, country brief: Austria, European Commission, DG Information Society and Media, ICT for Health Unit (October 2010); http://ehealth-strategies.eu/ database/documents/Austria_CountryBrief_eHStrategies.pdf.

[Schanner 2007] Schanner, A., Healthcare transformation and the role of EHR: Views from government. In: *Joint EuroRec—EHTEL Workshop, WHIT 2007 PreConference* (2007); http://www.ehtel.org/references-files/2007-10-whit-presymposium/EHTEL-EuroRec-2007_Schanner-ELGA.pdf.

[Vogla et al. 2006] Vogla, R., Wozak F., Breu, M., Penz, R., Schabetsbergerc, T., and Wurzd, M., Architecture for a distributed national electronic health record system in Austria. In: *Proceedings of EuroPACS* (2006); https://oncourse.iu.edu/access/content/ group/FA06-IN-INFO-I617-28592/Additional%20Articles/Architecture%20for% 20Distributed%20Electronic%20Health%20Record%20System.pdf.

[Wozak 2007] Wozak, F., Medical data grids as a base-architecture for interregional shared electronic health records, Doctoral Thesis, University for Health Sciences, Medical Informatics and Technology (UMIT), Institute for Health Information Systems (2007); http://iig.umit.at/dokumente/phd_wozak.pdf.

CHAPTER TWENTY-TWO

Canada's EHRS Blueprint

22.1 Introduction

Canada started its EHR implementation program with a vision to provide a seamless, highly accessible, and secure platform for delivering fast and accurate diagnosis and treatment of patients' health problems. The federal government of Canada collaborated with Canada Health Infoway Inc. (Infoway), provincial and territorial governments, and other health organizations to implement EHR in Canada.

Infoway is an independent not-for-profit corporation created by Canada's First Ministers in 2001 to foster and accelerate the development and adoption of EHR systems. Funded by the Government of Canada, Infoway works with the country's ten provinces and three territories.

22.2 Overview

Canada's national framework for interoperable EHR enables healthcare applications from hospitals to exchange health-related data through a service-based infrastructure situated in each jurisdiction of Canada. Canada's approach to develop a common EHR framework is based on the idea to support the development of heterogeneous solutions that can share health information across the country and thereby make health information accessible for patient care independent of a patient's or healthcare provider's location.

Electronic Health Record: Standards, Coding Systems, Frameworks, and Infrastructures, Pradeep Sinha, Gaur Sunder, Prashant Bendale, Manisha Mantri, and Atreya Dande.
© 2013 by The Institute of Electrical and Electronics Engineers, Inc. Published 2013 by John Wiley & Sons, Inc.

Electronic Health Record Solution (EHRS) Blueprint, a business and technical framework, is implemented in each jurisdiction to provide interoperable EHR in Canada [Infoway EHRS Blueprint].

The overall framework contains an *Electronic Health Record Solution* (EHRS) that uses the *Electronic Health Record Infostructure* (EHRi) and *Point of Service* (PoS) *applications.*

Electronic Health Record Solution (EHRS). EHRS is a combination of people, organizational entities, business processes, systems, technologies, and standards that interact and exchange clinical data to provide high quality and effective healthcare. EHRS is viewed as an ecosystem providing a blend of business and technology services for building an interoperable EHR. EHRS contains EHRi, which provides technology services.

Electronic Health Record Infostructure (EHRi). EHRi is a collection of common and reusable software services accessed by a diverse set of health information management applications. It describes software services for EHR, EHR data definitions, and messaging standards that are accessible to PoS. Such an EHRi is deployed at each province or territory [Infoway EHRS Blueprint].

Point of Service (PoS) applications. PoS applications are located at healthcare provider's site. For example, a pharmacy system, laboratory system, EMR system, radiology system, and so on, are PoS applications. All these applications access the services of EHRi to push or pull patient health information. These applications may not maintain the complete data of a patient's EHR, but can access or retrieve the complete set of patient EHR data from common data repositories through software services provided by EHRi.

The architecture and major components of these three elements of the framework are explained in the next section.

22.3 Architecture

22.3.1 ELECTRONIC HEALTH RECORD SOLUTION (EHRS)

Infoway's Electronic Health Record Solution (EHRS) comprises the following:

- An electronic health record with patient-centric view
- Support for workflow and management of studies and cases
- Services to identify patient and health care providers and healthcare locations
- Services to provide customized views of records
- Services to standardize the information contained in EHR and enable interoperability across systems of care
- Cover privacy and confidentiality of content of EHR

- Provide decision support, health surveillance, and research
- Has countrywide network communication infrastructure to support these services

EHRS includes individual electronic health records (EHR), Health Information Management Systems in large and small healthcare settings called Point of Service (PoS) applications, health information repositories and warehouses, and software services that screen and manage health information as it is transmitted from one point to another.

For maintaining and accessing health information across the country, Infoway has developed EHRi, which is Service Oriented Architecture (SOA)-based EHR management solution.

22.3.2 ELECTRONIC HEALTH RECORD INFOSTRUCTURE (EHRi)

Figure 22.1 shows the architectural components of EHR Infostructure. They are described below.

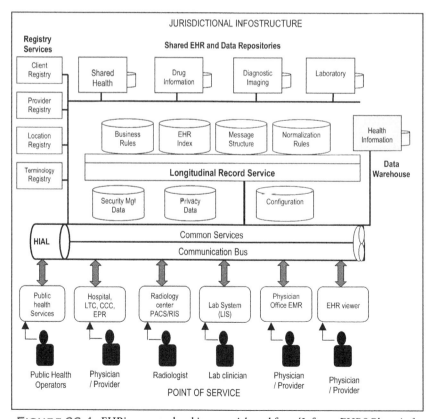

FIGURE 22.1   EHRi conceptual architecture. Adapted from [Infoway EHRS Blueprint].

Registry Services. These registries are implemented for the centrally managed information that identifies various actors and resources in EHRi. The four registries maintained in EHRi are:

1. *Provider Registry.* It maintains the information required to uniquely identify a healthcare provider. Each provider is registered and assigned a unique identifier. These registries are accessed before initiating any health information transaction for verification of the related actors and their locations.

2. *Client Registry.* It maintains the information regarding the patients to identify them uniquely.

3. *Location Registry.* It maintains the location information of healthcare providers and patients.

4. *Terminology Registry.* It maintains the codes provided by the coding systems and the terminologies for clinically relevant information such as disease names, laboratory tests and observations, and common meanings and terms.

Shared EHR and Data Repositories. The Shared Health Record repository maintains the basic information about health encounters, health service events, and clinical observations associated with those events for each patient. It provides a quick view of a patient's recently updated part of EHR.

Data repositories store and manage the contents of patients' EHRs. These repositories are implemented jurisdictionwise and are accessed by local Point of Service (PoS) applications for retrieving patient health information. Separate repositories are maintained for storing diagnostic images, reports generated during patient studies, drug information from medications, and laboratory related events and results.

Longitudinal Record Services (LRS). Longitudinal record services mainly access the EHR index that maintains the minimum data required to search a document, record, or event in an EHR. The EHR index maintains information such as patient id, type of record, date, provider id, and location of actual record in data repositories. This indexed information is required to identify the actual location (data repositories) of records and thereby respond to requests coming from PoS applications. For example, when PoS requests to verify a patient's or provider's identity, or retrieve the contents of EHR from different data repositories, these services respond with information. These services are responsible for maintaining the EHR index to support faster retrieval of information. LRS also provides replication services that replicate EHR data across multiple locations. However, no technologies or policies used in each of these services are available in public documentation.

Health Information Access Layer (HIAL). Every PoS application interacts with EHRi through Health Information Access Layer (HIAL). HIAL covers

Communication and Common services. This layer enables exchange of data between two EHRi located across jurisdictions when PoS applications request to access patient data available in other jurisdictions. This might happen in the case when a patient is provided care in multiple jurisdictions of the country.

1. **Communication Services.** These services involve support for various network and application protocols including routing, encoding and decoding, and encryption and decryption. Communication services act as interfaces or connectivity points for PoS applications to connect with EHRi.

2. **Common Services.** Common Services are a set of services on top of communication services which provide a security and interoperability layer for EHR.

Other than the above-described services, there are miscellaneous services such as Interoperability and Internationalization Services. These services are implemented based on HL7 v3 [HL7 v3] messages. PoS applications adhering to HL7 v3 as messaging standard can directly access data from EHRi by using it. For PoS that do not support HL7 v3, mapping and conversion services are provided that map PoS data schema with HL7 v3 message schemas and convert PoS data to HL7 v3 messages. These internationalization services are used for sharing EHRs in different languages.

EHR Viewer. Apart from PoS applications that access EHR data from EHRi, an EHR viewer is also provided separately that enables end-users to access, search, and view relevant and authorized health care data about patients. The viewer provides a single seamless view of the available, relevant healthcare information of a patient regardless of its source. It can be used by the patients to view their records and track their past and ongoing treatments.

Privacy and Security Services. Infoway provides the following eight services for protection of patient health information [EHRi Privacy].

1. **User Identity Service.** This service protects the user identity by using identification registries for patient, provider, and location of care. IHE PIX PDQ profile, based on HL7 v2.4 and HL7 v3 messages, is used to validate a user's identity while accessing any data repository from EHRi.

2. **Consent Directives Management Service.** This service is based on the common vocabulary of consent directives that are in-line with the current data protection and privacy laws of Canada. A messaging schema on top of the vocabulary provides means to manage the status of consent directives.

3. **Identity Protection Service.** This service is based on the idea of separately storing patient identifiers that uniquely identify a patient and patient's health information such as laboratory reports, diagnostic images, and so on, in order to reduce the potential impact of privacy breach. This service involves linking a patient's public identifiers (PIDs) with a unique number which is EHRi Client ID (ECID) used internally across EHRi. Federated identifiers

are dummy identifiers created to protect ECID from being exposed to secondary users such as researchers, students, and so on. Mapping tables are created to map PIDs to ECID, ECID to FIDs, and ECID to Client Registry where the original identity information of a patient resides. Federated identifiers are used while transferring patient information between EHRis located across jurisdictions. Since in another jurisdiction, the records would contain FID as the unique-id to link a patient's records, his/her original identity is still secured at the primary EHRi. The PIDs are normally used by healthcare providers to locate the health information. In the same way, federated identifiers are assigned to the same ECID, which are actually used by anonymous users such as researchers. This mechanism protects the ECID, which is the actual identifier, from being disclosed and provides mapped identifiers for accessing of information.

4. *Access Control Service.* This service uses three different approaches for managing user privileges on a patient's EHR. These are role-based, group-based, and discretionary. The role-based approach specifies privileges based on professional credentials of a user such as physician or nurse. The group-based approach specifies privileges for a set of users such as all care-givers working in a primary clinic or an emergency ward of a hospital. The discretionary approach involves users having specific relationship with a patient such as blood relatives. The discretionary approach is actually very similar to access control policy maintained by operating systems. It gives the owner of any file a privilege of sharing access with any other user(s) created in the same system or network.

5. *Anonymization Service.* This service enables retrieval of anonymized data for researchers and students. It provides the rules for replacing the contents such as identifiers, personal information, and so on, with dummy characters when data are requested from a Point of Service (PoS) application.

6. *Encryption Service.* This service provides a private keys (PKI)-based encryption mechanism for data storage, database encryption, and message encryption. Key management is an integral part of this service that includes creation, storage, and revocation of encryption keys. This service encrypts data during storage operations in data repositories, archives, and message transmission.

7. *Digital Signature Service.* This service provides the facility to request digital signatures to secure health information while it is transmitted over the network.

8. *Secure Audit Service.* It provides the services for logging of events such as update, insert on contents of the EHR and for storing them securely in the EHRi.

22.3.3 EXCHANGE

Contents of EHR are exchanged mainly between EHRi and PoS or between two EHRis of different jurisdictions. Application of existing technologies, standards, terminologies, and codes to provide semantic and syntactic interoperability makes it possible to seamlessly integrate and exchange EHR across jurisdictions.

EHRS uses medical and business standards, and their use is listed below [EHRi DICOM].

1. *Content and Messaging.* For exchanging contents between EHRi and PoS applications, standards like HL7 v2.x and HL7 v3 [HL7 v3], CDA R2, and DICOM are used.

2. *Terminology.* For standardizing clinical information in EHR, code sets of SNOMED CT [SNOMED CT 2011], LOINC [LOINC 2011], Canadian Classification of Health Interventions (CCI), and ICD 10-CA [ICD 10-CA and CCI 2011] are used.

3. *IHE Integration Profiles.* XDS/XDS-I [IHE XDS 2011] profile is used for clinical document exchange. It is specifically used to support exchange of diagnostic imaging data in the EHRi. PIX/PDQ is used to provide services for patient identification. The Audit Trial and Node Authentication (ATNA) profile provides workflow for user authentication, connection authentication, and record of audit trials.

4. *Electronic Business Standards.*

   - ebXML—Using ebXML [ebXML 2011], companies now have a standard method to exchange business messages, conduct trading relationships, communicate data in common terms, and define and register business processes.

   - Web services—EHR services provided by EHRi are hosted using SOA architecture by effectively using web services.

22.3.4 LEGAL FRAMEWORK

To govern the rights for access to electronic information, the Government of Canada has introduced various acts and guidelines.

Following is a list of legal frameworks published in Canada to cover EHRS activities:

- Government of Canada's Personal Information Protection and Electronic Documents Act (PIPEDA) [PIPEDA].
- Canadian Standards Association's Model Code for Protection of Personal Information—CAN-CSA-Q830-03.
- International Organization for Standardization's Code of Practice for Information Security Management—ISO 17799:2005.

22.4 Discussion

Clinical Process Model. From the documentation available, it appears that the EHR clinical process model is not part of EHRS implemented in Canada.

Structural Model. From the documentation available, it appears that there are two concepts related to EHR: a shared EHR that comprises of the latest summary of records and an EHR index that contains the minimum information required to search a record mapped to its actual location for all the records of a patient. Both these are used to view the patient health information.

Security/Privacy Considerations. EHRi framework by Infoway specifies, in detail, the various services involved in security and privacy of EHR contents. The approach is a good example of achieving secure interoperability of EHR through adherence to medical informatics standards.

The guidelines specified for implementation of role-based, group-based, and discretion approaches for access control can be implemented in any EHR system. However, for the role-based approach a clear distinction between roles maintained by PoS applications and EHRi is necessary. Separate policies need to be implemented to map roles of end-user applications and roles maintained by EHRi since it is important to log the actual user's credentials along with the hospital's credentials in the audit trial.

Legal Aspects. Introduction of acts, suitable laws, and codes help control user rights to access patient information to protect an individual's information when it is accessed electronically. These are integrated with the overall scope.

Exchange Specifications. The Canadian approach involves implementation of EHRS based on the EHRS Blueprint. Just publishing the Blueprint will not help achieve interoperability. Hence, to achieve interoperability in the true sense through adherence to medical informatics standards, the certification process is initiated by the implementing agency, Infoway. It examines each implemented component of the EHRS architecture on specific criteria [Infoway Certification].

Apart from the certification criteria, EHR Infostructure (EHRi) uses HL7 v3 messages for exchange of health information from PoS systems to data repositories and patient and provider registries. However, no public document is available that describes the internal storage schema or mechanisms.

For reports and diagnostics images, EHRi uses DICOM images, DICOM Structured Reports (SR), and CDA R2.

Canadian implementation surely is a good example of adhering to medical informatics standards not only for data content and its structures, but also for workflow. IHE Profiles for Cardiology, Access Control, and so on, are supported.

Technical Guidelines. EHRi framework is based on the Service-Oriented Architecture (SOA) and uses web services to provide different services in EHRi. SOA is part of communication services provided in Health Information Access Layer (HIAL). For digital certificates, PKI X.509 [PKI X.509] certificates are used.

22.5 Conclusion

Canada's implementation of the foundation for an interoperable EHR through a common EHRS provides one of the best ways to achieve interoperability through application of medical informatics standards and putting continued effort toward regulating implementation of such a solution in all jurisdictions of the country.

The access control service and policies considered by this implementation is a point of interest to evolve role-based, group-based, and discretion-based approach in distributed environment.

SOA is another area of consideration that must be focused on for implementation of health services on a national healthcare scenario.

The legal framework of Canada should certainly be considered for improving legal framework in a country to protect patient healthcare information.

BIBLIOGRAPHY

[**Arnold et al.**] Arnold, S., Wagner, J., Hyatt, S. J., and Klein, G. M., Electronic Health Records: A Global Perspective (2001).

[**Cornwall**] Cornwall, A., Electronic health records—An international perspective *Health Issues*, Number 73, 19–23 (2002); http://www.healthissuescentre.org.au/documents/items/2008/05/206744-upload-00001.pdf.

[**ebXML 2011**] Electronic Business Using eXtensible Markup Language; http://www.ebxml.org.

[**EHR Canada Audit**] Canada Audit Offices, An Overview of Federal and Provincial Audit Reports (April 2010); http://www.oag-bvg.gc.ca/internet/English/parl_oag_201004_07_e_33720.html.

[**EHRi DICOM**] Canada Health Infoway—Update DICOM Standards Committee (December 2008).

[**EHRi Privacy**] Electronic Health Record Infostructure (EHRi) Privacy and Security Conceptual Architecture; https://knowledge.infoway-inforoute.ca/EHRSRA/doc/EHR-Privacy-Security.pdf.

[**HL7**] Health Level 7; http://www.hl7.org.

[**HL7 v3**] Introduction to HL7v3; http://www.cihi.ca/cihiweb/en/downloads/v3Intro_e.pdf.

[**Giles et al. 2007**] Giles, G., Hagens, S., Kraetschmer, N., Hunter, C., and Muttitt, S., Towards evaluating quality, access and productivity—The creation of a pan-Canadian electronic health record evaluation framework. In: *CNIA Conference* (2007).

[**ICD-10 CA and CCI 2011**] Canada (ICD-10-CA) and the Canadian Classification of Health Interventions (CCI); https://secure.cihi.ca/estore/productSeries.htm?pc=PCC189.

[**IHE XDS 2011**] Integrated Health Enterprise XDS Implementation Profile; http://wiki.ihe.net/index.php?title=XDS.b_Implementation.

[**Infoway Certification**] Canada Infoway Certification Services; http://www.infoway-inforoute.ca/lang-en/working-with-ehr/solution-providers/certification.

[Infoway 2006] Canada Health Infoway and Health Council of Canada, Beyond Good Intentions: Accelerating the Electronic Health Record in Canada. In: *Policy Conference* (June 2006); http://www.healthcouncilcanada.ca/docs/papers/2006/infoway.pdf.

[Infoway EHRS Blueprint] Canada Health Infoway Inc., EHRS Blueprint – an interoperable EHR framework, (April 2008); https://www2.infoway-inforoute.ca/Documents/EHRS-Blueprint-v2-Exec-Overview.pdf.

[LOINC 2011] Logical Observation Identifiers Names and Codes; http://loinc.org.

[Morris 2010] Morris, A. A., The electronic health record in Canada—The first steps, *Health Law Review* (October 2010); http://www.law.ualberta.ca/centres/hli/userfiles/2_Morris.pdf.

[PIPEDA] Canada's Personal Information Protection and Electronic Documents Act (PIPEDA); http://laws.justice.gc.ca/eng/P-8.6.

[PKI X.509] X.509 standard for Public Key Infrastructure (PKI); http://www.itu.int/rec/T-REC-X.509/en.

[SNOMED CT 2011] SNOMED CT® homepage, (2011); http://www.ihtsdo.org/snomed-ct.

[Ulieru and Ionescu 2004] Ulieru, M., and Ionescu, D., Privacy and security shield for health information systems (e-Health). In: *IECON* (2004).

CHAPTER TWENTY-THREE

Denmark's MedCom

23.1 Introduction

Danish Electronic Health Record Observatory (EHR Observatory) in Denmark comprises of the Danish Centre for Health Telematics, Aalborg University and the consulting company MEDIQ. Since 1998, EHR Observatory is monitoring the development of EHR in Denmark.

Danish healthcare infrastructure is a nationwide healthcare network that facilitates sharing of healthcare information among the citizens of Denmark. It uses MedCom as the underlying data network for communication among healthcare services. The infrastructure development started in 2003 and is gradually moving toward the delivery of healthcare across the nation. It includes a process model of EHR, security infrastructure, and adherence to data exchange standards. *Basic Electronic Health Record (GEPJ) (Grundstruktur for Elektronisk Patientjournal* in Dutch) defines the structural model based on the conceptual process model [Vingtoft 2005].

23.2 Overview

Danish healthcare infrastructure provides access to the centralized healthcare information store through the national health portal and a set of web services. It has a well-defined security infrastructure to authenticate and authorize the users

Electronic Health Record: Standards, Coding Systems, Frameworks, and Infrastructures, Pradeep Sinha, Gaur Sunder, Prashant Bendale, Manisha Mantri, and Atreya Dande.
© 2013 by The Institute of Electrical and Electronics Engineers, Inc. Published 2013 by John Wiley & Sons, Inc.

of the system. Its EHR model is based on a well-planned clinical process model. In this model, an EHR is eventually a collection of medical records.

23.3 Architecture

23.3.1 EHR CONCEPT

The clinical process model of Danish Healthcare describes the "Period of Care" paradigm. It depicts a clinical process that revolves around a specific problem. The problem-oriented nature of the model requires linking of medical records generated by clinicians in different hospitals with the treatment of a particular problem. This concept matches with the patient's view of healthcare. From the patient's perspective, a health problem is the center point and a patient often visits multiple healthcare providers for its treatment. Eventually, what is relevant for a new doctor is the episode of care that took place until the current date for a particular problem.

Figure 23.1 depicts the Period of Care concept in a sequence of steps in delivering effective care.

When a patient visits a clinician, the clinician assesses the patient's health condition and reaches a diagnosis stage. After reaching a particular diagnosis, he/she sets a goal as a target health condition of the patient. Toward meeting this goal, the clinician plans for treatment. The patient follows the treatment plan for the specified period, and the clinician evaluates the outcome at each follow-up to compare it with the predefined goal. If the patient's health condition is not moving towards the goal, then the clinician may change the plan or reassess its symptoms. This way the cycle repeats until the clinician achieves the goal.

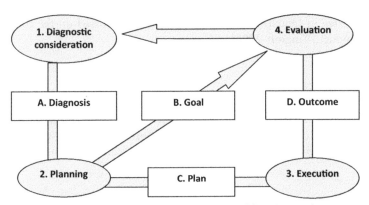

FIGURE 23.1   Danish EHR conceptual model. Adapted from [Asp and Petersen 2003].

23.3.2 EHR DESIGN

An integration process of existing healthcare IT systems in nationwide healthcare network triggered the development and refinement of the EHR structure. Initial development of the EHR structure was in the form of *Standardized Extracts of Patient's Data (SUP)* that gradually evolved as the *Basic Electronic Health Record (GEPJ in Danish)*. GEPJ follows the *Electronic Health Record Architecture standard (CEN/ISO EN 13606)* defining *Folder* containing *compositions* that can have Headed Section and Data Items [CEN EN 13606].

Standardized Extracts of Patient's Data (SUP). MedCom has developed the SUP standard for extracting administrative and clinical information from local systems in the form of XML files and for storing it in a centralized manner. Patients can view this data through national health portals but cannot download or update it. This is the initial stage conducted by MedCom to gather clinical information. When all the local systems will adhere to the MedCom standards, then the SUP will extract data more frequently and communication among the systems will be possible [Gartner 2006].

Basic Electronic Health Record (GEPJ in Danish). The National Board of Health in Denmark manages the structural model of the Basic Electronic Health Record. Based on the clinical process model and its different identified stages, the structural model of Danish EHR defines the contents for the following record types:

- Diagnosis
- Intervention
- Medication
- Patient Administration

GEPJ defines the summary level medical information of a patient that healthcare professionals can refer to during the present treatment. Data types in GEPJ are of two types: *Basic Primitive* and *Composite*. The composite data types are composed using the primitive data types. Detailed structure of record types in GEPJ is not available in public documentation [GEPJ and HL7 v3 2006].

23.3.3 DANISH HEALTH DATA NETWORK

The *Danish Centre for Health Telematics* started developing the *Danish Health Data Network*, called MedCom, in 1995. MedCom provides the underlying network for electronic communication of healthcare information across the nation. Initially, MedCom used the *Electronic Data Interchange For Administration, Commerce and Transport (EDIFACT)* as a standard for healthcare information communication. EDIFACT is an older specification adopted by ISO as a standard ISO 9735. EDIFACT has hierarchical structure containing segments with symbol to delimit segments with its own data types. It is another structural standard like HL7 v2.x standards. Later on, with the introduction of XML-technology, MedCom started using XML-based messages for interaction among systems. The current Danish healthcare infrastructure acts as a set of services hosted on the MedCom network.

23.3.4 SECURITY INFRASTRUCTURE

The Danish infrastructure also describes a comprehensive security mechanism for accessing information in the network. It uses the service-oriented approach to ensure secure access to healthcare information over MedCom.

Figure 23.2 shows secure access to healthcare infrastructure that is composed of web services. A Web Service user first authenticates itself with the Security Token Service (STS) that issues a short-lived PKI certificate to the user. Subsequent interactions of the user with the system include this certificate. The short-lived certificate provides single sign-on facility that enables the user to log on with the Certificate Authority (CA) server and allows web services to check authentication of the requesting user from the short-lived certificate itself.

23.3.5 NATIONAL HEALTH PORTAL (Sundheds.dk)

The Danish National Health Portal provides web-based access to medical records and healthcare services. This portal allows access based on the access policies defined for the users. Users need to provide digital certificates for accessing medical records of a patient [Danish Health Portal].

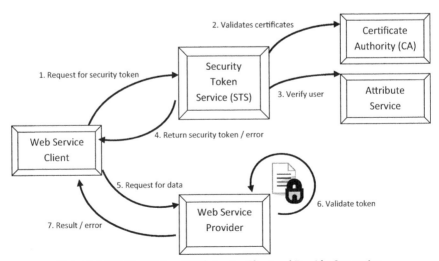

FIGURE 23.2 PKI-based Web Service Client and Provider Interaction.

23.3.6 EXCHANGE

The Danish infrastructure uses MedCom EDIFACT messaging standard for communication in earlier stages. Now the network is gradually moving toward adopting HL7 v3 messaging support along with EDIFACT support for backward compatibility with the older systems. For clinical terminologies in medical records, Danish healthcare infrastructure uses the localized SNOMED CT standard and also adopted SundTerms [Sundterms], a clinical terminology for describing local clinical terms in Denmark. EDIFACT is being mapped to HL7 v3 model.

The Danish model of healthcare IT infrastructure has a Service-Oriented approach. This infrastructure, called *Service-Oriented Systems Integration (SOSI)*, allows the systems in the network to interact with each other in a standard manner in which web services communicate. SOAP protocol is used which can carry XML information to the web service providers.

23.4 Discussion

Clinical Process Model. The Danish process model of EHR describes the thought process of clinicians, reflecting the real-life health problem-solving approach. This process describes the steps involved while solving a particular problem. This approach spans health records across hospitals because treatment of a health problem may involve many practitioners at different times. This is a good and helpful approach while designing any EHR model. The model is a sequential model starting with Diagnostic Consideration to Evaluation. EHR designers can refer to this clinical process model because it gives semantic meaning to the structural design of an EHR model.

Structural Model. GEPJ defines the summary level attributes for various types of medical records. Hence, considering the variety of medical records in a patient's life, the structural model needs to be more comprehensive in nature. Because it follows archetypes model, it is flexible enough to add archetypes for identified record types in the future. However, custom archetypes also create issues where different systems have different archetypes and thus are unable to interoperate. Along with this, the model needs to provide mapping with existing standards like HL7 v3, CDA, CCR, and so on, to be more flexible for changes in the infrastructure in the future.

Because the Danish EHR structural model follows the CEN/ISO EN 13606 standard, various types of archetype development are in progress. An issue with the archetype-based model is that while exchanging these records, a mapping needs to be there with exchange standards such as HL7 v3 messaging standard if not all the systems in a network are adhering to the same standard.

Security/Privacy Considerations. Security/privacy infrastructure in Denmark is clear and comprehensive for healthcare infrastructure. EHR system designers can refer to the approaches described in Danish healthcare infrastructure. They are as follows:

- *PKI* infrastructure-based security along with short-lived certificates ensures better security.
- *Security Assertion Markup Language (SAML)* for providing attribute-based policy specifications helps tackle complex conditions of access to health information.
- Single sign-on feature, which reduces the requirement of authentication to every healthcare service is guarded by introducing time-out security for short-lived certificates in the security framework.

Legal Aspects. Public documentation available for MedCom–Healthcare Data Network and Danish EHR Model do not explicitly describe the specifications for legal scenarios of health IT service in Denmark.

Exchange Specifications. MedCom was developed as healthcare data network having adherence to a set of exchange standards like XML, EDIFACT, and HL7 for communication over the healthcare network [MedCom 2003]. The EDIFACT standard is similar in structure to HL7 v2.x messaging standard. It lacks an information model and merely defines communication level segments' collection and data types. In a network where all systems adhere to the same standard, there will be no issue of data loss. However, it restricts systems to adhere to a single standard.

23.5 Conclusion

MedCom–Danish Healthcare Infrastructure uses the service-oriented approach for delivering healthcare services. Some of the notable points about it are:

- The healthcare network takes excellent care of security through PKI and SAML technologies.
- Adherence to EDI standards and making the existing systems adhere to a single standard is difficult where systems adhering to diverse medical informatics standards are present.
- EHR designers can refer to its clinical process model to realize a thought process behind the EHR model.

BIBLIOGRAPHY

[**Asp and Petersen 2003**] Asp, L., and Petersen, J., A conceptual model for documentation of clinical information in the HER. In: *Proceedings of PubMed* (2003); http://www.ncbi.nlm.nih.gov/pubmed/14663993.

[**Bernstein et al.**] Bernstein, K., Bruun-Rasmussen, M., Vingtoft, S., Andersen, S., and Nøhr, C., Modelling and Implementing Electronic Health Records in Denmark. http://www.epj-observatoriet.dk/publikationer/Bernstein-EHR-models.pdf.

[**CEN EN 13606**] CEN 13606-1 Reference model; http://www.gillogley.com/ehr_-cen_13606_reference_model.shtml.

[**Dalsgaard 2008**] Dalsgaard, E., Kjelstrøm, K., and Riis, J., A Federation of Web Services for Danish Health Care (2008); http://middleware.internet2.edu/idtrust/2008/papers/08-kjelstrom-health-federation.pdf.

[**Danish Health Portal**] Danish National Health Portal; https://www.sundhed.dk/.

[**Frank and Andersen 2010**] Frank, L., and Andersen, S. K., Evaluation of different database designs for integration of heterogeneous distributed electronic health records. In: *Proceedings of IEEE/ICME International Conference on Complex Medical Engineering (CME)* (2010).

[**Gartner 2006**] Gartner Industry Research, Case Study: Denmark's Achievements with Healthcare Information Exchange; http://www-03.ibm.com/industries/ca/en/healthcare/files/gartner-case_study-denmarks_achievementswHIE.pdf.

[**GEPJ and HL7 v3 2006**] Danish Standards, Comparing GEPJ and HL7 V3 (2006); http://www.epj-observatoriet.dk/konference2006/powerpoints/Comparing%20GEPJ%20and%20HL7%20v3.pdf.

[**MedCom 2003**] The European e-Business Watch, Case Study: MedCom—The Danish Healthcare Data Network (2003); http://www.ebusiness-watch.org/studies/case_-studies/documents/Case%20Studies%202004/CS_SR10_Health_1-MedCom.pdf.

[**MedCom 2006**] European Commision Information Society and Media, MedCom, Denmark—Danish Health Data Network," In: *Proceedings of DG INFSO,* (2006); http://ec.europa.eu/information_society/activities/health/docs/events/open-days2006/ehealth-impact-7-7.pdf

[**Sundterms**] Danish Local Coding System; http://www.sundterm.dk/.

[**UN/EDIFACT 2008**] UN/EDIFACT, Electronic Data Interchange for Administration, Commerce and Transport; http://en.wikipedia.org/wiki/EDIFACT.

[**Vingtoft 2005**] Vingtoft, S., Bruun-Rasmussen, M., Bernstein, K., Andersen, S., and Nøhr, C., EPJ-Observatoriet Statusrapport 2005. In: *Proceedings of EPJ-Observatoriet* (2005); http://www.epj-observatoriet.dk/publikationer/Statusrapport2005.pdf.

CHAPTER TWENTY-FOUR

Hong Kong's eHR Sharing System

24.1 Introduction

Hong Kong has set up an ecosystem of computerized health records in Hong Kong territory. However, lack of participation of the private sector was a hurdle in achieving nationwide e-Health delivery in Hong Kong. The government's initiative, known as the *E-Health Engagement Initiative (EEI),* is now attracting the private sector to join e-Health efforts in the country. For this purpose, the government has started a pilot with the vision to complete it by 2014 for adoption of a nationwide *eHR Sharing System.* The eHR Sharing System will enable public and private sectors to view, share, and add health information of patients upon their consent.

The government of Hong Kong has set up an *eHR Office* to set out national information infrastructure for making eHR sharing possible. Efforts for this initiative are underway, and currently the eHR office has released *eHR Content Index* and *eHR Codex Index* along with *eHR Interoperability Specifications* [EEI 2010].

24.2 Overview

Hong Kong has *Hospital Authority (HA),* which manages all public hospitals in the country. HA has taken the initiative to computerize healthcare delivery

Electronic Health Record: Standards, Coding Systems, Frameworks, and Infrastructures, Pradeep Sinha, Gaur Sunder, Prashant Bendale, Manisha Mantri, and Atreya Dande.
© 2013 by The Institute of Electrical and Electronics Engineers, Inc. Published 2013 by John Wiley & Sons, Inc.

primarily starting with the Patient Registration System in 1991. This effort led to an authorized patient registration database. This data was used to form *Hong Kong Patient Master Index (HKPMI)* with public hospitals. A later initiative in 1995 by HA to establish a *Clinic Management System (CMS)* in Hong Kong public hospitals resulted in capturing healthcare information electronically in all public hospitals. Experiences have shown that the CMS system helped the government in capturing information in cases of disease outbursts, epidemics, and other statistical information across the country. The private sector is yet to become involved in these efforts. To achieve this, the government of Hong Kong has rolled out the EEI program targeting the adoption of the eHR Sharing System across the country by the year 2014.

24.3 Architecture

The Hong Kong eHR initiative has two phases. The first phase is to develop the eHR Information Standard in Hong Kong for the *eHR Sharing System*. The second phase is to enable the private healthcare sector to contribute to the eHR Sharing System. This involves enabling their existing EMR/eHR systems to adopt information, security, and interoperability standards specified by the eHR Sharing System infrastructure.

24.3.1 E-HEALTH ENGAGEMENT INITIATIVE (EEI)

Hong Kong's EEI program is a two-stage program. Since there is already a wide proliferation of IT in the public healthcare domain through HA, the eHR Office decided to leverage the same model and bring the private healthcare sector into it. The eHR Office started implementation of the program in the year 2009. This two-stage program will run for 10 years starting in 2009 [EEI 2010].

First Stage. The eHR Office started the first stage in the year 2009 and plans to end in 2014 with the following objectives:

- Development of eHR Sharing System connecting public and private hospitals.
- Development of *electronic Medical Record/electronic Patient Record (eMR/ePR)* systems for healthcare providers in the private sector to connect to eHR Sharing system.
- Development of legal framework for ensuring privacy of healthcare information.

The public healthcare sector is already using the Clinical Management System to manage patient's records and share them among all clinics/hospitals in the public sector. The eHR Office decided to build an eHR Sharing System leveraging the same infrastructure following the standards in EHR architecture, terminology, and messaging. They have defined the following guiding principles for development of the eHR Sharing System:

- Patient-focused and patient-controlled system.
- Operated by government for patients and clinics/hospitals.
- Managing patient privacy considering legal, ethical, and technical issues.
- Built on "Hub and Spoke" model where medical practitioners can continue using their existing systems while contributing a defined set of healthcare information to the eHR Sharing System.

Second Stage. The eHR Office plans the second stage to run from 2015 to 2019 for expanding the reach of the eHR Sharing System in the nation. The second stage mostly involves private sector engagement in wide usage of the eHR Sharing System. The second stage will be more concretely planned, depending upon the outputs of the first stage.

24.3.2 eHR SHARING SYSTEM

The Healthcare information infrastructure of Hong Kong takes care of almost all aspects of national EHR efforts. Figure 24.1 shows its components [EEI 2010].

The vision of the eHR Sharing System is to build an EHR core acting as an EHR repository. The government, public and private healthcare sectors, along with central clinic management software, can contribute healthcare information to this repository. The access portal having a patient-centric view will provide access to this eHR repository.

eHR Sharing Infrastructure. The eHR Sharing Infrastructure is built on the "Hub and Spoke" model and is based on the following principles:

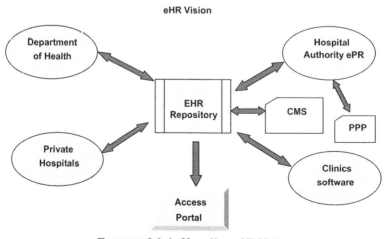

FIGURE 24.1 Hong Kong eHR Vision.

- **Building block approach:** To develop a large infrastructure through smaller components and refinement as per user requirements.
- **Service-oriented architecture:** To ensure extensibility and reusability.
- **Building security in:** To ensure secure access to healthcare information.
- **Built-in sustainability:** To ensure preservation of healthcare information beyond the life of a patient having a lifetime view of a patient's records.
- **High-level system serviceability:** To ensure 99.9% service availability in the healthcare domain.

Development of eHR Sharing System involves two major components:

1. *CMS Adaptation.* Since HA is already using the Clinic Management System (CMS) throughout the public healthcare sector, the eHR Office decided to develop CMS adapters that will help existing eMR/ePR systems in the private sector to connect to the central eHR Sharing System and share information in expected format.

2. *CMS on-ramp.* With the vision to provide low-cost solution to the private sector, eHR Office started the development of CMS on-ramp, an open source Clinic Management System. It is usable directly by the private sector, ensuring data sharing with the central eHR Sharing system.

eHR Contents. The eHR Office defines eHR as the *womb-to-tomb electronic longitudinal health record comprising all health data of a person.* The purpose of the eHR, according to the eHR Office, is to ensure sufficient information during the transfer/discharge of a patient. For this, it follows the identification of record types from ASTM CCR standard. eHR Contents include the following record types [eHR Contents]:

- Person demographics
- Healthcare practitioner
- Encounters
- Referral
- Episode summary
- Adverse reactions/allergies
- Problems
- Procedures
- Assessment/Physical examination
- Social history
- Past medical history
- Family history
- Medication

- Immunization
- Clinical requests
- Diagnostic test results (laboratory/radiology/others)
- Care and treatment plan

Guidelines given by the eHR Office include specification for the minimum information to be provided while sharing healthcare information with eHR Sharing system. This information includes:

- Person's eHR identifier
- Person's identification data
- Data creation/updation information
- Practitioner's information who creates clinical data

24.3.3 EXCHANGE

Use of HL7 v2.5. To describe data types and contents of each of the above-mentioned record types, the eHR model specifies the use of HL7 v2.5 standard as the base. For example, to describe immunization report, the model identifies various fields required for immunization information and specifies HL7 v2.5 standard data types for each of these fields.

Use of HL7 v3 and CDA. Current specifications by the eHR Office specify the usage of HL7 v3 and HL7 CDA standards for the eHR Information Model. It defines the communication framework involving two components. One is Event (such as patient registration) and the other is Document (such as any clinical record or report). Thus, the eHR Office specifies the use of HL7 v3 for Patient Administration-related activities to update the *Hong Kong Patient Master Index (HKPMI)* maintained by HA for all patients visiting public healthcare hospitals, and CDA is used for representing any other clinical information. The eHR Data Interoperability Standard document describes the mapping for fields in these record types with the HL7 v3 and CDA standards [eHR Interoperability 2009].

Use of Integrated Terminology Standard. The Hong Kong eHR Sharing System has developed the Hong Kong Clinical Terminology Table (HKCCT), which maps clinical concepts used in Hong Kong healthcare practices with international terminology standards such as LOINC, SNOMED CT, ICD and HA's own Hong Kong Clinical Vocabulary Table (HKCVT) [Lau 2012].

24.3.4 SECURITY/PRIVACY GUIDELINES

The standardization study conducted by the eHR Office recommends using security guidelines given by ASTM E31.20, ISO/TC 215 Working Group 4, and CEN/TC 251 Working Group 3 on security and privacy. It gives importance to the process of assigning unique identifiers to patients and healthcare providers. It suggests using the Hong Kong Identifier Number (for age above 11) and the Birth Certificate Number (for age below 11) as identifiers in the eHR Sharing System. The infrastructure relies on digital certificates and biometric information available to the government through HKID smart cards as the primary means of validated access [Fung 2006].

24.4 Discussion

Clinical Process Model. The Hong Kong eHR information infrastructure identifies a collection of clinical record types that can be part of an EHR. From the clinical process model perspective, the Hong Kong EHR is not representing any specific EHR process as such. The Information Standard given by the eHR Office is very specific about the structural content descriptions of clinical information.

Structural Model. The structural model of the eHR Sharing System is essentially a collection of clinical record types. All obvious record types are included. Record types in the model also include clinical requests. A clinical request describes who has requested what kind of records at what time. This informs the owner of the EHR to decide whether the request needs to be approved or not. However, having it as a part of the model is different from EHRs where this information is stored as audit and log only. EHR designers can refer to these record types for defining a comprehensive set of record types while designing an EHR framework. The attribute structure set is almost the same as CDA.

Security/Privacy Considerations. In the eHR Sharing System, identification of a user is very important from a security and privacy perspective. Hong Kong has the national unique ID infrastructure in place. As the security model of the eHR Sharing System follows the guidelines given by standards bodies, it is a good approach and covers the identity issues in IT systems. Use of smart cards ensures a user's authentication and authorization approved by some authority such as HA.

Legal Aspects. The eHR Sharing System in Hong Kong does not have Hong Kong-specific legal guidelines for e-health delivery. The Hong Kong model describes that patient information should be shared only in anonymized form for research and statistical purposes, and any additional information should be shared only on patient consent. For this purpose, clinical request record type is added to the patient record. On this basis, the system records a patient's consent. However, guidelines do not mention the exact attributes to be anonymized.

Exchange Specifications. The eHR Sharing System uses HL7 v3 (earlier used HL7 v2.5) and CDA for recording clinical information. This ensures that the captured data are all homogenous and that, once part of the system, all participating systems can access it easily. However, this approach has two drawbacks: One, it is not future proof when new revisions of the standard come out; and second, while converting from original to the specified format, not only possible data loss occurs, but the original format is not captured at all and may be lost forever. Without an external safeguard, this may have legal implications.

The second-stage implementation includes development of a national shared Image Archive and a Browser for radiological data supporting DICOM as exchange standard.

Recommendable Approach of Integrated Terminology. Use of the Hong Kong Clinical Terminology Table (HKCTT) is a recommendable approach in the eHR Sharing System. Comprehensive study of existing terminology standards and their applicability in the Hong Kong healthcare domain will help in coming out with the HKCTT. It will keep the map of not only international terminologies but also local terminologies. It will also provide terminologies for local concepts for which there is no equivalent mention in the international terminologies.

24.5 Conclusion

The overall infrastructure of the eHR Sharing System is in line with the development of an EHR framework. The approach taken toward integrating local EMR/EHR or HIS systems to contribute healthcare information to the central eHR Sharing System is recommendable with a concrete national program with long vision. However, the approach of promoting the same Clinic Management System (CMS) for all healthcare providers may turn out to be less interesting for private players.

A very useful and recommendable approach in this infrastructure is the development of HKCTT for terminologies that will cater to existing terminology standards along with the support for local clinical terms. However, the *Unified Medical Language System (UMLS)* is one such effort available in international terminologies. Maybe extension to UMLS vocabulary including mapping to local terminologies can also serve the same purpose.

The mapping provided with HL7 v3 for patient demographics and CDA for other medical records is quite clear. However, this approach demands adherence to these standards by every healthcare provider contributing to the eHR Sharing system.

BIBLIOGRAPHY

[EEI 2010] eHealth Record Office Food and Health Bureau, *Second Stage Electronic Health Record Engagement Initiative (2nd Stage EEI)*, (2010); http://www.ehealth. gov.hk/en/doc/invitation_booklet_en.pdf.

[eHR Development Overview] Hong Kong Hospital Authority, *Overview of eHR Development.*

[eHR Interoperability 2009]   eHR Information Standards Office, *eHR Data Interoperability Standards* (2009).

[eHR Contents]   eHR Standards Office, *Appendix i—eHR Contents;* http://www.ehealth. gov.hk/en/information_standards/information_standards_documents/appendix_ i_ehr_contents.html.

[eHR Allergy Specifications]   eHR Standards Office, *Appendix i—eHR Contents: Allergy;* http://www.ehealth.gov.hk/en/doc/annex1/allergy.pdf.

[eHR Assessment Specifications]   eHR Standards Office, *Appendix i—eHR Contents: Assessment;* http://www.ehealth.gov.hk/en/doc/annex1/assessment.pdf.

[eHR Care Treatment Plan Specifications]   eHR Standards Office, *Appendix i—eHR Contents: Care Treatment Plan;* http://www.ehealth.gov.hk/en/doc/annex1/care_ and_treatment_plan.pdf.

[eHR Drug Dispense Specifications]   eHR Standards Office, *Appendix i—eHR Contents: Drug Dispense;* http://www.ehealth.gov.hk/en/doc/annex1/drug_ dispense.pdf.

[eHR Drug Order Specifications]   eHR Standards Office, *Appendix i—eHR Contents: Drug Order;* http://www.ehealth.gov.hk/en/doc/annex1/drug_order.pdf.

[eHR Encounter Specifications]   eHR Standards Office, *Appendix i—eHR Contents: Encounter;* http://www.ehealth.gov.hk/en/doc/annex1/encounter.pdf.

[eHR Episode Summary Specifications]   eHR Standards Office, *Appendix i—eHR Contents: Episode Summary;* http://www.ehealth.gov.hk/en/doc/annex1/episode_ summary.pdf.

[eHR Family History Specifications]   eHR Standards Office, *Appendix i—eHR Contents: Family History;* http://www.ehealth.gov.hk/en/doc/annex1/family_ history.pdf.

[eHR Immunization Specifications]   eHR Standards Office, *Appendix i—eHR Contents: Immunization;* http://www.ehealth.gov.hk/en/doc/annex1/immunisation.pdf.

[eHR Laboratory Result Specifications]   eHR Standards Office, *Appendix i—eHR Contents: Laboratory Result;* http://www.ehealth.gov.hk/en/doc/annex1/laborator-y_result.pdf.

[eHR Order Specifications]   eHR Standards Office, *Appendix i—eHR Contents: Order;* http://www.ehealth.gov.hk/en/doc/annex1/order.pdf.

[eHR Past Medical History Specifications]   eHR Standards Office, *Appendix i—eHR Contents: Past Medical History;* http://www.ehealth.gov.hk/en/doc/annex1/past_ medical_history.pdf.

[eHR Person Specifications]   eHR Standards Office, *Appendix i — eHR Contents: Person;* http://www.ehealth.gov.hk/en/doc/annex1/person.pdf.

[eHR Practitioner Specifications]   eHR Standards Office, *Appendix i—eHR Contents: Practitioner;* http://www.ehealth.gov.hk/en/doc/annex1/practitioner.pdf.

[eHR Problem Specifications]   eHR Standards Office, *Appendix i—eHR Contents: Problem;* http://www.ehealth.gov.hk/en/doc/annex1/problem.pdf.

[eHR Procedure Specifications]   eHR Standards Office, *Appendix i—eHR Contents: Procedure;* http://www.ehealth.gov.hk/en/doc/annex1/procedure.pdf.

[eHR Radiology Result Specifications]   eHR Standards Office, *Appendix i—eHR Contents: Radiology Result;* http://www.ehealth.gov.hk/en/doc/annex1/radiology_ result.pdf.

[**eHR Referral Specifications**]   eHR Standards Office, *Appendix i—eHR Contents: Referral;* http://www.ehealth.gov.hk/en/doc/annex1/referral.pdf.

[**eHR Social History Specifications**]   eHR Standards Office, *Appendix i—eHR Contents: Social History;* http://www.ehealth.gov.hk/en/doc/annex1/social_history.pdf.

[**EHR Benefit and Challenges**]   eHealth Record Office Food and Health Bureau, *Electronic Health Record Sharing—Benefits and Challenges.*

[**Fung 2006**]   Fung, V., *White paper on Standardization of Health Data* (2006); http://www.openclinical.org/whitepaperHKstandards.html.

[**HK eHR Authority 2010**]   eHR Record Office (2010); http://www.ehealth.gov.hk/en/index5.html.

[**HK Terminology Standards 2010**]   eHR Information Standards Office, *Position Paper on Terminology Management for Electronic Health Record* (2010).

[**Lau 2012**]   Briefing on eHR Content – Problem and Procedure; http://www.ehealth.gov.hk/en/doc/slides/5_DxPx.pdf.

CHAPTER TWENTY-FIVE

India's Health IT Initiatives

25.1 Introduction

Like many other countries, India has also taken several initiatives for creating IT infrastructure for healthcare in the nation. The key initiatives toward this are:

1. *Information Technology Infrastructure for Health (ITIH) Framework.* It provides guidelines for standardizing the collection, storage, and transmission of electronic health data across different entities.

2. *Recommendations on Guidelines, Standards & Practices for Telemedicine in India (RGSPTI).* It provides recommendations for standardizing Telemedicine practices to enable Interoperability and Continuity of Care through telemedicine.

3. *Indian Health Information Network Development (iHIND).* It is a recommendation and development plan for promoting use of ICT in health care and knowledge management.

Apart from these, there are several ICT-based healthcare programs initiated by the Indian Union Ministry of Health & Family Welfare (*UMoH&FW*). Indian state governments have also, in recent years, moved to adopt ICT in healthcare delivery.

Electronic Health Record: Standards, Coding Systems, Frameworks, and Infrastructures, Pradeep Sinha, Gaur Sunder, Prashant Bendale, Manisha Mantri, and Atreya Dande.
© 2013 by The Institute of Electrical and Electronics Engineers, Inc. Published 2013 by John Wiley & Sons, Inc.

25.2 Overview

The Information Technology Infrastructure for Health (*ITIH*) framework is a collaborative effort of the *Ministry of Communication & Information Technology (MCIT)* with *Apollo Health Street Ltd. (AHSL)* as the supporting agency. It aims to standardize electronic healthcare practices across the country to enable interoperability.

Recommendations on Guidelines, Standards, and Practices for Telemedicine in India are developed by the *Union Ministry of Health and Family Welfare* under the *National Task Force for Telemedicine in India* for streamlining the practices for Telemedicine in India. It aims to standardize telemedicine practices for seamless flow of data while treating a patient through telemedicine [Telemedicine Guidelines 2007].

The Indian Health Information Network Development (*iHIND*) is an initiative/recommendation by the *National Knowledge Commission (NKC)* [NKC] (it is an advisory body to the Prime Minister of India) under healthcare as one of the knowledge areas. It aims to develop an Indian health information network to facilitate connectivity between healthcare providers across the country and provide a medium for transmitting healthcare data in electronic form.

Some other ongoing national initiatives/projects in the country built over ICT include:

- Integrated Disease Surveillance Project (*IDSP*)
- National Rural Telemedicine Network (*NRTN*)
- National Medical College Network (*NMCN*)
- Formation of EHR standardization committee

25.3 ITIH Framework

The vision of the ITIH [ITIH] for Indian healthcare system is quoted as:

> *To define Information Technology Infrastructure for Health in India that will standardize the capture, storage, and exchange of health information in an environment supported by a robust legal framework and a mature health informatics education system that will bring administrative simplification and improve patient care services by providing a continuum of care.*

ITIH provides recommendations in the following areas of HIT:

1. ***Billing Formats.*** It recommends eight billing formats for use in health insurance area such as subscription and un-subscription plans, insurance payments, billing for covered services, insurance claims, and so on. The aim is to upgrade from a paper-based billing system to an electronic form.

2. *Clinical Data Representation.* It recommends ICD-10-CM for disease codes, ICD-10-PCS for procedure codes, and LOINC for observation codes. The selection of coding systems was done through analysis for usability, cost effectiveness, stability, and information provided in specific context. In its analysis, the ITIH committee recorded that ICD codes are cost effective, widely used, and easily adaptable and contain in-depth information of diseases and procedures. Similarly, LOINC codes are widely used for providing detailed specifications for observation codes across the world.

3. *Data Elements.* It provides detailed list of data elements for Patient Demographics, Hospital Administration, and Health Insurance.

4. *Health Identifiers.* It provides detailed specification for the structure of identifiers for patients, healthcare providers, and organizations for seamless identification of participants in care activities.

5. *Messaging Standards.* It analyzes different standards for information exchange in healthcare IT such as HL7 for messaging in health information systems, X12 for communication of insurance data, and DICOM for imaging. The recommendations include a separate guideline for proposing standards for data transfer and development of Indian version of HL7.

6. *Minimum Data Sets.* It recommends Minimum Data Sets (*MDS*) to enable sharing of minimally required data for treating a patient from one hospital to another. It divides MDS into two types: MDS common for all kinds of diseases and MDS for specific diseases in India. The diseases considered for the latter type include:

   a. Cancer

   b. Diabetes

   c. Cardiovascular diseases

   d. Gastroenterology-related diseases

MDS recommendations for specific diseases include:

   a. Disease assessment

   b. Disease stage

   c. Risk factors

   d. Complications

   e. Treatment

   f. Outcomes

The recommended MDS common to all kinds of diseases includes:

   a. Referrals

   b. Demographics

A detailed attribute list for each MDS is provided in the guideline.

7. *Health Informatics Education.* It provides the guidelines for health informatics courses that can be useful to all players in healthcare industry for efficiently using IT in healthcare.

8. *Privacy and Confidentiality of Health Information.* It proposes to formalize a law covering legal aspects of healthcare industry while using health informatics such as security, accessibility, accountability, legal policies, and so on.

25.4 Recommendations on Guidelines, Standards, and Practices for Telemedicine in India

This set of recommendations is the result of year-long deliberation involving experts from UMoH&FW, MCIT, R&D institution, major hospitals in India, and industry representatives. This document is the most comprehensive recommendation that builds on the ITIH created earlier. Although the scope is to cover the guidelines for telemedicine, it goes beyond that and makes important recommendations for standards, concepts, codes, format, and so on. In fact, its recommendations for each of these domains are fully applicable in any domain of healthcare.

It provides specifications for the following components involved during telemedicine practices:

1. *Guidelines for Patient Management Process.* It specifies that during telemedicine, a common standard process for treating patients should be followed across organizations in the country. The process involves Patient Interview Assessment, Final Diagnosis and Treatment, and Follow-up. The cycle can repeat with reassessment.

2. *Guidelines for Civil and Support Infrastructure.* It specifies that a civil infrastructure used for telemedicine, called *Telemedicine Node*, should support proper functioning of the system, patient privacy, safety from environmental conditions, and proper connectivity during telemedicine sessions.

   Additionally, it mentions about provision of supportive services and infrastructure for overall better patient care during telemedicine such as Ambulatory Services, Pharmaceutical support at *Remote Consultation Centers (RCCs)*, and so on.

   It also specifies that every telemedicine node should be registered with the *National Telemedicine Grid* through a proposed regulatory body, called *Telemedicine Promotion Board of India (TPBI)*. This is to ensure that it meets the specifications for hardware, software and supported HIT standards. A unique registration identifier will be given to each telemedicine center called *Unique Telemedicine Service Provider ID (TSPID)*.

3. *Standards for Hardware.* It provides hardware specifications for supporting the minimally required configurations for working of telemedicine. The

hardware specifications includes telemedicine interface, video conferencing system, hardware used for interfacing telemedicine systems with communication networks, and so on.

4. ***Standards for Software.*** It provides software specifications for telemedicine such as operating system, telemedicine software, and user interface. It also specifies various functionalities that telemedicine software should possess. The functionalities include capture, storage, display and transmission of patient information, scheduling, and device integration for data capture from clinical devices.

5. ***Standards for Data Format.*** The data format suggested for telemedicine includes Textual data (ASCII text or Human readable), Still Image data (includes JPEG, GIF, PNG, TIFF, Bitmap, DICOM, etc.), Motion Pictures (includes MPEG, DICOM, AVI), Audio Signal (PCM, AIFF/AIFF-C, WAV, MP3, Lossless FLAC, TTA, WMA), signals, waveforms, and binary data.

It also gives recommendations for the use of clinical codes such as ICD-10 for Diseases, ICD-10-PCS for Procedures, and LOINC for Observations. It has recommended CDT-2 specifically for Dental Procedures.

6. ***Standards for EMR/HER.*** Because EMR/EHR is one of the required components for telemedicine for sharing of medical data during tele-consultation, the recommendations for standards for EHR/EMR in terms of structure, storage, security, data sets, and so on. are suggested.

It suggests the following records to be maintained in an EMR/EHR:

a. Patient Information

b. History

c. Case (episode or problem for which a patient needs care)

d. Visit (record of encounters for an episode)

e. Procedures

f. Follow-ups

g. Clinical data for supported modalities such as Cardiology, Pathology, Radiology, and so on.

h. Opinion/Advice

EHR must follow the "As-Is principle" for data storage to preserve the meaning of data. An explicit consent should be taken from the user before changing the format of the data in the system. It does not impose any restriction for internal storage of data but suggests W3C XML schema.

It suggests the use of compression techniques during data transmission over network (suggested techniques include *Run Length Encoding (RLE)*, IEEE standard, ZIP, Huffman Encoding-based compression, Shannon–Fano Encoding-based compression). In order to provide data security, it suggests the use of *Triple Data Encryption Standard (3DES)* and *Advanced Encryption Standard (AES)* encryption techniques.

For standardizing data sets in suggested records, it recommends to follow the Minimum Data Sets (*MDS*) defined in ITIH. Based on that, it has defined Common/Minimum Data Sets (CDS/MDS) for the following records:

a. Protected Patient Health Information (Patient Identification information)
b. Demographics other than identification
c. Clinical Data
d. Investigation Data
e. Clinical Opinion

The standard suggests the use of national unique integer identification number, for which Government of India has already started a project named "Aadhar" [UIDAI Aadhar].

7. **Standards for Data Transmission.** It specifies the transmission mechanisms for application-to-application communication and transmission through other media such as e-mail, fax, and so on. It recommends different data exchange standards such as ANSI/HL7 v3 compatible with ANSI/HL7 v2.5, CDA for clinical documents, and NEMA DICOM PS 3-2004 for image data. It also suggests that the standard should be updated periodically for being up-to-date with the evolution of newer data exchange standards in future.

8. **Security Aspects.** It specifies the minimum requirements for different security aspects including authentication, integrity of data, privacy, security, and so on, and suggests the mechanisms for achieving them. The guidelines are compliant with *IT Act of India*. It also suggests the provision of transport level security through Secured Socket Layer (*SSL*), Transport Layer Security (*TLS*), and Virtual Private Network (*VPN*). It recommends use of *3DES* and *AES* as encryption algorithms for transmitting data over networks. It also suggests the provision of audit log for access, update, or insert of data.

9. **Standards Data Encoding.** It specifies the use of *ASCII* and *Unicode* (UTF-8, UTF-16) as data encoding formats for textual data. It gives emphasis on using Unicode for supporting multiple languages and for making data convertible from one language to another.

10. **Legal Aspects.** It suggests the various legal policies such as data retention policy, consent management, dispute resolution, data ownership, and so on. Additionally, it specifies that while sharing a patient's data there should be consideration of the patient's rights.

It also specifies the inclusion of records related to insurance in the context of telemedicine and educational course for healthcare professionals toward health informatics.

25.5 iHIND

National Knowledge Commission (*NKC*) of India has the mandate to study and propose solutions for a host of issues. NKC created an expert group under the project iHIND to study and propose improvements in healthcare delivery using ICT, especially in rural India [iHIND].

NKC has given the following recommendations for the improvement of healthcare delivery in the country [NKC Recommendations]:

1. Initiate the development of Indian Health Information Network.
2. Establish national standards for clinical terminology and health informatics.
3. Create a common HER.
4. Frame policies to promote the use of IT in healthcare.
5. Create appropriate policy framework to protect health data of citizens.
6. Medical Informatics to be part of medical and paramedical curriculum.
7. Create an institutional framework for implementation.

iHIND proposes to provide connectivity between healthcare providers throughout the country and enable electronic transaction of health records. This network will be used as the backbone for implementing nationwide EHR, where health records of all individuals would be stored in a secured manner enabling preservation of clinical knowledge. Sharing of information between scientists and end users will ultimately improve healthcare quality in the country. iHIND would be helpful in national disaster management because real-time connectivity will allow improved care. Similarly, it can be utilized in various areas of healthcare such as drug surveillance, reduction in medical errors, insurance, and so on.

iHIND project aims to:

1. Identify the technologies and network infrastructures.
2. Define standards for data sharing, data protection, and business practices.
3. Identify strategies for widespread use of health information network.
4. Define strategies for promoting health information exchange.

25.5.1 ARCHITECTURE

iHIND proposes a national health information network that follows a "hub-and-spoke" model. Each district of the country will act as a Hub and all healthcare provider organizations including hospitals, institutes, insurance agencies, and so on. will act as spokes, responsible for sharing data at *District Hub*. Each District Hub will be connected to its *State-Level Data Warehouse* having a network server. A diagrammatic representation of the architecture is given in Figure 25.1.

A pilot project for its implementation is in progress. It includes implementation of the same architecture in two districts so that on success, same model can be replicated. Each district will represent a model of *Regional Health Information Organizations* (*RHIO*). It defines RHIO as a multi-stakeholder organization that

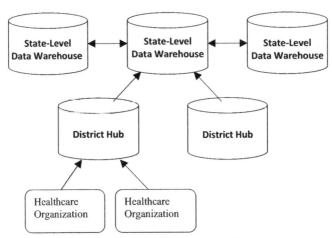

FIGURE 25.1 iHIND network architecture.

enables exchange and use of health information in a secure manner for promoting improvement of health quality, safety, and efficiency.

iHIND will store data from all healthcare organizations in a secured manner and provide its retrieval in real time, depending on the applied access policies. It is mentioned that *National Health Information Authority* (*NHIA*) should be responsible for applying those security and access policies.

iHIND describes a generic healthcare process. However, the described process appears to be more specific to storing Encounter details of a patient. It provides a list of required attributes for Encounter, Clinical Record, and Demographic Records.

25.5.2 CONFIDENTIALITY, ACCESS, AND SECURITY

iHIND considers a patient as the owner of his/her health record. Privacy and security of data will be maintained through the authorization mechanisms. A written authorization letter signed by a patient's authorized doctor will be required for giving access permissions to any other user. The patient data will be used in anonymized manner for public health, medical education, and research purpose.

iHIND provides general data security using symmetric key encryption. The exchanges of data should take place over Secured Socket Layer (*SSL*). Every action on an EHR will be audit logged.

25.5.3 STANDARDS

For incorporating data attributes as per national requirements, iHIND uses multiple standards depending on the type of clinical information. It has listed all possible clinical coding systems used for recording codes for observations, procedures, disease, allergies, and so on. It has considered HL7 v2.5, CDA, and DICOM for data exchange while SOAP over TCP/IP as transmission protocol.

25.6 Other Initiatives

There are other projects and initiatives for promoting the use of HIT in clinical practices in the country. Some of them are described below:

25.6.1 INTEGRATED DISEASE SURVEILLANCE PROJECT

In response to the need of early detection of potential epidemic diseases in the country, Government of India started a project named Integrated Disease Surveillance Project (*IDSP*) in the year 2004. The project takes a decentralized approach for surveillance of diseases, where every state in the country independently runs this project. Each state represents a State Surveillance Unit (*SSU*). All SSUs have to report to a Central Surveillance Unit (*CSU*). A SSU has several District Surveillance Units (*DSUs*) and every DSU constitutes Reporting Units (*RUs*). The project helps in delivering timely and effective public health information for health challenges in the country [IDSP].

Survey data are collected for 13 major diseases occurring in the country. The data are collected and reported to the SSUs on a weekly basis, depending on surveillance need of a disease (whether it needs a regular, sentinel, or periodic surveillance). At every SSU, these data are converted in electronic form and sent to the CSU with analysis reports.

IDSP initiative uses both paper system and electronic system for covering information. It has electronic forms at SSU level and CSU level for each disease covered in the program. These forms have been designed to capture all relevant details for statistical as well as analytical study.

Data collected by IDSP across the country are helpful in the following ways:

1. Preparation for high-priority diseases and risk factors can be done at early stages.
2. The occurrence of disease can be prevented and efficiency of existing healthcare programs can be improved

Currently, the project is implemented and running in many states of the country [IDSP Karnataka].

25.6.2 NATIONAL RURAL TELEMEDICINE NETWORK (NRTN)

To enable access to healthcare services in rural parts of the country, the Ministry of Health & Family Welfare started a mission program named National Rural Health Mission (*NRHM*) in the year 2005. It aims to provide accessible, affordable, and accountable quality health services to the people living in remote parts of the country [NRHM; NRHM Mission].

One of the requirements of the program is to develop a network for bringing such health services at the doorstep. To address this need, a project called National Rural Telemedicine Network (*NRTN*) was proposed. The technical architecture for building a low-cost telemedicine network for the nation is formulated in NRTN [NRTN].

The NRHM program is implemented separately at different states by the state government to make it a nationwide activity. As part of the pilot project. Union Government funded the states for setting up and running the service professionally.

NRTN architecture covers different regions of the country with specifications for healthcare services depending on technical accessibility and population. It includes the following four levels of healthcare centers:

1. **Level 1** - It could be a Primary Healthcare Center (*PHC*) that connects to Level 2.

2. **Level 2** - It could be a District Hospital that connects to Level 3.

3. **Level 3** - It could be a State Hospital that connects to every other Level.

4. **Level M** - It is a Mobile Telemedicine Unit covering some villages connected to the nearest Level 1 or directly to Level 2.

The architecture provides the complete specification of the technical infrastructure with an estimated cost of building this network for the identified number of District Hospitals, PHCs, State Hospitals, and Mobile Telemedicine Units.

25.6.3 NATIONAL MEDICAL COLLEGE NETWORK

Union Ministry of Health and Family Welfare under the National Task Force on Telemedicine has planned a project called National Medical College Network. The project aims to provide telemedicine services for medical education by connecting medical collages with academic medical institutes of the nation. These institutes will act as *Regional Hubs* while each connected medical college will act as a *Node*. Data will be collected at all the nodes and will be stored at the respective Regional Hubs.

A pilot project for Phase 1 implementation of this network is planned where few Regional Hubs are identified with their corresponding regional hospitals. Users at hospitals in a region will send data to their respective Regional Hub and experts at the Regional Hub will respond to their queries through telemedicine. This will lead to knowledge sharing and better patient care [Mishra; Mishra et al. 2008; Mishra 2011].

25.6.4 STANDARDIZATION OF EHR

Penetration and development of health informatics applications in India have picked up significantly in the last decade. This led to many EMR applications placed in different hospitals. The applications developed are not always interoperable due to lack of standard guidelines for EMR in the country. To address the issue of use of standard healthcare data representation and format by healthcare applications in the country, Ministry of Health and Family Welfare had constituted an EMR Committee in the year 2010 (Later the scope of this committee was increased and named an EHR committee). The objective of this committee is to study the existing standards for data representation, exchange, and content and propose a set of EHR standards and guidelines for the country. The EHR committee is currently working on finalizing the first draft of the standards. The standards considered include the following [EHR Committee]:

- HL7 2.5/ HL7 v3 for exchange
- HL7 v3 RIM for Information model
- CDA for clinical documents
- DICOM for images
- XML/SOAP for communication
- CCR (ASTM) for summary documents
- Coding systems from all medical disciplines

The committee has also proposed a minimal data set based on the earlier recommended ones that will be required by a healthcare organization for treatment of patients. It is called the *Proposed Portable Health Record*. The recommendations are in draft stage and may become standard guidelines in the near future for implementation of EHR systems.

25.7 Discussion

Clinical Process Model. ITIH and RGSPTI are guidelines and do not include a clinical process model for national healthcare workflow. On the other hand, iHIND is a development plan and does not propose any EHR process model.

Structural Model

ITIH. ITIH covers all aspects of healthcare infrastructure including (a) billing formats against insurance claims, (b) clinical content standard for a specific generic type of data such as observations, procedures, and diseases, (c) a common minimum data set for the mentioned types of diseases, (d) recommendations for healthcare identifier, (e) messaging standards, and (f) legal and educational framework.

However, it does not provide any guidelines for various clinical modalities that are needed for implementing a comprehensive health informatics application. It only focuses on the commonly occurring diseases in the country mainly for public health. Also, there are no structural guidelines to build on EMR/EHR.

RGSPTI. It specifies what all records should be present in an EHR/EMR and defines the functions of EHR/EMR. However, it does not specify any standard information model that should be adhered to. Additionally, the records that it has mentioned are more specific to telemedicine and can be considered as a subset for an EHR system.

iHIND. iHIND does not specify any information model for storing data, but it specifies the requirements that should be fulfilled by an EHR structure. It specifies that the information model should be able to incorporate all types of already existing/generated standard format of data to promote easy adaptability.

In case of RGSPTI, it follows the MDS provided by ITIH, which is a prior recommendation, with some specialized CDS/MDS as per the requirements in telemedicine context. However, iHIND has provided a new list of attributes as part of an Encounter, Demographics, and Clinical Record.

Security/Privacy Considerations

ITIH. It only gives the recommendations for security of health identifiers of patients. However, it does not cover other security aspects such as data security while storing and transmitting data. It proposes bringing in a law for defining the rules for security, access policies, audit, and mandates in health informatics.

RGSPTI. It covers almost all security aspects including authentication, integrity, privacy, and security of data for minimum requirements, and suggests mechanisms for achieving them. The guidelines are compliant with the IT Act of India. Although the recommendations for security are specific to telemedicine, some of them can be applicable to EHR systems such as specifications for transmission, storage, and access to data.

iHIND. It considers security at different levels including data and transmission level security and proposes encryption techniques. However, it is not as comprehensive as RGSPTI.

Legal Aspects. RGSPTI mentions various legal aspects that should be covered including mandates, data retention policies, privacy, and confidentiality but it does not impose them as mandatory guidelines. ITIH suggests to formulate the law covering legal aspects of HIT systems. iHIND does not mention any legal policies at current pilot stage.

Exchange Specifications. All ITIH, RGSPTI, and iHIND have suggested versions of HL7, DICOM, and CDA for data communication. As suggested in the recommendation, applications may choose one of the standards for data communication. Considering the case of large EHR, data from all these applications will be collected. Hence, a nationwide EHR needs to support all the suggested standards. Also, due to continuous updates in standards and evolution of new standards, it becomes an essential requirement that a national EHR should be capable of incorporating all types of standard data.

Attention should be given to popular data formats such as PDF, JPG, DOC, and so on, produced by many of the existing healthcare applications in the country. Among suggested standards, CDA or CCR can be used to incorporate these clinical documents.

Technical Guidelines

ITIH. ITIH has proposed different codes for different clinical modalities such as LOINC and ICD. In such a case, a system may have to provide mappings between these supported clinical coding systems as provided by the Unified Medical Language System (*UMLS*).

iHIND. iHIND provides only a basic architecture for network infrastructure. It specifies connectivity between healthcare organizations and District Hub and District Hub to State level Data Warehouse, but it does not specify the connectivity mechanism between the State Level Data Warehouses to make it a complete nationwide connected network. In addition, the functional specifications of components of District Hub are not clear.

25.8 Conclusion

ITIH is a good initiative for providing the guidelines for collecting, storing and analyzing health information for prominent diseases across the country. It is considered the basis for emerging activities of standardizing healthcare IT sector in the country. The guidelines with new variants in the course of time may be considered to be mandated by the government in the area of health informatics.

Although recommendations are for standardizing telemedicine practices, RGSPTI provides the specifications for standards for data exchanges, data contents, and security that can be considered while developing EHR systems.

iHIND is intended for developing national network for health information exchange. Its purpose is to bring in a nationally connected infrastructure for health information.

Although no concrete measure for EHR is yet initiated in India at a national level, research and proofs of concepts in the form of various pilot projects are going on for evolving a national EHR framework [DIGHT].

BIBLIOGRAPHY

[**DIGHT**] Centre for Development of Advanced Computing (CDAC), India and Swedish Institute of Computer Science (SICS), Sweden, *Technology Development for Building Distributed, Scalable, and Reliable Healthcare Information Store/Distributed Infrastructure for Global Healthcare Technology (DIGHT);* http://medinfo.cdac.in/projects/ongoing_project/technology.aspx. http://dight.sics.se/files/docs/ehr-proposal.pdf.

[**EHR Committee**] Ministry of Health and Family Welfare Department of Health and Family Welfare, *Office Memorandum for Standardization of Electronic Medical Records* (September 2010) http://www.itbhuglobal.org/chronicle/EMR-Standards-Committee-MoHFW-GoI.pdf.

[iHIND] National Knowledge Commission, Implementation proposal of Indian health information network development submitted to Ministry of Health (March 2010).

[IDSP] Integrated Diseases Surveillance Project; http://idsp.nic.in.

[IDSP Karnataka] Integrated Diseases Surveillance Project, Karnataka; http://stg2.kar. nic.in/healthnew/IDSP/Home.aspx

[ITIH] Ministry of Communication and Information Technology, *Framework for Information Technology Infrastructure for Health in India, by Department of Information Technology* (2003).

[Mishra] Mishra, S. K., National network of all India medical colleges, Sanjay Gandhi Postgraduate Institute of Medical Sciences, Lucknow, India; http://www.stbmi.ac. in/matter/international%20pub/24_National%20Network%20of%20all%20india %20medical%20colleges.pdf.

[Mishra 2011] Mishra, S. K., Laying country wide e-infrastructure for Distance Medical Education Network Design, Pilot and scaling up Deployment for National Medical College Telemedicine Network: India Case Study. In: *31st meeting, SPAN Ashia-Pasific advanced Network* (February 2011); http://www.apan.net/meetings/ HongKong2011/Session/Slides/Medical/6-4.pdf.

[Mishra et al. 2008] Mishra, S., Ganapathy, K., and Bedi., B. S., The current status of eHealth initiatives in India, *Making eHealth Connections* (2008); http://www. ehealth-connection.org/files/conf-materials/Current%20Status%20of%20eHealth %20Initiatives%20in%20India_0.pdf.

[NKC] National Knowledge Commission; http://www.knowledgecommission.gov.in.

[NKC Recommendations] National Knowledge Commission, Report of the Working Group on Health Information Network (2007); http://www.knowledgecommission. gov.in/downloads/recommendations/HINPM.pdf. http://www.knowledgecommis-sion.gov.in/downloads/documents/wg_health.pdf.

[NRHM] National Rural Health Mission; http://mohfw.nic.in/NRHM.htm.

[NRHM Mission] National Rural Health Mission, *Mission Document (2005–2012)*; http://www.mohfw.nic.in/NRHM/Documents/Mission_Document.pdf.

[NRTN] Ministry of Health & Family Welfare, Government of India, *National Rural Telemedicine Network, Suggested Architecture and Guidelines.*

[Sinha and Gaur Sunder 2009] Sinha, P., and Gaur Sunder, A national framework for EMR storage—The next step in e-Health services. In: *Proceedings of the 5th National Congress of Telemedicine Society of India (Telemedicon'09)* (November 2009).

[Sinha and Gaur Sunder 2011] Sinha, P., and Gaur Sunder, Addressing India's skewed-doctor-to-patient ratio issue through ICT. In: *Proceedings of National Conference on Future Trends in Information & Communication Technology & Applications (NCICT -2011)* (September 2011).

[Telemedicine Guidelines 2007] Ministry of Health & Family Welfare, *Government of India, Recommendations on Guidelines, Standards & Practices for Telemedicine In India, under Task Force for Telemedicine in India* (2007).

[UIDAI Aadhar] Unique Identification Authority of India (UIDAI), Planning Commission, Government of India, *Aadhar*; http://uidai.gov.in/.

CHAPTER TWENTY-SIX

Netherlands' AORTA

26.1 Introduction

Dutch National ICT Institute for Healthcare (*NICTIZ, Nationaal ICT Instituut in de Zorg* in Dutch) in the Netherlands initiated a program called "AORTA" in the year 2007 to establish a nationwide health informatics infrastructure providing secure access to healthcare information of patients across the country. NICTIZ called the program AORTA after the largest artery in the human body to represent the importance and cruciality of the program [Spronk 2008].

26.2 Overview

NICTIZ has the overall responsibility of establishing the nationwide healthcare IT infrastructure in Netherlands. NICTIZ works in two areas toward healthcare IT infrastructure: AORTA infrastructure and the "Continuity of Care"-based Electronic Patient Record (EPR).

AORTA Infrastructure. AORTA has a decentralized architecture. It is because the law in Netherlands prohibits primary care practitioners from transferring medical records of a patient to other doctors. In the Netherlands, every citizen is assigned a General Practitioner (GP) and a dentist along with a citizen number. The assigned GP maintains the dossier for the patient and is not supposed to transfer it to other practitioners.

Electronic Health Record: Standards, Coding Systems, Frameworks, and Infrastructures, Pradeep Sinha, Gaur Sunder, Prashant Bendale, Manisha Mantri, and Atreya Dande.
© 2013 by The Institute of Electrical and Electronics Engineers, Inc. Published 2013 by John Wiley & Sons, Inc.

These legal restrictions prohibit any possibility of storing the entire health-care information centrally over the nationwide infrastructure. Hence, AORTA infrastructure connects all healthcare information sources with a secured link on which patients, healthcare providers, and healthcare insurers can access medical records without actual transfer of the records. It also takes care of privacy and security through nationally identified mechanisms.

Electronic Patient Record (EPR). The Netherlands standardized EPR for clinical domains like Radiology, Dentistry, Diabetic, Acute Care, and so on. EPR catering to a particular domain adheres to the standards suggested by the EPR Committee. These EPRs are collectively referred to as the *Dutch Electronic Patient Dossier (EPD) System.*

26.3 Architecture

26.3.1 DUTCH ELECTRONIC PATIENT DOSSIER (EPD) SYSTEM

Figure 26.1 shows the overall architecture of the EPD system that includes the following components [Carenini et al. 2009]:

Qualified Healthcare Information Systems (QHIS). QHIS systems fulfill a set of requirements for securely connecting with the national information hub and communicating with the hub in defined messaging standards. It makes use of Unique Healthcare Provider Identifier (UZI) and Citizen Service Number (BSN, Burgerservicenummer, in Dutch) cards for user authentication, adheres to medical domain-specific EPR standard for patient records, and HL7 v3

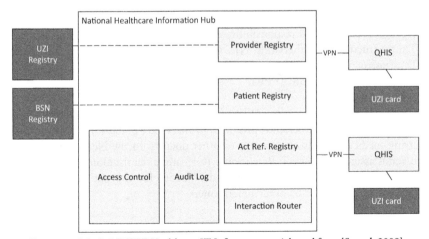

FIGURE 26.1 NICTIZ Healthcare IT Infrastructure. Adapted from [Spronk 2008].

messaging standard for transmission of healthcare information. This set of features enables every system certified as QHIS to communicate over the national healthcare infrastructure.

UZI Registry. The UZI registry maintains the list of all healthcare providers registered to use the national healthcare infrastructure. It includes healthcare providers and health insurers. *UZI cards* are smart cards issued to healthcare providers through which they can access the system in a secure manner. UZI is the Dutch acronym for Healthcare Provider Identifier.

BSN Registry. The BSN registry maintains a list of all citizens according to their national identifiers. BSN is the national unique identifier assigned to every citizen of the Netherlands. BSN is the Dutch acronym for Citizen Identification Number.

National Healthcare Information Hub (NHIH). National Healthcare Information Hub is the central part of AORTA infrastructure that manages access to information by healthcare providers and patients and makes the information available to them by fetching it from healthcare information sources.

Messaging Infrastructure. AORTA infrastructure uses HL7 v3-based messaging. HL7 v3 messages are wrapped in SOAP envelopes to transmit to NHIH over secure connection.

Act Reference Registry. It is an HL7 v3 concept used in AORTA infrastructure to maintain a registry of medical records and custodian of these medical records (i.e., healthcare practitioners). It helps NHIH in routing requests for healthcare information to the proper source of information [Spronk 2007].

26.3.2 NICTIZ HEALTHCARE IT INFRASTRUCTURE WORKFLOW

The National Health Information Hub (NHIH), being the central entity, makes use of a Provider Registry (UZI Registry) and a Patient Registry (BSN Registry) to authenticate requestors. The NHIH then uses the Act Reference Registry to figure out what healthcare information is present with which healthcare provider. For this purpose, the NHIH makes use of metadata to figure out the type of record and identification of the healthcare information source. Technical description of metadata is not available in public documentation of the Dutch healthcare infrastructure.

Once NHIH figures out the location of the requested information, it uses HL7 v3 messaging wrapped in SOAP envelope and transmits this information to the requestor. In summary, NHIH uses the web services infrastructure to facilitate communication among all QHIS in the Netherlands.

26.3.3 EXCHANGE

Dutch infrastructure uses HL7 v3 messaging for communication. For representing clinical terms, AORTA infrastructure uses SNOMED CT and LOINC terminologies. The profiles defined over HL7 v3 messaging are not available in public documentation.

26.3.4 SECURITY/PRIVACY GUIDELINES

The System and Network Engineering Group at the University of Amsterdam, Netherlands has studied security infrastructure of Dutch Healthcare IT Infrastructure. AORTA infrastructure incorporates the recommendations of this study. It uses registries for identification of patient, healthcare providers, and health insurers. It also uses cryptographic communication for healthcare information among QHIS systems and NHIH. A role-based access model allows proper authorization during access through QHIS systems [Noordende].

26.4 Discussion

Clinical Process Model. AORTA architecture works as a federated system like a broker, facilitating requester-filler entities. Hence, it does not have a central entity at the national level that stores and represents healthcare information. Due to this, there is no representation of EHR process model.

Structural Model. AORTA infrastructure provides another approach for building a national level healthcare IT infrastructure. Some of the notable points of this architecture are:

- The AORTA model is distributed with healthcare information sources being local and not collecting information at the central level. This scenario may give more trust to hospital administrators and practitioners as healthcare information is available in their own custody.

- Access to health information remotely is restricted to the legally authorized users only, requiring no sharing of record whatsoever.

- The Web-services approach is useful for large-scale networks because it involves communication in XML-based messages, which is an open information representation standard. However, adherence to only HL7 v3 for communication may lead to issues involved in transforming healthcare information from existing form to HL7 v3 format. In addition, it requires continuous update in the entire infrastructure whenever an underlying standard is updated.

Security/Privacy Considerations. The Netherlands healthcare IT infrastructure takes care of security and privacy through the already established registries at the national level. These security mechanisms are helpful in authenticating and authorizing users of the system. Some of the notable points are:

- Use of citizen number registry (BSN) and healthcare provider and insurer registry (UZI) ensures right authorization.
- Cryptographic communication of healthcare information offers safeguard against eavesdropping over network.
- Role-based access is necessary for ensuring the privacy of a patient's healthcare information.

Legal Aspects. EHR framework designers can consider AORTA infrastructure as an ideal example for replication in those geographies where laws restrict data sharing. AORTA infrastructure is a complete framework catering to such legal needs and still provides nationwide access to healthcare information, achieving better healthcare services in the nation.

Exchange Specifications. *European eHealth Research Area (eHealth ERA)* has studied e-health strategy in the Netherlands. Adherence to HL7 v3 messaging by Dutch infrastructure is suitable for their architecture because they are storing their medical records locally and just exporting them in HL7 v3 messages to the requestors for viewing purpose. Hence, the inherent problem of data loss during conversion to an HL7 v3 message for particular important healthcare information may not cause a serious issue. The original record will always be with the primary care practitioner [eHealth ERA].

The entire infrastructure will need to be upgraded continuously with upgrades in HL7 v3 standard. Experience of major architectural transition in HL7 standard from HL7 v2.x to HL7 v3 shows that such transitions will need massive investment in improvement of the national healthcare infrastructure.

AORTA infrastructure uses HL7 v3 standard for communication because it allows transfer in XML format that is very flexible and easy to understand technology. In addition, SOAP protocol can carry XML data, making it simple to build a web service based architecture [Haveman 2007].

26.5 Conclusion

AORTA infrastructure is a good example for building distributed access to local healthcare systems across the nation instead of managing a central healthcare information store. Some of the observed points are as follows:

- Adherence to a specific messaging standard and terminology standards causes inherent problems of standard lock-up, data loss, and major possible requirement of improvements in infrastructure if the standard itself is revised considerably.

- The approach of keeping metadata in the national healthcare information hub is a good idea, which facilitates efficient searching of medical records when requested. EHR framework designers can think of such an approach while designing large-scale frameworks.

BIBLIOGRAPHY

[**Carenini et al. 2009**] Carenini, A., Krummenacher, R., Marcos, D., Momtchev, V., and La, M., Assessment of the developed solution with regards to the detected indicators. In: *Proceedings of Triple Space Communication* (2009).

[**eHealth ERA**] European eHealth Research Area; http://ehealth-strategies.eu/.

[**Haveman 2007**] Haveman, H., eHealth strategy and implementation activities in the Netherlands. In: *Proceedings of eHealth ERA towards the Establishment of a European e-Health Research Area*, (2007); http://www.ehealth-era.org/database/documents/ERA_Reports/eHealth-ERA_Report_Netherlands_03-10-07_final.pdf.

[**HL7 v3**] Health Level 7; http://www.hl7.org/.

[**NICTIZ**] Dutch National ICT Institute for Healthcare; http://www.nictiz.nl/page/Home/English.

[**Noordende**] Noordende, G., A Security Analysis of the Dutch Electronic Patient Record System; http://d1sx0yagqoiea4.cloudfront.net/epd/Techreport-VWS.pdf.

[**Smet 2011**] Smet, K., The Dutch Nationwide Electronic Health Record: Why the centralized services architecture? In: *Proceedings of IEEE/IFIP Conference on Software Architecture (WICSA)*, pp. 181–186 (2011).

[**Spronk 2007**] Spronk, R., Act Reference Registries: An Infostructural Core Concept (2007); *http://www.ringholm.com/docs/00950_en.htm.*

[**Spronk 2008**] Spronk, R., AORTA, the Dutch National Infrastructure; http://www.ringholm.de/docs/00980_en.htm.

[**UZI registry**] Dutch Healthcare Providers and Insurers Registry; http://www.uziregister.nl/english/.

CHAPTER TWENTY-SEVEN

Singapore's NEHR

27.1 Introduction

In 1999, the Ministry of Health (MOH), in Singapore [MOH] initiated the National EHR [Singapore HIT] to connect hospitals, clinics, and other care-related organizations through two major clusters, SingHealth [SingHealth] and NHG [NHG], the two major healthcare providers in Singapore. Both Sing-Health and NHG took steps to automate the healthcare scenario with different approaches. EMR Exchange (EMRX) is another such program started to achieve interoperability across healthcare applications connected via SingHealth and NHG clusters. The most recent initiative is the National Electronic Health Record (NEHR) project, which is underway to implement a national EHR System that includes the implementation of Information Technology (IT) in polyclinics and primary care clinics by developing integrated RIS/PACS systems and by using Software-as-a-Service (SaaS) technology for connecting private clinics.

27.2 Overview

Implementation of IT in Healthcare in Singapore is in three stages, namely, Health Clusters, Electronic Medical Record Exchange (EMRX), and National Electronic Health Record (NEHR).

Electronic Health Record: Standards, Coding Systems, Frameworks, and Infrastructures, Pradeep Sinha, Gaur Sunder, Prashant Bendale, Manisha Mantri, and Atreya Dande.
© 2013 by The Institute of Electrical and Electronics Engineers, Inc. Published 2013 by John Wiley & Sons, Inc.

27.3 Architecture

27.3.1 HEALTH CLUSTERS

There are two major groups of healthcare organizations in Singapore. They are more than organization groups in the sense that they define the processes and norms to be followed for interoperability of healthcare systems.

Singapore Health Services (SingHealth). SingHealth has a centrally controlled and accessible health-service-based system that stores and provides access to patient health information generated by any of the periphery institutions.

National Healthcare Group (NHG). In contrast to SingHealth implementation, NHG developed a patient record sharing system that integrates and shares health data across periphery institutional EMR systems.

However, exchange of health data among periphery institutions across these two clusters was not possible. To solve this and other issues related to the exchange of health data, Singapore began work toward building an EMR Exchange. Recently, the healthcare clusters were divided into five major health clusters for better collaboration and sharing of health services [NEHR Phase I].

27.3.2 EMR EXCHANGE (EMRX)

Focus of the EMRX project is to improve patient safety and care by achieving interoperability between the two major clusters implemented at SingHealth and NHG. EMRX is a clinical document exchange broker working between Sing-Health and NHG. It is based on ANSI HL7 v2.3 standard [HL7] [Singapore HIT]. This project now supports exchange of different clinical documents across various health institutions in the country.

The first phase of this project focused on exchange of patient discharge summaries between SingHealth and NHG clusters. As Figure 27.1 shows, EMRX is a central broker that exchanges data between general practitioners, community hospitals, and other network of hospitals. It was further extended to include hospital in-patient discharge summary, laboratory test results (e.g., blood test results), X-ray and other radiological test results, medical operation reports, drug allergies, medicines, cardiac reports, and emergency department reports.

EMRX allows an implied consent model to access patient information. All clinical documents can be shared across EMRX. However, Singapore regulations impose restrictions over sharing of certain clinical data such as data related to termination of pregnancies, HIV-positive status, and mental illness. Note that the data sharing policies are controlled by the health clusters and not by the Ministry of Health (MOH).

Authentication and access control in this project are based on a two-level approach using password and access token. Each user has a password and an access token stored on a smart card. The EMRX system is secured by various

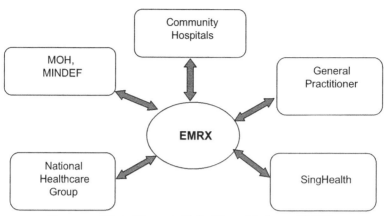

FIGURE 27.1 Electronic Medical Record Exchange (EMRX).

intrusion detection mechanisms that identify and alert the concerned authorities on detecting an intrusion.

Figure 27.1 depicts EMRX as a central entity that enables sharing of clinical documents across MOH, Ministry of Defense (MINDEF), Community Hospitals, General Practitioners, NHG, and SingHealth.

27.3.3 NATIONAL ELECTRONIC HEALTH RECORD (NEHR)

iN2015 (Intelligent Nation 2015) [iN2015], a 10-year plan of Singapore, includes the vision to develop a National Electronic Health Record (NEHR) system across the country. Phase I of this plan has gone live in June 2011 [NEHR Phase I]. Phase I includes establishment of Summary Care Records and the EHR model, along with services in major health clusters and other healthcare providers such as polyclinics, community hospitals, 50 clinics, and MINDEF [Muttitt].

In this project, various contracts were signed with IT companies to implement Enterprise Services, Core Clinical Data Repository, Enterprise Master Patient Index (EMPI), Clinical Viewer, and Message communication [Li 2010]. This project includes the following major components:

1. **EHR Services.** Development work related to EHR in the project is categorized into five different domains, namely, EHR, National Health Identification Service, Identity and Access Management, Terminology, and Integration. EHR Services required in these domains are further categorized based on the type of data processed. Some of the categories are Demographic services, Diagnosis services, Terminology services, Immunization services, Interoperability services, Drug services, and so on. Each of the services provides operations for adding, updating, and retrieving data. For better management and reuse, implementation of these services is based on the Service-Oriented Architecture (SOA). Healthcare applications can access these EHR services through national healthcare Enterprise Service Bus (ESB) distributed across major healthcare groups in Singapore [Lam et al. 2011].

2. *EHR Architecture.* An individual's EHR in Singapore is called the Summary Care Record (SCR). Each SCR contains various entities such as Episodes and Encounters of care, Health Problems, Laboratory and Diagnostic test results, Clinical Documents, Procedures, Immunization, Events, Alerts, Medicines, and so on. The EHR model designed under this project is based on a Logical Reference Model that supports interoperability based on its ability to be transformed into medical standard information models. The EHR model is developed using archetypes and templates defined by openEHR [openEHR; Brooks 2011].

3. *National Health Portal (NHP).* The iN2015 plan envisions providing cost-effective and quality healthcare to citizens of Singapore, manage chronic disease programs, promote use of IT among citizens, and help them manage their care records. The National Health Portal (NHP) attempts to implement a nationwide, shared, patient-centric EHR system for providing clinical decision support, tele-health, health management tools, and health education resources and for promoting research activities.

4. *RFID Bracelets.* Under the iN2015 plan, Singapore plans to provide a RFID bracelet to each citizen. These RFID bracelets will contain EMR data and identification information of an individual that can be used to access the Patient Health Record.

5. *Security.* Role-based access control policies are implemented for secure access to the Summary Care Record (SCR) of a patient. Patient consent management in giving access to parts of his/her EHR is done through an implied consent model, since operating explicit patient consent is practically difficult, especially under emergency situations [Tan and Seng 2009].

Information regarding the architecture and technical details of the project is sparsely available in public domain. Hence, minimal information is provided in the chapter.

Following is a list of medical data standards, technologies, terminologies, and integration standards being adopted in the NEHR project [Payne 2009].

1. *Medical Practice Policies.* This project focuses on medical practice guidelines such as AU Red Book [AU Red Book 2009] and Ministry of Health (MOH), Singapore Guidelines [Lee et al. 2011] to take preventive measures in general medical practice.

2. *Messaging Standards.* This project envisages to develop data level support for HL7 v3 [HL7 v3] and earlier versions of HL7 v2.x [HL7], HL7 CDA [HL7 CDA], and ASTM CCD [CCD] to ensure supporting multiple standards.

3. *Terminologies and Coding Systems.* This project standardizes the clinical terms and meanings used in healthcare by supporting the use of various coding systems and terminologies. For example, it supports the use of SNOMED CT [SNOMED CT], ICD 9 and ICD 10 [ICD], and LOINC [LOINC].

4. *Health Integration Standards.* The enterprise services architecture in this project supports health integration standards such as Integrated Health

Enterprise (IHE) Profiles and Continua Health Alliance [Continua], which is a consortium of healthcare organizations working as a certifying agency for healthcare products.

5. *Technical Standards.* The project makes use of cutting-edge technologies to host a reliable healthcare technology platform. Enterprise and EHR Services are based on SOA [SOA], which makes use of Web Services. The National Health Portal (NHP) is based on ADF JSF (Java Server Faces).

27.4 Discussion

Clinical Process Model. From the documentation available for EMRX and NEHR projects, it appears that no process model is designed for EHR.

Structural Model. The information model specified in the Summary Care Record (SCR) developed under the NEHR project is evidence-based and implementation-independent model. It is based on a logical reference model to support various medical standards. The information model contents comprise openEHR archetypes and templates that define the structure for clinical data [Brooks 2011]. EHR Model-related documentation is sparsely available in public domain.

Security/Privacy Considerations. EMRX implements access control based on a smart card and a password assigned to each user. Due to this two-level approach, it is possible to secure a patient's EHR even if the smart card is stolen, since the password is still with the patient.

Intrusion detection mechanisms implemented by EMRX is a topic of further study because it claims to secure the system from any kind of attacks from intruders who want to misuse the information. No detailed mechanisms used in NEHR or EMRX were discussed in publicly available documents.

Access control policies in NEHR are implemented using the role-based approach. However, it will be interesting to study the way in which users are legitimately identified and how dummy users are restricted access to EHR.

Legal Aspects. Singapore provides a legal framework for securing electronic health information through ethical and professional acts. These contain the Computer Misuse Act, unauthorized access, modifications to computer material acts [CMA], and so on. The Ministry of Health (MOH) has made it mandatory for healthcare applications not to share sensitive health information of patients such as HIV test data. It is researching and confirming with other countries approaches in this regard and is evolving a legal framework for protecting electronic transmission of healthcare data.

Exchange Specifications. To enable interoperability between the two major clusters (SingHealth and NHG), HL7 v2.3 was adopted. However, it was identified that achieving complete interoperability was difficult [Singapore HIT].

EMRX has a major drawback: It is essentially a document-level exchange, with no standardized or structured data support. Seamless sharing of data beyond documents is very difficult, if not impossible. For example, diagnostic images, including X-rays, cannot be exchanged over EMRX, because various institutions under the two major clusters use different vendors and their current viewers use different versions of image protocols. Images from one institution are therefore not easily readable in another institution without degradation of quality and significant translation effort [NEHR Update].

Lack of structured data also means that anything beyond information exchange, such as making the system "smarter" to aid clinical decisions, research, and disease surveillance, is technically impossible.

EMRX supports exchanging of data without any legal binding that could protect privacy of patient healthcare data. Different approaches taken by both the health clusters to implement EHR created two disparate healthcare applications with a distinct feature set. Due to this issue, the EMRX standard could not support exchange of all kinds of clinical documents generated in healthcare environment. This made achieving interoperability between them further difficult, which was the primary aim behind introducing EMRX. To solve such issues, the National Electronic Health Record (NEHR) project was initiated [Tsai 2010].

Technical Guidelines. In implementation of the National Health Portal (NHP), latest technologies are followed. For example, ADF JSF (Java Server Faces), AJAX, JSR-168 Portlet compliant, Service-Oriented Architecture (SOA) Development platform, Web Service-enabled application, Application as Service, and Business Process Execution Language are some of the technologies used.

27.5 Conclusion

Implementation of EMRX as a methodology to connect various healthcare organizations can be further studied to identify challenges and benefits in achieving interoperability across healthcare applications. Also, study of EHR services can help in understanding SOA-based implementation of EHR in healthcare. Use of the latest and cutting-edge technologies in NEHR is the next point of study since such technologies help in designing and developing robust and future-proof healthcare applications.

BIBLIOGRAPHY

[AU Red Book 2009] AU Red Book, Guidelines for Preventive Activities in General Practice (The Red Book); http://www.racgp.org.au/guidelines/redbook.

[Brooks 2011] Brooks, C., Clinically driven logical information modeling and data exchange in Singapore. In: *12th International HL7 Interoperability Conference*

(IHIC), (May 2011); http://www.hl7.org/events/ihic2011/papers/saturday/S_Q1_ 4_IHIC%202011brooks%20-%20Slides%20V%200.3.pdf.

[CCD] Continuity of Care Document; http://en.wikipedia.org/wiki/Continuity_ of_Care_Document.

[CMA] Computer Misuse Act; http://agcvldb4.agc.gov.sg/non_version/cgi-bin/cgi_ retrieve.pl?&actno=Reved-50A&date=latest&method=part.

[Continua] Continua Health Alliance; http://www.continuaalliance.org/index.html.

[Gan 2004] Gan, G. L., The EMR Exchange and Beyond (2004); www.sma.org.sg/ sma_news/3605/commentary_glg.pdf.

[HL7] Health Level 7; http://www.hl7.org.

[HL7 v3] Introduction to HL7v3; http://www.cihi.ca/cihiweb/en/downloads/v3Intro_ e.pdf.

[HL7 CDA] Health Level 7 Clinical Document Architecture (CDA); http://www.hl7. org/implement/standards/cda.cfm.

[ICD] International Statistical Classification of Diseases and Related Health Problems (ICD); http://www.who.int/classifications/icd/en/.

[iN2015] Intelligent Nation 2015(iN2015); http://www.ida.gov.sg/About%20us/ 20070903145526.aspx.

[Infoway Connects] Infoway Connects, National Electronic Health Record Perspectives: Singapore (March 2011); http://infowayconnects.infoway-inforoute.ca/blog/global-perspectives/343-national-electronic-health-record-perspectives-singapore/ #axzz1bKVPcX5q.

[Kwee 2009] Kwee, H. N., Transforming Healthcare Delivery in Singapore (2009); http://news.sma.org.sg/4110/Healthcare%20Delivery.pdf.

[Lam et al. 2011] Lam, T., Fai, W. F., and McKinnon, S., Singapore Healthcare's Journey Towards Interoperability, Sharing and Reuse; http://www.omg.org/news/ meetings/workshops/HC-Australia/Lam.pdf.

[Lee et al. 2011] Lee, K. M. T., Chan, H. N., Cheah, B., Gentica, G. F. C., Guo, S., Lim, H. K., Lim, Y. C., Noorul, F., Tan, H. S., Teo, P., and Yeo, H. N.,"Ministry of Health (MOH); http://smj.sma.org.sg/5206/5206cpg1.pdf.

[Li 2010] Li, J., Asia Pacific Future Gov; http://www.futuregov.asia/articles/2010/jun/ 25/singapore-awards-us144-million-national-ehr-tender/.

[LOINC] Logical Observation Identifiers Names and Codes (LOINC) http://loinc.org/.

[MOH] Ministry of Health; http://www.moh.gov.sg

[Muttitt] Muttitt, Dr. S., Developing a National Electronic Health Record.

[NEHR Phase I] Asia Pacific Future Gov News; http://www.futuregov.asia/articles/ 2011/may/03/first-phase-singapore-national-ehr-goes-live/.

[NEHR Update] Ministry of Health, Update on National Health Record Systems (03-Mar-2010); http://www.moh.gov.sg/mohcorp/parliamentaryqa.aspx?id=23922.

[NHG] National Health Group; http://www.nhg.com.sg.

[openEHR] Government and openEHR; www.openehr.org/shared-resources/usage/government.html.

[Oracle HTB] Oracle Health Transaction Base (HTB); http://www.oracle.com/us/ industries/healthcare/046614.html.

[Payne 2009] Payne, A.G., Innovation in Healthcare—The Singapore National Health Portal.

[**Singapore HIT**] Singapore HIT Case Study; http://www.pacifichealthsummit.org/downloads/hitcasestudies/economy/singaporehit.pdf.

[**SingHealth**] Singapore Health Services; http://www.singhealth.com.sg.

[**SNOMED CT**] Systematized Nomenclature of Medicines—Clinical Terms (SNOMED CT); http://www.ihtsdo.org/snomed-ct/.

[**SOA**] Service Oriented Architecture (SOA); http://en.wikipedia.org/wiki/Service-oriented_architecture.

[**Stein 2009**] Stein, M., Evolution of Personal Health Records in Singapore (August 2009); www.hisa.org.au/system/files/u2233/hic09-1_MichaelSteine.pdf.

[**Tan and Seng 2009**] Tan, P., Seng, O. L., Singapore's National Electronic Health Record Architecture. In: *SOA in Helathcare Conference* (2009); http://www.omg.org/news/meetings/workshops/SOA-HC/presentations-09/04-03_Tan-Seng.pdf.

[**Tsai 2010**] Tsai, F.S., Security Issues in E-Healthcar (2010); http://140.116.84.13/index.php/bme/article/viewFile/484/772.

CHAPTER TWENTY-EIGHT

Sweden's NPO

28.1 Introduction

National IT Strategy for eHealth is an initiative of Swedish National Board of Health and Welfare [National IT Strategy]. This strategy was formulated in the year 2006. One of the action areas of this strategy was to introduce an interoperable nationwide EHR framework. For this, a project named National Patient Summary (NPO) (Swedish name: Nationell Patientöversikt (NPÖ)) was started, whose objective is to implement a nationwide EHR framework for improving patient security and quality of healthcare. The project is divided into phases for delivering a solution for the nationwide EHR framework.

NPO [Bergh 2009] implementation and deployment contract [EHI eHealth Insider] is given to TieTo (an IT service company) [Tieto] and InterSystems (a software development company that provides software for high-performance database management systems, healthcare systems, and rapid application development) [InterSystems]. The project completed its first phase of implementation in the year 2009 [ProHealthServiceZone 2009].

Electronic Health Record: Standards, Coding Systems, Frameworks, and Infrastructures, Pradeep Sinha, Gaur Sunder, Prashant Bendale, Manisha Mantri, and Atreya Dande.

28.2 Overview

The National IT Strategy for eHealth in Sweden includes the following six action areas:

1. Bringing laws and regulations in sync with increase in data exchange.

2. Creating a common information exchange rules for data interoperability in healthcare and supporting EN 13606 standard to create a European standard similar to HL7 (HL7 v3).

3. Creating a common technical infrastructure for communication, electronic directory of users and organizations, identification of healthcare providers, and infrastructure for security and access control.

4. Implementing interoperable IT systems for exchanging/maintaining the nationwide EHR framework, administrative support, and prescription support.

5. Developing the national infrastructure for access to health information across organizational boundaries.

6. Making information and services easily accessible to citizens via web.

A number of national projects were started to initiate work towards the above-mentioned areas [Status Report 2008; Status Report 2009]. Most notable among them are:

1. Patient Data Act 2008, which defines legal requirements for health data exchange of patients. The law became effective on July 1, 2008.

2. Regulatory framework for information interoperability in healthcare.

3. A national eHealth network that connects healthcare applications across the country.

4. A national health directory for keeping details of all health providers.

5. Electronic ID cards for every individual who is employed in the healthcare sector.

6. A national service for dealing with security and access related rules and enforcements (it is under development and implementation).

7. Development of national EHR process and information models considering business processes under National Information Structure through the *National Information Structure* (NI) Project (finished in 2009).

8. A national project for incorporating interdisciplinary terminology. It promotes use of SNOMED CT as nationwide terminology with translation and modification as per Swedish requirements.

9. National infrastructure for health data exchange incorporating all the above-mentioned supportive services with EHR and interoperability framework called the National Patient Summary (NPÖ) [NPO a]. The NPO involves

national information structure, national terminology adoption, and integration of all services to form a national infrastructure for the nationwide EHR framework.

10. A National web portal named My Care Contact was developed [EHR Impact Report 2009]. It supports a number of healthcare services.

28.3 Architecture

28.3.1 CLINICAL PROCESS MODEL

Building a generic process model was one of the primary requirements of the NPO for identifying generic concepts in healthcare process in the country. A concrete information model can be built on top of such a generic process model.

Figure 28.1 shows the Swedish generic process model of EHR for clinical process (also called core process in healthcare).

The generic process model of Swedish national EHR focuses on changing the health state of a patient for which it has two aims [Swedish Process Model]:

1. Finding the problem (diagnosis)
2. Treating the problem (treatment)

In Figure 28.1, the upper lobe depicts the process for finding a patient's health problem and covers assessment, orders (e.g., order for blood test), and

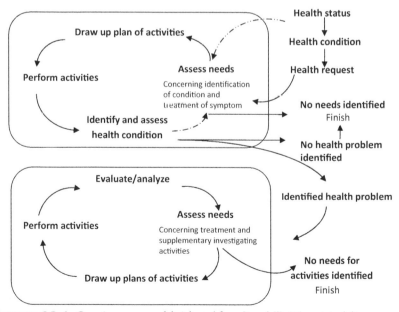

FIGURE 28.1 Generic process model. Adapted from [Lundell]. (The original diagram was published by the National Board of Health and Welfare in 2009).

diagnostic activities (e.g., blood test), and diagnosis/reassessment. On the other hand, the lower lobe describes the process for treating the identified problem, which also repeats the same cycle but produces different artifacts depending on the process of treatment. Here *Health request* corresponds to referral activities.

Based on the process model and study of business processes in healthcare, several models were generated for Swedish healthcare scenarios. A separate project called Structured Architecture for Medical Business Activities (SAMBA) was carried out for modeling business processes in Sweden [SAMBA 2003]. SAMBA was influenced by CEN/TC 215 EN13940-1 (CONTsys) [EN 13940-1 2007] standard and includes various concepts for administrative and legal processes from it.

SAMBA describes the process of "Caring for the individual patient" in a three-layer process model, where different processes interact with different refinement objects. They include:

1. *Clinical process* for clinical activities.
2. *Management process* for decision making and controlling the overall healthcare processes.
3. *Communication process* for transfer of information.

Based on these three core processes, the project describes the process flow for various use cases considering the activities in healthcare settings in Sweden.

28.3.2 INFORMATION MODEL

Swedish national information model called *Applied Operational Information Model* (V-TIM) (Swedish name: Verksamhets tillämpad informationsmodell) reflects the Swedish national process model for incorporating clinical and business requirements of Swedish healthcare environment [V-TIM] [Broberg and Rosenälv 2010].

Swedish information model is based on EN 13606 (EHRcom) standard covering all parts of the standard (representation, exchange, security, exchange protocol, and terminology). V-TIM modifies EN 13606 as per the requirements of Swedish Patient Data Law 2008 and the national process model of Sweden. The information model is continuously improving through reviews and its current version in use is V-TIM 2.0.

The national EHR project in Sweden has adapted the following standards:

- Terminology standard—SNOMED CT with translation in Swedish [SNOMED CT]
- Standards for EHR content and exchange—EN 12967(HISA), EN13940 (CONTsys), and EN13606 (EHR-com), which is interoperable with open-EHR and HL7.

28.3.3 Sjunet

Sjunet [Hyppönen et al. 2007] is a Swedish communication network for healthcare that enables communication between hospitals, primary care centers, and home care. Every county with all government and a number of private health care providers is connected to Sjunet network. This optical-fiber network facilitates secure and reliable information exchange. Sjunet is used for many healthcare services such as *Telemedicine, e-Learning*, and *e-Prescription* throughout the country.

28.3.4 ELECTRONIC CATALOG FOR HEALTH AND SOCIAL CARE

Electronic Catalog for Health and Social Care (Swedish name: Hälso och Sjukvårdens Adressregister (HSA-katalog) (HSA) is a national electronic directory that keeps information about the organizations dealing with health and social care, healthcare professionals, and services provided by healthcare providers and professionals. HSA includes the counties, regions, municipalities and private care providers, and additional actors in healthcare.

It is useful in searching different healthcare services and providers at national level and used for providing access control for national EHR implementation. The HSA database uses SQL technology for enabling data queries and retrieval.

28.3.5 SECURE IT IN HEALTH SERVICES

Secure IT in Health Services (SITHS) is a national security service for electronic communication within and outside the organization by healthcare professionals. In SITHS mode, every person who is providing healthcare services has a personal electronic ID card through a Public Key Infrastructure (PKI) certificate. Every issued certificate is published in HSA Directory to ensure its validity. SITHS ensures the identity and legal responsibility of a health service provider while transferring patient data from one organization to another at any point of time. Carelink maintains SITHS. Carelink is a supportive partner in Swedish national projects for development of IT in healthcare. It also manages other healthcare services, such as Sjunet healthcare network and HSA directory services.

28.3.6 BASIC SERVICES FOR INFORMATION

Basic Services for Information (Swedish name: Bastjänster för informationsförsörjning) (BIF) is responsible for protecting the privacy and security of a patient's health data and for providing the national security infrastructure for healthcare. BIF covers all aspects of security as per Patient Data Law 2008. It provides the following nine basic IT services:

1. *Authentication Service.* It validates the electronic ID provided to healthcare professionals from HSA. It enables Single Sign-On and unified logging for all systems.

2. *Access Service.* It provides access to users, depending on the access rights stored in HAS.

3. *Consent Service.* It manages consents of patients for sharing and keeping healthcare records with healthcare professionals.

4. *Log Service.* It logs all events for read–write and administrative activities.

5. *Healthcare Relationship Service.* It provides information for care relation between a doctor and a patient. This helps in providing different health services.

6. *Disclosure Service.* It allows sharing of EHR with confirmation of a healthcare provider to ensure correctness of data.

7. *Patient Context Control Service.* It manages updates on an EHR from different healthcare systems, that is, version control.

8. *Log Analysis Service.* It provides access log to detect unauthorized access to an EHR.

9. *Notification Service.* It notifies a user or system for changes in roles and rights.

28.3.7 REGULATORY FRAMEWORK FOR INFORMATION INTEROPERABILITY IN HEALTHCARE

Regulatory Framework for Information Interoperability in Healthcare (Swedish name: Regelverk för interoperabilitet inom Vården) (RIV) [Pallinder 2006] includes the following components:

1. *Technical Instructions.* It includes the instructions for communication wrapper over the data, such as headers, enveloper, security tokens, and so on, for interaction in the network.

2. *RIV Directory Service.* It includes the rules for keeping information for referencing care providers.

3. *RIV for Interoperability with other Frameworks.* It includes the guidelines for data conversion between other frameworks and Swedish information model.

4. *RIV Conformity Process.* It includes the instructions for software providers for achieving conformity with RIV, such as documenting service specifications.

RIV provides the specifications for design and communication of services to achieve interoperability to enable service-oriented architecture in healthcare in Sweden at national level.

RIV instructions are based on SITHS, HSA, and Sjunet. The message structure includes *Envelop*, *Header Element*, and *Body Element* that must be complaint with EHRcom and HL7v3.

28.3.8 NATIONAL PATIENT SUMMARY

National Patient Summary (NPO) aims to provide good and safe care to patients. It stores and manages access of patients' critical health information regardless of where patients seek care.

Figure 28.2 shows the technical architecture of NPO, which uses the standards and components of health infrastructure in the country. It uses BIF, RIV for rules during exchange, SITHS, HSA, National web portal for patients, and Sjunet. [NPO b]

28.4 Discussion

Clinical Process Model. A generic process model helps in achieving inter-operability at concept level and in building meaningful information models of an EHR. Being generic enough, it can be specialized in different requirement contexts.

The Swedish process model covers all aspects of healthcare process, including clinical and management. It is influenced by the legislative requirements and business processes in the country. This model can be referred to for implementing national process-based EHR with changes according to the national requirements.

Structural Model. Swedish information structure is based on the EN 13606 (EHRcom) standard that defines generic reference model for exchanging part of or a complete EHR through *Archetypes*. The EN 13606 standard provides the means to achieve interoperability with HL7 v3 and openEHR. Both of these are popularly used in European countries.

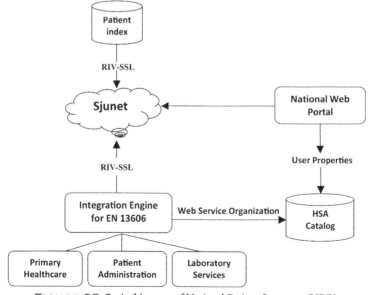

FIGURE 28.2 Architecture of National Patient Summary (NPO).

Security/Privacy Considerations. In NPO, BIF deals with protection of patient data. It uses the *Attribute-Based Access Control* (ABAC) mechanism for controlling access of data through *eXtensible Access Control Markup Language* (XACML).

BIF may get loaded due to repetitive request for data, such as Electronic-ID Card details and fetching huge data every time. Such a load may increase the response time. For reducing the load on BIF, an access service is designed. This service will be installed at every application that needs to share/access patient data. It stores permission data locally and pushes specific authorization information for every record access.

ABAC [Yuan and Tong 2005] provides access control policies based on attributes presented by a patient. It is more powerful in terms of flexibility than Role-Based Access Control (RBAC), which provides access policies based on roles given to a user. ABAC makes it more suitable for distributed environment (Web services). Thus, it can be considered as a useful technology for implementation of access control for a nationwide health store. However, ABAC is more complex to implement than RBAC. Efficient use of ABAC should be analyzed considering its complexity of implementation.

Legal Aspects. NPO implementation follows the national regulation (Patient Data Act 2008) for patient data privacy and safety. It specifies access policies for accessing patient data by any healthcare provider. A patient can block some of his/her records, access log details, specify contents to be logged, and specify the duration for keeping the logs.

Exchange Specifications. Swedish national strategy included development of national infrastructure for health to enable secured transfer of patient data. Additionally, rules for interoperability were defined for implementing healthcare services across the nation.

Since the Swedish EHR model is based on the EHRcom standard, the exchange of the data is supported through Archetypes. Additionally, it is interoperable with HL7 v3 and openEHR.

Technical Guidelines. Prior to the implementation of NPO, various national services were already implemented and working (such as HSA, SITHS, and BIF). Existence of the national services and infrastructure resulted in smoother implementation of national EHR.

NPO uses the HealthShare [HealthShare] product of InterSystems that enables decentralized storage of data and keeps data as is with healthcare organization, enabling the use of already existing systems. It provides connectivity among these systems for data exchange via the national network.

28.5 Conclusion

Swedish National IT strategy for eHealth is one of the most well-planned and successful examples of implementation of a countrywide national EHR system.

NPO has adapted international standards for data structure, content, and communication. Various aspects of use of technology and Swedish generic process are a good example to follow while building a nationwide EHR system.

BIBLIOGRAPHY

[**Bergh 2009**] Bergh, C., *The Swedish National Patient Overview (NPO) Background and Status*, Tieto Corporation (May 2009).

[**Broberg and Rosenälv 2010**] Broberg, H., and Rosenälv, J., CEN/ISO EN13606 in Sweden. In: *CEN/ISO EN13606 Invitational Workshop, Madrid, Spain* (June 2010); http://en13606.webs.upv.es/web13606/images/docs/workshop2010/08-EN13606-Sweden-Broberg-Rosenalv-CEHIS.pdf.

[**EHI eHealth Insider**] Special Report, TietoEnator wins Swedish electronic healthcare record contract with InterSystems HealthShare, *EHI eHealth Insider* (2009); http://www.e-health-insider.com/Features/item.cfm?docID=261.

[**EHR Impact Report 2009**] EHR IMPACT European Commission, DG INFSO & Media, *The Socio-economic Impact of the Regional Integrated EHR and ePrescribing System in Kronoberg, Sweden* (September 2009).

[**EN 13940-1 2007**] European Committee for Standardization (CEN), *Health Informatics—System of Concepts to Support Continuity of Care—Part 1: Basic Concepts, EN 13940-1*; http://www.tc215wg3.nhs.uk/docs/isotc215wg3_n386.pdf.

[**HealthShare**] InterSystems Product, HealthShare; http://www.intersystems.com/healthshare/index.html.

[**Hyppönen et al. 2007**] Hyppönen, H., Doupi, P., and Tenhunen, E., eHealth strategy and RTD progress in Sweden, *Report in the Framework of the eHealth ERA Project* (September 2007); http://www.ehealth-era.org/database/documents/ERA_Reports/eHealthERA_CountryReport_SWEDEN_final%2017-09-07.pdf.

[**InterSystems**] InterSystems Corporation; http://www.intersystems.com.

[**Lundell**] Lundell, K., Swedish National Board of Health and Welfare, Generic Process Model for Health Related Services; http://www.contsys.net/documents/Swedish_national_ process_model2.pdf.

[**National IT Strategy**] Ministry of Health and Social Affairs, Sweden, *National Strategy for eHealth in Sweden*; http://www.sweden.gov.se/content/1/c6/06/43/24/f6405a1c.pdf.

[**NPO a**] National Patient Summary Web site; http://www.cehis.se/vardtjanster/npo.

[**NPO b**] Örebro University Hospital, *NPÖ—National Patient Summary*; http://www.flexlab.com/labdays/Ia%20Jansson%20NP%C3%96%20Malm%C3%B6%20 20090918.pdf.

[**Pallinder 2006**] Pallinder, A., E., Walking the talk of interoperability, *eHealth Conference* (2006); http://www.ehealthconference2006.org/pdf/Pallinder.pdf.

[**ProHealthServiceZone 2009**] InterSystems, Swedish National Patient Summary project completes first stage, *News at ProHealthServiceZone* (June 2009); http://www.prohealthservicezone.com/News/It_and_communications_in_healthcare/ Medical_records_and_document_management/Swedish_national_patient_summary_project_completes_first_stage_4691.asp#ixzz1d17p6EYj. http://www.prohealthservicezone.com/Customisation/News/

IT_and_Communications_in_Healthcare/Medical_records_and_document_management/Swedish_National_Patient_Summary_project_completes_first_stage.asp.

[SAMBA 2003] Structured Architecture for Medical Business Activities (SAMBA), *Process and Concept Analysis of the Workflow in Swedish Health Care for Care of One Individual Subject of Care*, (Nov 2003); http://www.contsys.eu/documents/samba/samba_en_short_1_3.pdf.

[SNOMED CT] National Board of Health and Welfare, Sweden, *SNOMED CT - should Sweden join now or wait?*, Status Report, (November 2006); http://www.socialstyrelsen.se/Lists/Artikelkatalog/Attachments/9742/2006-131-32_200613132.pdf.

[Status Report 2008] Ministry of Health and Social Affairs, Swedish Association of Local Authorities and Regions (SALAR) and National Board of Health and Welfare, Sweden, *Swedish Strategy for eHealth - safe and accessible information in health and social care, 2008 Status Report*, (2008); http://www.regeringen.se/content/1/c6/11/48/75/39097860.pdf.

[Status Report 2009] Ministry of Health and Social Affairs, Swedish Association of Local Authorities and Regions (SALAR), National Board of Health and Welfare, and Association of Private Care Providers Sweden, *Swedish Strategy for eHealth—Safe and Accessible Information in Health and Social Care, 2009 Status Report* (2009); http://www.regeringen.se/content/1/c6/12/48/02/a97569e9.pdf.

[Tieto] Tieto Corporation; http://tieto.com.

[V-TIM] Specification for Information Structure of V-TIM Swedish version;http://www.arkitekturledningen.se/undermappar/Dokument/V-TIM_v2_091013_English_attributes.pdf.

[Yuan and Tong 2005] Yuan, E., and Tong, J., Attributed Based Access Control (ABAC) for Web Services. In: *Proceedings of IEEE International Conference* (November 2005).

CHAPTER TWENTY-NINE

Taiwan's Health Information Network

29.1 Introduction

Taiwan initiated implementation of ICT in the healthcare domain as early as in the 1980s. Development of National Health Information System and use of Health Information Technology (HIT) led to better, efficient, and safe medical care. A pilot project to develop a National Health Information Network (HIN) was conducted in phases from 1989 to 1991 and 1991 to 1993. HIN was extended to other regions of Taiwan in the next phase (1994–1996). Initial network architecture of HIN was based on TCP/IP over a frame-relay backbone. Soon the network faced bandwidth issues since healthcare applications require more bandwidth due to the use of more multimedia data. Numerous healthcare applications and thin uncommon data structures made interoperability difficult. Phase II of HIN (2001) focused on such issues. The issue of bandwidth and security was resolved by providing bandwidth upgrades. On the other hand, for security, Virtual Private Network (VPN) was introduced as the base network and smart cards were used for user identification [Li 2010].

In 2004, the Taiwan Medical Record Template (TMT) project was initiated to use TMT as base data schema for exchanging healthcare information across

Electronic Health Record: Standards, Coding Systems, Frameworks, and Infrastructures, Pradeep Sinha, Gaur Sunder, Prashant Bendale, Manisha Mantri, and Atreya Dande.
© 2013 by The Institute of Electrical and Electronics Engineers, Inc. Published 2013 by John Wiley & Sons, Inc.

healthcare applications. This was the first step toward achieving interoperability [Rau et al. 2010].

Such development projects provided a health information technology platform for achieving national goals in areas such as electronic clinical care, insurance management, disease management, surveillance and reporting, consumer health informatics, biotech development, standards, interoperability, incentives and ethics, legal, and social security.

29.2 Overview

Broadly, implementation of HIT in Taiwan is a set of initiatives under the following:

National Health Information Network (HIN) and Virtual Private Network (VPN). HIN is a nationwide network for connecting public government hospitals, pharmacies, and clinics to securely exchange health information. The network is a combination of frame-relay network and virtual private network between government organizations and health care providers.

Taiwan Medical Record Template (TMT). To resolve the issue of interoperability between healthcare applications and for managing and exchanging health information, the Taiwan Association for Medical Informatics (TAMI) [TAMI] research group developed a common reference structure based on CDA R2 and XML.

29.3 Architecture

In 1987, Taiwan initiated a project to establish a nationwide infrastructure for health information exchange. This network has three regional information centers and a frame-relay communication network connecting public hospitals. The project's initial target was to support basic public health administration, hospital regulation, and cancer registries. Figure 29.1 represents the network architecture based on frame relay. The frame-relay network connects the Department of Health (DOH), Service Center (SC), Health Certificate Authority (HCA), and National Health Information Infrastructure's (NHII) Internet Data Center (IDC), including its branches with Government Health organizations, Hospitals, Clinics, Blood Donation Centers, Health Business entities, and Mental Health Centers [Li 2005].

The frame-relay based network architecture soon faced bandwidth problems due to the increase in exchange of multimedia content in healthcare domain. Need for a stable and more reliable security infrastructure was also identified. To address these issues, work began toward building the next level of network architecture based on VPN. This work led to the development of HIN 2.0.

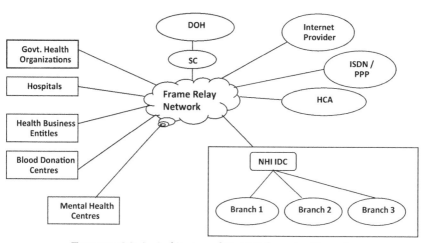

FIGURE 29.1 Architecture of Health Information Network.

29.3.1 NATIONAL HEALTH INFORMATION NETWORK (HIN) 2.0

Figure 29.2 shows the architecture of the new HIN, called the Medical Information Exchange Centre (MIEC). It consists of the following major components:

1. **Gateway.** Gateway is located at the healthcare provider site. It retrieves data from the local Health Information System (HIS). Local database format is customized to give mandated format using data mapping schemas. Gateway

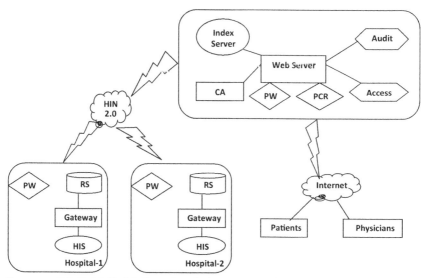

FIGURE 29.2 Medical Information Exchange Centre (MIEC), Taiwan. Adapted from [Li et al. 2001].

can be configured to check changes in the local database at specific intervals for the type of tests and results being shared. Gateway sends the data to Resource Server and reads the data back.

2. **Resource Server (RS).** Resource Server resides at the healthcare provider's location. It receives data from the Gateway and maintains it in local relational database storage. It continuously updates the Index Server with the information that the data is available with itself.

3. **Index Server.** Index Servers are maintained at separate central servers accessible to Resource Servers. An Index Server maintains the minimum patient identification information and links to Resource Server locations where actual patient healthcare data resides. To search a patient's record in HIN, requests from Physician Workstation (PW) or Patient Centered Retrieval (PCR) are sent to such Index Servers that return the Resource Server's location, if a matching record is found.

4. **Physician Workstation (PW).** This web-based interface is used by a physician to access a patient's health records. It displays a chronologically ordered records list containing images and text for gaining faster access to recently generated records.

5. **Patient-Centered Retrieval (PCR).** This web-based interface is used by the patients to view their own records. For ease of understanding, the interface is simplified and represents health terms in both Chinese and English languages.

6. **Health Certificate Authority (HCA).** Health Certificate Authority generates private keys for gaining access to HIN's VPN. The keys are generated for various types of users such as health professionals, patients, physicians, and so on. These users receive a smart card containing the basic user identification and security information. A smart card also contains a summary of his/her medical record.

7. **Access Server.** Access Server identifies each user based on the key provided by HCA and validates the user's access to patient health records. To decide the access rights of a user, it maintains a security matrix based on the user's role and type of data to be accessed.

8. **Audit Server.** All kinds of access to patient records are recorded on an audit server. These can be used to generate audit reports and hold any user accountable for changes done on patient records.

29.4 Exchange

29.4.1 TMT STANDARD

The Taiwan Medical Record Template (TMT) project, started in 2004, was initiated to develop a reference information structure for building interoperable EHR. TMT is a document-based information standard built using XML. The

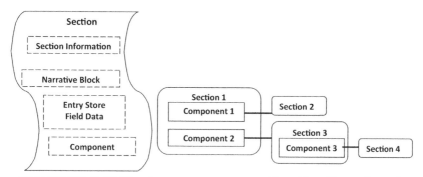

FIGURE 29.3 TMT section–component structure. Adapted from [Rau et al. 2010].

development work involved collecting documents, forms from different hospitals, clinics, and segregating them into clinical and administrative categories as per their usage in real environment. These categories help in identifying various EHR content heads representing health information in an EHR. Researchers, experts, and specialists then researched through these collected formats and developed a single format for each category. The first version of the TMT standard was thus created. In the next version, formats for other specialist departments were developed. Training programs for healthcare professionals and physicians were conducted for understanding applications and their usage in exporting EHR formats based on TMT standard.

Figure 29.3 depicts the basic section–component structure defined for TMT templates. Various structural elements of a TMT template are described below:

1. **Section.** Section in a TMT template represents the title of the document. Title contains information about the author, title, and identifier of the document. Sections can be nested using components. The narrative block represents textual data that contains section description. An example of a section can be patient demographic information or family history. Reusable sections for most commonly used health information are readily available in TMT.

2. **Component.** Components are used in sections to refer to other sections. The combination of sections and components provides a tree-view structure for an EHR.

3. **Entry.** Entry contains the actual health information represented in machine-readable text format. A section can contain multiple entries as required. For example, patient information section contains entries such as patient id, patient name, and so on.

From a security perspective, inclusion of digital signatures is possible in these templates enabling health providers to exchange documents securely over the network. Apart from structure, content types are defined for representing health information in standards-based and terminology-specific form. A complete EHR is a collection of various template forms.

One way to achieve interoperability with other EHR systems is to transform TMT XML files into CDA Release 2.0 document format using XSLT [XSLT] technology and exchange it [Rau et al. 2010]. Other exchange mechanisms to transfer TMT templates-based EHR that enable sharing of EHR among patients and healthcare providers are as follows:

1. Use of Patient-Centered Retrieval (PCR) web application to access patient's EHR that is located anywhere in the Health Information Network (HIN).
2. Exporting TMT-based EHR on removable media such as CD-ROM and importing it in the Hospital Information System (HIS).
3. Exchange of TMT XML files using the Gateway located across hospitals.

29.5 Discussion

Clinical Process Model. The model of Taiwan for EHR does not define the clinical process model. It is based on a technical framework to enable network communication across hospitals, clinics, pharmacies, and a standard for exchange of clinical and administrative information among them.

Structural Model. Taiwanese researchers have transformed physical forms and documents used in healthcare environment into XML-based templates that can be transformed to CDA [HL7 CDA] format. These templates are constituted inside an EMR profile that is identified as complete health profile of an individual. Adhering to a template for each category and each specialist department does give a structure for information that must be captured. However, like HL7, this structure is aimed toward exchange of information only and does not affect information model of individual health stores. Each hospital or clinic must map its records to the given template while exchanging them.

Security/Privacy Considerations. The new network architecture introduces a virtual private network to which access can be gained by using the private key issued by the Health Certificate Authority (HCA). A smart card that contains the private key is provided. Patients can access their records online using the smart card; and any physician, with help from patients, can send records to other doctors for referral. Smart cards are tracked for usage patterns to check an individual's frequency of hospital visits. This information assists in the generation of health reports for tracking an individual's health, thereby providing better healthcare [Reid 2008].

For a physician, to access a patient's record, it is mandatory to use the smart cards issued to both the physician and the patient. Apart from this, for secure data transmission, the TMT standard provides attachment of a digital signature with TMT documents and specifies sending of health organization's certificate and a timestamp during transmission. This ensures authentication, confidentiality, and integrity of the TMT document.

Data transmission technologies used in Taiwan can be a basis for developing a distributed, secure health record exchange framework.

Legal Aspects. The Taiwan Government holds that a patient is the owner of his/her EHR, but data still reside under the custody of hospitals. The TMT standard follows the existing laws of the land for data protection and medical care.

Exchange Specifications. Taiwanese researchers defined the need for evolving a TMT standard on the basis of the following interoperability definition.

Interoperability Definition, IEEE: *The ability of two or more systems or components to exchange information and to use the information that has been exchanged* [Jian et al. 2007].

The definition suggests two dimensions:

1. Functional or syntactic interoperability, which defines the message structures and functions used in exchange of information between these systems.
2. Semantic interoperability, which defines the use of information shared between systems, should be understood at the level of defined domain concepts so that information can be processed by systems in the same manner [Jian et al. 2007].

To define the need of a new standard (TMT), various existing exchange standards and specifications such as CDA [HL7 CDA], ASTM's CCR [ASTM CCR], *open*EHR [openEHR], and IHE XDS [IHE XDS] were studied. During this study, it was analyzed that none of these standards support exchange of complete contents of EHR. The Taiwanese study inferred that existing standards support only textual data exchange in the form of either summaries or images.

Presently, some SDOs have collaborated to develop exchange standards that cover most of the data represented in an EHR. For example, HL7 [HL7] and ASTM [ASTM 2011] developed the Continuity Care Document (CCD) [CCD QSG]. Currently, work is ongoing to integrate DICOM with it.

Based on the specific needs of local healthcare environment in Taiwan, decision was made to customize existing standards and then build specifications on it. This thought led to the development of TMT standard. CDA structure and Reference Information Model (RIM) [HL7 v3 RIM 2011] (CDA is based on HL7 v3 RIM) were customized to build TMT standard for exchange.

It may be noted that the task of collecting and reforming all physical forms, sheets, and documents used in health care environment and then standardizing each form contents at a national level is a long exercise. Moreover, such standardized forms must be acceptable to all healthcare organizations, ISVs, and OEMs.

For successful implementation of a standard like TMT, it should ideally be complemented with healthcare applications and viewers that are adaptable to changes in any of the electronic document templates, and support any changes, enhancements, addition of data types or new form of content.

Any customization made to an existing standard is always local and cannot be implemented outside the local environment. This might create an ecosystem where semantic interoperability between customized versions of a standard is not possible. However, development of a health ecosystem that crosses jurisdictions of a country is still a dream.

Technical Guidelines. Building a nationwide exchange system for medical information based on VPN is a good example of a secure communication network across health care organizations.

The HIN architecture does the following:

- It connects healthcare organizations and hospitals over a single network to form a heath exchange network.
- It provides secure access to the network.
- It takes care of optimization and reliability for large data transmission.

The idea behind building such a network is to keep data with hospitals but provide data sharing mechanisms and network infrastructure. This makes the HIN lighter without being concerned about large data storage as hospitals maintain their existing applications used in patient care delivery. The network architecture includes the centrally located servers that maintain the index of links to the locations (hospitals) where actual patient data exists. The architecture also includes applications that locally reside at a hospital and update the central index from time to time. Such a detailed architecture specification can guide development of a nationwide distributed record exchange.

29.6 Conclusion

Initiative to build a network communication infrastructure across the country to connect public hospitals, clinics, pharmacies, and other health organizations builds foundation for implementation of a nation-wide Exchange for electronic health information. Development of such a network architecture becomes a major task in the implementation of distributed, scalable health information store.

The MIEC architecture, as depicted in Figure 29.2, is a good attempt toward building a medical information exchange by developing applications based on cutting-edge technologies. As can be understood from Figure 29.2, this work also involves mechanisms to achieve seamless integration of data from existing healthcare applications residing at hospitals with their individual databases.

The TMT standard can be effective in achieving interoperability across heterogeneous healthcare applications by customizing the existing standard. Such a standard may be referred as a guide to initiate work toward creation of standardized contents and structures for clinical documents used in healthcare environment.

Use of smart cards with integrated circuits containing personal identification information and private keys that secure access to HIN is a point of further study as its short-term and long-term implications are yet to emerge.

BIBLIOGRAPHY

[**ASTM 2011**] American Society for Testing and Materials (ASTM); http://www.astm. org/.

[**ASTM CCR**] ASTM E2369-05e1 Standard Specification for Continuity of Care Record (CCR); http://www.astm.org/Standards/E2369.htm.

[**CCD QSG**] CCD Quick Start Guide; http://www.lantanagroup.com/resources/quick-start-guides/.

[**HL7**] Health Level 7; http://www.hl7.org.

[**HL7 CDA**] Health Level 7 (HL7), Clinical Document Architecture (CDA); http://www.hl7.org/implement/standards/cda.cfm.

[**HL7 v3 RIM 2011**] Health Level 7 (HL7), Reference Information Model (RIM); http://www.hl7.org/implement/standards/rim.cfm.

[**IHE XDS**] IHE Cross-Enterprise Document Sharing; http://www.ihe.net/Participation/ upload/iti6_ihewkshp07_xds_majurski.pdf.

[**Jian et al. 2007**] Jian, W.-S., Hsu, C-Y., Hao, T-H., Wen, H-C., Hsu, M-H., Lee, Y-L., Li, Y-C., and Change, P., Building a Portable Data and Information Interoperability Infrastructure-Framework for a Standard Taiwan Electronic Medical Record Template; http://ehrkorea.org/newsletter/files/Taiwan_EMR_Template.pdf.

[**Li 2010**] Li, Yu-Chuan., Taiwan HIT Case Study. In: *Pacific Health Summit*, National Bureau of Asian Research (2010); http://www.pacifichealthsummit.org/downloads/ HITCaseStudies/Economy/TaiwanHIT.pdf.

[**Li 2005**] Li, Yu-Chuan., National Health Information Infrastructure (NHII) and International Standards—A Taiwan Perspective. In: *GHIT Standards Summit* (2005); http://www.himss.org/content/files/GHIT-SSummit2005/Taiwan% 20Healthcare%20Smart%20Card-n-NHII-Japan-20050920-v2.1.pdf.

[**Li et al. 2001**] Li, Yu-Chuan., Kuo, Hsu-Sung., Jian, Wen-Shan,, Tang, Dali-Dian., Liu, Chien-Tsai., Liu, Li., Hsu, Chicn-Yeh., Tan, Yong-Kok., and Hu, Chung-Hong, Building a Generic Architecture for Medical Information Exchange Among Healthcare Providers; http://libir.tmu.edu.tw/bitstream/987654321/11618/2/ 17++Building+a+generic+architecture+for+medical+information+exchange+ among+healthcare+providers.pdf.

[**openEHR**] openEHR; http://www.openehr.org.

[**Rau et al. 2010**] Rau, Hsiao-Hsien., Hsu, Chien-Yeh., Lee, Yen-Liang., and Jian, Wen-Shan., Developing Electronic Health Records in Taiwan (2010); http://ieeexplore. ieee.org/xpls/abs_all.jsp?arnumber=5439509.

[**Reid 2008**] Reid, T.R., Taiwan Takes Fast Track to Universal Healthcare, (April, 2008); http://www.npr.org/templates/story/story.php?storyId=89651916.

[**TAMI**] Taiwan Association of Medical Informatics (TAMI); http://www.medinfo.org. tw/html/intro_eng.html.

[**XSLT**] Extensible Stylesheet Language; www.w3schools.com/xs

CHAPTER THIRTY

United Kingdom's Spine

30.1 Introduction

The National Health Service (NHS) in United Kingdom is responsible for delivering quality health services. It conducts National Program for IT (NPfIT) to proliferate usage of information technology in healthcare domain. Under this program, the NHS aims to establish a nationwide infrastructure that will provide a platform for hosting electronic patient records to facilitate anytime, anywhere access to any patient's health information. The NHS program includes a service-oriented EHR framework having Care Records Service (CRS). CRS provides standards for summary and detailed patient records applicable nationwide. CRS will hold sufficient information for knowing a patient's allergies, previous treatments, major problems, and so on. Based on this information, a physician can base the diagnosis and course of treatment, ensuring better analysis of problems and better treatment. The NHS also aims to develop UK-wide EHR service known as *Spine*, where CSR will be one of the services in the EHR service stack. Spine has been implemented in England.

30.2 Overview

Spine includes a national-level IT infrastructure for hosting summary care records. These records are accessible to patients whenever needed. Service-oriented architecture of Spine is a large-scale infrastructure in healthcare domain in England.

Electronic Health Record: Standards, Coding Systems, Frameworks, and Infrastructures, Pradeep Sinha, Gaur Sunder, Prashant Bendale, Manisha Mantri, and Atreya Dande.
© 2013 by The Institute of Electrical and Electronics Engineers, Inc. Published 2013 by John Wiley & Sons, Inc.

30.3 Architecture

30.3.1 SPINE INFRASTRUCTURE

Spine uses a service-oriented infrastructure for providing healthcare services. It has several component services for different purposes. They are as follows:

Spine. Spine is the main part for hosting electronic patient records of citizens. Spine hosts a number of services on top of the EHR store facilitating access to medical records anytime, anywhere [NHS NPfIT 2011].

Figure 30.1 shows the components of Spine architecture. These are:

1. ***Personal Demographic Service (PDS).*** PDS is a single, central source of patient identification and demographic details. It acts as a gateway for accessing medical records of every individual.

2. ***National Care Record (NCR).*** NCR manages a patient's clinical information. Together, PDS and NCR constitute the patient's summary care record.

3. ***Legitimate Relationship Service (LRS).*** ACF keeps track of registration, authentication, and authorization of users of Spine. It performs the functions like audit, authentication, and management of patient's preferences for accessing medical records.

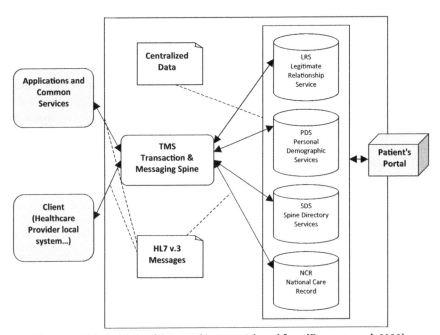

FIGURE 30.1 National Spine architecture. Adapted from [Ferronato et al. 2003].

4. **Spine Directory Service (SDS).** SDS provides information to the users about additional services provided over Spine, Healthcare Organizations, and their details in a secure manner.

5. **Secondary Uses Service (SUS).** To facilitate clinical research, epidemic reporting, healthcare planning and related events, Spine provides Secondary Uses Service (SUS) under secure and privacy-managed access control.

6. **Transaction and Messaging Spine (TMS).** Applications/services over Spine use TMS to transmit clinical information from one entity to another. This service also provides notifications whenever any clinical-information-related activity happens in any application/service.

7. **Clinical Spine Application (CSA).** CSA provides web-based access to Spine infrastructure. Using this portal clinicians, patients, administrators, researchers, and so on, can manage clinical records [Carenini et al. 2009].

N3. N3 is the national broadband network of England connecting hospitals, medical institutions, and clinics providing underlying communication backbone for IT applications. British Telecommunications plc (BT) started developing the N3 network in 2004, and since then it has become the major backbone for NHS [NHS N3 2008].

Currently, N3 network hosts many healthcare IT services benefitting citizens of England. These services are:

1. **Electronic Booking Service, Choose and Book.** It provides a central appointment booking service for patients across all hospitals and clinics in England.

2. **Electronic Transmission of Prescriptions (ETP).** It provides the flexibility in making/presenting paperless prescriptions for medical practitioners, pharmaceutical agencies, and patients across England.

3. **Picture Archival and Communications System (PACS).** It provides a central mechanism for medical image storage, retrieval, distribution, and display across medical practices in England.

4. **NHS Care Records Service (CRS).** It is a major component of Spine infrastructure enabling patients to access their healthcare records over the network from anywhere.

Local Service Provider (LSP). BT plc is working with NHS in modernizing healthcare IT systems in hospitals, medical institutions, and clinical practices to make use of healthcare services over N3 network. It acts as a Local Service Provider to migrate existing IT systems in healthcare practices in England to systems capable of communicating with national database and healthcare services available through the Spine program.

30.3.2 STRUCTURE OF SUMMARY CARE RECORD

Spine infrastructure provides a summary care record available to the patients in multiple stages [NHS SCR 2006].

Stage 1: Text-Only Summary Care Record. The summary care record contains the minimum patient demographics and a set of clinical information including text-only information related to prescriptions, and adverse and allergic reactions to medication. The Royal College of General Practitioners has standardized the components of summary care record [Hassey and Robinson 2007]. The summary care record is supposed to include textual summary initially as a patient's record. The components that are included in the summary are:

- Drugs
- Allergies
- Adverse drug reactions
- Major diagnoses
- Chronic conditions
- Major operations
- Significant therapies and treatment plans
- Immunizations

Stage 2: Coded Summary Care Record. The coded summary care record will replace the text-only summary care record. It will include detailed diagnoses and problems associated with a patient's health. Systems compliant to use coding systems in summary care record will help clinicians determine which fields are mandatory in the summary. This will ensure data quality and validity in summary care records.

30.3.3 CONTENT OF SUMMARY CARE RECORD

The NHS captures clinical information in categories mentioned in the text-only summary care record along with codes in SNOMED CT attached with the records. For this, the record types identified are:

- Current medications
- Allergies
- Adverse reactions
- Hospital admission
- Handover note
- Discharge summary

The NHS has developed standard guidelines specifying the contents of the above-mentioned record types [Clinician's Guide to Record Standards 2008].

30.3.4 SECURITY INFRASTRUCTURE

Figure 30.2 shows the national level security infrastructure required by the NHS for securing a nationwide EHR framework.

Major actors in the infrastructure are *National Health Services (NHS Portal)*, *Health Care Organization (HCO) Server,* and *Index Server*. Index Server acts as an index of all electronic health records. The HCO Server actually hosts electronic health records. NHS Portal, Index Server, and HCO Server have the *Open Architecture for Secure Interworking Services (OASIS)* Access Control Management Mechanism. OASIS security architecture provides a Role-Based Access Control (RBAC) mechanism.

OASIS certificates extend the X.509-based certificates to include role information. The security infrastructure provides these certificates to users including patients and healthcare providers. When a user requests for access to an EHR, the request goes to the index server. Based on the user's role and access rights, it filters out the list of records and then sends this list to NHS portal. Based on the click on a particular record, the user interface retrieves that EHR record from the HCO server. Because the role-based privilege is already determined by the Index Server for a list of records, no extra privilege check is done at the HCO server.

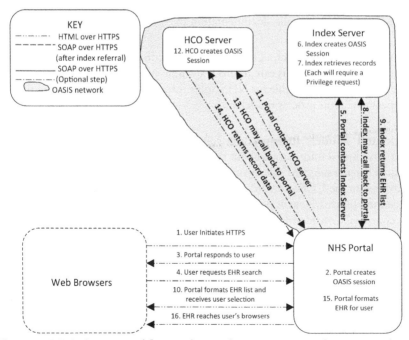

FIGURE 30.2 Access control framework using the OASIS security infrastructure. Adapted from [Eyers et al. 2006]. Reproduced by permission of the Institution of Engineering and Technology.

30.3.5 EXCHANGE

HL7 CDA or ASTM CCR standards can represent the summary care record as a document. It consists of a *Header* and a *Section*. The Header includes document and patient identification parameters. Section includes clinical information related to defined record types. Since HL7 CDA or ASTM CCR standards can represent clinical information in XML format, it is easy to manage and render the contents of the summary care record. Applications can transmit these documents in HL7 v3 messages ensuring interoperability.

The NHS provides *NHS Classifications Service (NCS)* that standardizes the use of clinical terminologies across England. NCS provides guidelines and standards for use in healthcare practices in England. The *Office of Population Censuses and Surveys (OPCS)* in England defines the coding terminologies called OPCS-4. The standards mandatory from NCS perspective are *OPCS Classification of Interventions & Procedures (OPCS-4)* and *ICD-10*. The NHS holds the license of these terminology uses in the country and makes it available in healthcare practices in England [NHS CS 2011; NHS Coding Standards 2011].

30.4 Discussion

Although the NHS Spine program is for the United Kingdom, it is currently only in England. All the public documentation of Spine is attributed to England.

Clinical Process Model. The NHS CRS describes a patient summary in the form of a care record. This care record is a simple structural content record. From the documentation available for NHS Spine infrastructure, it appears that there is no specific clinical process model.

Structural Model. Presently, the summary care record is text-only, having summary clinical information about the allergies and adverse reactions to medications. When the standard will encompass all clinical record types, it may actually be equivalent to the CCR standard. The summary care record will also include local procedures for treatment as per the practices and their associated coding terminology concepts. Considering the structural model of summary care record as of now for representing EHR model is a long way to go. As it is not supposed to hold the entire clinical information of a patient, one cannot refer it as the standard for EHR of a patient.

The nature of the standard is like a report-based representation of clinical record types. This approach is useful if the EHR framework is holding clinical information internally in a particular standard. However, adhering to a particular standard has disadvantages of data loss associated with it during conversion. However, the summary care record standard can help while defining the summary information in a patient's EHR.

Security/Privacy Considerations. Spine describes the security infrastructure clearly. Some of the notable points are as follows:

- Multifactor authentication at local systems
- Multifactor authentication for web access to national distributed EHR
- Nationally hosted service for patient registration for authentic demographics information
- Role-based access control to the EHR to manage privacy
- Online registry of available services over national distributed EHR store and authenticated access to them
- Single sign-on facility for hosted set of health services
- Use of strong authentication and data protection policies in the network

These techniques are important from security perspective of a large-scale EHR framework.

The OASIS Security infrastructure is an example architecture for security in a nationwide EHR framework. It uses role-based access control for authentication and authorization. However, EHR framework also requires attribute level authorization for which different frameworks like XACML needs to be evaluated. For example, a lab technician can access healthcare information only during a particular period of the day.

Large-scale EHR security infrastructures can utilize some of the technical methodologies in Spine, such as (a) using digital certificates for authentication and (b) using SOAP over HTTPS for secure transmission while designing security framework for EHRs.

Legal Aspects. As such, Spine-infrastructure-related documentation does not describe legal aspects/guidelines. However, nonrepudiation and patient consents can be the two issues that this infrastructure takes care of may have legal implications. Authentication, authorization, and patient preferences management handle these issues.

Exchange Specifications. The summary care record has the structure of report that HL7 CDA and ASTM CCR standard can represent in document format. The only issue is to provide mapping between the types defined by HL7 CDA and the types followed in summary care records. Then exchange is possible through HL7 v3 messages including CDA or CCD documents. However, no mapping between the data types of summary care record and CDA is available in public documentation.

For standardization of coding systems, NHS took an approach of developing their own standard called OPCS-4. NHS classification service added local procedures to OPCS-4, which are not there in ICD-10. Localization leads to the design of an EHR framework that is geography-specific in nature but serves the purpose better there.

30.5 Conclusion

The NHS initiative of the national healthcare IT network is an important case study to understand architectural decisions and corresponding pros and cons. Some important points about this initiative are:

1. The approach of having a nationwide patient demographic service is important from the perspective of a national framework.
2. The security infrastructure utilizes efficient techniques for ensuring secure access to national EHR framework.
3. SCR standard should provide one-to-one mapping with CDA standard data types to ensure lossless representation.
4. SCR standard's information model is not comprehensive enough to hold a patient's entire health record.

BIBLIOGRAPHY

[Carenini et al. 2009] Carenini, A., Krummenacher, R., Marcos, D., Momtchev, V., and La, M., Assessment of the developed solution with regards to the detected indicators. In: *Proceedings of Triple Space Communication* (2009).

[Clinician's Guide to Record Standards 2008] Health Informatics Unit, Clinical Standards Department, Royal College of Physicians, A Clinician's Guide to Record Standards—Part 2: Standards for the structure and content of medical records and communications when patients are admitted to hospital. In: *Proceedings of Digital and Health Information Policy Directorate* (2008); http://www.rcplondon.ac.uk/sites/default/files/clinicians-guide-part-2-standards_0.pdf.

[Eyers et al. 2006] Eyers, D., Bacon, J., and Moody, K., OASIS Role-based Access Control for Electronic Health Records. In: *Proceedings of IEE*, Software, pp. 16–23, (2006).

[Ferronato et al. 2003] Ferronato, P., Lotti, S., and Berardi, D., Architectural strategy for eHealth (March 2003); http://www.funzionepubblica.gov.it/media/566290/tse-ibse-strategia_architetturale-v01.00-def.pdf.

[Hassey and Robinson 2007] Hassey, A. and Robinson, P., The GP summary of summary care record. In: *Proceedings of RCGP Health Informatics Standing Group*, (2007); http://www.connectingforhealth.nhs.uk/systemsandservices/scr/documents/rcgpscrl.pdf.

[NHS Coding Standards 2011] Coding Standards in England, (2011); http://www.connectingforhealth.nhs.uk/systemsandservices/data/clinicalcoding/codingstandards.

[NHS CS 2011] NHS Classifications Service, (2011); http://www.connectingforhealth.nhs.uk/systemsandservices/data/clinicalcoding.

[NHS N3 2008] NHS N3 Network (2008); http://n3.nhs.uk/TheN3Story/N3Enabling21stCenturyhealthcarefortheNHS.cfm.

[NHS NPfIT 2011] NHS National Programme for IT (2011); http://www.btplc.com/Health/NHSIT/NPfIT/index.htm.

[NHS SCR 2006] NHS Connecting for Health, *The Initial Generation and Continuing Refreshment of the GP Summary Care Record—The Way Forward* (2006).

CHAPTER THIRTY-ONE

USA's EHR Meaningful Use

31.1 Introduction

In the United States of America, several organizations were created in the past to improve healthcare service delivery through the use of ICT. These organizations are still contributing in different areas of healthcare domain such as Standardization of Health Information, Health Processes, Messaging and Communication, EHR Systems Development, EHR Security and Privacy, Supportive Health Services Management, Health Insurance Automation, and Regulation of ICT in Health through Legal Framework. Some healthcare standards that evolved as a result of these contributions have already been covered in the earlier chapters. Hence, this chapter primarily focuses on those initiatives of the United States of America that are targeted toward implementation of EHR in the country.

The *Department of Health and Human Services (HHS)* is the parent governing organization of the United States. It has undertaken several nationwide initiatives toward implementing ICT in healthcare. *Office of National Coordinator (ONC)* [ONC] for Health Information Technology is an agency under the HHS that greatly contributes in the area of research in healthcare and quality management. This chapter presents some of these initiatives and describes their approach toward use of ICT to improve healthcare services in the nation.

Electronic Health Record: Standards, Coding Systems, Frameworks, and Infrastructures, Pradeep Sinha, Gaur Sunder, Prashant Bendale, Manisha Mantri, and Atreya Dande.

31.2 Overview

The two initiatives of the United States targeted primarily toward EHR implementation and covered in this chapter are:

EHR Meaningful Use. In the United States, to promote usage of the EHR in clinical practices among healthcare organizations and adhere to the standard practices, the *American Recovery and Reinvestment Act of 2009* (ARRA) [ARRA 2009] was introduced. Under the ARRA, the Department of Human Health Services (HHS) was assigned the responsibility to define statutory and regulatory guidelines. Thus, EHR Meaningful Use program was initiated. Centres for Medicare and Medicaid Services (CMS), which is an agency under HHS, administers these activities. The CMS and the HHS established regulatory guidelines in July 2010 for EHR Meaningful Use. These regulations govern the requirements of EHR Meaningful Use and related incentive payments.

National Health Information Network (NHIN). The NHIN is a common health information exchange platform covering standards, communication protocols, specifications, and services to provide secure exchange of health information across healthcare applications. It helps in achieving the goals of *Health Information Technology for Economic and Clinical Health (HITECH)* Act [HITECH].

31.3 EHR Meaningful Use

From the guidelines of EHR Meaningful Use, it is clear that the regulation incentivizes adoption. Hence, the guidelines talk about the incentives and qualifying criteria. These regulations were established in July 2010. As per the guidelines, the healthcare applications that will not comply with EHR Meaningful Use by 2015 may be penalized. Different requirement specifications are available under EHR Meaningful Use program. In these publications, *Core Set* defines the minimum clinical or patient information that should be available in an EHR, *Menu Set* describes the set of functions that should be provided by an EHR system, and *Final Rule Document* published by the Code of Federal Regulations (CFR) specifies the requirements to be fulfilled by healthcare applications. These requirement specifications are covered later in the chapter.

The EHR Meaningful Use program is divided into the following three stages:

Stage 1. The main objective of Stage 1 is to enable healthcare applications to capture the relevant clinical and patient-related information and then share it across healthcare applications. Under *Stage 1, CMS*, the administrative authority has released two regulations, namely, *Incentive program for Electronic Health Records,* and *Standards and Certification Criteria for Electronic*

Health Records. The first regulation defines the objectives that healthcare application providers must achieve to qualify for payment of incentives. The second regulation describes the technical functions to be implemented by an EHR system. This regulation is named as the Final Rule Document [HHS Health IT Portal 2011].

Stage 2. The main objective of Stage 2 is to define requirements for clinical processes and regulate their adoption in healthcare applications. At the time of writing, as the program is running in this stage, a set of recommendations are defined and are available for public comments. The recommendations are based on the outcomes from Stage 1 [HHS Health IT Portal 2011]. Stage 2 also includes the development of a Health Information Exchange to enable a patient's health information access from anywhere.

Stage 3. The main objective of Stage 3 is to validate the objectives achieved in the first two stages and take necessary actions for completion of stated objectives under the program.

31.3.1 REQUIREMENT SPECIFICATIONS

The requirements defined in the Final Rule Document are categorized into the following three sets:

1. **Core Set:** It defines the categories of patient health information to be supported by an EHR system.
2. **Menu Set:** It defines the functions to be implemented by an EHR system.
3. **Standards, Implementation Specifications, and Certification Criteria:** These are the rules that an EHR system should adhere to.

The three sets of the Final Rule Document are discussed below:

Core Set It describes the requirements for EHR content that an EHR system should adhere to. It defines the minimum information to be contained in different record types in an EHR. It also specifies the requirements for security and privacy, exchange, and clinical processes. The Core Set is categorized into the following:

Patient Demographics	Clinical Quality Reporting
Vital Signs	Electronic Copy of Health Information
Problem List	Electronic Prescription
Medication List	CPOE - Medication Orders
Medication Allergy List	Drug–Drug or Drug Allergy Checks
Smoking Status	Electronic Exchange
Clinical Summaries	Clinical Decision Support Rule
Discharge Instructions	
Privacy and Security	

Menu Set It specifies the requirements for the availability of medical information for research, education, and reporting purposes. These are the basic functions that an EHR system should follow in order to qualify for certification under EHR Meaningful Use. The guidelines covered are as follows:

- Formulary Checks
- Clinical Lab Results
- Patient Lists
- Patient Education
- Medical Reconciliation
- Summary of Care Record
- Immunization Registries
- Syndromic Surveillance Data
- Advanced Directives
- Public Health Reportable Lab Results
- Patient Reminders
- Patient Electronic Access

The Menu Set, as evident from the listing above, is expected to stimulate health information generation for national use in statistical reporting of diseases, conducting research, and nationwide surveys about health.

Standards, Implementation Specifications, and Certification Criteria - This part of the Final Rule Document is released under Stage 1. These requirements must be fulfilled by the EHR systems to interoperate EHR data and to qualify for incentives payment. Here, a summary of these requirements is described to highlight the important points [e-CFR 2011].

The requirements are divided into the following four sections:

- Content Exchange Standards
- Vocabulary Standards
- Standards for Electronic Health Record Protection
- Certification Criteria

Content Exchange Standards. This section specifies the medical standards and implementation specifications for healthcare applications and EHR systems that must be followed while exchanging EHR contents such as patient summary record, prescriptions, laboratory results, and so on. Similarly, the standards are specified for other contents of an EHR.

The content structure of a patient summary record is defined using the CDA Release 2 [HL7 CDA R2] standard. Continuity of Care Document (CCD) [CCD] is used to exchange such a summary care record. The implementation specification that can be used in this regard is *Healthcare Information Technology Standards Panel (HITSP)—C32 Summary Documents* using CCD Component [HITSP C32].

The *National Council for Prescription Drug Programs (NCPDP) SCRIPT* [SCRIPT] standard is specified for representing and exchanging prescriptions electronically. HL7 v2.5.1 standard is specified for exchanging laboratory results and HL7 v2.3.1 for immunization results.

Vocabulary Standards. This section specifies the codes, terminologies, and nomenclatures used for representing clinical information in an EHR.

SNOMED CT [SNOMED CT] is specified for representing the health problems encountered by a patient. LOINC [LOINC] is specified for representing the laboratory test results and clinical observations. For representing immunizations, HL7 Standard Code Set CVX—Vaccines Administered [CDC HL7 CVX] is specified.

Standards for Electronic Health Record Protection. This section specifies the EHR security and privacy guidelines. Final Rule Document acknowledges the importance of securing health information contained in an EHR and while exchanging information across health care systems. It provides the guidelines to record access, update, or exchange EHR. The recorded information should contain details such as date, time, patient identification, and user identification. It suggests the use of encryption algorithms specified by *Federal Information Processing Standards (FIPS)* 140-2 [NIST 2001] for securing EHR contents.

Certification Criteria. The certification criteria should be followed by healthcare applications and EHR systems to qualify for incentives payment. These certification criteria are mandated to be followed unless specified as optional. The three subsections under the certification criteria are discussed below [e-CFR 2011].

1. *General Certification Criteria.* The certification requirements defined under this subsection are as follows:

   a. The general criteria mandates EHR systems to generate notifications for drug-to-drug contradictions, drug allergy checks based on medication list, and medical allergy list maintained by the system. It specifies that EHR systems should support configuration of such notifications to add, remove, or create a new notification as needed.

   b. It specifies that an EHR system should maintain updated patient demographics information, problem list, active medication list, vital signs, body mass index, smoking status, and laboratory test results for a patient.

   c. It specifies that an EHR system should be able to provide syndrome-based retrieval of information, which helps in public health surveillance and reporting.

d. It directs an EHR system to record each action taken on an EHR, provide access control permissions, and follow specifications of Federal Information-tion Processing Standards (FIPS) 140-2 [NIST 2001] for applying security functions in the system.

2. ***Specific Certification Criteria for EHR Systems for an ambulatory setting.*** This subsection extends the general certification criteria described earlier and defines the criteria for an EHR system implemented in ambula-tory setting (outpatient). These certification criteria are mandated to be followed unless specified as optional. The certification requirements defined under this subsection are as follows:

   a. It specifies that a Computerized Provider Order Entry (CPOE) system in ambulatory setting should allow a user to create, retrieve, and update order types such as, medications, laboratory, imaging, and prescriptions.

   b. It specifies that an EHR system should provide electronic clinical decision support rules based on the contents of an EHR such as problem list, medication list, test results, and so on.

   c. It specifies that exchange of a part or complete EHR should be supported using the medical standards and implementation specifications listed in the Final Rule Document.

3. ***Specific Certification Criteria for EHR Systems for an inpatient setting.*** This subsection also extends the general certification criteria as described earlier and specifies the particular criteria to be adhered by an EHR system for inpatient setting.

   a. It specifies that an EHR system should support the creation of a copy of complete or part of EHR in human readable format or copy it on an electronic media.

   b. For maintaining quality guidelines, it specifies that an EHR system should support CMS quality measures and reporting [PQRI 2009].

Apart from specifying the certification criteria, test certification programs are arranged for testing and evaluating them. Software tools for creating test cases and evaluating them on an EHR system are developed. To understand the rules and implement systems conforming to them, training programs are arranged for providers/vendors of EHR systems, Physician Order Entry systems, etc. The EHR system certifications are given by Certification Commission for Health Informatics Technology (CCHIT) [CCHIT].

The guidelines also talk about security and privacy of EHR. The software advice website [Software Advice 2010] describes EHR security guidelines as per "EHR Meaningful Use" specifications as a list of the following functionalities:

- Assign unique user names.
- Permit certain users to access health information during emergency.
- Terminate an electronic session after a predetermined time of inactivity.

- Encrypt and decrypt electronic health information that is stored and exchanged.
- Record actions (e.g., deletion) related to electronic health information.
- Track alterations of electronic health information.
- Set up user verification measures.
- Record disclosures made for treatment, payment, and healthcare operations.

31.4 National Health Information Network (NHIN)

The objectives behind the implementation of *National Health Information Network (NHIN)* are [Shah 2010]:

- Provide secure internet-based private network.
- Ensure trusted entities participation and access control.
- Achieve interoperability across healthcare applications through requirement specification and certifications.
- Enable privacy and security management using legal policies.
- Make indexed information available on the network that helps locate information easily.
- Provide an operating model that defines activities, roles, and responsibilities to trusted entities and manages them.

NHIN is more like a specification that can be implemented in any type of healthcare environment. The discussion on NHIN is divided into several parts, namely, NHIN Architecture, Exchange Services, Transaction Profiles, and Authorization Framework. Two implementation projects based on this specification are also covered in the discussion.

31.4.1 NHIN ARCHITECTURE

Fundamentally, NHIN is a network of networks based on a federated implementation model where no centralized health store or service is maintained. It consists of the following four major components [NHIN DRAFT April 2010]:

1. **NHIN Node.** The *Health Information Organizations (HIOs)* are NHIN nodes. An HIO is a hospital, clinic, and so on, of any size. Each HIO has a healthcare application and a NHIN Gateway. An HIO setup can have numerous EMR systems, Laboratory Information Systems (LIS), Radiology Information Systems (RIS), and so on. Each healthcare application in an HIO tries to access patient health information from other HIOs through an NHIN Gateway. Patient health information is stored at an HIO and not on

any of the NHIN Gateways. Policies to allow or deny access to a part of health information are regulated by each HIO. It is also accountable for the accuracy and correctness of the information provided over NHIN.

2. ***NHIN Gateway.*** Each NHIN Gateway enables secure exchange of health information through the use of interoperability standards and technologies. Each HIO implements a NHIN Gateway based on the specifications of NHIN. NHIN Gateways are implemented using the Service-Oriented Architecture (SOA). Web services are the basis for transport, service discovery, and exchange of information. Each NHIN Gateway defines the functions provided by it using the Web Services Description Language (WSDL) document. The web services are based on Web Services Interoperability (WS-I) profiles. The two profiles used in NHIN architecture specifications are WS-I Basic v2.0 [WS-I Basic Profile 2.0] and WS-I Security v1.1 [WS-I Security Profile 1.1].

3. ***NHIN Service Registry.*** The NHIN service registry is implemented using the Universal Description Discovery and Integration (UDDI) version 3.0 specification [UDDI]. It contains location information about NHIN Gateway web services. NHIN nodes can access this registry through a secure channel using the PKI (Public Key Infrastructure) interfaces. This registry can be distributed among HIOs that can maintain subregistries locally. However, a central master registry of all these services is maintained with the NHIN governance bodies.

4. ***NHIN Security Infrastructure.*** A security service is provided in NHIN, which manages PKI-based (X.509) keys [X.509] for each NHIN node Figure 31.1. It provides the capabilities to create, update, or revoke the keys.

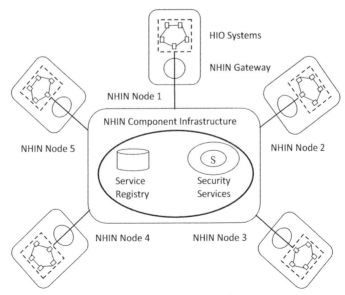

FIGURE 31.1 NHIN service infrastructure.

However, this function is limited to the NHIN governance bodies. It is used to establish a two-way Secure Socket Layer (SSL) interaction between two NHIN nodes.

31.4.2 EXCHANGE SERVICES

These services are invoked while exchanging patient health information across NHIN nodes. The technologies for implementing these services are the same as NHIN Gateway. Following are the four services specified under Exchange Services:

1. ***Patient Discovery.*** Before initiating a transaction to retrieve a patient's health information, it is necessary to identify the patient. Hence, in such a scenario, an NHIN node first attempts to query all NHIN Gateways from NHIN Service Registry to find a match for a patient based on his/her demographic attributes. In response, each NHIN node tries to match the queried attributes with entries from the Master Patient Index maintained locally at each HIO, and it returns a Patient Identifier in case of a successful match. A successful match enables the requestor NHIN node to query for further information based on the patient identifier.

2. ***Document Query and Retriev.*** This service endpoint helps in finding a clinical document based on the patient identifier and query attributes that define part of the contents described in the document so that it can be searched across NHIN nodes. Each document can be retrieved using the document identifier also.

3. ***Health Information Event Messaging (HIEM).*** This is a subscription and notification service used by an NHIN node to subscribe to various health related events generated by other NHIN nodes.

4. ***Document Submission.*** This service is used to send a single or a batch of documents from one NHIN node to another. To perform this operation, it is required to identify the patient whose documents are being exchanged.

31.4.3 TRANSACTION PROFILES

Transaction profiles are defined to facilitate service providers (HIOs) to follow the guidelines and implement services that support uniform features. These profiles define the specification of services provided that can help to use the service. It defines the constraints and functions provided by the service. For example, a Document Submission Profile would put a constraint of including the patient identifier in each document submitted. Each of the exchange services are implemented based on such profiles. For example, an HIEM GIPSE profile is used for Geocoded Interoperable Population Summary Exchange (GIPSE), used by the U.S. Centres for Disease Control and Prevention (CDC). A Continuity Assessment Record and Evaluation (CARE) Profile is used by the Centre for Medicare and Medicaid Services (CMS) for exchanging patient discharge summaries.

31.4.4 AUTHORIZATION FRAMEWORK

An authorization framework is based on the web service constructs and defines the information to be exchanged to authorize an NHIN node to access information from another NHIN node. It specifies the usage of Security Assertion Markup Language (SAML) 2.0 specification [SAML]. Authentication is done on the basis of requestor NHIN node's key and optionally using the Domain Name System (DNS) address or Internet Protocol (IP) address. NHIN Access Consent policies are defined that enable a node to obtain authorization for accessing another NHIN node directly. Such assertions can be specified using SAML.

31.4.5 NHIN TRIAL PROJECT

To implement and demonstrate a working model of NHIN specification, NHIN Trial Project was implemented using open source CONNECT. CONNECT is a Health Information Exchange (HIE) software solution implemented based on the standards and governance principles stated under NHIN [CONNECT]. However, CONNECT is more based on the principles of enabling communication from HIE-to-HIE solutions rather than from a Point-to-Point solution that includes healthcare applications. NHIN specifications are more like the second case. Hence, NHIN Direct Project was initiated by the Office of National Coordinator (ONC) to practically implement NHIN specifications.

31.4.6 NHIN DIRECT PROJECT

The NHIN Direct Project [NHIN Direct] evolved from the NHIN Trial Project and is currently being regulated by ONC to allow users to implement NHIN Gateway specifications in less time and effort. NHIN Direct helps in creating a network of simple to complex set of systems in an HIO. The project is gaining importance since it supports a wide variety of users, such as clinics, small-to-large hospital setups, and nationwide architecture. The NHIN Direct Project expects its specifications and services to be used to exchange different formats such as structured (text, PDF, etc.), semistructured (CDA-base templates, HL7 MDM), and fully structured (CCR, CCD). These will be implemented as separate profiles so that users (HIOs) can implement any of them as per the local environment. It will make use of the Representational State Transfer (REST) [REST] protocol to implement web services.

31.5 Discussion

EHR Meaningful Use. The US Government laid down the EHR Meaningful Use guidelines to clarify the type of tasks involved in clinical processes, the kind of EHR software used for fulfilling these tasks, and incentivize the adopters for right usage. The guidelines are covered from the perspective of EHR description, security and privacy specifications, and exchange specifications.

NHIN. The National Health Information Network (NHIN) is being implemented to achieve interoperability across various healthcare setups in the country. The project is receiving wide support from major players in healthcare in the United States.

Clinical Process Model

EHR Meaningful Use. EHR Meaningful Use is a statutory and regulatory guidelines specification for right usage of EHR systems. There is no clinical process model defined by the guidelines. It describes the types of clinical information with partially defined contents. It also specifies the functional requirements for EHR systems in each of these categories.

NHIN. NHIN is a specification for Health Information Exchange and policies for exchange. It does not involve a process model of EHR.

Structural Model

EHR Meaningful Use. Being regulatory guidelines for deciding the qualifiers for national incentive program in healthcare, EHR Meaningful Use defines the expectations to use certified EHR systems, where CCHIT is responsible for certifying an EHR system for use. It does not specify the structural details of the clinical information types and associated functional components such as CPOE. At some places, the guidelines briefly specify the types of contents; for example, Patient Demographics can contain Gender, Race, Ethnicity, Date of Birth, Preferred Language, and so on. However, there is no comprehensive list of parameters under each clinical type. This is apparently not in the scope of these guidelines.

NHIN. From the available documents, it appears that NHIN describes the structure for exchanging health information but does not describe a complete structural model or information model for EHR. It specifies the use of certain health information attributes while accessing its exchange services.

Security/Privacy Considerations

EHR Meaningful Use. The guidelines given are more toward making use of EHRs and converting the current clinical processes and associated business processes in an electronic format as a normal practice. That is why the incentive to motivate the healthcare industry is provided. The security and privacy guidelines described earlier in the EHR Meaningful Use section can help in providing considerations while designing security model of an EHR system for a national EHR. The certification criteria specified in *Title 45, Code of Federal Regulations (45 CFR 170), Part 170* describe each of the components of Core Set and Menu Set of "EHR Meaningful Use" and specify the applicable standard in that category. The detailed specification listed is very useful for identifying which existing standard techniques should be used for meeting these goals.

NHIN. NHIN uses X.509-based certificates as keys to identify the users and NHIN nodes. Access to various architectural components is provided only on successful validation of these keys. Security Assertion Markup Language (SAML) is used for exchanging security-related transactions, which can be studied to identify its usage in implementing authorization frameworks.

Legal Aspects The identified list of components and associated functionalities by EHR Meaningful Use need adherence to the guidelines given by 45 CFR 170. This approach can be useful in implementing a distributed EHR system by establishing regulatory guidelines for streamlining the usage of information technology in healthcare domain.

Exchange Specifications

EHR Meaningful Use. EHR Meaningful Use provides detailed description of specific exchange standards to be used for each of the identified topics in Core Set and Menu Set. For example, for submission of laboratory reports, the committee suggests using the HL7 v2.5.1 standard. Similarly, for submission of health information to public health agencies for reporting and survey, the committee suggests using the HL7 v2.3.1 standard. For the Patient Care Summary record, it suggests using the HL7 CDA R2 or Continuity of Care Document (CCD) standard. This approach makes EHR technologies adhere to multiple standards and ensures that a record type is actually bound to a specific standard. The approach, however, has the disadvantage that not every EHR vendor will like to adhere to the suggested standards, thereby compromising flexibility. This technique suggests a nice way of adhering to multiple standards, but information-type-wise standard specification may be problematic in the long run.

NHIN. The main objective of NHIN specification is to simplify and regulate health information exchange between diverse healthcare applications. To achieve this, it provides several exchange services and transaction profiles. NHIN Direct uses CDA R2, CCR, and CCD for exchange of health information. Apart from the standards, it specifies profiles to exchange structured and nonstructured data. Supporting several standards provides flexibility to users in implementing any of the supported standards and eliminates the problems of supporting a single standard.

Technical Guidelines

EHR Meaningful Use. Clear technical guidelines are available for specific EHR functions like content exchange, security, nonrepudiation, privacy, and so on. The specifications given by National Institute of Standards & Technology (NIST) [NIST 2001] for security techniques are well-known techniques for security and are widely used globally for protecting electronic information. The techniques suggested like Encryption, Hashing algorithms, could be used in any national EHR system for information security.

NHIN. NHIN being a pure technical specification, it provides the details of technological specifications to be used. It explicitly specifies the usage of SAML for authorization framework, WS-I profiles and web service features, and UDDI for web service registry. The specification is a good reference for studying various technological specifications that can be used in small- to large-scale health environments.

31.6 Conclusion

EHR Meaningful Use specifies the regulatory guidelines laid by the U.S. Government for determining qualifying organizations/software under EHR incentives program. The regulatory guidelines given are in the areas of content, exchange, and security of EHR. These guidelines can be referred by any country while setting up similar guidelines for a national EHR model.

NHIN is a specification for Health Information Exchange to enable exchange of patient health information across various regions of the United States using a common framework of services. The standards and technologies specified in the specification are well suited for implementing such a setup in a country.

BIBLIOGRAPHY

[ARRA 2009] Internal Revenue Service (IRS), American Recovery and Reinvestment Act of 2009 (ARRA); http://www.irs.gov/newsroom/article/0,,id=204335,00.html.

[CCD] Continuity Care Document (CCD), Health Level 7 (HL7); http://wiki.hl7.org/index.php?title=Product CCD.

[CCHIT] Certification Commission for Health Informatics Technology (CCHIT); http://www.cchit.org/about/commission.

[CDC HL7 CVX] Center for Disease Control and Prevention (CDC), *HL7 Standards Code Set CVX—Vaccines Administered*; http://www2a.cdc.gov/nip/IIS/IISStandards/vaccines.asp?rpt=cvx.

[CONNECT] CONNECT Open Source Portal; http://www.connectopensource.org.

[e-CFR 2011] Electronic Code of Federal Regulations (e-CFR) publication for Title 45, PART 170, Subpart B (November 2011); http://ecfr.gpoaccess.gov/cgi/t/text/text-idx?c=ecfr&sid=3e82ac8332cbd3613a64aedb850f7c08&rgn==div6&view=text&node=45:1.0.1.4.79.2&idno=45.

[Final Rule 2010] Standards and Certification Criteria Final Rule Document, (July 2010); http://edocket.access.gpo.gov/2010/pdf/2010-17210.pdf.

[Gantz 2010] Gantz, S., Privacy and Security Considerations for EHR Incentives and Meaningful Use (2010); http://www.securityarchitecture.com/docs/SecPriv_MU.pdf.

[HHS Health IT Portal 2011] Department of Health and Health Services, Health IT Portal; http://healthit.hhs.gov/portal/server.pt?open=512&objID=2996&mode=2.

[HITECH] Health Information Technology for Economic and Clinical Health (HITECH) Act; http://www.hipaasurvivalguide.com/hitech-act-text.php.

[HITSP C32] Health Information Technology Standards Panel (HITSP), C32, *HITSP Summary Care Document using HL7 Continuity of Care Document (CCD) Component*; http://www.hitsp.org/Handlers/HitspFileServer.aspx?FileGuid=bad7c178-0e4a-4dab-8144-0bfa45d6325b.

[HL7 CDA R2] Health Level 7, Clinical Document Architecture (CDA), Release 2; http://www.hl7.org/implement/standards/cda.cfm.

[IEEE-USA NHIN 2009] IEEE-USA Recommendations for NHIN, (2009); http://www.ieeeusa.org/policy/positions/NHINInterooperability1109.pdf.

[Jespen 2005] Jespen, T., Interoperability for the NHIN. In: *IEEE USA Medical Policy Technology Committee Meet* (2005); http://www.google.com/url?sa=t&rct=j&q=nhin+papers+ieee&source=web&cd=2&ved=0CCEQFjAB&url=Mei http%3A%2F%2Fwww.ieeeusa.org%2Fvolunteers%2Fcommittees%2Fmtpc%2FInteroperability070505.ppt&ei==avnJTpnhHomHrAfWlIGhDg&usg=AFQjCNFN5lrWCGYVumV51VqhrPS5DAezgw&cad=rja.

[Laurentis et al. 2007] Aurentis, D.D., Dickerson, C., DiMario, M., Gartz, P., Jamshidi, M. M., Nahavandi, S., Sage, A. P., Sloane, E. B., and Walker, D. R., A case for an International Consortium on System-of-Systems Engineering, *IEEES Systems Journal*, Vol. 1, No. 1, (September 2007); http://www.deakin.edu.au/dro/eserv/DU:30007797/nahavandi-caseforaninternational-2007.pdf.

[LOINC] Logical Observation Identifiers Names and Codes (LOINC); http://loinc.org/.

[NHIN Direct] NHIN Direct Project; http://directproject.org.

[NHIN DRAFT April 2010] National Health Information Network (NHIN) Exchange, Architecture Overview DRAFT v0.9 (April 2010); http://www.google.co.in/url?sa=t&rct=j&q=nhin+overview+draft&source=web&cd=1&ved=0CB0QFjA-A&url=http%3A%2F%2Fhealthit.hhs.gov%2Fportal%2Fserver.pt%2Fgateway%2FPTARGS_0_11113_911643_0_0_18%2FNHIN_Architecture_Overview_Draft_20100421.pdf&ei=PxTNTovAEci4rAfh1tnkDA&usg=AFQjCNG9Cf4-Z_Rxij UNWMblb0Ed_kxGDQ.

[NHIN Specifications] National Health Information Network (NHIN) Specifications (October 2010); http://healthit.hhs.gov/portal/server.pt?open=512&objID=1407 &parentname=CommunityPage&parentid=8&mode=2&in_hi_userid=11113& cached=true.

[NIST 2001] National Institute of Standards and Technology (NIST), *Federal Information Processing Standards (FIPS)—PUB 140-2(Annex A)*; http://csrc.nist.gov/groups/STM/cmvp/standards.html#02.

[ONC] Office of the National Coordinator for Health Information Technology (ONC); http://healthit.hhs.gov/portal/server.pt/community/healthit_hhs_gov__onc/1200.

[PQRI 2009] Quality Reporting Standard, Centers for Medicare and Medicaid (CMS), *Physician Quality Reporting Initiative (PQRI) 2009 Registry XML Specification*; https://www.cms.gov/PQRI/downloads/PQRI2009RegistryXMLSpecsFinal508.pdf.

[REST] Restful Web Services; http://www.oracle.com/technetwork/articles/javase/index-137171.html.

[SAML] Security Assertion Markup Language (SAML); http://www.oasis-open.org/committees/download.php/27819/sstc-saml-tech-overview-2.0-cd-02.pdf.

[SCRIPT] National Council for Prescription Drug Programs (NCPDP, *SCRITP—e-Prescribing Standard*; http://www.ncpdp.org/eprescribing.aspx.

[Shah 2010] Shah, N. S., An overview of NHIN and NHIN Direct software developers; http://www.ibm.com/developerworks/web/library/wa-nhindirect/index.html.

[Sloane et al. 2007] Sloane, E., Way, T., Gehlot, V., Beck, R., Villanova University, Villanova, Conceptual SOS model and simulation systems for a next generation National Healthcare Information Network (NHIN-2): Creating a net-centric, extensible, context aware, dynamic discovery framework for robust, secure, flexible, safe, and reliable healthcare. In: *Systems Conference, IEEE* (2007); http://ieeexplore.ieee.org/xpl/freeabs_all.jsp?arnumber=4258867.

[SNOMED CT] Systematized Nomenclature of Medicines—Clinical Terms (SNOMED CT); http://www.ihtsdo.org/snomed-ct/.

[Software Advice 2010] Meaningful Use, Certified EHR technology and Stimulus Bill; http://blog.softwareadvice.com/articles/medical/the-stimulus-bill-and-meaningful-use-of-qualified-emrs-1031209/.

[UDDI] Universal Description Discovery and Integration (UDDI) version 3; http://www.uddi.org/pubs/uddi_v3.htm.

[WS-I Basic Profile 2.0] Web Services Interoperability (WS-I), *Basic Profile version 2.0*; http://www.ws-i.org/Profiles/BasicProfile-2_0%28WGD%29.html.

[WS-I Security Profile 1.1] Web Services Interoperability (WS-I), *Basic Security Profile version 1.1*; http://www.ws-i.org/Profiles/BasicSecurityProfile-1.1.html.

[X.509] X.509 Certificates; http://www.ietf.org/rfc/rfc2459.txt.

PART SIX

Findings and Conclusion

CHAPTER THIRTY-TWO

Findings and Conclusion

Earlier parts of the book introduced and discussed various international and national healthcare IT standards, Coding systems, EHR frameworks, and case studies for implementations of national EHR frameworks/systems. The description of each standard, framework, or case study also included the discussion on its suitability for developing a robust and complete EHR system. Their suitability was discussed based on certain requirements that included healthcare process, information model, EHR exchange specifications, security and privacy considerations, and legal aspects. The suitability of coding systems and terminologies was discussed based on their scope, structure, and significance in representing health information.

While the suitability of a standard, coding system, framework or case study was discussed individually in its respective chapter, this chapter compares and assesses them collectively for their suitability in designing an EHR system.

32.1 EHR Standards

ISO/TS 18308 standard specifies the requirements for an EHR system. The standard lists the requirements to be fulfilled by the structure of an EHR for accommodating clinical records, clinical data, and terminologies. It also specifies the requirements for exchange, usage, and sharing of data between healthcare applications, security and privacy of data, clinical activities that should be followed, legal and ethical requirements, requirements from consumer point

Electronic Health Record: Standards, Coding Systems, Frameworks, and Infrastructures, Pradeep Sinha, Gaur Sunder, Prashant Bendale, Manisha Mantri, and Atreya Dande.
© 2013 by The Institute of Electrical and Electronics Engineers, Inc. Published 2013 by John Wiley & Sons, Inc.

of view, and so on. Being an international standard, an EHR framework should conform to the requirement specifications provided by it.

CEN/TC 215 EN 13940 (CONTsys) has helped in concretizing the idea of defining the care process. It describes the standard clinical concepts and processes in order to provide a common view for the care processes followed in different hospitals. The basic concepts defined in this standard include the actors involved in healthcare processes, health issues, healthcare episode comprising patient–physician encounters, clinical decisions taken during patient care, and concepts in records and data management. These concepts help in identifying the various entities involved in healthcare processes. Healthcare Processes described in this standard specify the usage of the basic concepts to define different workflows in EHR systems. EHR systems adhering to this standard would reflect the real-world healthcare processes into their EHR models.

HL7 EHR-S Functional Model provides the functional requirements of an EHR system. It describes the various functional profiles categorized as Direct Care, Supportive Functions, and Information Infrastructure that individually enlist the various functions involved in patient care management, clinical decision support, administration and financial management, security, record management, registry, and standard terminology and related services. It can be used for analyzing and evaluating the functions that should be present in an EHR system.

CEN/ISO EN13606 is a five-part standard for EHR Communication that provides the specifications for a Reference Model. It describes the architecture for representing a part or whole of EHR that can be exchanged along with an archetype interchange specification adopted from *openEHR Archetype Model*. Reference Archetypes and Term Lists provide the structures for representing clinical terminologies independent of the coding systems and reference archetypes for providing interoperability between existing standards/frameworks (HL7 v3 and openEHR). It also provides the specifications for data exchange and components for security of EHR. The specifications provided by CEN/ISO EN13606 are based on ISO/TS 18308 requirements of EHR, and it is also accredited by ISO as ISO/CEN 13606. Technical specification for an interoperable EHR can be developed through this standard.

HL7 v2.x standard facilitates exchange of data across healthcare applications. The standard has a notion of information model that is given as message exchange format and not EHR model. The message exchange format is not based on object-oriented development. Though it provides the flexibility of defining one's own field set in messages, it makes it harder to achieve interoperability. Despite having few shortcomings due to its older design, it is the most widely used HIT standard world over.

HL7 v3 was developed to address the shortcomings in HL7 v2.x and is based on object-oriented methodology. It provides a Reference Information Model (RIM) and Vocabulary Domain that describe the contents and content types in an EHR for exchange. It uses XML for data exchange. It also provides an Interaction Model that describes the various interactions that take place between healthcare applications during data exchange. HL7 v3 is widely used for data exchange in recently implemented EHR systems and nationwide EHR implementations.

CDA is an XML document-based standard that uses the basic components of HL7 v3 RIM. It was developed specifically to incorporate the structure for representing various clinical documents exchanged in healthcare domain. It provides a document structure based on Sections, Headings, Contents, and so on.

The structure of CDA, openEHR Information Model, and CEN 13606 EHR EXTRACT (Reference Model) are similar. It is due to continuous harmonization between them for structure, data types, and exchange of EHR data.

CCD is a XML document-based standard developed for exchanging patient discharge and referral related information between healthcare applications. It uses HL7 v3 RIM and CDA's document structure to define document structure for various clinical artefacts.

DICOM is a widely used standard for medical image exchange in medical devices and RIS. Hence, to integrate data from such systems, adoption of DICOM in EHR is a primary step toward achieving interoperability and a uniform device interface mechanism. It is one of the most comprehensive standards in radiology/pathology domain.

CCR is helpful in identifying clinical record types in an EHR system. The CCR Information Model provides the content structure and types for developing patient transfer and discharge summaries. Various categories of health information provided by CCR can be studied to identify the searchable attributes for medical records for accessing patient records across organizational boundaries.

All of the above-mentioned standards with focus on different areas of EHR have varying requirements. HL7 v2.x focuses on exchange of clinical data. However, its newer version, HL7 v3, covers the specification for the information model. DICOM, on the other hand, gives emphasis on image data transfer. ISO/TS 18308 only provides the requirements; hence, systems adhering to it may vary in implementation. CEN/ISO EN 13606 provides a compressive specification for EHR communication using Archetypes for data exchange. However, it does not give a concrete list of clinical records that should be supported through Archetypes. CEN/TC 215 EN 13940 standardizes clinical concepts and clinical processes in healthcare.

Requirements of an EHR system differ from application to application and from country to country. Hence, adherence to a single standard for a national EHR system, where data from different healthcare applications are integrated, is not a feasible idea in the long run. Additionally, every standard has its own importance in the area for which it was evolved. Therefore, it is not possible to favor one standard over the other across all domains and functions of EHR system. Work is continuing to harmonize among some of the standards to support interoperability between them.

A comparative table of these EHR standards under the criteria for supporting healthcare process, information model, security and privacy considerations, and legal aspects is shown in Table 32.1.

TABLE 32.1 Comparison of Standards

Criteria	ISO/TS 18308	EN 13940	HL7 EHR-S FM	EN 13606	HL7 v2.x	HL7 v3	CCD	CDA	DICOM	CCR
Requirement specifications	✓	✗	✓	Partial	✗	✗	✗	✗	✗	✗
Process model	✗	✓	✗	✗	✗	✗	✗	✗	✗	✗
Structural model	✗	✗	✗	✓	Partial	✓	✓	✓	Partial	✓
Security/privacy	✗	✗	✗	✓	✗	✓	✓	✓	✓	✓
Legal aspects	✗	✗	✗	✓	✗	✗	✗	✗	✗	✗
Exchange specifications	✗	✗	✗	✓	✓	✓	✓	✓	✓	✓
Technical guidelines	✗	✗	✗	✓	✗	✓	✗	✗	✓	✗
Others	NA	Refers EN 13606 for clinical data representation	NA	ISO/TS 18308 compliant	NA	NA	NA	Document structure similar to EN 13606	NA	NA

*a*NA, not available.

32.2 Coding Systems

ICD provides the classification and groupings of diseases and related health problems. This is useful in carrying out statistical analysis of prevailing diseases in specific regions. Lack of details regarding diagnostic procedures in ICD codes made healthcare bodies build expanded versions of ICD codes such as ICD-9-CM, ICD-10-CM for clinical modifications and ICD-10-PCS for supporting procedure codes. ICD can be used in EHR frameworks to incorporate disease names and symptoms from the health problems recorded in an EHR.

LOINC is universally used to identify laboratory tests, results, and clinical observations. This coding system is listed as the standard for representing laboratory results in Final Rule Document under Stage-I of "EHR Meaningful Use" program in the United States. It is adopted in almost all the studied national EHR programs. However, coverage of health information in LOINC is limited to representing laboratory tests, results, and observations.

CPT provides standardized code-set for medical procedures or services performed during healthcare activities. CPT's scope restricts its usage in other categories of health information. It is best suited for use in financial transactions and legal considerations in medical procedures that help in managing administrative, financial, and legal processes in a healthcare environment.

HCPCS extends CPT's code set to provide codes for standardizing external health services carried out during healthcare service delivery such as supplies, pharmacies, medical equipments, and so on. This code-set is used in billing and insurance claim processing of such external health services. These codes can be used to interpret insurance-related information in an EHR.

SNOMED CT is a comprehensive terminology as compared to other coding systems. Many standards and frameworks such as HL7 v3 and openEHR have provided integration of SNOMED CT. It provides extensive support for technical implementation of coding terminology that facilitates rapid development of these codes in software applications. SNOMED CT is mandated for use in representing patients' health problems in Final Rule Document under Stage I of the EHR Meaningful Use program in the United States as well as in several national healthcare programs.

UMLS specifically targets mapping between existing coding terminologies. It provides mapping with almost all existing coding systems. However, it requires individual licenses of all specific coding systems (if licensed) for use. Hence, in EHR system design, UMLS can be considered as a framework for providing mapping between coding systems rather than a coding system database. UMLS is continuously growing with newer versions to support newer concepts, upgradations, and mapping.

A comparison of the studied coding systems in terms of covered clinical specialties is shown in Table 32.2.

Different coding terminologies and classifications are included to understand each one's applicable scope in the development of models for electronic health record. It is clear that the use of coding systems in electronic health records support semantic interoperability and decision making. Hence, developing data

TABLE 32.2   **Comparison of Coding Systems**

Clinical Specialties	LOINC	SNOMED CT	ICD-10	CPT	HCPCS
Procedures	✓	✓	✓	✓	✓
Admin	✗	✓	✗	✓	✓
Diseases	✗	✓	✓	✗	✗
Test Observations	✓	✓	✗	✗	✗
Findings	✗	✓	✗	✗	✗
Disorders	✗	✓	✓	✗	✗

representation structures for each of the coding standards in the electronic health record is important. However, with the number of coding systems and terminologies already implemented and many more waiting to be released, the task becomes complex for providing data representation structures for each one of them. There should be a single data representation structure that can accommodate values of existing and future code sets.

An electronic health record architecture should build indexes on the records that contain these code sets and host a search mechanism to locate these records faster. However, in a heterogeneous standards-based model of EHR, searching for similar terms and concepts should be provided across different code sets. For example, a search query for a record representing an ICD code should also search for records with similar SNOMED CT code. This task raises the need for providing mapping between similar terms and concepts represented by different code sets, where a framework like UMLS can be used.

32.3 Standard Frameworks

Though the archetype model of *openEHR* is very comprehensive and can be defined as per the requirements of users, it is complex in terms of its applicability to the already existing health information systems (since openEHR uses two-level modeling approach, existing systems need considerable time for upgrading). Additionally, flexibility for building archetypes (if they are unshared) may affect data interoperability. This can be tackled by adopting similar kind of approach taken by NEHTA, by putting a regulatory body for creation of archetypes at the national level. openEHR also provides integration archetypes for providing mapping between a known data representation format and an openEHR model. Because openEHR meets the requirement specifications provided by ISO/TS 18308 and CEN/ISO EN 13606 and is compatible with HL7 v2.x, it can be a good approach to build an EHR system.

Currently, *IHE Integration Profiles* provide interoperability specifications only for specific standards, that is, DICOM, HL7 v2.x, and HL7 v3 messaging standards. The records represented in other standards such as CCD, CCR, and openEHR will still require mapping. The mechanism defined by IHE Cross

Enterprise Data Sharing (XDS) profile is recommendable where it maintains a document registry of CDA, and CCD documents and systems can exchange it through registry lookup among each other.

An information model and an exchange model of EHR are the main concerns in developing an EHR system. openEHR is a complete framework that can be used to build an EHR system, and IHE aims at enabling workflow-based interoperability between systems adhering to diverse communication standards.

32.4 Case Studies: National EHR Efforts

The national EHR programs presented in the book reveal the fact that implementing a nationwide healthcare IT infrastructure is a long process involving a planned, phased activity. Countries such as Australia, Austria, Taiwan, United States, and many others have gone through phases such as study and analysis, building supporting infrastructures like security, standardization of EHR, standardization of communication mechanisms, and legal guidelines. These activities are then followed by prototype implementation for a set of stakeholders, and then a national rollout plan is created and executed.

The core component of healthcare IT infrastructure is its EHR model. All these countries have taken different approaches in designing the structure of their EHR. Many countries have defined their own templates that can be mapped to CDA templates. HL7 v3 is preferred communication mechanism for these CDA documents. However, defining of the template will face the serious problem of acceptance by existing solution providers. There are many issues like existing models not fitting in the template. Hence, most of these templates claim themselves as a summary part of the record and not the complete representation. This design is more acceptable but renders the EHR partially ineffective because many records are not covered or are considered not important enough to be included in a summary record. Usually clinicians do not make summary documents of minor ailments or what most HSP cover under the OPD section. Hence, there is a risk that such EHR models may not cover all medical events, transactions, and encounters in the lifetime of a patient.

For security, most countries have taken an approach of PKI-infrastructure and service-oriented architecture for building secure nationwide healthcare IT infrastructure. These infrastructures use the known exchange standards for information exchange, which mostly leads to conversion of existing data into standard data formats. This strategy may result in data loss due to mismatch or no-match between the standard data format and existing data format, and between one standard format and another. One thing that all the countries have emphasized is the need for unique identification not only for the patients, but also for the healthcare providers and insurers. Most countries have used an RBAC-based authorization mechanism to ensure security and access, with only Sweden using a more sophisticated mechanism, called ABAC.

England, Austria, Australia, and Sweden license the terminology standards for use in the country. This enables them to localize and customize the clinical terms as per their local use. However, this approach may be counterproductive when taken across national boundaries because it works only for the country. The approach taken by Hong Kong in this regard is different. They have come up with the Hong Kong Clinical Terminology Table (HKCTT), which maps local concepts in Hong Kong with related terms in all known terminology standards. From these approaches, it seems that the model should not bind to a particular terminology standard but should make room for any terminology that it wishes to use.

Countries such as Hong Kong, Australia, and Taiwan require local healthcare applications to upgrade to support the EHR model that is accepted as a nationwide EHR model. It also requires to upgrade in the existing systems to adhere to the communication standards supported by national infrastructure. Due to the diversity of healthcare applications across a nation, this activity itself would require years to finish, at a considerable cost that local hospitals may not be willing to bear. Hence, such a model would not work or may take a longer time in most situations. Denmark has used a technique of standardizing a pull process for required data from local hospitals. It is called as *Standardized Extract of Patient Data* (SUP). A standard is defined for the minimum required data as the summary data for a particular record type and extract that data through the mapping provided by local applications and put it in the national store. The mechanism of pulling data based on mapping is innovative. However, use of existing standards like DICOM, HL7 v2.x, v3, CDA, ASTM CCR, and CCD appears to be a better idea rather than defining a new national standard.

A countrywise comparison of the architectural components for a national EHR program is drawn in Table 32.3. The table lists the countries in rows and the architectural components required for a national EHR program as criteria in columns.

With several nations deploying healthcare IT infrastructure, there is a good corpus available for newcomers to learn from their experiences. Based on the available information, a quantitative and qualitative assessment of these efforts is given later. For this assessment, the evaluation criteria include a clinical process model, a structural model, exchange specifications, security/privacy considerations, and legal aspects.

32.4.1 QUANTITATIVE ASSESSMENT

After review of the national healthcare IT infrastructures of few countries, a quantitative assessment for the countries and standards is provided. It is observed that very few countries among the covered case studies (i.e., Denmark and Sweden) use process model for describing the workflow of the generic healthcare process in the country.

Table 32.4 shows the analysis of use of existing standards in these countries that helps in the design time decisions for new frameworks. Toward this, the assessment shows the use of different standards in each country. This matrix plots 10 countries and 10 standards. If a country is using a particular standard, then the corresponding cell information represents "Y" otherwise "N".

TABLE 32.3 Architectural Components of National EHR Programs

Criteria	Australia	Austria	Canada	Denmark	United Kingdom	Hong Kong	India	Netherlands	Singapore	Sweden	Taiwan	USA
Clinical Process Model	✗	✗	✗	✓	✗	✗	NA	✗	✗	✓	✗	✗
Service-based Framework	✓	✓	✓	✓	✓	✓	NA	✓	✓	✓	✓	✓
Authentication	PKI	PKI	PKI	PKI	PKI (OASIS)	PKI	NA	PKI	PKI	PKI	PKI	PKI
Authorization	RBAC	RBAC	RBAC	RBAC	RBAC	RBAC	NA	RBAC	RBAC	ABAC	RBAC	RBAC
Infrastructure (Central (C), Federated (F))	C	F	C	C	C	C	NA	F	F	F	F	F
Patient Index	✓	✓	✓	✓	✓	✓	NA	✓	✓	✓	✓	✓
Provider Registry	✓	✓	✓	✗	✓	✗	NA	✓	✗	✓	✗	✓

TABLE 32.4 Country-wise Usage of Standards

Standards	Australia	Austria	Canada	Denmark	United Kingdom	Hong Kong	India[a]	Netherlands	Singapore	Sweden	Taiwan	USA
HL7 v2.x	Y	N	N	N	N	Y	Y	N	Y	N	N	Y
HL7 v3	N	Y	Y	Y	Y	Y	Y	Y	Y	Y	N	N
CDA	Y	Y	Y	N	Y	Y	N	N	Y	N	Y	Y
ASTM CCR	N	N	N	N	Y	N	N	N	N	N	N	N
HL7/ ASTM CCD	N	N	N	N	N	N	Y	N	Y	N	N	Y
openEHR	Y	N	N	Y	N	N	N	N	Y	Y	N	N
IHE	N	Y	Y	N	N	N	N	N	Y	N	N	N
DICOM	N	Y	Y	N	N	N	Y	N	N	N	N	Y
EHRCom	N	N	N	Y	N	N	N	N	N	Y	N	N

[a]Recommended.

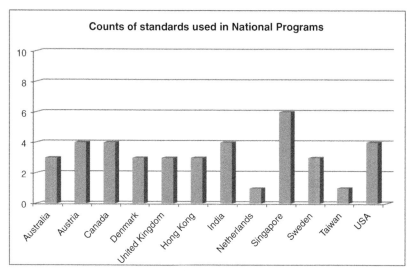

FIGURE 32.1 Count of standards used in National Programs.

It helps in drawing statistics for average usage of each standard in these 10 countries for identifying the widely and commonly used standards. It also helps in drawing the statistics for adoption of a number of standards in each country. The analysis shows how many countries support multiple standards and to what extent.

The graph in Figure 32.1 shows that most of the countries have adapted more than one standard to fulfill different national, regional, and organizational requirements. The graph in Figure 32.2 shows that HL7 v3 and CDA are the most widely supported standards.

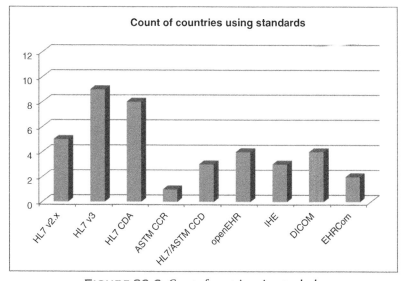

FIGURE 32.2 Count of countries using standards.

32.4.2 QUALITATIVE ASSESSMENT

Qualitative assessment for the various criteria is as follows:

1. *Clinical Process Model*

   a. Clinical Process Models are useful in providing uniformity in describing clinical concepts and business processes in healthcare.

   b. The National EHR Model should be generic and process oriented.

   c. Information models based on the Clinical Process Model represent semantic meaning of the contents of the model.

2. *Information Model*

   a. The selection of a standard greatly affects the design of information model.

   b. An EHR information model should support data from multiple standards so that the systems already adhering to one or the other standard as per the requirement of the organization do not need to upgrade or provide mapping to another particular standard. This helps in achieving The As-Is principle where healthcare information should be preserved as it is received without any modification.

   c. A distributed model implementation and resources is more flexible than central-hub based designs. It allows for the organic growth of network and resources.

3. *Exchange Standard*

   a. Use of a single standard for data exchange provides easy flow of information across a network, whereas for supporting multiple standards it is required to support their respective data exchange formats.

   b. In addition, use of a single standard will require conversion of data from existing EHR applications or may need to upgrade the existing local systems to adhere to that single standard.

   c. Some data in an existing EHR system may not fit in the selected single standard and thus need to work for that kind of data. This would cause either data loss or lack of access to the actual original data. This can lead to medico-legal issues as well.

   d. If the standard selected upgrades into a newer version, then the issues of complete upgradation or consistency with the previous version (if not provided) have to be handled.

4. *Security/Privacy Consideration*

   a. Most countries use a PKI-based security model.

   b. Almost all countries have used the Service-Oriented Architecture that provides a futuristic approach of building different national services.

   c. Use of Role-Based Access Control is not sufficient in providing access to the patient data in a healthcare domain. EHR information requires security/privacy at the level of attributes in each of the records. For this, EHR designers can look for additional mechanisms like the Attribute-Based Access Model.

d. Security and Privacy techniques applied should be compliant with the national and international regulations and standards.

5. *Legal Aspects*

a. Implementation of a national EHR system has many legal challenges, since it involves sharing of sensitive health data of patients.

b. Most countries have faced several problems in implementing a national EHR system, despite having stronger laws for security/privacy with various mandates for sensitive clinical data.

32.5 Recommended Phases for Implementing A National EHR System

Implementation of a national EHR system needs phased planning because it requires legal guidelines in the area of security, privacy and ethics from IT perspective. It also requires availability of infrastructures like national registries for patients, healthcare providers, and insurers. Existing infrastructures in various countries and their approaches for implementing a national EHR system in the countries covered in the book reveal that it requires a planned implementation in phases to achieve an all-inclusive solution. All these countries have planned for these efforts for decades in the following four different phases:

- *Phase I.* It includes study and analysis to gather requirements and feasibility study for those requirements.

- *Phase II.* It includes parallel work toward achieving standardization in healthcare information representation, establishing national registries for unique identification of stakeholders in healthcare, and coming out with regulatory guidelines in the area of security, privacy, and legal requirements.

- *Phase III.* It mainly includes implementation of different healthcare services. It actually develops the glue between these efforts and makes national healthcare IT infrastructure available in the nation.

- *Phase IV.* Depending on the success of Phase III, this phase involves the expansion of these implementations to cover the entire nation that requires a nationwide program for execution, proliferation, and adaption of technology.

Glossary

AAFP: See *American Academy of Family Physicians.*

ABAC: See *Attribute-Based Access Control.*

ADA: See *American Dental Association.*

ADL: See *Archetype Definition Language.*

AHFS DI: See *American Hospital Formulary Service DI.*

AMA: See *American Medical Association.*

American Academy of Family Physicians (AAFP): AAFP is a national medical organization involving family physicians, students, family medicine residents to transform healthcare. It is involved in clinical research, educational, and policy making for better healthcare.

American College of Radiology (ACR): ACR is an association of radiologists, physicists, and nuclear medicine physicians working toward the advancement of radiology science, educating professionals, and improving patient care quality.

American Dental Association (ADA): ADA is a consortium of American dentists that promotes good oral health to the public.

American Hospital Formulary Service Drug Information (AHFS DI): AHFS DI coding system provides classification and identification of drugs. It was formerly known as AHFS.

American Medical Association (AMA): AMA is the leading association of medical practitioners and students in the United States (US). It aims to bring all healthcare providers together for solving professional and public health issues.

American National Standards Institute (ANSI): ANSI is a nonprofit organization that manages and administers US standardization activities.

American Society of Health-System Pharmacists (ASHP): ASHP is a national association of pharmacists in America and aims to enhance patient safety by improving the use of medication.

Electronic Health Record: Standards, Coding Systems, Frameworks, and Infrastructures, Pradeep Sinha, Gaur Sunder, Prashant Bendale, Manisha Mantri, and Atreya Dande.
© 2013 by The Institute of Electrical and Electronics Engineers, Inc. Published 2013 by John Wiley & Sons, Inc.

American Society of Testing Materials (ASTM): ASTM is an international organization involved in developing standards in various industry domains to improve product quality, increase safety, and enhance consumer satisfaction. It has already developed standards in health-related areas such as 3D imaging, medical devices and implants, electronic health data exchange, and so on.

Anonymization: Anonymization is a way of removing information related to patient identification from medical records. The information is replaced sometimes with dummy characters. Such anoymized information is used for statistical, research, or educational purposes. Some regulatory requirements mandate anonymization before sharing of medical data.

ANSI: See *American National Standards Institute.*

Archetype Definition Language (ADL): ADL is a standard language for describing clinical concepts. The clinical concepts are called Archetypes. ADL is adapted by openEHR, CEN, ISO, and so on.

ASHP: See *American Society of Health-System Pharmacists.*

ASTM: See *American Society of Testing Materials (ASTM).*

Attribute-Based Access Control (ABAC): ABAC is a technique for controlling access to the resources for performing a particular task based on the attributes of the requestors, resources, and environment. The attributes are a set of key-value pairs used to describe requestors, resources, and environment for authorization purposes. ABAC is more flexible than RBAC where Role could be one of the attributes for authorization. See also: *RBAC.*

CCR: See *Continuity of Care Record.*

CDT: See *Current Dental Terminology.*

CEN: See *European Standardization Committee.*

CEN EN 12967—Health informatics-service architecture (HISA): HISA provides specifications for enabling the development of distributed open systems in healthcare. It specifies the architecture of a generic healthcare information system where all the communication between applications is through a middleware layer of common services. The standard provides the structure of the data maintained and retrieved by those middle layer services retaining the flexibility of internal management of the structure.

CEN EN14822—General-purpose information components (GPIC): The GPIC standard defines a set of general-purpose information components using UML modeling. These components are different health informatics business objects, which are frequently required within during communication in healthcare. The components are defined by referring to HL7 v3 RIM classes for making CEN standards interoperable with HL7 v3. See also: *CEN, HL7 v3, UML.*

CEN TC 251: It is a technical committee of CEN and responsible for the development of standards in medical domain. See also: *CEN.*

CEN/ISO EN 13606—Health informatics—Electronic health record communication (EHRcom): EHRcom is a European standard that focuses on interoperability between diverse healthcare systems. It provides technical specifications for standardizing the structure, content, communication, and security aspects during communication between EHR systems. See also: *CEN, CEN TC 215*.

CEN/TC 251 EN 13940—Health informatics—System of concepts to support continuity of care (CONTsys): CONTsys is a European standard that defines the concepts and processes in healthcare. See also: *CEN, CEN TC 215*.

Centers for Medicare and Medicaid Services (CMS): CMS is an agency in the US Department of Health and Human Services. It controls Medicare, Medicaid, Children's Health Insurance Program, HIPAA, Laboratory Improvement Amendments (CLIA), implementation of EHR incentive, and other services. See also: *HIPAA*.

Classification of Diseases for Oncology (ICD-O): ICD-O coding system is developed by WHO and provides the codes for tumor diseases. See also: *WHO*.

Clinical and Laboratory Standards Institute (CLSI): CLSI is a nonprofit standards development organization that promotes the development of clinical and laboratory standards to improve quality of care. CLSI was formerly known as National Committee for Clinical Laboratory Standards (NCCLS).

CLIS: See *Clinical and Laboratory Standards Institute*.

CMS: See *Centers for Medicare and Medicaid Services*.

Computer-Based Patient Record (CPR): CPR is the lifetime health record of a patient that includes data from all healthcare organizations and requires full interoperability. Currently, CPR is only a concept and may be implemented in near future. See also: *EHR, EMR, PHR*.

Continuity of Care Record (CCR): CCR is a standard developed by *ASTM* defining patient health related summaries that can be exchanged between healthcare providers. Each summary contains the minimum important information required to take decision in further course of treatment. See also: *ASTM*.

CONTsys: See *CEN/TC 251 EN 13940*.

CPR: See *Computer-Based Patient Record*.

CPT: See *Current Procedural Terminology*.

Current Dental Terminology (CDT): CDT coding system provides the codes for dental procedures and services. CDT is developed by ADA and is incorporated in HCPCS codes. See also: *ADA, HCPCS*.

Current Procedural Terminology (CPT): CPT provides the codes for identification of medical, surgical, and diagnostic services. CPT code sets are maintained by AMA and majorly used by physicians for reimbursement from insurance companies. See also: *AMA*.

DICOM: See *Digital Imaging and Communications in Medicine.*

Digital Imaging and Communications in Medicine (DICOM): DICOM is a standard defined by *NEMA* for exchanging patient health information along with images using a composite structure across healthcare applications and medical devices. This standard is primarily used in radiological devices for capturing and communicating images with healthcare applications.

ebXML: See *Electronic Business using eXtensible Markup Language.*

EDIFACT: See *Electronic Data Interchange for Administration, Commerce and Transport.*

EHR: See *Electronic Health Record.*

EHRcom: See *CEN/ISO EN 13606.*

Electronic Business Using eXtensible Markup Language (ebXML): ebXML is a standard specification for exchanging business messages over the Internet. It is developed by OASIS and the United Nations/ECE agency CEFACT. ebXML is also known as e-business XML. See also: *OASIS, XML.*

Electronic Data Interchange for Administration, Commerce, and Transport (EDIFACT): EDIFACT is an international Electronic Data Interchange (EDI) standard developed by the United Nations (UN). The standard is also known as UN/EDIFACT.

Electronic Health Record (EHR): EHR is a longitudinal electronic medical record of an individual that contains clinical information captured from different encounters. It is shared between healthcare providers through different healthcare applications ensuring availability of required clinical information for care of an individual. See also: *CPR, EMR.*

Electronic Medical Record (EMR): EMR is a computerized record of a patient's clinical, demographic and administrative data. It is limited to the electronic medical document activity at a single health care organization. EHR is a broader concept than EMR and involves a level of interoperability across healthcare organizations. See also: *EHR, PHR.*

EMR: See *Electronic Medical Record.*

European Standardization Committee (CEN): (French: Comité Européen de Normalisation) CEN is a nonprofit standards body that is responsible for proliferating European Standards in various domains in European Union (EU) and some associated countries outside the EU.

eXtensible Access Control Markup Language (XACML): XACML is a standard XML-based *ABAC* language for specification of access control policies. It is an OASIS ratified standard. It also defines the framework for communication and evaluation of those policies. See also: *ABAC, OASIS, XML.*

eXtensible Markup Language (XML): XML provides a set of rules for encoding documents so that they can be correctly interpreted during transport and storage-retrieval. World Wide Web Consortium (W3C) has defined the XML specifications.

eXtensible Stylesheet Language Transformations (XSLT): XSLT is a XML-based language used for the transformation of XML documents into other formats such as HTML, PDF, XHTML, etc. It is mostly used for converting data between XML schemas or to render XML data on web pages. See also: *XML.*

FDA: See *Food and Drug Administration.*

Food and Drug Administration (FDA): FDA is an agency of the US Department of Health and Human Services. FDA aims to protect and support public health by overseeing food safety, tobacco products, and regulatory operations and policies for food products.

GPIC: See *CEN EN14822—General-purpose information components.*

HCPCS: See *Healthcare Common Procedure Coding System.*

Healthcare: Healthcare refers to a system or systems that offer, provide, or deliver health care.

Health care: Health care (different from Healthcare) refers to the care (treatment) provided to a patient. This is an action taken by a person who works in healthcare. See also: *Healthcare.*

Health Informatics: It deals with the integrated usage of information, communication and electronics technologies for optimizing acquisition, storage, retrieval and usage of data in health and medicine. It is also referred as health care informatics, healthcare informatics, medical informatics, nursing informatics, and so on.

Health Information Management and Systems Society (HIMSS): HIMSS is a not-for-profit organization involved in using Information Technology (IT) to optimum level for developing management systems for providing better health care. It was involved in the development of *CCR* standard. See also: *CCR.*

Health Insurance Portability and Accountability Act (HIPAA): HIPAA was enacted in United States in the year 1996. It specifies the regulations and guidelines for health insurance policies protecting workers and their families. It also mandates the use and development of standards in electronic exchange of data related to a patient's health, health administration, and financial transactions. See also: *CMS.*

Health Level 7 International (HL7): HL7 is a not-for-profit, ANSI-accredited standards developing organization working on standards for exchange of health information contained in an Electronic Health Record (EHR) (See *Electronic Health Record*). See also: *ANSI.*

Healthcare Common Procedure Coding System (HCPCS): HCPCS provides the codes for identification of medical services, supplies and equipment. They are based on the CPT Codes. See also: *CPT.*

HIMSS: See *Health Information Management and Systems Society.*

HIPAA: See *Health Insurance Portability and Accountability Act.*

HIS: See *Hospital Information System.*

HISA: See *CEN EN 12967—Health informatics-service architecture.*

HL7 v2.x: HL7 v2.x is a series of application-level standards defined by HL7 for electronic data exchange in all types of healthcare environments, prominently working toward defining exchange mechanisms between health IT systems implemented at Hospitals.

HL7 CDA: See *HL7 Clinical Document Architecture (CDA).*

HL7 Clinical Document Architecture (CDA): CDA is a standard for exchanging clinical documents across healthcare applications. It specifies a document structure based on XML and is used to create health-related document templates. It uses HL7 v3 RIM classes and attributes for defining the content of such clinical documents. See also: *XML, HL7 v3 RIM.*

HL7 EHR-S FM: See *HL7 EHR-System Functional Model.*

HL7 EHR-System Functional Model (HL7 EHR-S FM): EHR-S FM is developed by HL7 EHR-SIG committee. It defines a functional specification for EHR systems that specifies various guidelines as a functional profile. These functional profiles are categorized into direct care, supportive, and information structure.

HL7 v3 RIM: See *Reference Information Model (RIM).*

HL7 v3: HL7 v3 is a standard defining specifications for messages, data types, and health related terms based on Reference Information Model (RIM). The standard is based on a model-driven approach where domain-specific messages are developed through continuous harmonization. It is used in clinical information exchange.

HL7: See *Health Level 7 International.*

Hospital Information System (HIS): HIS supports management of healthcare workflows and data (includes medical, administrative, legal and financial data) in the hospital. There are some other similar titles and acronyms for such a system, namely; Health Information System (HIS), Healthcare Information System (HIS), Clinical Information System (CIS), Patient Data Management System (PDMS), and so on.

ICD: See *International Statistical Classification of Diseases and Related Health Problems.*

ICD-O: See *Classification of Diseases for Oncology.*

ICF: See *International Classification of Functioning, Disability and Health.*

IHE: See *Integrating Healthcare Enterprise.*

IHE Cross Enterprise Document Sharing (XDS): XDS profile defines the workflow for sharing of clinical documents between institutions. See also: *IHE*.

IHE XDS: See *IHE Cross Enterprise Document Sharing*.

IHTSDO: See *International Health Terminology Standards Development Organization*.

Implementable Technology Specification (ITS): ITS is a specification given by HL7 ITS Special Interest Group (SIG) that defines HL7 artefacts encoding and transportation related guidelines. It also specifies the procedure for dealing with errors.

International Classification of Functioning, Disability and Health (ICF): ICF coding system provides identification and classification of disabilities. It is developed by WHO with the support of World Health Assembly. See also: *WHO*.

International Health Terminology Standards Development Organization (IHTSDO): IHTSDO is an international nonprofit organization that owns and maintains SNOMED CT and related terminology standards.

Integrating Healthcare Enterprise (IHE): IHE is an international organization that focuses on the development of frameworks for exchanging health information across various healthcare applications. The frameworks developed are called IHE Integration Profiles.

International Statistical Classification of Diseases and Related Health Problems (ICD): ICD codes describe diseases or conditions and provide classification of diseases. ICD codes are maintained by WHO. See also: *WHO*.

ISO/TC 215: ISO/TC 215 is a technical committee of International Organization for Standardization (ISO) working in health informatics for standardizing health information and achieving interoperability across health IT systems.

ISO/TS 18308: ISO/TS 18308 is a requirement specification that defines the user and technical requirements for EIIR architecture.

ITS: See *Implementable Technology Specification (ITS)*.

Laboratory Information System (LIS): LIS is a computer information system that accepts, processes, and stores information generated during medical laboratory operations.

LDAP: See *Lightweight Directory Access Protocol*.

Lightweight Directory Access Protocol (LDAP): LDAP is a protocol used for searching and maintaining information from a server over the Internet.

LIS: See *Laboratory Information System*.

LLP: See *Minimum Lower Layer Protocol*.

Logical Observation Identifiers Names and Codes (LOINC): LOINC is an international standard coding system that provides codes for identifying laboratory and other clinical observations. Regenstrief Institute maintains LOINC database. See also: *Regenstrief Institute, Inc.*

LOINC: See *Logical Observation Identifiers Names and Codes.*

Massachusetts Medical Society (MMS): MMS is a Massachusetts statewide professional association involved in educating physicians, healthcare professionals, and students on advanced medical knowledge and healthcare processes to achieve standardization in medical practice and healthcare management. It was involved in the development of *CCR* standard. See also: *CCR.*

MIME: See *Multipurpose Internet Mail Extensions.*

Minimum Lower Layer Protocol (MLLP): MLLP is a protocol defined for identifying start and end of each *HL7* message while transporting it over a network protocol layer such as TCP/IP. MLLP defines the header and trailer characters to be included with the *HL7* message before transmission so that the receiving application can differentiate between multiple messages. See also: *HL7.*

MLLP: See *Minimum Lower Layer Protocol.*

MMS: See *Massachusetts Medical Society.*

Multipurpose Internet Mail Extensions (MIME): MIME is an internet standard that specifies the type of content exchanged over the Internet. Communication protocols such as HTTP use this standard to describe the type of content being transferred.

NANDA: See *North American Nursing Diagnosis Association.*

National Council for Prescription Drug Programs (NCPDP): NCPDP is an ANSI-accredited nonprofit standards development organization that promotes healthcare through education and standards. See also: *ANSI.*

National Drug Code (NDC): NDC is a unique identifier used in the United States for identifying medicines.

National E-Health Transition Authority (NEHTA): NEHTA is a constitutional authority of Australian government. It is responsible for promoting e-health in Australia by developing standards, specifications, policies, necessary infrastructure, and so on.

National Electrical Manufacturer's Association (NEMA): NEMA is a trade association involved in developing products and standards in medical imaging, utility, commercial, and industrial applications. *DICOM* is a standard developed by NEMA's Medical Imaging and Technology Alliance division.

National Library of Medicine (NLM): NLM is the US national library of medicine that provides material and research services for biomedicine and healthcare domain.

NCCLS: See *US National Committee for Clinical Laboratory Standards.*

NCCLS LIS5-A: The standard provides the specification for transferring clinical observations between heterogeneous healthcare systems. The standard was formerly an ASTM standard called ASTM E1238. See also: *CLIS,* NCCLS.

NCPDP: See *National Council for Prescription Drug Programs.*

NDC: See *National Drug Code.*

NEHTA: See *National E-Health Transition Authority.*

NEMA: See *National Electrical Manufacturer's Association.*

NIC: See *Nursing Interventions Classification.*

NLM: See *National Library of Medicine.*

NOC: See *Nursing Outcomes Classification.*

North American Nursing Diagnosis Association (NANDA): NANDA is an association that promotes standardization especially for nursing. NANDA has developed a standard vocabulary that provides the classification of nursing diagnosis, which is also called NANDA.

Nursing Interventions Classification (NIC): NIC is a standardized nursing terminology that provides the classification of nursing care activities in clinical settings.

OASIS: See *Organization for the Advancement of Structured Information Standards.*

Object Constraint Language (OCL): OCL is a declarative language that describes the constraints on object-oriented modeling languages. OCL is part of Unified Modeling Language (UML) and it helps in analyzing the software for various pre and post conditions and constraints. See also: *OMG, UML.*

Object Management Group (OMG): OMG is an organization that focuses on the development of standards for modeling programs, systems, and business processes, enabling effective visual design, implementation and maintenance of software and other processes.

OBR: See *Observation Request Segment.*

Observation Request Segment (OBR): OBR is a mandatory segment used in HL7 v2.x observation reporting messages for representing header-related information in a report. It contains identification information related to recorded observations, order, report generation location, specimen, and so on. See also: *HL7 v2.x.*

Observation/Result Segment (OBX): OBX is a HL7 v2.x segment used to transmit the smallest unit of information related to each observation recorded in a report. Apart from coded observation unit, it can contain an *HL7 CDA* document or a *DICOM* image as well. See also: *DICOM, HL7 v2.x, HL7 CDA.*

OBX: See *Observation/Result Segment.*

Ocean Informatics Pty. Ltd.: Ocean Informatics is an Australian health informatics company. It is actively involved in the research and development of open source health software and standards.

OCL: See *Object Constraint Language.*

OMG: See *Object Management Group.*

openEHR: openEHR is an open-source specification for storage, retrieval and management of EHR. The name openEHR is used for both foundation and specification. openEHR also provides the open-source implementation of openEHR specification in different implementing technologies. See also: *EHR.*

OpenMRS: OpenMRS is an Open Source Medical Record System. It uses openEHR Archetypes for defining clinical constraints on its data model. Its data model is based on Regenstrief concept model. Regenstrief is one of the leading organizations for the development of OpenMRS.

Organization for the Advancement of Structured Information Standards (OASIS): OASIS is a nonprofit organization that promotes the development and implementation of open standards especially for security, Web Services, Grid, and other areas.

Nursing Outcomes Classification (NOC): NOC is a standard terminology that provides classification of patient outcomes, depending on nursing intervention.

PACS: See *Picture Archival and Communications System.*

Personal Health Record (PHR): PHR is a patient-centric electronic health record. It is managed and controlled by the patient herself/himself. See also: *EHR, EMR.*

PHR: See *Personal Health Record.*

Picture Archival and Communications System (PACS): PACS is a central repository of medical images that enables storage, retrieval, distribution, and display of images across medical practices.

PKI: See *Public Key Infrastructure.*

Public Key Infrastructure (PKI): PKI is a security framework, which enables a user to securely exchange information over an insecure public network through the use of digital certificates.

Radiological Society of North America (RSNA): RSNA is an international association of radiologists, along with other medical professionals, headquartered in Oak Brook, Illinois, United States.

Radiology Lexicon (RadLex): RadLex is a coding system developed by RSNA and provides identification and classification of terms related to radiology domain.

RadLex: See *Radiology Lexicon.*

RBAC: See *Role-Based Access Control.*

Reference Information Model (RIM): RIM is an information model defined by *HL7 v3* used for developing message structures for exchanging clinical and administrative information across healthcare applications. It is an object model that defines the content for HL7 clinical domains and state-transition cycle of messages or group of messages in exchange.

Regenstrief Institute, Inc.: Regenstrief Institute is an informatics and healthcare research organization that aims to improve health care by improving quality and cost-effectiveness. It has developed several widely used and standardized systems such as Regenstrief Medical Records System (RMRS), LOINC system, and so on. See also: *LOINC.*

Role Based Access Control (RBAC): RBAC is a technique for controlling access to the resources for performing a particular task based on the roles of individual users in a system. The roles could be defined according to the authority and responsibility of the user within the system.

RxNorm: RxNorm terminology is developed by NLM. It compiles all the drug-related coding systems and provides mapping among them. See also: *NLM.*

SAML: See *Security Assertion Markup Language.*

Security Assertion Markup Language (SAML): SAML is a *XML* based standard specification by OASIS for authentication and authorization between distributed service environments. See also: *XML.*

Service-Oriented Architecture (SOA): SOA provides a set of specifications for the design and development of software called services. The services are defined business processes interoperable with each other. The services could be different software components.

SNOMED CT: See *Systematized Nomenclature of Medicine—Clinical Terms.*

SOA: See *Service-Oriented Architecture.*

Systematized Nomenclature of Medicine—Clinical Terms (SNOMED CT): SNOMED CT is a comprehensive coding system that provides classification and identification of diseases, observations, procedures, organisms, substances, and so on. It is maintained by IHTSDO and provides multilingual support. See also: *IHTSDO.*

UCL: See *University College London.*

US National Committee for Clinical Laboratory Standards (NCCLS): See *Clinical and Laboratory Standards Institute.*

UML: See *Unified Modeling Language.*

UMLS: See *Unified Medical Language System UMLS.*

Unified Medical Language System (UMLS): UMLS is a coding system that aims to integrate the concepts/codes from different national and international medical vocabularies. It provides mapping between similar codes from different coding systems that helps in converting codes from one coding system to another. UMLS is maintained by NLM and mappings are freely available for use. See also: *NLM*.

Unified Modeling Language (UML): UML is a standardized modeling language for developing visual models of object-oriented systems. UML specifications are defined by OMG. See also: *OMG*.

University College of London (UCL): UCL is a public, multidisciplinary research university located in London, UK.

Uniform Resource Identifier (URI): URI is an identifier used to locate any content on the Internet. Content can be a textual web page, video, or a sound clip. It describes information regarding, the protocol used to access the content, the computer where the content resides, and the file name.

URI: See *Uniform Resource Identifier*.

Virtual Private Network (VPN): VPN is a tunnel protocol to establish a secure network over a public network to connect remote sites such as offices, remote users of an organization, business partners, and so on.

VPN: See *Virtual Private Network*.

Web Services: Web Services are the technologies that enable connections between machines for communication in a network. Web Services uses Web Service Description Language (WSDL) for defining the protocol and services provided by a service provider. The service user uses WSDL for sending a request to the service provider.

WHO: See *World Health Organization*.

World Health Organization (WHO): WHO is responsible for directing and managing public health in United Nations (UN). It is responsible for monitoring and assessing health issues around the globe. It is also responsible for defining the standards, regulations, and policies that will help in improving health care in the countries.

XACML: See *eXtensible Access Control Markup Language*.

XML: *eXtensible Markup Language*.

XSLT: See *eXtensible Stylesheet Language Transformations*.

Z-Segment: Z-Segment is used for populating data that is not covered by existing HL7 v2.x messages. Each Z-Segment should start with a mandatory MSH segment, which contains syntactic information related to any HL7 v2.x message. Users can create a local Z-message which contains Z-Segments as well as existing HL7 v2.x Segments. See also: *HL7 v2.x*.

Index

Electronic Health Record: Standards, Coding Systems, Frameworks, and Infrastructures, Pradeep Sinha,
Gaur Sunder, Prashant Bendale, Manisha Mantri, and Atreya Dande.
© 2013 by The Institute of Electrical and Electronics Engineers, Inc. Published 2013 by John Wiley & Sons, Inc.

Printed and bound by CPI Group (UK) Ltd, Croydon, CR0 4YY

16/04/2025

14658363-0005